WINGS
OF FAME™

Aerospace Publishing Ltd
AIRtime Publishing Inc.

Published quarterly by
Aerospace Publishing Ltd
179 Dalling Road
London W6 0ES
UK

Copyright © Aerospace Publishing Ltd
1996

ISSN 1361-2034

Aerospace ISBN 1 874023 71 9
                (softback)
                1 874023 77 8
                (hardback)
AIRtime ISBN 1-880588-23-4

Published under licence in USA and
Canada by AIRtime Publishing Inc.,
10 Bay Street, Westport,
CT 06880, USA

Editorial Offices:
WINGS OF FAME™
Aerospace Publishing Ltd
3A Brackenbury Road
London W6 0WE UK

Publisher: Stan Morse
Managing Editor: David Donald
Assistant Editors: Robert Hewson
                   Jim Winchester
Sub Editor: Karen Leverington
Editorial Assistant: Tim Senior
US Correspondent: Robert F. Dorr

Artists: Chris Davey
         Tim Maunder
         John Ridyard
         Mark Rolfe
         John Weal
         Iain Wyllie

Origination by
   Chroma Graphics, Singapore
Printed by
   Officine Grafiche DeAgostini,
   Novara, Italy

The editors of WINGS OF FAME™
welcome photographs for possible
publication, but cannot accept any
responsibility for loss or damage to
unsolicited material.

The publishers gratefully acknowledge
the assistance given by the following
people:

Anthony Galbraith and Douglas Young
for their assistance with the *Coastal
Command Strikes* feature.

Warren M. Bodie, Larry Davis, John
Guttman, David W. Menard, Dr. Jacob
Neufeld and Gary Padrtra for their help
with the *94th Fighter Squadron* article.

**WINGS OF FAME™ is published
quarterly and is available by
subscription and from many fine
book and hobby stores.**

**SUBSCRIPTION AND BACK
NUMBERS:**

**UK and World (except USA and
Canada) write to:**
Aerospace Publishing Ltd
FREEPOST
PO Box 2822
London
W6 0BR
UK
**(No stamp required if posted in
the UK)**

USA and Canada, write to:
AIRtime Publishing Inc.
Subscription Dept
10 Bay Street
Westport
CT 06880, USA
(203) 838-7979
Toll-free order number in USA:
1 800 359-3003

**Prevailing US subscription rates
are as follows:**
**Softbound edition for 1 year:
$58.00**

**Softbound edition for 2 years:
$108.00**

**Softbound back numbers
(subject to availability) are
$19.00 each. All rates are for
delivery within mainland USA,
Alaska and Hawaii. Canadian
and overseas prices available
upon request. American Express,
Discover Card, MasterCard and
Visa accepted. When ordering
please include your card
number, expiration date and
signature.**

**U.S. Publisher:
   Mel Williams**
**Subscription Director:
   Linda DeAngelis**
**Retail Sales Director:
   Jill Brooks**
**Charter Member Services
Manager:
   Joanne Harding**
**Shipping Manager:
   E. Rex Anku**

WINGS OF FAME™

CONTENTS

Volume 4

Coastal Command Strike

Coastal Command entered World War II with only two squadrons equipped and trained to attack enemy surface ships. These were No. 22 at Thorney Island in Sussex and No. 42 at Bircham Newton in Norfolk, both equipped with the Vickers Vildebeest III, a slow and obsolete biplane of a basic design which dated back to 1928. This aircraft was normally armed with a single 18-in (46-cm) torpedo and two machine-guns, and carried a crew of two or three.

In addition, Coastal Command boasted two squadrons of Lockheed Hudsons, a new American aircraft which was being introduced to replace the slow but reliable reconnaissance-tasked Avro Anson with which eight other squadrons were equipped. There were five other squadrons equipped with flying-boats:

Short Sunderlands, Saro Londons or Supermarine Stranraers. These aircraft comprised the whole of Coastal Command's force, although of course there were also maritime squadrons serving with other RAF commands in the Mediterranean and the Far East.

This tiny anti-shipping strike force was not quite so ridiculous as it might seem in retrospect. Before the war, the main threat to Britain from the German Kriegsmarine was rightly perceived as the U-boat, which could cut the country's vital supply lines, principally those with America and the Commonwealth. Coastal Command thus concentrated on escort duties for ocean convoys, its aircraft armed with anti-submarine bombs or later with depth charges. It worked in close collaboration with the Royal Navy and its Fleet Air Arm. Germany's coast

along the North Sea was quite short, and the destruction of enemy ports which harboured warships was considered the province of the RAF's Bomber Command. At sea, these warships could be countered by the Royal Navy's Home Fleet, which was still extremely powerful. Nobody could have foreseen the extraordinary outcome of the German Blitzkrieg in the West and the demands which Coastal Command's small anti-shipping force would be called upon to fulfil.

The pilots of Coastal Command were considered an elite. They were highly trained as both pilots and navigators, having undergone a 'general reconnaissance' course at the end of their normal training, for their flights over the sea required special skills. A few had passed an additional 'long navigation' course, which took

The low priority given to Coastal Command in the inter-war years is shown by this view of Vildebeests of No. 22 Squadron, which were the only aircraft available to the strike squadrons in 1939. The torpedoes are angled downwards for better entry into the water.

Below: Beaufort Is of No. 217 Sqn are seen at St Eval in mid-1941. The Beaufort was the first purpose-built torpedo bomber operated by Coastal Command. Despite its faults, it served the command well until mid-1942, and led to its far more successful derivative, the Beaufighter.

Above: A Beaufighter TF.Mk X of No. 455 Squadron (RAAF) lets loose a salvo of rockets low over the sea, a scene repeated many times in the waters of northwest Europe from the middle of the war. A barrage of rockets had the effect of a broadside from a small warship.

Coastal Command was the poor relation of the three RAF combat commands. For the early part of the war it was hampered by equipment that was either ancient, underdeveloped or handed down from other commands. Early results were disappointing and achieved at a terrible cost. By the end of the war, the new strike wings would introduce specialised aircraft and develop sophisticated tactics, and were to wreak havoc on shipping around the enemy-held coasts. Nonetheless, attacking defended ships in daylight took great courage, and many brave crews were lost severing the supply lines of the Third Reich.

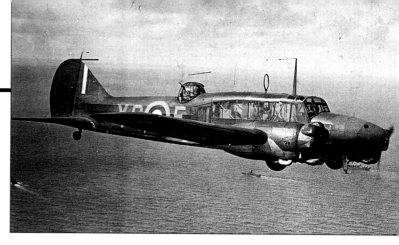

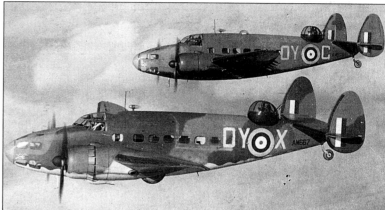

them deeper into the theories and practice of navigation, particularly astro-navigation. This qualification was roughly equivalent to a university degree. There were few officers trained solely as navigators, or 'air observers' as this function was known at the time. The other members of the crews – wireless operators and gunners – were usually non-commissioned and of low rank but highly trained and competent. However, anti-shipping tactics against surface vessels were out of date, equipment was inadequate, and the command did not have the benefit of good intelligence.

Wartime role

On the outbreak of war, Coastal Command was called upon to act at full stretch, primarily in the anti-submarine role around Britain's coastline and patrols in the North Sea hunting for potential surface raiders. The crews were under orders not to attack merchant ships unless these could be identified as surface raiders. The Ansons and Hudsons suffered some casualties from well-armed enemy floatplanes and single-

engined fighters, but a Hudson of No. 220 Squadron from Thornaby in Yorkshire scored the RAF's first victory in air combat when the crew shot down a Dornier Do 18 flying-boat over the North Sea on 8 October 1939. The 'phoney war' of those early months did not apply to Coastal Command.

Meanwhile, efforts to provide more effective anti-shipping aircraft, which had begun before the war, met with only limited success. The Ansons were steadily withdrawn from front-line service and most of the squadrons were equipped with Hudsons which, although not ideal as attack aircraft, at least had the range to reach the Norwegian coast. The Bristol Beaufort entered service with No. 22 Squadron at Thorney Island in November 1939 as 'the world's fastest torpedo bomber', with a crew of four, but suffered initially from technical faults. It was employed at first on minelaying and low-level duties, although later it became Coastal Command's standard torpedo bomber. The need for a long-range fighter escort was recognised, but the best that could be provided

Top: The Avro Anson, which first entered squadron service in 1936, was the standard reconnaissance aircraft in Coastal Command at the outbreak of war. Armed with only a single machine-gun firing forward and another in the turret, this aircraft is from No. 502 Squadron based at Aldergrove in Northern Ireland.

Above: The Lockheed Hudson, modified from an airliner design, began to replace the Ansons in May 1939 for maritime reconnaissance, and was later employed as a strike aircraft. A range of 2,160 miles (3476 kg) and up to seven machine-guns made it a marked improvement on its predecessor. These Hudsons are No. 48 Squadron aircraft.

Below left: Mk XII torpedoes are wheeled out to Beauforts of No. 22 Squadron. The first torpedo sorties by Beauforts were made by this squadron in September 1940 from North Coates. In the background is a Swordfish, possibly one of the Fleet Air Arm aircraft under Coastal Command control.

Below: The Handley-Page Hampden was known by its crews as 'the Flying Suitcase'. When the type reached obsolescence with Bomber Command, it found a fair degree of success with the strike squadrons as a torpedo bomber. Five squadrons used the Hampden TB.Mk 1 in action, and later many were ferried to Canada for use as trainers.

Above: A Spitfire PR.Mk IV of 'B' Flight, Photographic Reconnaissance Unit sits at readiness at St Eval. The PRU was controlled by Coastal Command, and the Spitfires did valuable work in hunting enemy shipping.

Above right: The prime concern of Coastal Command in the early war period was large surface raiders such as the heavy cruiser Admiral Hipper, photographed here at Brest by a PRU Spitfire from St Eval on 26 January 1941.

was the Bristol Blenheim Mk IV light bomber, some of which were fitted with a four-gun pack beneath the fuselage in addition to the two guns in the turret. By the time the Wehrmacht attacked in the west, three Coastal Command squadrons were equipped with Blenheim IVs.

The success of the German invasion of Denmark and Norway, followed by the Blitzkrieg of 10 May 1940 and the fall of France, transformed the situation for the few strike squadrons of Coastal Command. Within a few brief weeks, the short enemy coastline facing Britain was increased immensely, from the Arctic Circle to the Franco-Spanish border. Within this lay superb harbours from which enemy warships or armed merchant ships could operate, backed by modern airfields to provide air cover.

On 4 May, the RAF had received a directive allowing attacks against enemy merchant ships, but after the defeat in the West it became obvious that the Hudsons and Beauforts of Coastal Command were inadequate in numbers to cope with the enormous task they faced. During the period of the Blitzkrieg, most operational aircraft of the RAF were heavily engaged in efforts to protect the withdrawing British forces. Thereafter, one of the main duties of Coastal Command was the interdiction of the supply of high-grade iron ore from Sweden, which was shipped via Narvik in Norway to feed the German armament and munitions industries, in return for shipments of coal. During the summer months this ore, which was vital to the German war machine, could be carried with some difficulty across the Baltic Sea to German ports, but the Baltic was frozen up in winter. With the German occupation of the Netherlands, a more convenient port of entry was Rotterdam, from where it

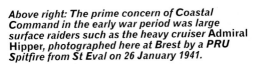

Above left: The Blenheim Mk IV was used by both Bomber Command and Coastal Command on anti-shipping attacks in the 1940-41 period, as illustrated by this attack by No. 2 Group Bomber Command on the Danish merchantman Delaware and other ships. This 1941 encounter was a far cry from later in the war, when multiple anti-aircraft guns and escort ships dictated co-ordinated attacks, specialist anti-flak aircraft, and rockets and torpedoes as the primary offensive weapons.

Left: An escorting minesweeper takes a direct hit from a Beaufort of the North Coates Strike Wing on 18 April 1943, the date of their first successful attack. On this day, off Ijmuiden, Holland, the Norwegian merchant ship Hoegh Carrier of 4,096 tons was sunk by a torpedo, and several M-class minesweepers were damaged. No aircraft (from Nos 143, 236 and 254 Squadrons) were lost.

was carried in barges down the Rhine to the industrial centre of the Ruhr. German convoys were instituted immediately, escorted by minesweepers and trawlers packed with anti-aircraft guns to serve as flak-ships, coupled with air cover. This enemy merchant fleet was increased by large numbers of vessels captured in Norway, Denmark, the Netherlands and France. At the same time, the ports of western France became available for German U-boats, battleships, cruisers and surface raiders. These could wreak havoc on Atlantic convoys and had the potential to destroy Britain's capacity to continue the war.

Battle of Britain efforts

For the months of the Battle of Britain and until the end of 1940, the strike aircraft of Coastal Command were mainly engaged on patrols and the bombing of enemy invasion ports. Three bomber squadrons equipped with Blenheim Mk IVs were transferred to the Command in July 1940 to help. They were accompanied by a squadron of Swordfish torpedo bombers from the Fleet Air Arm.

However, some notable attacks were made against shipping. On 21 June, six Swordfish of the Fleet Air Arm from Hatston in the Orkneys attempted to torpedo the heavily-escorted battleship *Scharnhorst* off Bergen. The torpedoes missed and two Swordfish were shot down by

flak. Coastal Command followed soon afterwards with a medium-level attack by four Hudsons of Nos 224 and 233 Squadrons from Leuchars in Fife, each carrying two 500-lb (227-kg) bombs. These also missed, and two Hudsons were shot down by Messerschmitt Bf 109s. The last attack was made by nine Beauforts of No. 42 Squadron from Wick in Caithness, which dive-bombed with a similar bomb load. The bombs straddled the battleship but did not hit it, and three Beauforts were shot down by Bf 109s. Even if their bombs had scored direct hits, it is unlikely that they would have attained sufficient impact velocity to penetrate the armoured deck of the battleship. Thus, seven aircraft were lost for no result, in spite of the bravery of the crews.

Up to this time there had been a shortage of torpedoes available for the Beaufort squadrons, but some began to arrive in the late summer of 1940. In the meantime, bombing attacks against shipping were made by the Hudsons, Blenheims, Beauforts and Swordfish, achieving some results at the cost of heavy losses. Another method of attack, which was later proved to

Above: This pair of No. 42 Sqn Beaufort Is was based at Leuchars. The leading aircraft is fitted with a rear-facing machine-gun, aimed by the navigator with the aid of a mirror. This weapon, fitted to ward off belly attacks by Bf 109s, often jammed due to a convoluted ammunition feed.

Above: In the long run, the air-dropped mine inflicted more damage to enemy shipping than did direct attack, and at less cost. This is a 1,650-lb (748-kg) land mine, but the sea mine was of similar appearance and weight. A Beaufort could only carry one of these weapons.

Below: Beaufort Mk Is of No. 22 Squadron run up at Thorney Island, Sussex. The early Beaufort Mk I suffered from engine and other faults, and the Bristol Taurus was supplanted by the lower-powered, but more reliable, Pratt & Whitney Twin Wasp.

Above: In addition to increasing flak defences, enemy fighter attacks were an ever-present danger on operations close to enemy-controlled coasts. This Beaufighter Mk IC of No. 236 Squadron at North Coates crash-landed after a battle with Bf 109s on 3 June 1943.

Above right: The first Beaufighters to serve with Coastal Command were Mk IC fighters which were received by No. 252 Sqn at Chivenor (as seen here) in December 1940. They were initially used as long-range fighters and escorts and, despite being too unstable at low level, had success against German patrol aircraft.

Top right: The Whitley was not a great success in Bomber Command, but Coastal Command GR.Mk VIIs equipped with air-to-surface-vessel radar (in this case, ASV.Mk II) made useful long-range patrol aircraft. Although primarily employed against submarines, Whitleys sometimes attacked surface vessels.

Coastal Command Strike Wings

Base	Squadrons	Dates
North Coates	143, 236, 254	Nov 42 - May 45
Wick	144, 404	Oct 43 - May 44
Leuchars	455, 489	Mar 44 - Apr 44
Langham	455, 489	Apr 44 - Oct 44
Davidstow Moor	144, 404	May 44 - Jul 44
Portreath	235, 248	June 44 - Sept 44
Strubby	144, 404	Jul 44 - Sep 44
Banff	143, 144, 235, 248, 404	Sep 44 - May 45
Dallachy	144, 404, 455, 489	Oct 44 - May 45

produce far more cost-effective results, was the dropping of magnetic mines, codenamed 'cucumbers'. These weighed about 1,650 lb (748 kg) and were dropped with a small parachute from about 800 ft (244 m) near harbour entrances. They were activated by the steel hull of a vessel passing above and blew up with tremendous force. Unfortunately, they sometimes exploded in the air and blew the aircraft to tiny fragments. A land mine version of the same weapon, known as a 'TIM' bomb, was also used against dock areas.

On 17 September, six Beaufort crews of No. 22 Squadron at North Coates in Lincolnshire were briefed to make a night torpedo attack against shipping in Cherbourg harbour, while 14 Blenheims of Nos 53 and 59 Squadrons were detailed to bomb the docks. The weather proved a problem, but a single Beaufort flown by Flight Sergeant Norman Hearn-Phillips penetrated the outer harbour and torpedoed the 1,626-ton merchant vessel *Johann Blumenthal*.

The Beaufort was very badly hit by flak, but the pilot nursed it home to make a skillful belly landing at Thorney Island. Another Beaufort was shot down by flak over the target. The Blenheims dropped their bombs and badly damaged the German torpedo boat *T-11* (the size of a small destroyer), set oil tanks on fire and caused much destruction in the dock area.

Enter the Beaufighter Mk IC

In December 1940 a new aircraft entered service with No. 252 Squadron at Chivenor in North Devon. The Bristol Beaufighter Mk IC incorporated much of the structure of the Beaufort but carried a crew of only two, a pilot and a navigator who also performed the duties of wireless operator. Armed with four 20-mm cannons and six 0.303-in (7.7-mm) machine-guns in the wings, it was originally intended as a long-distance fighter but later adaptations of this more powerful machine were to prove the scourge of German-controlled shipping.

By the end of the year, the strike force had sunk only six enemy ships by direct attack and badly damaged 14 others. Coastal Command entered 1941 with a force of eight Blenheim squadrons, six of Hudsons, three of Beauforts, two of FAA Swordfish and one of Beaufighters. The author joined one of the Beaufort squadrons in January as a commissioned air observer and served in it for 14 months. By this time, intelligence had improved, partly as a result of information passed by courageous agents in the occupied countries and partly from the magnificent work carried out by the Spitfire pilots of the Photographic Reconnaissance Unit, which was also controlled by Coastal Command.

The combination of the Beaufighter and the air-launched rocket was to provide, arguably, the deadliest weapon in the long anti-shipping war. In June 1942 the Beaufighter Mk VIC introduced RPs (rocket projectiles) and a dihedralled tailplane, bringing better low-level stability.

The power and strength of the Beaufighter is emphasised in this classic (if posed) shot of an operational 'Torbeau' and crew. On the extreme nose is the camera housing from which many spectacular pictures were taken.

The author's squadron operated mainly over the west coast of France, although there were sometimes detachments to other areas. Most of the sorties were mine-laying or low-level bombing attacks against enemy ports at first or last light. The usual load dropped on the ports consisted of two 500-lb (227-kg) and four 250-lb (113-kg) general-purpose bombs, although sometimes one of the bombs was replaced with a canister of incendiaries. These attacks were met with intense light flak

and probing searchlights. The Germans used different chemicals in their tracer bullets and 20-mm shells – strontium nitrate giving a red trail, copper resulting in a luminous shade of green, sodium the more normal orange and potassium a shade of mauve – so that the gunners could pick out their own trajectories. The air gunner fired down the searchlight beams and the wireless operator threw out empty beer bottles, believing that they produced an eerie whistling note which caused the enemy gunners to duck, while the air observer in the nose directed the pilot and aimed the bombs. The Beaufort jolted upwards as the bomb load fell away, and the gunner counted the explosions and reported

on the fires while the pilot skidded violently to avoid more flak and then turn on a homeward course.

Attacks on enemy vessels

Other Beaufort and Hudson squadrons made daylight sorties over the North Sea, along the coasts of the Netherlands and Norway, hunting enemy vessels. Usually they operated singly or in small flights, taking advantage of cloud cover. In addition, the Beauforts and Swordfish dropped mines near harbour entrances, and bombing attacks were made on ports at night. Sinkings of enemy vessels increased, but so did the losses suffered by the squadrons.

In this period there were two major attacks

On 15 October 1944, the Banff Strike Wing attacked escorted merchant ships off south Norway and sank the **Inger Johanne,** *a Norwegian merchant vessel of 1,202 tons and the 426-ton flak ship* **Mosel.** *These are probably No. 404 Squadron aircraft attacking the latter ship.*

The Beaufighter was never an aerobatic aircraft and could not turn with single-engined enemy fighters, but in the right hands could be thrown around with some flair. Surprisingly, a torpedo had little impact on performance, and the 'Torbeau' was the fastest torpedo carrier of the war.

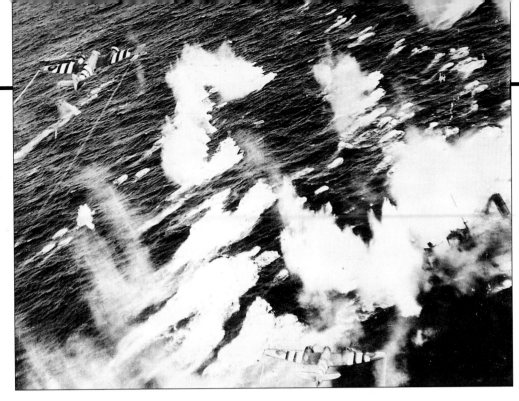

against enemy warships, both made by Beauforts operating singly. The first was in the early morning of 6 April, after a reconnaissance Spitfire had responded to an agent's report from Brest to the effect that the battleship *Gneisenau* had moved out of dock to moorings in the outer harbour. Its photographs confirmed the accuracy of this report, although it was not known at the time that the Germans were making safe an unexploded bomb in the dock. Six torpedo-carrying Beauforts of No. 22 Squadron were dispatched from St Eval in Cornwall to this target, but in increasingly bad weather only one, flown by Flying Officer Kenneth Campbell, found the battleship. He released a torpedo which ran true and blasted a 40-ft (12.2-m) hole in the *Gneisenau*. It nearly sank but was towed back into dock and remained out of commission for five months. The Beaufort was shot down into the harbour and all crew members were killed. Their bodies were recovered by the Germans and given a full military funeral. Campbell was awarded a posthumous Victoria Cross, the only award of its kind received by any crew member of Coastal Command's strike squadrons.

Damage to *Lutzow*

The other attack occurred on 13 June, when a Beaufort of No. 42 Squadron from Leuchars, flown by Flight Sergeant Ray Loveitt, attacked the pocket-battleship *Lutzow*. This warship was known by British Intelligence to have left Kiel Bay and to be heading north. Its general movements had been monitored by the Government Code and Cypher School at Bletchley Park in Buckinghamshire, which had been able to

decrypt the wireless traffic of the Kriegsmarine in home waters, following the capture of Enigma cypher material from *U-110*, a U-boat which had surrendered on 9 May to the Royal Navy. Nevertheless, the British did not know the exact position of the *Lutzow*, and the Beaufort flown by Loveitt was the only one of eight machines from Nos 22 and 42 Squadrons to find the ship, off southwest Norway. It was escorted by destroyers but Loveitt achieved surprise from low cloud and skimmed over their masts to drop a torpedo which scored a hit, without a shot being fired in return. The pocket-battleship was very badly damaged but managed to return to Kiel, where it remained in dry dock for over six months.

In the meantime, the equivalent of four Blenheim squadrons of Bomber Command's 2 Group were diverted from their normal tasks to make daylight attacks against enemy vessels along

Pulling streamers from their wingtips in the moist air above the sea off the Frisian Islands, Beaufighters from No. 236 Squadron pull up from a rocket and cannon attack on a German armed trawler. Two such ships, the Falkland *and the* A. Pilsche, *were sunk by the North Coates Strike Wing in this attack on 22 July 1944.*

the Dutch and French coasts, while the Coastal Command strike aircraft carried out most of their sorties on moonlit nights. The Bomber Command crews set about their new task with great verve and by July 1941 claimed to have sunk 104 vessels and badly damaged 72 more.

However, a post-war analysis based on German records showed that the true figures were seven vessels sunk and six seriously damaged, giving a poor return for heavy losses of Blenheims, which averaged 23 per cent per attack. These Bomber Command operations continued for two more months and then tailed off.

Dangers to crew

In the latter part of 1941, air-to-surface-vessel (ASV) radar was installed in some coastal aircraft, helping considerably in locating enemy vessels, especially at night. By the end of the year, the coastal strike squadrons had sunk 28 merchant vessels by direct attack and badly damaged 20 more, but their losses continued at an intolerable rate. It is not generally realised, even by some air historians, that these activities were extremely dangerous. During the author's operational tour, 34 Beauforts and crews were lost in his squadron, from a strength which seldom exceeded 12 at any one time. On 12 November 1942, RAF statistics showed that aircrew stood only a 17 per cent chance of surviving an operational tour in torpedo bombers or 25 per cent in light bombers, compared with 44 per cent in heavy or medium bombers and 43 per cent in day fighters. A later analysis showed that even the 17 per cent survival rate for torpedo bomber crews was optimistic and that the true figure was merely 2 per cent. Of course, such percentages varied from month to month and from squadron to squadron, but on average the strike aircraft of Coastal Command and their equivalents abroad were suffering the heaviest casualties of all RAF squadrons.

By the beginning of 1942, the strike force consisted of five squadrons of Beauforts, three of Beaufighters and three of Blenheims. There

The term 'low-level attack' meant just that. While one Banff Wing 'Beau' climbs away, the following aircraft blasts over an escort ship at yard-arm height. The bridge of the dazzle-painted ship sports a kill marking from a previous engagement.

Bristol Beaufighter TF.Mk X No. 489 Squadron, RNZAF angham, July 1944

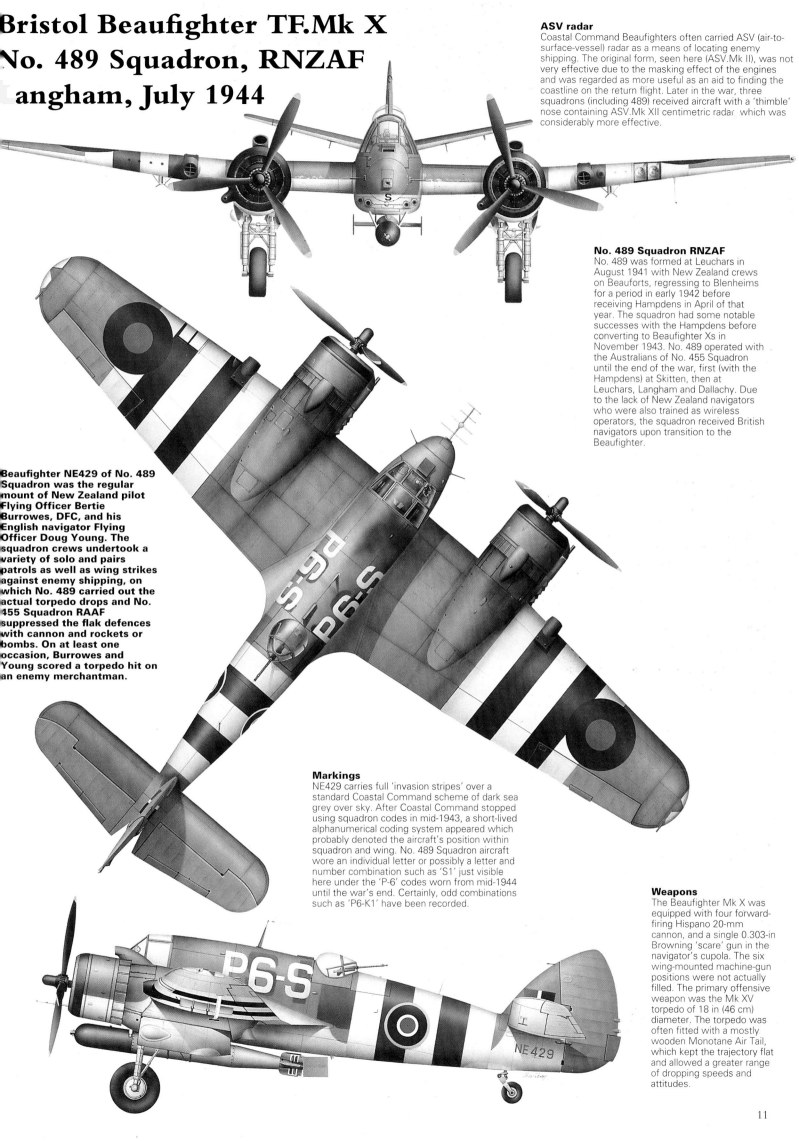

ASV radar

Coastal Command Beaufighters often carried ASV (air-to-surface-vessel) radar as a means of locating enemy shipping. The original form, seen here (ASV.Mk II), was not very effective due to the masking effect of the engines and was regarded as more useful as an aid to finding the coastline on the return flight. Later in the war, three squadrons (including 489) received aircraft with a 'thimble' nose containing ASV.Mk XII centimetric radar which was considerably more effective.

No. 489 Squadron RNZAF

No. 489 was formed at Leuchars in August 1941 with New Zealand crews on Beauforts, regressing to Blenheims for a period in early 1942 before receiving Hampdens in April of that year. The squadron had some notable successes with the Hampdens before converting to Beaufighter Xs in November 1943. No. 489 operated with the Australians of No. 455 Squadron until the end of the war, first (with the Hampdens) at Skitten, then at Leuchars, Langham and Dallachy. Due to the lack of New Zealand navigators who were also trained as wireless operators, the squadron received British navigators upon transition to the Beaufighter.

Beaufighter NE429 of No. 489 Squadron was the regular mount of New Zealand pilot Flying Officer Bertie Burrowes, DFC, and his English navigator Flying Officer Doug Young. The squadron crews undertook a variety of solo and pairs patrols as well as wing strikes against enemy shipping, on which No. 489 carried out the actual torpedo drops and No. 455 Squadron RAAF suppressed the flak defences with cannon and rockets or bombs. On at least one occasion, Burrowes and Young scored a torpedo hit on an enemy merchantman.

Markings

NE429 carries full 'invasion stripes' over a standard Coastal Command scheme of dark sea grey over sky. After Coastal Command stopped using squadron codes in mid-1943, a short-lived alphanumerical coding system appeared which probably denoted the aircraft's position within squadron and wing. No. 489 Squadron aircraft wore an individual letter or possibly a letter and number combination such as 'S1' just visible here under the 'P-6' codes worn from mid-1944 until the war's end. Certainly, odd combinations such as 'P6-K1' have been recorded.

Weapons

The Beaufighter Mk X was equipped with four forward-firing Hispano 20-mm cannon, and a single 0.303-in Browning 'scare' gun in the navigator's cupola. The six wing-mounted machine-gun positions were not actually filled. The primary offensive weapon was the Mk XV torpedo of 18 in (46 cm) diameter. The torpedo was often fitted with a mostly wooden Monotane Air Tail, which kept the trajectory flat and allowed a greater range of dropping speeds and attitudes.

The most feared of the German escort ships was the Sperrbrecher. These were converted merchant vessels, strengthened for exploding mines as well as dotted with flak positions. This is Sperrbrecher 7, formerly the Sauerland, which was badly damaged by Davidstow Moor Beaufighters on 12 August 1944 off Royan.

were also 12 squadrons of Hudsons in Coastal Command, but only five of these were engaged on anti-shipping attacks while the remainder carried out anti-submarine work or air-sea rescue. On 12 February there was a humiliating experience for Coastal Command, and indeed for the whole of the RAF and the Royal Navy, when the battleships *Scharnhorst* and *Gneisenau*, together with the heavy cruiser *Prinz Eugen*, broke out of Brest and passed unharmed through the English Channel, although both

battleships were damaged by magnetic mines laid by the RAF before reaching Germany.

By this time, all the Beaufort squadrons carried torpedoes and had been responsible for a high proportion of the sinkings in 1941, but their future in the UK was cut short in the following spring when they were dispatched to the Mediterranean, where their presence was urgently required to destroy supplies reaching the Axis forces in North Africa. A substitute for this aircraft was found with the Handley Page Hampden, a machine which Bomber Command no longer wanted and which was converted to this new role, equipping four Coastal Command strike squadrons. These carried out some effective work, mainly off the southwest coast of Norway. Armstrong Whitworth Whitley VIIs were also employed for bombing attacks against

shipping in the Bay of Biscay. In September, 32 Hampdens of Nos 144 and 455 (RAAF) Squadrons were sent to Vaenga in north Russia, in order to attack the battleship *Tirpitz* if it attempted to leave Altenfjord and attack Convoy PQ18, which was heading for Murmansk. Nine of these Hampdens were lost en route, and the remainder did not carry out any operation. They were handed over to the Russians in mid-October and the crews returned to Britain in RAF Catalinas.

Meanwhile, two new versions of the Beaufighter were developed for anti-shipping work. In mid-1942, the Mk IC was replaced with the Mk VIC, with more powerful engines, better stability at low level and a backward-firing machine-gun for the navigator. The other was the 'Torbeau', a torpedo-

Anti-shipping Tactics

Enemy defences
Defences include flak of 105-mm, 88-mm, 40-mm, 37-mm and 20-mm calibre, as well as numerous light machine-guns. In addition to these weapons, parachute and cable rockets and barrage balloons, a mast-mounted flamethrower was sometimes used, although it was found that an aircraft could fly through the flame with little damage, and the device proved hazardous to the ships operating it.

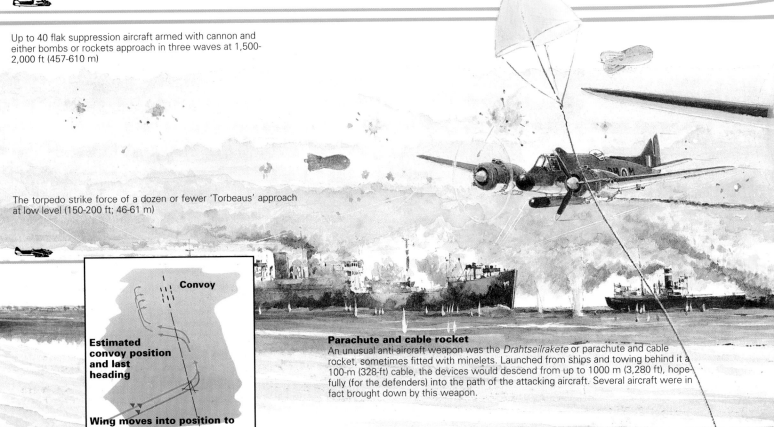

Escorting fighters weave above, height dependent on cloud cover

Up to 40 flak suppression aircraft armed with cannon and either bombs or rockets approach in three waves at 1,500-2,000 ft (457-610 m)

The torpedo strike force of a dozen or fewer 'Torbeaus' approach at low level (150-200 ft; 46-61 m)

Convoy

Estimated convoy position and last heading

Wing moves into position to attack out of sun

Parachute and cable rocket
An unusual anti-aircraft weapon was the *Drahtseilrakete* or parachute and cable rocket, sometimes fitted with minelets. Launched from ships and towing behind it a 100-m (328-ft) cable, the devices would descend from up to 1000 m (3,280 ft), hopefully (for the defenders) into the path of the attacking aircraft. Several aircraft were in fact brought down by this weapon.

The effect is obvious of a 20-mm cannon shell on the armoured windscreen of this Beaufighter TF.Mk X of No. 248 Squadron on 2 August 1943. Despite being temporarily blinded by dust and splinters, the pilot managed to land the aircraft back at Predannack in Cornwall.

Some idea of the strength of defences faced by the strike crews can be seen in this view, taken on 25 September 1944 of an attack by the North Coates and Langham Wings near Den Helder, Holland. Two small escort ships were sunk by the Beaufighters.

carrying adaptation of the Mk VIC. This retained the four cannons and the single machine-gun but carried a new Mk XV torpedo which had been developed for dropping at the higher speed of the Beaufighter. In November 1942, the first Strike Wing was formed at North Coates, consisting of Nos 236 Squadron with the Beaufighter VIC and 254 Squadron with the 'Torbeau'. However, the first attack, on 20 November, was not a success. Twenty-five Beaufighters took off for a German convoy off the Hook of Holland and

sank a naval tug of 449 tons, slightly damaging two other vessels, while Bf 109s set about the attackers. Three Beaufighters were shot down, two more crashed on landing and five more were badly shot up.

Changing tactics

During 1942 the strike aircraft of Coastal Command sank 25 enemy vessels and badly damaged 20 more. This was not a high return for the heavy losses, in spite of the efforts and courage of the crews. Obviously, something was wrong with the tactics and method of attack. The Beaufighter squadrons at North Coates did not operate again as a strike wing for five months, although individual sorties took place.

Coastal Command's strike force began 1943 with six squadrons of Beaufighters, four of

Hampdens, five of Hudsons (although three of the latter were mainly employed on reconnaissance) and two of FAA Swordfish. The solution to the defective tactics was found with the appointment of Wing Commander Neil Wheeler as commanding officer of No. 236 Squadron soon after the attack of 20 November. He was able to base his recommendations partly on the experiences of the Beaufort crews who had operated from Malta. These squadrons had sunk several vessels supplying the Axis forces in North Africa, but at

Barrage balloons
These tethered balloons on steel cable often remained unseen by the attackers until the last minute (if at all). Not particularly effective, they sometimes proved the success of an attack to post-strike reconnaissance by remaining flying above a sunken ship.

Beaufighter Strike Wing Attack 1944-45
This illustration depicts a typical late-war Coastal Command wing strike at the point when the small force of 'Torbeaus' is making its attack run on an enemy convoy consisting of merchant vessels escorted by a *Speerbrecher* (left). The defences have already been softened up by the first and second waves of rocket, bomb and cannon-equipped flak suppression aircraft (sometimes called 'Flakbeaus'), and the third wave is diving in to keep the defenders' heads down as the torpedo bombers make their run. The aircraft are late production Beaufighter TF.Mk Xs with ASV.Mk VIII radar in a thimble radome and the fin leading-edge extension added to further increase stability at low level.

Flying through dense cloud and led by Mosquito FB.Mk VIs of No. 333 (Norwegian) Sqn, Beaufighters of Nos 144 and 489 (RNZAF) Squadrons, Dallachy Strike Wing attacked shipping in Dalsfjord on 23 March 1945. The attacking force flew over mountains and up the longest and narrowest of the Norwegian fjords to sink the Norwegian vessel Lysaker of 910 tons, but at the cost of two Mosquitoes.

Above: The Mosquito Mk XVIII had the heaviest-calibre gun of any operational British combat aircraft. The 2.25-in (57-mm) Molins gun mounted under the nose weighed nearly 1 ton (1016 kg), but gave the 'Tsetse' Mosquito unequalled firepower until the advent of rocket-armed Mosquitoes. Only 27 'Tsetses' were built.

the cost of very heavy casualties. The remnants of the squadrons were gathered into No. 39 Squadron at Luqa under Wing Commander Patrick Gibbs, who had formerly flown with No. 22 Squadron in Britain. Gibbs insisted on employing the Beaufighters of No. 227 Squadron to suppress the flak from enemy ships and their escorts, while the torpedo aircraft followed immediately and dropped their weapons in very quick succession. Losses continued to be heavy but the tactics had a devastating effect on the Axis convoys, with numerous sinkings.

Wheeler recommended that the home-based squadrons should attack in wing formation only after prior reconnaissance and intelligence, that each anti-flak Beaufighters should be given a target in advance and thus protect the 'Torbeaus', which should operate in 'fluid pairs' against specific ships. Above all, the attacks should not take place unless the force was protected by fighter escorts.

After some argument, these tactics were adopted in the first attack of the year, which took place on 19 April off Texel. Fifty-one

Beaufighters took part, including those of No. 143 Squadron, which had joined the North Coates Strike Wing. Some of the anti-flak aircraft also carried bombs. They were escorted by 22 Spitfires of Nos 118 and 167 Squadrons. On Wheeler's command of "Attack attack attack", the Beaufighters turned to their target in well-drilled precision, with startling results. Four of the escorting vessels were damaged and one of the main merchant ships was sunk by torpedoes. Moreover, every aircraft returned, to be met by a cheering crowd of ground personnel who

Coastal Command Strike Aircraft Comparisons

Type/date introduced	Engines	Top speed	Initial climb	Range	Armament
Vickers Vildebeest III/1935	1 x 635 hp (476 kW)	143 mph (230 km/h)	630 ft (192 m)/min	1,250 miles (2011 km)	2 MGs, 1 torpedo or 1,100 lb (499 kg) of bombs
Avro Anson I/1936	2 x 350 hp (262 kW)	188 mph (303 km/h)	720 ft (219 m)/min	660 miles (1062 km)	2 MGs (1 fwd), 360 lb (163 kg) of bombs
Lockheed Hudson I/1939	2 x 1,100 hp (75 kW)	246 mph (396 km/h)	1,200 ft (366 m)/min	2,160 miles (3477 km)	5 MGs (2 fwd), 750 lb (340 kg) of bombs
Bristol Beaufort I/1939	2 x 1,130 hp (847 kW)	265 mph (426 km/h)	1,200 ft (366 m)/min	1,035 miles (1666 km)	4-7 MGs (2 fwd), 1 torpedo
Bristol Blenheim IV/1940	2 x 920 hp (690 kW)	266 mph (428 km/h)	1,500 ft (457 m)/min	1,460 miles (2350 km)	5 MGs (1 fwd), 1,320 lb (599 kg) of bombs
Handley-Page Hampden I/1941	2 x 1,000 hp (750 kW)	254 mph (409 km/h)	980 ft (299 m)/min	1,885 miles (3034 km)	4 MGs (2 fwd), 1 torpedo
Bristol Beaufighter VIc/1942	2 x 1,600 hp (1199 kW)	306 mph (492 km/h)	2,005 ft (611 m)/min	2,800 miles (4,500 km)	4 cannon, eight rockets
Bristol Beaufighter TF.Mk X/1943	2 x 1,772 hp (1328 kW)	333 mph (536 km/h)	1,430 ft (436 m)/min	1,470 miles (2366 km)	4 cannon, 1 MG, 1 torpedo or eight rockets or 1,500 lb (680 kg) of bombs
de Havilland Mosquito VI/1944	2 x 1,635 hp (1228 kW)	380 mph (611 km/h)	1,870 ft (570 m)/min	1,205 miles (1939 km)	4 cannon, 4 MGs, eight rockets or 4 500-lb (227-kg) bombs

unexpectedly lined the runway at North Coates.

This attack marked a turning point in the fortunes of the strike squadrons. Another significant improvement was the introduction of the rocket projectile shortly afterwards. The Beaufighter could carry eight of these in rails under the wings, and each was fitted with a 25-lb (11.3-kg) solid-shot warhead. The rockets were aimed at the water in front of the ships so that they curved upwards and penetrated the hulls, on the principle that one hole below the

waterline was worth 10 above. The first attack was made on 1 June 1943 in a Beaufighter of No. 236 Squadron flown by Flying Officer Mark Bateman, on detachment at St Eval, when *U-418* was sunk with all hands. Rockets were fitted to the anti-flak squadrons of the North Coates Strike Wing later in the month, but the crews took some time to perfect their techniques with the new weapon and the first results were disappointing.

From July, the new Beaufighter TF.Mk X was supplied to the squadrons. This was fitted

On 12 August 1944 the Portreath Strike Wing, consisting of the Mosquito VIs of Nos 235 and 248 Squadrons, flew to the Gironde Estuary near Bordeaux and attacked enemy vessels with bombs and rockets. Two German minesweepers, the M370 and the Mari Therese, were sunk.

with even more powerful engines and an extended tail fin which gave better stability at low level, and could be employed as a torpedo carrier or for anti-flak. There was some doubt in Coastal Command about the effectiveness of the strike wing concept, but in October another was formed at Wick, consisting of Nos 144 and 404 (RCAF) Squadrons, both equipped with the new TF.Mk X. By this time, Swedish companies had refused to allow their vessels to sail as far as Rotterdam. Unloading of Swedish ships took place at Emden, increasing transport

The Molins gun of a 'Tsetse' Mosquito produces a blaze of light as another shell streaks towards the Wartheland, a German vessel of 3,768 tons. The Wartheland was sunk by No. 248 Squadron in Eid Fjord on 12 December 1944. 'Tsetses' retained two 0.303-in guns for sighting.

Right: One of 34 Mosquitoes that attacked shipping in Sande Fjord on 4 April 1945 fires its cannon and rockets on two of the nine ships found there. A dry dock containing a tanker blew up during the assault, and four of the ships were left burning.

Above: Rocket-equipped Mosquitoes were a devastating weapon against enemy-controlled shipping in the latter part of the war. The pilot could fire them in pairs or as a single salvo of eight. In training, they were often fired in pairs at decreasing ranges, but this proved too dangerous operationally and usually they were salvoed at the target in one go.

A Mosquito VI of No. 143 Sqn of the Banff Strike Wing is seen in February 1945. The versatile Mosquito could carry small depth charges as well as bombs, rockets, cannon and machine-guns, and experiments with mines were undertaken.

problems for the Germans. In the course of 1943, the strike squadrons sank 32 enemy vessels. Although this was little improvement on the previous year, morale among the crews was high, the ratio of successes to losses was improving and the Germans were forced into a ship-building programme coupled with an increase in the number of escort vessels.

Strike wings formed

At the beginning of 1944, there were 11 squadrons equipped with Beaufighters, five of which had been combined into strike wings. All the Hampdens and Hudsons had been phased out as strike aircraft and for the time being no FAA squadrons were under Coastal Command control. The move towards combining the remaining Beaufighter squadrons into strike wings gathered pace. In March, Nos 455 (RAAF) and 489 (RNZAF) Squadrons were officially formed into the Leuchars Strike Wing with the new Beaufighter TF.Mk X, although these 'ANZAC' squadrons had frequently operated in concert for some months. They moved to Langham in Norfolk during April, from where they could work with the North Coates Strike Wing. During this month two more units, Nos 144 and 404 (RCAF) Squadrons, were combined into the Davidstow

An armourer secures a 60-lb (27-kg) high-explosive warhead rocket to a Mosquito at Banff in the winter of 1944-45. There were two types of warhead for the standard 3-in (7.6-cm) rocket – 60-lb HE and 25-lb (11-kg) solid head – designed to pierce a ship below the waterline.

Above: The Banff Strike Wing was guided by Mosquitoes of No. 333 (Norwegian) Squadron to an attack on shipping of Alesund, Norway on 17 March 1945. The attack was very successful, and the German merchant vessels Iris of 3,323 tons and Remage (1,830 tons) plus the Norwegian Log (1,684 tons) were sunk, and the German Erna (865 tons) was very badly damaged.

Below: The tranquillity of a Norwegian fishing village is wrecked by the Mosquitoes and Beaufighters of the Banff Wing as they attack shipping at anchor in Rekefjord on 13 November 1944. In this attack, the Norwegian Rosenburg I, seen here, was badly damaged and the German minesweeper R32 and the ASR boat 529 were sunk.

On 20 March 1945, Mosquitoes of the Banff Wing attacked enemy shipping in the Norwegian harbour of Porsgrunn as well as a factory on the quayside. Due to collapse of the German organisational system at this stage of the war, no confirmation of the several vessels claimed sunk can be made. The pall of black smoke comes from a Mosquito that crashed during the attack.

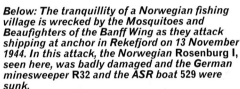

forced with concrete against magnetic mines.

The strike squadrons were in position to protect the flanks of the invasion force from D-Day, 6 June. They were joined by eight squadrons of the FAA before Operation Overlord began, five of Avengers and three of Swordfish. All squadrons made a series of effective attacks, against German destroyers moving up from the west and against German R-boats and E-boats in the east. The attacks were carried out with the help of the new Portreath Strike Wing, which was formed in early June with two Mosquito squadrons. One of these was No. 235 Squadron, which converted from Beaufighters to Mosquito VIs at the time of D-Day. This aircraft carried four 20-mm guns and four machine-guns, together with eight rocket rails. The other was No. 248 Squadron, which had converted from Beaufighters to Mosquito VIs during the previous January. There was also a special detachment of Mosquito XVIIIs in No. 248 Squadron. This aircraft, known as the 'Tsetse', was fitted with a Molins anti-tank gun in the nose, capable of firing 6-lb (2.7-kg) shells at the rate of two per second from a magazine of 25 rounds. A U-boat had been sunk by one of these 'tsetses' on 25 March, and No. 248 Squadron shared in the destruction of another on 10 June.

By the end of June, the Davidstow Strike Wing moved to Strubby in Lincolnshire, to concentrate on the coastal traffic off Norway. In September it moved further north to Banff, where it was joined by the Portreath Strike Wing, after all German surface vessels operating from France had been wiped out. From here

Moor Strike Wing in Cornwall, from where their TF.Mk Xs could disrupt enemy shipping along the west coast of France.

Sinkings increased steadily, but this type of operation remained extremely hazardous. All attacks took place at very low level, when the aircraft and the defending ships could fire at point-blank range. Although the weapons of the Beaufighter could be devastating, the Germans had packed their ships with defensive armament. Among the escorts were many of the formidable *Sperrbrecher*, a large merchant ship converted into a flak ship equipped with numerous guns of all calibres and a hull rein-

Xs. By this time, the use of torpedoes had been abandoned by the RAF and the squadrons employed the rocket as a more effective weapon.

During the course of 1944, the RAF strike squadrons and their FAA companions sank about 175 enemy vessels of all types, an enormous increase on their past results. At the same time, Bomber Command continued attacks on ports and ship-building yards, assisted by Halifaxes of Coastal Command, while mining of enemy waters took another heavy toll of enemy shipping. The remainder of this enemy merchant fleet and its escorts faced annihilation. Germany's desperate problems were compounded by Sweden's decision in September 1944 to close its Baltic ports to the country.

The remnants of the coastal shipping were duly torn to pieces in the final months of the year. As the Russians advanced in the east, German ships and U-boats in the Baltic moved west and became additional targets for the strike wings. By this time, the strike squadrons operated off Denmark and the North Sea coast of Germany, as well as off Norway. Before the war was over, they sank 10 U-boats on the surface and 86 other vessels. The North Coates Strike Wing also sank 10 midget submarines off the Dutch coast.

German ship-building suffers

Although the anti-shipping offensive did not stop Germany's import of Swedish iron ore and other vital minerals until late in the war, the campaign resulted in mounting difficulties for the country from early 1943. Aerial minelaying at night sank more ships than the strike aircraft, especially in the Baltic, while other enemy ships were destroyed in harbour by Bomber Command and the US Eighth Air Force, but the combined effect of the campaign was overwhelming. The German ship-building programme was unable to keep pace with the rate

the Mosquitos and Beaufighters ranged along the coasts of Norway. Most of the enemy ships moved only at night, but they sheltered in harbours or fjords during the day and could still be attacked. The Banff Strike Wing was often protected by long-range Mustangs during their daylight attacks. It also had the invaluable services of No. 333 (Norwegian) Squadron, which was equipped with Mosquito VIs. The Norwegian crews were familiar with their home terrain and acted as outriders for the main

The main Coastal Command effort against U-boats was made by flying-boats and Liberator bombers, but the strike wings scored against enemy submarines too. On 2 May 1945, the Banff Wing attacked U-boats in the Kattegat, sinking the U-2359 and damaging two others.

force, guiding them to targets in the fjords.

By September. the Allies had advanced into Belgium and the southern part of Holland, rendering Rotterdam useless to the Germans and enabling the North Coates Strike Wing to concentrate on Denmark and the south coasts of Norway. One of its number, No. 143 Squadron, converted to Mosquito VIs and flew up to Banff in October. The squadrons in Scotland were then split into two, with Nos 143, 235 and 248 Squadrons remaining in the Banff Strike Wing and equipped with Mosquitos, while Nos 144 and 404 Squadrons moved to Dallachy in Morayshire where they were joined by Nos 455 and 489 Squadrons from Strubby. The new Dallachy Strike Wing was equipped entirely with Beaufighter TF.Mk

of sinkings and the repair of damaged ships became an insuperable problem, while the Kriegsmarine had great difficulties in finding sufficient seamen to replace casualties and man its dwindling number of ships. German war production was tied up in this area of operations and numerous units of the Luftwaffe were kept in constant readiness against day and night attacks. The strike force of Coastal Command seldom numbered more than about 12 squadrons, all of which were engaged solely on attacks against legitimate military targets. Their contribution to the ultimate victory was of far greater significance than is generally recognised.

Roy C. Nesbit

Right: The demanding nature of many of the anti-shipping missions flown along the Norwegian coast is demonstrated by this view of Beaufighters of the North Coates or Dallachy Wings picking off concealed shipping along the walls of a fjord.

Below: Ships were not the only victims of the strike wings. On 21 April 1945, the Banff Wing, led by Wing Commander Christopher Foxley-Norris, encountered a force of about 18 Ju 88s, Ju 188s and He 111s while returning from a fruitless anti-shipping patrol in the Kattegat. Nine of the German aircraft (some of which were carrying torpedoes) were claimed shot down by the Mosquito pilots, for no loss, but post-war evidence suggests that only two aircraft managed to return to Norway, and these made belly-landings. Here, one of the bombers explodes on the water as two Mosquitoes pull away.

94th Fighter Squadron
'Hat in the Ring'

When the public thinks of American air power in World War I, the image that immediately comes to mind is the 'Hat in the Ring' emblem that became possibly the best-known squadron badge in US history. Today, the unit flies the F-15, a far cry from the SPADs of the Great War. Between the two lies a proud history.

This P-38 pilot from the 94th provides an abiding image of a World War II American fighter pilot. The 'Hat in the Ring' badge, restored to the unit early in the war, was worn with great pride.

Today, 'tossing a hat into a ring' has become the term for announcing a political candidacy, but in the early years of this century the act signified readiness for a fight. Unfortunately, the United States was not nearly as ready to fight as this impudent symbol suggested.

It was the 94th's commander, Major John S. Huffer, who had the idea for what has become one of the most famous of military emblems. One of the pilots, Lieutenant Johnny Wentworth, was an architect and was asked to design a distinctive insignia. Huffer suggested Uncle Sam's stovepipe hat with the stars and stripes for a hatband. The flight surgeon, Lieutenant Gary Walters, mentioned the old American custom of throwing a hat in the ring

as an invitation to battle. Thus, the 'Hat in the Ring' was created.

The 94th Aero Squadron came into being at Kelly Field, Texas on 20 August 1917 and went to Europe as part of the 1st Pursuit Group. The Great War was the first full-sized test of combat aircraft. Americans were late entering the war, and by 1917 air combat was no longer a curiosity. But aircraft, weapons, tactics and people were all evolving and the 94th Aero Squadron – joined, from the beginning, by the 95th Aero Squadron – was there early enough to be a pioneer. The 94th went into action at Villeneuve-les-Vertus, commanded by Major John S. Huffer. Both the 94th and 95th squadrons were initially equipped with Nieuport 28C-1s.

The Germans launched a massive attack

against the British lines north of Villeneuve on 21 March 1918. The Nieuports of the 94th and 95th still lacked guns. Worse, staff officers in Paris reported that the pilots were not proficient enough to withstand an onslaught. Villeneuve was too close to the front to be occupied by partially-trained units, so the 1st Pursuit Group Organization and Training Center moved to a quieter sector. Someone in headquarters also realised that most of the pilots had not received any formal air-to-air gunnery training. Consequently, on 21 March 1918, 95th pilots went off for the training while the 94th set up

shop at what one pilot called 'a mud patch' at Epiez on 1 April. Soon afterward, the squadron moved to dryer ground at Gencoult and began flying patrols.

In its Nieuport 28C-1s, the 94th made the first patrol flown by an all-American squadron in France. This took place on 6 March 1918. Major Raoul Lufbery led two young first lieutenants, Douglas Campbell and Edward V. Rickenbacker, on a two-hour patrol near Rheims. A German anti-aircraft battery challenged the flight, but it encountered no aerial opposition. This was fortunate because neither Campbell's Nieuport nor Rickenbacker's carried any armament. The two neophytes believed they had flown an uneventful patrol. To their surprise, the more experienced Lufbery pointed out that he had spotted no less than 10 SPADs, four German fighters, and a German two-seat observation aircraft during the mission. He also showed Rickenbacker holes in the fabric skin of the younger pilot's aircraft, a reminder of their brush with the German battery.

Rickenbacker remembered in his biography that the new 'Hat in the Ring' emblem proudly adorned his Nieuport on the morning of 14 April 1918 when he, Captain Peterson and Lieutenant Reed Chambers took off for a patrol of American lines in their sector, to be followed aloft by Campbell and Winslow. This was the first combat mission ever ordered by an American commander of an American squadron of American pilots – and it was a fiasco. Fog closed in. Peterson became disorientated in the weather and returned to the airfield. Rickenbacker remembered that, "[Chambers] and I continued on. We became separated in the fog and were nearly lost. Two German planes pursued us and they really became lost."

First American kills

Hearing the German aircraft over the field, Lieutenants Douglas Campbell and Allan Winslow of the 94th took off and shot down a German Albatros D.III and an Albatros D.V over their own airfield. Lieutenant Winslow's victory is recognised as the first of World War I for the US Army Flying Corps. At the time, Campbell's plane had only one machine-gun installed because the squadron had just received its first shipment of Vickers .303s and there were not enough for two per plane.

The American pilots landed about 10 minutes after having scrambled aloft for their baptism of fire. Bad weather settled in, so the 94th remained on the ground for several days, basking in the glow of its initial success. Captain James N. Hall and Lieutenant Rickenbacker shared a kill on 29 April 1918, the squadron's only other victory that month. Soon after this, the 27th Aero Squadron joined the 94th and 95th in the field.

The 1st Pursuit Group suffered a devastating loss on 19 May 1918 when Major Lufbery, part of the group staff but flying with the 94th, took off to intercept a German intruder. He attacked the two-seater but the German gunner hit Lufbery's Nieuport in its fuel tank. The aircraft burst into flames. Lufbery rode the blazing machine down to about 3,000 ft (915 m) where he apparently jumped out of the aircraft. He wore no parachute. French villagers who witnessed his fall reported that he struck a fence, staggered briefly to his feet, then fell over dead. Lufbery had received credit for 17 kills at the time of his death, although he may have scored at least that many more that were never confirmed. First Lieutenant Kenneth P. Culbert, who spoke eloquently at Lufbery's funeral, was himself killed in action the next day.

As for the Nieuport 28 with its 160-hp (119-kW) Gnome 9N rotary piston engine, the sprightly French-built biplane suffered from engine problems and a tendency to shed upper-wing fabric in long dives – neither a trait that endeared it to pilots. The Nieuport was typically armed with two fixed, forward-firing 0.303-in (7.7-mm) Vickers machine-guns. A poll of pilots showed that not one in the 94th believed the Nieuport was the equal of German fighters.

Misgivings aside, the Nieuport worked for First Lieutenant Douglas Campbell who became the first American air ace on 31 May 1918. Campbell shot down a German Rumpler observation plane over American lines near the village of Menil-la-Tours. 94th pilots introduced the 27th squadron to action by leading their first patrols on 2 June 1918.

Headquarters for the 1st Pursuit Group was shifted to Tonquin on 29 June 1918, the same

front and predicted a drive on Paris. To provide air cover for the upcoming offensive, the Germans deployed 46 of their 71 fighter squadrons, including Hermann Göring's Jagdeschwader I, the famed 'Richthofen Flying Circus'. The quality and numbers of the opposition, along with the demanding requirements of the group's missions, forced the 1st Pursuit Group to adopt new tactics.

Observation support

Colonel William 'Billy' Mitchell, First Air Brigade commander, assigned the 1st Pursuit Group three missions. The squadrons worked to allow American observation aircraft to operate freely, to prevent enemy observation aircraft from completing their missions, and to "cause such other casualties and inflict such other material damage on the enemy as may be possible." The tactics adopted to protect American observation aircraft subsequently caused unnecessary losses, but the most immediate problem the group faced came from the numerically superior, aggressive, and experienced German squadrons.

Only by suffering heavy observation and fighter losses did the American fliers discover successful tactics: the observation aircraft flew in larger formations, forcing attacking Germans to face the concentrated gunfire of their defensive

armament. Escort support took the form of squadron-strength fighter sweep flown ahead of and around the observation formations. This gave the fighters the initiative, since they could now attack as the Germans climbed toward the observation formation. Epic air battles involving several squadrons on both sides sometimes developed.

The 94th in particular experienced difficulties with Nieuports coming apart in mid-air – the ultimate fate for a fragile aircraft with a notorious reputation for shedding fabric from its wings during violent manoeuvres. The Americans expressed frustration with their Nieuports and thoroughly disliked the tricky flying characteristics of the Camel. They opted to change over to the SPAD S.XIII, and ultimately gained considerable success with this excellent scout. The conversion to the SPAD (a term which quickly became a dictionary word in American aviation) took place during July 1918 and was seen at the time as adding to the challenges confronting the pilots. Among the SPAD's greatest exponents were Rickenbacker (26 victories) and the companion squadron's Lieutenant Frank Luke (21 victories).

The SPAD XIII was powered by a 220-hp (165-kW) Hispano-Suiza 8Ba engine. Over 7,000 were eventually built and the aircraft became the best-known fighter of World War I in the USA. It was sturdier and more powerful than the little-lamented Nieuport, but its

day the group's 54 Nieuport 28s made the flight without incident. From here, the pursuit group was to have four months of continuous combat. The group's operations on the Marne marked the beginning of a period during which the Army Air Service began to develop operational and tactical procedures. Allied intelligence had detected a massive German build-up along the

Wings

Each wing was built around a two-spar construction, with five crosses of internal wire bracing and a thin shaped wooden strip for the leading edge and wingtip. The lower wings were joined to the fuselage, while the upper wings were mounted on a sturdy centre-section. The latter incorporated a cutout to improve visibility and featured padding to minimise injury in the event of a crash landing.

Powerplant

SPAD XIIIs were powered by various versions of the Hispano-Suiza 8B engine, the most common being the 8Bc which produced 220 hp (164 kW) at 2,100 rpm. The engine was cooled by a frontal radiator, with variable shutters, and a small header tank for coolant in the upper wing centre-section. Additional ventilation plates below and to the sides helped with cooling. Exhaust was collected from the cylinders and ducted, four per side, externally to behind the cockpit.

Gunsight

Several sight systems were employed on the SPAD, but the most common was this simple cross. It was mounted on a transverse beam between the guns, offset to starboard. It was as far forward from the pilot as possible to minimise angular discrepancies caused by the varying position of his head.

SPAD S.XIII
94th Pursuit Squadron
1st Pursuit Group

This SPAD was the mount of Captain Edward V. Rickenbacker, the highest-scoring American pilot of World War I. Born on 8 October 1890, Rickenbacker was commissioned in France in early 1918 and was assigned to the 94th Pursuit Squadron in March. On 29 April he downed his first victim, an Albatros D.Va, and racked up a further 21 aircraft and four balloon kills by the Armistice on 11 November. He took command of the squadron on 25 September.

Undercarriage

The main undercarriage was attached directly to the airframe, and was braced by four wires. The main axle consisted of three beams and elastic to absorb the shocks of ground operations. The tailskid was equipped with a steel shoe, and was pivoted around the attachment on the lower fuselage. A horn projected into the fuselage, with elastic shock absorbing.

Armament

The SPAD was armed with two Vickers 0.303-in (7.7-mm) machine-guns, mounted in troughs in the upper fuselage. Each gun was armed with 400 rounds, and had an external cocking lever just forward of the cockpit.

Fuel

SPAD XIIIs had two fuel tanks. The main 24-Imp gal (110-litre) tank was in the lower fuselage just forward of the pilot, the lower part forming part of the aircraft's lower skin. A smaller tank was located in the upper wing centre-section.

Above and right: To relieve squadron boredom following the end of the war, the 94th PS began painting its SPAD XIIIs in a wide array of 'show-bird' schemes with which they intended to celebrate over Paris.

Hispano-Suiza engine was more complex and more difficult to keep in tune. Pilot transition and the maintenance training process disrupted operations and effectively grounded the 94th squadron for several days.

The Chateau Thierry (or Aisne-Marne) campaign comprised two phases that lasted from 15 July to about 6 August 1918. The long-awaited German offensive formed phase one from 15 to 18 July. The Germans gained some ground, but the well-prepared Allied armies blunted the German drive. The Allies launched a counter-offensive that lasted from 18 July through early August. To a degree, the 94th was overshadowed by the other squadrons of the 1st Pursuit Group during this period but the 94th fought valiantly nonetheless.

Rickenbacker, who went to some lengths to lay his hands on a SPAD ahead of his colleagues, was elated with the improved performance offered by the new fighter. Conversely, he was distressed with his own side for not providing parachutes, which he understood were being routinely issued to the Germans.

In August 1918, a mid-air collision claimed the lives of First Lieutenants Walter Smyth and Alexander Bruce. "With parachutes on, both of those fine young men would have lived," remembered Rickenbacker. "It was absolutely criminal for our higher command to withhold

parachutes from us. Men perished in agony [needlessly]. What reward did Raoul Lufbery gain for his role in helping to develop American air mastery? Death on a picket fence when a parachute would have saved his life."

A major in Paris complained to Rickenbacker that, "If you pilots had parachutes, you'd use them on the slightest pretext and the Air Service would lose planes that might otherwise be brought down safely."

The group operated out of Tonquin and later Saints (occupied on 8 July) until about 20 August 1918. On 21 August 1918, Major Harold E. Hartney became group commander.

Hidden deployment

The 94th and its parent group moved again in early September 1918 from Saints to Rembercourt, 20 miles (31 km) west of the town of St Mihiel on the Verdun/St Mihiel front. This move became part of the American drive to eliminate the St Mihiel salient and the group made the trip under the utmost secrecy. As the squadrons arrived at Rembercourt they dispersed around the field and camouflaged their aircraft and other equipment. The group kept its deployment hidden while it attempted to mask the American build-up along its front from German observation aircraft.

The attack began on 12 September 1918. American forces eliminated the German positions in about four days. During the campaign the 1st Pursuit Group covered the front from Chatillion-sous-les-Cotes to St Mihiel, flying observation escort and anti-observation sorties.

Extremely bad weather during the first three days of the offensive forced American aircraft to low levels, where they attacked German observation balloons and harassed troops on the ground. The attack caught the Germans in the midst of evacuating the salient, and American aircraft took a heavy toll of the retreating enemy. The weather improved on 14 September 1918, but German air opposition centred on the southern flank of the salient covered by the American fighter units. As a result, the 1st Pursuit Group concentrated on ground attack throughout the campaign. Although ground operations ended on 16 September, air operations continued for another week or so.

Pilots flew many sorties each day, frequently landing only to take on more fuel and ammunition. The pace of action took its toll on both aircraft and pilots. As the ground campaign drew to a close, Hartney ordered the group to reduce its operations to give the mechanics time to make permanent repairs on the SPADs, many of which were beginning to look like flying sieves from ground fire. The pilots were as worn out as the aircraft: on 16 September 1918, First Lieutenant John Jeffers of the 94th fell asleep while returning from a patrol. His SPAD continued its flight on course, losing altitude slowly. Jeffers woke up in time to level out and crash on a hill not far from the airfield. He escaped injury.

On 25 September 1918, Lieutenant Rickenbacker replaced Major Kenneth Marr as commanding officer of the 94th Aero Squadron. Rickenbacker took command of a

Above: In 1922 the 94th PS began operating the Thomas-Morse MB-3A, the first effective fighter of US origin. In addition to this main combat type, the 94th had a collection of utility aircraft such as the Curtiss JN-4, Curtiss JN-6, Orenco D Pursuit, Fokker PW-5 and Airco DH-4.

Left: Following demobilisation in June 1919, a new 94th Pursuit Squadron was formed in the lean inter-war USAAC organisation. The first major equipment was the Royal Aircraft Factory S.E.5a, flown between 1919 and 1922.

The 94th flew aircraft from both of the famous American interwar biplane fighter families. Shown above is a Curtiss P-1B Hawk, which was assigned from 1925 to 1931 and which supplanted the Curtiss PW-8 as the main service type. The Boeing P-12B (right) was on strength from 1930 to 1932. These were augmented at times throughout the period by the Curtiss P-2, P-3, P-5 and P-6, all members of the Hawk family.

squadron which, in his view, "had never lived up to its early promise." When he checked on the status of the squadron's aerial victories he found that the "presumptuous young 27th [squadron] had suddenly taken a spurt, thanks to their brilliant [Frank] Luke, and now led the Hat in the Ring Squadron by six victories!" Rickenbacker immediately convened his pilots and announced that "no other American squadron at the front would ever again be permitted to approach our margin of supremacy." Within a week the 94th had overtaken the 27th and never again relinquished the lead.

After his talk with the pilots, Rickenbacker next approached the squadron's mechanics who, he reported, "felt the disgrace of being second more keenly than did we pilots." Not surprisingly, Rickenbacker later noted that from that time on the squadron's aircraft were always in top mechanical condition.

Rickenbacker resolved to lead by example. He found others to take care of paperwork and administrative duties so that he could fly. "I never spent more than 30 minutes a day upon the ground business connected with 94's operation."

The US Army launched its final offensive of the war on 26 September 1918 when the American First Army began the Meuse-Argonne offensive. The terrain favoured the defenders and the Germans had organised a formidable defensive system. The 1st Pursuit Group drew the task of providing low-level support during the advance. Committed to low-altitude defence suppression and air support operations, the 94th and its sister squadrons reverted to the small formations and stalking tactics that had characterised earlier service on the Toul front. During the last seven weeks of the war, most missions were flown at low altitude, attacking enemy observation aircraft and heavily-defended observation balloons, although pilots showed no reluctance to take on enemy fighters that slipped past the group's top cover. The loss of Lieutenant Frank Luke in the 94th's companion 27th squadron occurred during this period.

Rickenbacker's 94th squadron racked up 28 kills in the final six weeks of the war. This was a pace-setting tally for the 1st Pursuit Group. In October, the group's five squadrons destroyed 56 of the enemy at a cost of 13 American air-

One of the most attractive of the interwar biplanes was the Curtiss P-6E, a few of which were used by the 94th in 1932 prior to the squadron adopting the two-place P-16. The Indian head adorned the squadron's aircraft from 1924 to 1942.

craft. November was an even more remarkable month. During the first 10 days of the month, the group destroyed 45 German aircraft and balloons without a loss. The 94th, which had claimed America's first kill of the war, also received credit for the last, a Fokker destroyed by Major Maxwell Kirby on 10 November 1918. The armistice took effect the next day.

Rickenbacker finished the war as America's 'ace of aces' with 26 kills: 22 aircraft and four balloons. The 94th Aero Squadron received credit for 67½ kills. The 94th had suffered 18 combat casualties.

Army of occupation

On 17 November 1918 orders from the American staff in Paris relieved the 94th Aero Squadron from its assignment to the 1st Pursuit Group, assigned it to the 5th Pursuit Group, Third Army, and directed it to prepare to accompany elements of the American Army across the Rhine. The squadron departed Rembercourt on 25 November and occupied the former German airfield at Noers ('No Wheres', pilots called it) four days later.

In December 1918, 94th pilots – bored by inactivity brought about by the Armistice – sought to repaint their drab SPADs. With Rickenbacker's departure on a bond tour, squadron commander Captain Reed Chambers authorised the men to paint gaudy 'show bird' colour schemes on their fighters, and painted his own craft red, white and blue, calling it the American Flag. (Chambers lined up seven German Maltese crosses, signifying his aerial victories, inside the hat brim in the 'Hat in the Ring' insignia.) Intending to fly their aircraft to a planned banner celebration in Paris in April 1919, other pilots painted aircraft, described in a document at the time, as 'a giant wasp, a reclin-

On 8 April 1924 the 103rd Aero Squadron (formed 31 August 1917 from former members of the Lafayette Escadrille) was consolidated with the 94th. When the 'Hat in the Ring' insignia was banned in September 1924, the 94th Pursuit Squadron used the 103rd's World War I-vintage Indian head as its badge.

ing mermaid, a fish with silver scales outlined on a black [background], another of bright canary colour, another of blood red all over...' First Lieutenant Leo H. Dawson's Shamrock had vivid alternating green and white diagonal wing striping and green and white shamrocks spread about its fuselage. Other SPADs were painted to represent an Easter egg and the Japanese naval flag.

The aircraft were not flown over Paris as the men had hoped (although some travelled to the capital, flying part-way to Toul) but the brightly-coloured aircraft were displayed at several events after the 13th Aero Squadron took over the aircraft from the 94th in the spring of 1919.

The 94th ended its service with the Third Army on 9 April 1919 and arrived at Hoboken,

New Jersey on 31 May 1919. It demobilised at New York on 1 June. Even as the World War I squadrons completed their demobilisation, however, the War Department began organising a new 1st Pursuit Group at Selfridge Field, Michigan.

Inter-war years

In April 1919, the War Department despatched two-man cadres of the 94th Pursuit Squadron and three sister units to Selfridge, thus laying the foundation for a new 1st Pursuit Group. Activated on 22 August 1919, the group became one of three group-level organisations in the US Army's air arm for most of the next decade. After a brief sojourn at Ellington Field, Texas, the 1st Pursuit Group resettled in Michigan in 1922 under commander Major Carl Spatz (who, years later, changed the spelling of his name to Spaatz).

One of the aircraft flown by the 'Hat in the Ring' during this immediate post-war era was the S.E.5a, which squadron pilots had flown in Europe but had not adopted. The Royal Aircraft Factory S.E.5a had been regarded by many as the best scout aircraft of World War I. With its slender lines and fighting prowess, the S.E.5a was flown by famous aces like William 'Billy' Bishop, Ray Collishaw, and Edward 'Mick' Mannock. The tough, rugged S.E.5a was powered by a 200-hp (149-kW) Wolseley Viper V-8 engine and, in British use, was armed with a forward-firing synchronised 7.7-mm Vickers machine-gun and a Lewis gun mounted over the centre section of the upper wing.

The parent unit of the 94th finally got its own emblem in 1924 when the War Department sanctioned unit emblems. On 21 January 1924, the Adjutant General approved an insigne for the 1st Pursuit Group. The design of the device reflected the unit's history. The colours of the shield – green and black – represented the original Army Air Service. The five stripes stood for the group's five campaigns: Champagne-Marne, Aisne-Marne, St Mihiel, Verdun and Meuse-Argonne. The colours of the crest, with its golden winged arrow on a sky-blue disc, were the colours of the Army Air Corps. The crest bore the group's motto '*Aut Vincere Aut Mori*' ('Conquer or Die'). Revisions made in 1957 deleted the crest and added the scroll at the base of the shield, creating the version for today's 1st Fighter Wing.

The War Department decided it had no choice but to change the emblem of the 94th because of a commercial consideration that arose in the post-war years. In the 1920s Eddie Rickenbacker produced a line of automobiles that bore his name. Rickenbacker adopted, as the company's logo, the hat-in-the-ring device the 94th had used as a unit emblem during the war. Again in an effort to avoid the appearance that it was promoting a product, the Adjutant

Above: Major Ralph Royce was the 1st Pursuit Group commander in 1936, seen here in the cockpit of his Boeing P-26A. All of the three constituent squadrons converted to the monoplane fighter in 1934.

Left: Eighteen Boeing P-26As from the 94th Pursuit Squadron pose in vics for the camera. The P-26 had one foot in the future (first US monoplane fighter) and one in the past (open cockpit, non-retractable undercarriage and external wing and gear bracing).

General's office decided on 6 September 1924 that the 94th would use the Indian head device formerly used by the 103rd Aero Squadron. Even though the Rickenbacker automobile was not a commercial success and the company soon went out of business, the 94th continued to use the Indian head insignia until 1942.

In the early 1920s, the Thomas-Morse M.B.3a was among the fighters on the 'Hat in the Ring' squadron's roster. In the mid-1920s the principal fighters of the 94th and its sister squadrons were the Curtiss PW-8 and P-1 Hawk. In 1930, the 1st Pursuit Group picked up Boeing P-12Bs, some of which went to the 94th squadron. By 1932, however, the 94th Pursuit Squadron's strength consisted of 16 Y1P-16s.

Two-place fighter

The Berliner-Joyce Y1P-16 (later P-16) was roughly the same size as the more familiar Curtiss P-6 Hawk and Boeing P-12, but carried a two-man crew – pilot and rear gunner. Powered by a Curtiss V-1570A engine, the P-16 had a top speed of 175 mph (282 km/h), a service ceiling of about 25,000 ft (7740 m), and a range of 650 miles (1046 km). The US Army procured only 25 and apparently assigned all to the 94th. In January 1933, the squadron's Y1P-16s participated in cold weather tests at Selfridge. Together with two Keystone B-6A biplane bombers from another unit, the tests included all five pursuit types then used by the 1st Pursuit Group (P-6E, P-12C, D and E, and Y1P-16). The 94th Pursuit Squadron apparently operated its entire fleet of Y1P-16s at Selfridge, Sault Sainte Marie, Michigan and Duluth, Minnesota, with good results, until the test unit was disbanded on 15 March 1933.

The 1933 cycle for training manoeuvres included an Air Corps anti-aircraft exercise in southern Ohio and Kentucky. These were large exercises involving several Air Corps units. The 94th with its Y1P-16s was based at Patterson Field, Ohio, and assigned to the 3rd Attack Group.

The 1933 exercise tested the anti-aircraft net, and the applicability of radio to air defence. Some of the defending fighters carried radios, so the net spotted and tracked attackers and helped

Above: From 1934 to 1938 the Boeing P-26 was the 94th's main fighter, but a few Consolidated P-30A (later redesignated PB-2A) two-seat fighters were also used. These aircraft had an armament of two fixed 0.303-in guns in the upper fuselage, and a single trainable gun in the rear cockpit.

Right: Seversky P-35As arrived in 1937, the first of the modern monoplane fighters to serve the USAAC. This example has been restored by the USAF Museum in 94th Pursuit Squadron markings.

position interceptors for attacks. Although bad weather grounded the pursuits for several days, leaving the group staff to practise tracking attack formations, officials later concluded that the air defence manoeuvres were successful.

The 1st Pursuit Group participated in the 1933 World's Fair in Chicago where group commander Major George H. Brett led a 72-plane formation on 1 July 1933. On 15 July 1933 the group launched a 42-plane formation under its new group commander, Lieutenant Colonel Frank M. Andrews, to escort the Italian transatlantic flight of 21 Savoia-Marchetti S-55s under General Italo Balbo from Toledo, Ohio, to Chicago. Like so many of its leaders in the 1930s, these men were to become leaders of the war effort a decade later – Brett as the US air commander in Australia, Andrews with the Eighth Air Force in England.

The 1st Pursuit Group had 69 aircraft in service on 1 January 1934. These included one

P-6A, one XP-6C, and 16 Y1P-16s assigned to the 94th. On 9 February 1934 the group received a message from Major General Benjamin O. Foulois, chief of the Air Corps, advising it to be prepared to assign pilots and aircraft to air mail duty. Two days later, President Franklin D. Roosevelt ordered the Air Corps to carry the mail while his administration resolved contract problems with commercial carriers.

Difficulties with the mail

Air Corps pilots in general were ill-equipped for the mail-hauling task and their equipment was not up to the test. The pilots had little training in night flying, the aircraft lacked adequate instruments, and ground facilities for cross-country flights were lacking. Bad weather compounded the problems. The result was a disaster. From 11 February to 23 June 1934, when the last officer from the 94th returned

Above: Painted for the army war games in North Carolina in 1940 are the Seversky P-35As of the 94th PS, the Indian head markings showing through the hastily applied camouflage. During this period the 94th also operated a few Curtiss P-40s and Republic P-43s.

Right: The Curtiss P-36A also served with the 94th from 1938, flying alongside the P-35A until 1940. In 1941 the squadron gave up the last of its P-35s to begin operations with the much better Lockheed P-38.

The 94th Pursuit Squadron received the Lockheed P-38 Lightning in the summer of 1941, and it was to remain on this type of aircraft for the duration of the war. This a P-38D, photographed prior to Pearl Harbor.

This was Dallas 'Spider' Webb's P-38F, forced down on the Greenland ice-cap in July 1942 while attempting to cross the Atlantic to the war zone in England. Six P-38s and two B-17s suffered this fate and were later discovered and salvaged for restoration during the 1980s.

Flown by Captain Jim Harmon, this was one of two 94th aircraft which landed at Lisbon during the transit to North Africa. This aircraft was interned, and became a part of the Portuguese air force: the other was 'stolen' and flown away by Lieutenant Jack Ilfrey.

from air mail duty, 1st Pursuit Group pilots were involved in 10 crashes or forced landings that cost the Air Corps as many aircraft. On 22 February 1934, First Lieutenant Durwood O. Lowry of the 94th became the first of 12 Air Corps pilots to die carrying the mail when his parachute became entangled in the tail surfaces of a Curtiss O-39 biplane he was forced to abandon near Toledo.

On 22 February 1934, the same day Lowry died, another 1st Pursuit Group pilot escaped with serious injuries when he flew his P-12E into the side of a mountain near Uniontown,

Pennsylvania. The next day group pilots were involved in two crashes and two forced landings. All four aircraft – two O-39s, a P-6E, and a Y1P-16 – were destroyed, but the only injury was a broken leg when a pilot landed on a barn roof in Freemont, Ohio, after abandoning his aircraft. The group and the 94th Pursuit Squadron bid farewell to the air mail in June, and Andrews was replaced as commander of the 1st Pursuit Group on 10 October 1934 by Major Ralph Royce.

In 1935, the 94th converted to the metal-and-fabric, fixed-landing gear, open-cockpit Boeing P-26A Peashooter monoplane fighter. In August 1936, the squadron deployed 28 P-26As to Chanute Field, Illinois, for Second Army manoeuvres.

Modern fighters

The 1st Pursuit Group brought a new generation of fighters into inventory in 1937. Lieutenant Colonel Royce flew the first P-36 from the Curtiss plant at Buffalo, New York, to Selfridge Field on 7 April 1937. The group was still largely equipped with the P-26 and was slow to convert to the Seversky P-35 and Curtiss P-36 with their retractable landing gear, enclosed cockpit and all-metal construction. Powered by a 1,050-hp (783-kW) Pratt & Whitney R-1830-45 Twin Wasp engine, the P-35A had a top speed of about 235 mph (378 km/h). The P-35A with its 1,050-hp Twin Wasp had a maximum speed of about 305 mph (490 km/h). The aircraft delivered by Royce was a Y1P-36 service-test model. Following tests in May 1937, the Air Corps awarded Curtiss a contract for 210 Hawks – the largest US Army fighter order since World War I. These were the aircraft that formed a bridge between the P-26 and those the 94th would fly in World War II.

Although the 1st Pursuit Group was converting to more modern aircraft, it still took its P-26s and PB-2s to Muroc Dry Lake, California for 1937 Air Corps manoeuvres. On 1 May 1937, 16 transports carrying a 168-man advance party left Selfridge. This party arrived at Muroc the next day as the 27th squadron with 15 PB-2As, and the 94th squadron, with 28 P-26Cs, left for California. On 3 May 1937, the 55th

Pursuit Squadron, 28 P-26As from Barksdale, arrived and was attached to the 1st group. More aircraft arrived at Muroc on 4 May to bolster the 27th. The manoeuvres began on 10 May.

The exercise pitted the 1st Pursuit Group's fighters against bombers and attack aircraft in anti-aircraft tests, a scenario much like the one used in 1933 in southern Ohio. The group staff plotted intruders and vectored on-station pursuit ships to intercept them.

Muroc operations

Operations on 11 May 1937 were typical of the exercise: at 03.00 the group command post learned of bombers approaching the patrol area. The 27th squadron scrambled at 03.13, the 55th at 03.22, and the 94th remained in reserve. A formation of 18 attack aircraft entered the air defence zone at 03.27.

The 27th attacked the intruders at 03.41 and 03.51. The 94th scrambled at 04.00, just after the attackers gassed the airfield at Muroc with real tear gas and simulated mustard gas. Elements of the 27th intercepted a bomber formation at 04.37 while a third group faced still more attackers at 04.47.

The 27th picked up yet another attacking group over Muroc at 04.59. The fighters landed at dispersed airfields at 05.25. The three squadrons scrambled again at 14.30 and the 55th made its first interception five minutes later. The 55th picked up more attackers at 14.40, 14.55, 15.15, and 15.22. The group landed at 15.50.

The next day's battle began at 03.20. The surviving record of these mock battles – akin to today's Red Flag exercises – makes for dry reading and gives us little of the flavour of intrepid airmen facing the elements before dawn, of men caught up in mock battle with the wind rushing through the wires and fumes in the cockpit, of the noise and confusion as aircraft rushed over the location of the future Edwards Air Force Base dispensing noxious gas that would never be released in a practice manoeuvre in today's more sensitive climate. Unfortunately, action photography was still in its infancy and no images appear to exist of the 94th Pursuit Squadron defending democracy against an onslaught of rickety A-17s and B-10s. The 1st Pursuit Group maintained the rigorous exercise schedule for 12 days before returning to Selfridge on 26 May.

In 1939, the 1st Pursuit Group's P-36s were painted in experimental camouflage schemes that included such bizarre combinations as

A P-38F is seen at Youk-les-Bains shortly after the journey from England. The 94th was originally assigned to the 8th Air Force, which applied RAF-style two-letter unit codes, the 94th being assigned 'UN', followed by an individual aircraft letter.

green, yellow, orange, and white; lavender, bottle green, olive drab, orange and white; and grey, lavender, olive drab, and forest green. Most of these fighters belonged to the 27th, but some were the property of the 94th Pursuit Squadron.

On 6 December 1939, the word 'interceptor' was added in parentheses to the designations of the 1st Pursuit Group and the 94th Pursuit Squadron. On 1 January 1941, the First Pursuit Squadron (Interceptor) was activated at Selfridge and joined the 71st Pursuit Group as a companion squadron to the 94th – an association that continues today.

The 27th squadron jumped ahead of the 94th in July 1941 when it received its first Lockheed P-38 Lightning, described in a document at the time as "one of the most radical departures from tradition in American fighter development." The Lightning's wing span of 52 ft (16.09 m) was almost double the 28 ft (8.66 m) of the P-26 the 94th had taken to exercises in 1937. The P-38 Lightning's two turbo-supercharged Allison V-1710 inline piston engines each produced 1,475 hp (1100 kW), quite a contrast to the 660 hp (492 kW) of the P-26 of less than a decade earlier. The Lightning had a maximum speed of 414 mph (666 km/h) at 25,000 ft (7740 m), again a contrast to the Boeing fighter's 234 mph (376 km/h) at 7,500 ft (2322 m). The exact date of arrival of the P-38 Lightning with the 94th Pursuit Group seems not to have been recorded, but it occurred in the weeks after the 27th's receipt.

On 5 December 1941, Captain Ralph Garman led the air echelon of the 94th, consisting of 20 P-38s, to March Field, California for a planned 90-day temporary duty assignment. The 94th was at El Paso, Texas when it heard that Japanese carrier aircraft had attacked the US Pacific Fleet at Pearl Harbor.

World War II

The remainder of the 1st Pursuit Group under Major Robert S. Israel, Jr was at Selfridge when, at 18.00 on 7 December 1941, the group received a message from Headquarters First Air Force directing it to proceed to March Field. Group personnel stayed up all night preparing for the deployment, although the first echelon of support personnel did not leave Selfridge until 9 December. The 94th arrived at San Diego on 8 December; the 27th and 71st, flying 12 P-38s and 24 Republic P-43 Lancers, arrived two days later. The group reassembled on 14 December.

The pursuit group began 1942 with an assigned strength of 992 (81 officers and 911 enlisted), against an authorised strength of 1,260 (149 and 1,111). Newly assigned personnel began arriving to increase strength but the numbers gave no real sense of the situation. As

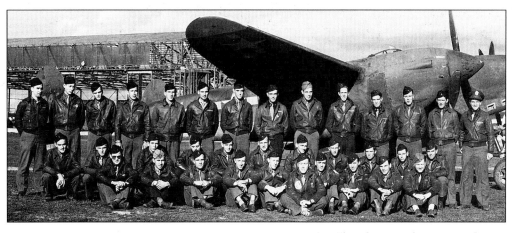

Above: This squadron group photograph was taken at Monserrato, near Cagliari on Sardinia. The date was December 1943 and the aircraft was the P-38H.

Right: The 'Hat in the Ring' emblem was rarely seen on squadron aircraft during World War II, but is painted on this unidentified Lightning. Standing in front, complete with their medals, are Lieutenants Lee, Theise, Vrilakas and Van Sice.

the Air Corps expanded between 1939 and 1941, it often called upon the group to provide cadres for new groups and squadrons. When the Air Corps organised new units after Pearl Harbor, it continued to use the 1st Pursuit Group as a source of cadres but on a much larger scale. On 3 January 1942 the group lost 124 men to the 51st Pursuit Group. On 1 February, 129 more returned to Selfridge where they became the core of the 80th Pursuit Group. Finally, on 25 April, as the group prepared to deploy to Europe, 474 enlisted men and 24 officers, including group commander Israel who had been promoted to lieutenant colonel, were reassigned and formed the cadre of the 82nd Pursuit Group. Morale and performance suffered as a result of these moves.

The War Department recognised that the problems plaguing the 1st Pursuit Group affected other units as well. In March 1942, General Henry H. 'Hap' Arnold, chief of Army Air Forces, contracted Eddie Rickenbacker, who was recovering from injuries suffered in an airliner crash more than a year before. Arnold gave Rickenbacker an aircraft, a crew and a mission: to visit flying units, "talk to these boys, inspire them, put some fire in them," and to look for reasons that morale and performance seemed to be lagging. Beginning 10 March 1942, Rickenbacker visited 41 groups in 41 states in 32 days.

Rickenbacker's travels took him to March Field where he met with his old squadron, the 94th. The pilots assembled and after giving them a pep talk that recalled the squadron's heritage, Rickenbacker asked the pilots to explain

what was wrong. Their complaints ranged from bad food to limited flying time, a familiar litany Rickenbacker heard elsewhere on his tour. But one pilot voiced a complaint that Rickenbacker resolved to handle personally. Why, the pilot asked, was the 94th using the Indian head insignia? What had become of the hat in the ring?

The return of the emblem

On his return to Washington, Rickenbacker broached this and other questions to Arnold who handled the easy one first: on 12 April 1942, he informed Rickenbacker that the hat in the ring would be reassigned to the 94th.

The other problems were not so easy to solve. Rickenbacker placed the blame for continuing morale problems not on the pilots – "There was nothing wrong with these boys. They were America's best: keen, alert, inspired, enthusiastic, fit. They craved action" – but on the AAF itself. As Rickenbacker saw it, the root cause of the morale problem was obvious: the pilots wanted to fly but the system forced them to undergo "severely curtailed training. They wanted to give it all they had, but we were not letting them." Half a century later, it is unclear why Rickenbacker paid attention only to pilots and did not address morale in the ground echelon, the term then in use to cover maintainers, armourers, and support and administrative personnel.

Events soon took care of any complaints about a shortage of flying time. As a result of strategic decisions made by the United States

An oil barrel provides an improvised platform for cleaning the barrels of a P-38H's nose guns. The photo was almost certainly taken at Salsola in Italy, in the spring of 1944. This airfield was in the Foggia complex, previously attacked by the 94th in a major raid in August 1943.

Above: Conditions were rudimentary in the Mediterranean theatre: this homely construction of empty crates was the headquarters building for the 94th FS at Youk-les-Bains in Algeria.

Right: During a visit to North Africa in late 1942/early 1943, Eddie Rickenbacker gives the crews of the 1st Fighter Group a pep talk. He was very active in spurring on US aircrew.

and Great Britain before the United States entered the war, America based its strategy in 1942 on the notion that Germany posed a more immediate threat than Japan and that the United States and its allies therefore would pursue a 'Germany first' strategy. To implement this decision, the AAF developed plans to deploy a large part of its air strength to England. Planners aimed to have American air units in combat over Europe by mid-1942, with an eye toward an invasion of continental Europe in 1943. If, however, either the German or Russian war efforts seemed near collapse, the air units could support an immediate cross-channel invasion in 1942. Both plans called for an accelerated build-up of American air strength in England. The War Department dubbed the move of AAF units to England in 1942 Operation Bolero.

The 1st Pursuit Group formed the vanguard of the Bolero build-up. On 23 April 1942, the War Department ordered continental commands to prepare various air units for overseas movement. The group received its alerting message on 29 April and movement orders on 14 May. They divided the group into two com-

An armourer works on a P-38J at Salsola in Italy. The J arrived during 1944, and was immediately recognisable thanks to its chin intakes on each engine nacelle.

ponents. The air echelon consisted of 85 P-38Fs, a like number of pilots, a maintenance officer and 65 crew chiefs, an armament officer and five weapons specialists, and a communications officer and five radio and flight instrument specialists. These 88 officers and 75 enlisted men moved by air throughout the deployment. Two flight surgeons and 200 additional enlisted men assigned to the air echelon made the initial movement across the United States by rail, but flew on C-47 transports for the transatlantic legs of the trip. The ground echelon, 99 officers and 872 enlisted men, moved from the United States to England by ship.

Across the 'Pond'

On 15 May 1942 the group and its squadrons dropped their 'pursuit' designation and took on the word 'fighter', the 94th Fighter Squadron among them. While the air echelon left California for Dow Field, Maine, the ground echelon moved to Fort Dix, New Jersey to board the *Queen Elizabeth* on 3 June. The ship sailed the next day and arrived at Gourock, Scotland five days later. The ground echelon of the 1st Fighter Group then moved to an RAF station at Goxhill, England, where it settled in to await the arrival of the air echelon.

The fighters had a more interesting time of it. By 25 May 1942, all three squadrons were at

Dow where they began training for the long flights ahead. The deployment from California afforded the group time to practise its long-distance, high-altitude formation flying, but during the stay in Maine the pilots continued to practise long formation flights. The Bolero deployment was to be a test: never before had the United States attempted to send fighters, even long-range, twin-engined aircraft like the P-38, on such a long over-water deployment in the face of uncertain weather conditions. The AAF believed that the confidence of pilots had to be developed, so the group continued to fly progressively longer flights "to accustom pilots to the rigours of long hours in the air." Official specifications on the P-38, used for planning the deployment, decreed that with 570 US gal (2158 litres) of fuel, cruising at 15,000 ft (4644 m) at 200 kt (369 km/h), the P-38 could fly for six hours and still have fuel for at least an extra hour's flying time as a reserve. AAF planners used 1,443 miles (2322 km) as a safe maximum ferry range.

Training progressed smoothly, for the 1st Fighter Group had a great deal of experience with this type of operation. The transoceanic legs were scheduled to begin in early June, the exact date depending on the weather, but events half a world away forced a change in plans. The Battle of Midway loomed in the

Above: Caught indulging in lunch are two of the 94th's P-38 aces, Ilfrey (left) and Lovell. Jack Ilfrey was already well-known for his exploits in Portugal, where his aircraft was interned. He somehow managed to get the ground crew to fuel it up so that he could continue his journey from England to North Africa.

Above: Lieutenant Meredith explains in traditional fighter-pilot style his manoeuvring against a German aircraft to other 94th FS pilots. The squadron was in Italy at the time.

Right: Colonel Ralph Garman was the commander of the 1st Fighter Group during its initial war period. Here he is seen in a P-38F or G in 1943 at a base in North Africa.

Pacific and the War Department decided to move units to the West Coast to defend the region if the Japanese succeeded in their plan to smash the US Pacific Fleet. The 1st Fighter Group, therefore – 94th Fighter Squadron included – headed back toward California. The group was at Morris Field, North Carolina, on 6 June 1942 when it was learned that the Japanese fleet, minus four aircraft-carriers, was in retreat in the Pacific. The group returned to Maine and began its Bolero deployment on 24 June.

Navigation support

The transatlantic ferry route comprised four sectors. The route ran from Maine to Goose Bay, Labrador, and from then to Greenland, Iceland and Scotland. The group generally travelled in cells of five aircraft, with a B-17 escorting five P-38s. The rest of the air echelon moved in C-47s.

The 1st Fighter Group began the Maine-Goose Bay leg on 24 June 1942, with flights departing throughout the day. On arrival at Goose Bay, after a flight of about 600 miles (966 km), pilots found a single gravel runway measuring 150 ft (46 m) wide and 1,500 ft (464 m) long. Electric lights illuminated its southern edge, but spruce trees served as runway markers on the other edge and at the ends. Still, the group completed this leg without incident.

The second, 780-mile (241-km) leg to a base in Greenland presented greater challenges and a

group of P-38s landed on the ice-cap. The third took the remainder of the group to Reykjavik, Iceland. The 27th squadron was left there to defend the island while the 71st and 94th pressed on. The first P-38s reached Prestwick, Scotland on 9 July 1942 when Colonel John N. Stone, the group commander, arrived with a flight of seven aircraft. It was not until at least 31 July that the group was fully on board in England. The 94th Fighter Squadron was separated from the rest of the group and stationed at Kirton Lindsay. By 1 September 1942, the first day the group was considered fully operational, group headquarters were co-located with the 94th. The 94th was assigned letter codes UN and the radio callsign SPRINGCAP.

Almost immediately, planners questioned whether the P-38 could survive in combat with

Right: Armourers hoist a bomb on to the inner wing pylon of a 94th FS P-38J at Salsola. The P-38 was widely used as a fighter-bomber in the theatre, its nose-mounted guns packing a heavy punch for the strafing mission.

Below: The Hog Caller was a P-38J of the 94th Fighter Squadron, seen here at its Italian base. The squadron saw out the war with this variant of Lightning. In the last few months of 1944 the squadron moved to Corsica for the invasion of southern France, before returning to the Foggia complex in December. The squadron remained there for the duration.

the smaller, supposedly more nimble Messerschmitt Bf 109. Eighth Air Force officers were reluctant to commit the group to fighter sweeps over the continent. Since the P-38 had been designed as an interceptor, the aircraft occasionally scrambled to meet German intruders over England, but these sorties resulted in few encounters and no victories.

Return of the emblem

On 30 September 1942, Rickenbacker visited the 94th again and distributed 'hat in the ring' pins to pilots. Rickenbacker does not seem to have paid much attention to others in the squadron, with one exception: intelligence offi-

Unit Heritage

When reactivated on 3 July 1946 at March AFB, California, the 94th FS was operating the Lockheed P-80A (above), followed soon after by the improved P-80B. This formation of P-80Bs (right) wears bright tail colours for a deployment to Ladd Field in Alaska at the end of 1947.

cer Major Alden B. Sherry was an old friend who had been in the 94th in World War I. He was the only man to serve in the squadron in both wars.

Although the 71st squadron flew some missions and lost a pilot, the 94th apparently saw no action before the air echelon was moved to North Africa on 14 November 1942. The 94th reported two pilots missing on the flight to Algeria. Captain James Harmon, the squadron commander, and First Lieutenant Jack Ilfrey both landed in Lisbon, where the neutral Portuguese showed every intention of holding the two Americans for the duration. Harmon persuaded the Portuguese to let him go after he volunteered to leave his well-travelled P-38 behind as a souvenir. Ilfrey talked his hosts into refuelling his aircraft and removing the chocks from the wheels. Suitably serviced, he took off in front of his surprised guards.

The 94th set up shop at Youks-les-Bains. The 'Hat in the Ring' squadron made the 1st Fighter Group's first combat sorties in North

In early 1951 the 94th attempted to recreate the 'Sabre Dancers' aerobatic team, which had performed many displays during 1949. The attempt got little further than this publicity photo showing a quartet of 94th F-86As with the sabre fin marking.

Africa on 29 November 1942 when six aircraft strafed the German airfield at Gabes. On the flight back to Youks-les-Bains, Captain Newell O. Roberts and the prodigal Lieutenant Ilfrey shared in the destruction of a Messerschmitt Bf 110. Later that day the squadron destroyed two Junkers Ju 88s and claimed two Bf 109s as probable kills.

On 3 December 1942, the 94th lost two of four aircraft despatched to strafe the airfield at Gabes. The 94th joined the 71st at Maison Blanche on 12 December, but between 15-17 December all three squadrons moved to a new station at Biskra.

Bomber escort

At the end of 1942, morale was low. Inexperienced American pilots were doing poorly against seasoned German veterans. The P-38s flown by the 94th and its two companion squadrons were in poor shape as a result of their travels from California to Maine to England to North Africa. Bad tactics, for the most part imposed by Twelfth Air Force operations officers, did nothing for morale and produced no aerial victories. Bomber units wanted fighter escort, and the P-38 was the only fighter in the

theatre that had the range to do the job. Bomber-oriented staff officers gave little thought to long-range escort tactics; lacking any better ideas, they simply directed the P-38s to fly close escort with the bomber formations. Ordered to fight defensively in close proximity to the bombers, the P-38s yielded the tactical initiative to the Germans.

Nor were fighter tactics any better when bombers were left out of the equation. The P-38s flew and fought in tight four-plane flights. Flight leaders selected targets and generally did the only aimed firing. The other three planes in a flight tried to stay close to the leader, and if they fired at all it was usually on the leader's cue and at the leader's target. Given the P-38's firepower, the resulting cone of fire was often lethal to any enemy aircraft that encountered it, but it was hardly an efficient way to use the aircraft. The group's pilots recognised the difficulties, but the herd instinct was difficult to overcome in the heat of combat. By mid-1943, the 94th was using more fluid formations composed of a pair of two-ship elements. Each element was theoretically independent but they usually worked together. Three flights (12 aircraft) made up a standard squadron formation. Operational procedures changed, too, and in time escort fighters received a longer leash. This allowed them to rove around the bomber formation and catch Luftwaffe fighters forming up for their attacks on the bombers.

Combat sorties were undertaken almost – but not quite – daily. On 7 January 1943, the Italians shot down and captured First Lieutenant J. C. Harrison Lentz of the 94th near Tripoli. They put Harrison on a submarine for the trip to a POW camp in Italy, but the British caught the submarine cruising on the surface and sank it. Lentz managed to escape. The ship that sank the submarine picked him up and took him to Malta. From there he made his way back to his squadron, which he rejoined on 19 January 1943.

Four Junkers Ju 88s bombed the airfield at Biskra on 10 January 1943, destroying three aircraft, damaging another, and wounding three enlisted men.

The 1st Fighter Group's three squadrons all happily uprooted themselves from Biskra in February 1943 and settled in a new station at Chateau d'un du Rhumel. On 17 February 1942, the group was assigned to the newly acti-

This Sabre was an F-86A-7, seen in 1953 after the squadron had moved to George AFB. The 1st Fighter Wing was mainly employed on training Sabre pilots for the Korean conflict during the early part of the decade.

vated North African Strategic Air Force, part of Air Marshal Sir Arthur Tedder's Mediterranean Air Command. At the end of February the War Department announced a new rotation policy: pilots with 50 combat missions and 150 hours in combat were reassigned to other duties.

On 5 April 1943, when attacking German transports being used to evacuate North Africa, the group (including the 94th) claimed 11 Junkers Ju-52s, a Bf 109, and a Fiesler Fi 156 Storch. The North African campaign ended with the capture of Tunis on 7 May 1943.

After a brief respite, on 25 August 1943 the 1st Fighter Group flew a long-planned secret mission. The target was the Foggia airfield complex in southern Italy. The group launched 65 aircraft under Major George A. Rush, group operations officer. After joining up with 85 more P-38s from the 14th and 82nd Fighter Groups, the 150-aircraft formation proceeded at extremely low altitude to the target area 530 miles (853 km) from base.

The P-38s split into squadron-strength formations and hit eight airfields in the Foggia complex. The group was credited with destroying numerous buildings, gun positions, and other targets on the ground and with destroying or damaging 88 German aircraft at the cost of two P-38s lost (none from the 94th). Although the 1st Fighter Group won a distinguished unit citation for this mission, many of its members felt that the raid had been less than a total success.

Allied forces invaded Sicily on 9 July 1943. On 9 September 1943, American troops invaded Italy at Salerno. During this period, the 94th Fighter Squadron made several brief changes in location, ending up on 9 December 1943 at Gioia del Colle, near Bari in the heel of Italy. Soon afterward came yet another change with a move to Salsola, a former German airfield in the Foggia complex.

The 94th and its sister squadrons began receiving newer P-38J Lightnings in the spring. On 16 April 1944, the 1st Fighter Group flew its 1,000th combat mission. Soon afterward, the group was escorting bomber missions to the oil refineries in Ploesti, Romania. On 11 August 1944, the group deployed 60 aircraft to Corsica to support Operation Dragoon, the Allied invasion of southern France. On 15 December, the group returned to the Foggia complex. Much of the remainder of the war was typical of January 1945, when the group flew only eight days because of the horrendous weather at Foggia.

Between 4 June 1942 and 6 May 1945, the 1st Fighter Group flew 20,955 sorties on 1,405 combat missions. The 94th Fighter Squadron claimed 124 of the group's 402½ aerial victories. The group also claimed 149 ground kills, 98 probables, and 231 damaged. The group lost 204 pilots killed or missing in action and 28 pilots to non-combat mishaps. The group demobilised quickly at the end of the war. On 15 September 1945, the group moved to Caserta near Naples where it was deactivated on 16 October 1945, ending 36 years of continuous service.

Post-war operations

On 3 July 1946, the 94th Fighter Squadron stood up once again as a component of the newly-activated 1st Fighter Group at March Field, California, equipped with Lockheed P-80 Shooting Stars. As before, sister squadrons were the 27th and 71st. The group pioneered day-to-day operational use of jet fighters, but with considerable difficulty. Pilot inexperience and mechanical difficulties gave the P-80 a high accident rate, while parts shortages were a persistent problem. Even so, the 1st Fighter Group maintained a heavy schedule of demonstration flights that introduced the jet fighter to a curious public. This effort was under way when the US Air Force became an independent service branch on 18 September 1947. The 'P' for pursuit designation was changed to 'F' for fighter on 11 June 1948. As a further part of post-war reorganisation, the 1st Fighter Wing was activated at March Field on 15 August 1947, marking the Air Force's shift from combat groups (which it retained until 1952, and reinstated in 1992) to combat wings.

The first North American F-86A Sabre assigned to the 94th Fighter Squadron arrived on 15 February 1949. By the end of June 1949, the 1st Fighter Wing had received 79 of its authorised 83 Sabres. During this period, the fighter wing was shifted from Tactical Air Command (3 July 1946) to Continental Air Command (20 December 1948) to Strategic Air Command (1 May 1949).

In 1949, a flight demonstration team called the 'Sabre Dancers' spent several months dazzling audiences at air shows. Interest in aviation was strong in those post-war years, and the sight of a quartet of F-86A Sabres performing precision manoeuvres was a real crowd-pleaser. Over the years, the myth has arisen that the 'Sabre Dancers' team belonged to the 94th squadron. It did not; the team was operated by the 27th squadron until it disbanded. Two years later, a much-published photo (dated from a T-33 Shooting Star on 3 January 1951) showed four F-86As of the 94th rehearsing for an air show. The four 94th pilots were trying to form an aerobatic team at the time and were even discussing using the 'Sabre Dancers' name, but the 94th team never became reality.

Not yet clear was the importance of the trail-

Above: Seen at George AFB in 1953, this line-up (which includes an aircraft with the 'Sabre Dancer' marks) is headed by the F-86E assigned to the squadron commander, as denoted by the fuselage stripes.

Below: Sabres of the 94th originally wore these markings while at March AFB, an F-86A being seen here in 1949. In 1950 the squadron moved to George, and was redesignated as a fighter-interceptor squadron.

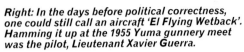

Above: The 94th began its transition to the F-86D in early 1953, flying the 'Dog' until late 1956. The E-4 airborne intercept radar gave only limited all-weather capability.

Right: In the days before political correctness, one could still call an aircraft 'El Flying Wetback'. Hamming it up at the 1955 Yuma gunnery meet was the pilot, Lieutenant Xavier Guerra.

blazing efforts being made with the F-86; the 1st Fighter Wing was training most of the pilots who would take the Sabre to war a year later. In 1949, however, the wing and the 94th squadron stayed close to home due to of a shortage of mounts for auxiliary fuel tanks, the lack of bases equipped to service the F-86, and the number of mechanical problems. First Lieutenant Robert E. Farley of the companion 71st squadron parachuted from an F-86 in late 1949, becoming the first US Air Force pilot to use an ejection seat during normal operations.

Mass formations

Wing and squadron made many efforts to fly large formations of Sabres. On 21 October 1949, the 94th put aloft three formations of 13 aircraft each but was bettered by the 27th which put two 21-machine formations into the air. The purpose of this exercise became clear in January 1950 when the wing deployed a size-able contingent of aircraft to participate in the filming of the RKO motion picture *Jet Pilot* with John Wayne and Janet Leigh. Apart from Leigh the film had little to commend it, but the wing claimed a final formation record on 4 January 1950 when it passed a 24-aircraft formation (eight Sabres from each squadron) in front of Hollywood's cameras.

On 20 May 1950, Captains Richard D. Creighton of the 71st, Wyman D. Anderson of the 94th and John D. Smith of the 27th shaved more than 16 minutes off the San Francisco to Los Angeles speed record, but it was a curtain call for the early F-86A fighters. The Sabre fleet was grounded in June so that engineers and

Between late 1956 and 1960 the 94th FIS flew the F-86L, similar to the 'Dog' but with a datalink to the SAGE system. These aircraft are on practice camp at Yuma, although the squadron's home had returned to its traditional ground at Selfridge.

mechanics from North American could modify them to the standard of later aircraft in the F-86A series.

Wing and squadron were redesignated 1st Fighter-Interceptor Wing and 94th Fighter-Interceptor Squadron on 16 April 1950. Returned to Continental Air Command on 1 July 1950 (a week after the start of the Korean War), the 94th was assigned to Victorville (later George) AFB, California. On 1 January 1951, while pilots trained in the 94th were battling MiGs in Korea, Continental Air Command was disestablished: wing and squadron reverted to Air Defense Command (ADC).

ADC became caught up in a rapid build up of its forces to defend North America against a Soviet atomic attack. The size of the Russian threat may have been exaggerated – it consisted of a few hundred Tupolev Tu-4 'Bull' bombers copied after the Boeing B-29 Superfortress and at most a few dozen atomic bombs; the term 'nuclear weapon' was not yet in general use – but ADC enjoyed high priority and got what it wanted.

The Air Defense Command staff successfully argued to its Pentagon bosses the need to disperse its air defence squadrons under a plan that made wing and even group headquarters unnecessary. The 1st Fighter Wing was reduced to a headquarters with no real job, while the three flying squadrons were spread around the US. Members of the 94th watched their sister squadron, the 71st, commanded by World War II ace Major Robin Olds, move across the country to Pittsburgh. Each of the flying squadrons was placed under an air defence wing (ADW) in a different location, the 94th Fighter-Interceptor Squadron being assigned to the 4705th ADW on 6 February 1952. The 1st Fighter-Interceptor Wing and the 1st Fighter Group were inactivated on 6 February 1952. The 470th was replaced on 1 March by the

activated 27th Air Division.

At times, the high priority enjoyed by ADC appeared to take precedence over other components of the US Air Force that were fighting a shooting war in Korea. The 94th flew F-86A Sabres – day fighters, without air-to-air radar – while these very Sabres were desperately needed in Korea to fight the MiG-15.

Interim fighter

The F-86D, which combined features of the Sabre day fighter with E-4 air-intercept radar and afterburner, was an 'interim' all-weather interceptor armed with 2.75-in folding-fin aircraft rockets (FFAR) instead of guns. Other aircraft being developed to confront attacking Soviet bombers (Northrop F-89 Scorpion, Lockheed F-94) required a second crew member to operate the radar, but the F-86D remained a single-seater. At George AFB, the 94th FIS converted to the F-86D on 1 February 1953. At the time, the 'Dog Sabre' was still afflicted with an unusual number of teething troubles. The radar, engine and afterburner all had problems.

Still, the public relations literature of the era portrayed the 94th, and Air Defense Command, as seamlessly defending the North American continent against attack. An ADC booklet was released in a vain effort to coin the acronym DIID (detect, identify, intercept, and destroy) to describe the interceptor's mission and to make it sound as important as fighting MiGs. There were far fewer Soviet bombers than the booklet implied, but the 'Dog Sabre' would have been far less effective in intercepting them than it said.

To ease the pilot's workload, the F-86D's 7,500-lb (33.36-kN) thrust J47-GE-17 turbojet with afterburner was fitted with an electronically-controlled fuel scheduling system. A single throttle level determined the amount of fuel fed to the engine, and matched the engine and afterburner for optimum efficiency. This system increased the response of the engine to changes of throttle setting and, by relieving the pilot of the need to constantly monitor engine behaviour, gave him a spare moment here and there to check his radar scope.

Another problem with the F-86D led to what pilots called the 'Jesus Christ manoeuvre'. By itself, the early F-86Ds would go into a pitch mode. When the pilot pulled back to compensate, it would start to pitch up, then begin to porpoise. "Guys would be bouncing off their cockpits," an engineer recalls. Adjustments to the size and shape of control surfaces eventually solved the problem.

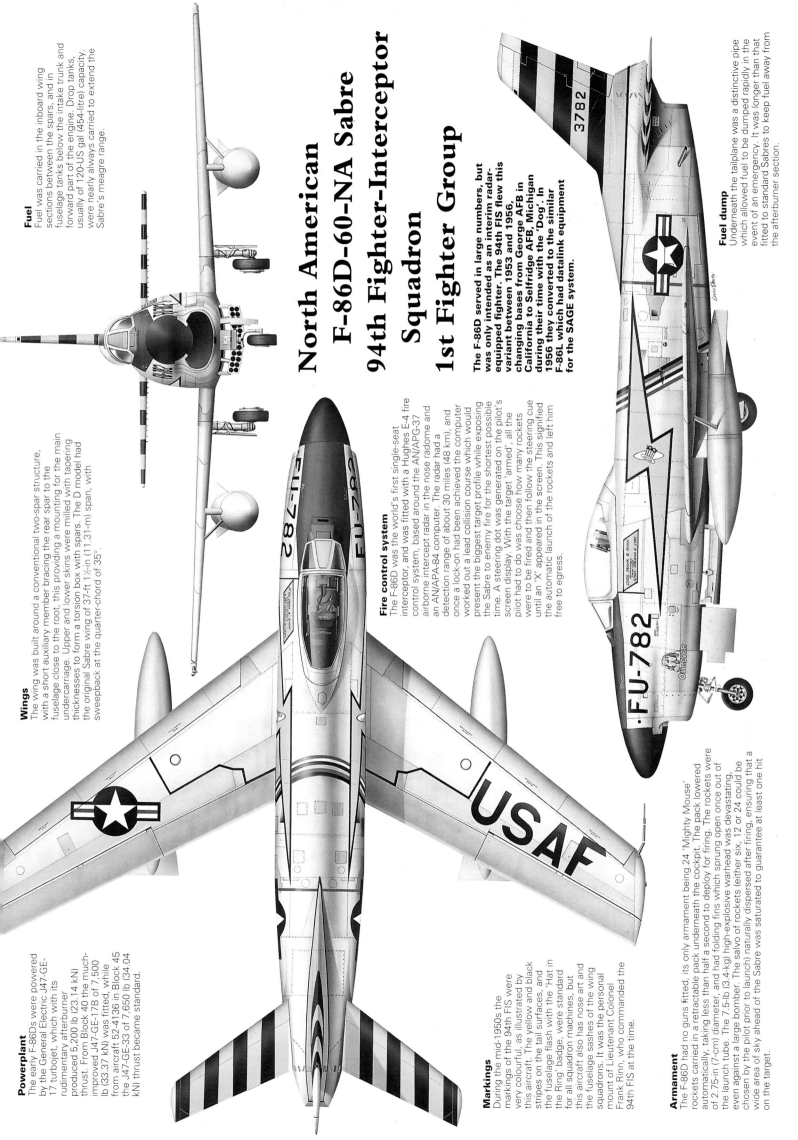

Fuel
Fuel was carried in the inboard wing sections between the spars, and in fuselage tanks below the intake trunk and forward part of the engine. Drop tanks, usually of 120-US gal (454-litre) capacity, were nearly always carried to extend the Sabre's meagre range.

Wings
The wing was built around a conventional two-spar structure, with a short auxiliary member bracing the rear spar to the fuselage close to the root, this providing a mounting for the main undercarriage. Upper and lower skins were milled with tapering thicknesses to form a torsion box with spars. The D model had the original Sabre wing of 37-ft 1½-in (11.31-m) span, with sweepback at the quarter-chord of 35°.

North American
F-86D-60-NA Sabre
94th Fighter-Interceptor
Squadron
1st Fighter Group

The F-86D served in large numbers, but was only intended as an interim radar-equipped fighter. The 94th FIS flew this variant between 1953 and 1956, changing bases from George AFB in California to Selfridge AFB, Michigan during their time with the 'Dog'. In 1956 they converted to the similar F-86L which had datalink equipment for the SAGE system.

Fire control system
The F-86D was the world's first single-seat interceptor, and was fitted with a Hughes E-4 fire control system, based around the AN/APG-37 airborne intercept radar in the nose radome and an AN/APA-84 computer. The radar had a detection range of about 30 miles (48 km), and once a lock-on had been achieved the computer worked out a lead collision course which would present the biggest target profile while exposing the Sabre to enemy fire for the shortest possible time. A steering dot was generated on the pilot's screen display. With the target 'armed', all the pilot had to do was choose how many rockets were to be fired and then follow the steering cue until an 'X' appeared in the screen. This signified the automatic launch of the rockets and left him free to egress.

Fuel dump
Underneath the tailplane was a distinctive pipe which allowed fuel to be dumped rapidly in the event of an emergency. It was longer than that fitted to standard Sabres to keep fuel away from the afterburner section.

Powerplant
The early F-86Ds were powered by the General Electric J47-GE-17 turbojet, which with its rudimentary afterburner produced 5,200 lb (23.14 kN) thrust. From Block 40 the much-improved J47-GE-17B of 7,500 lb (33.37 kN) was fitted, while from aircraft 52-4136 in Block 45 the J47-GE-33 of 7,650 lb (34.04 kN) thrust became standard.

Markings
During the mid-1950s the markings of the 94th FIS were very colourful, as illustrated by this aircraft. The yellow and black stripes on the tail surfaces, and the fuselage flash with the 'Hat in the Ring' badge, were standard for all squadron machines, but this aircraft also has nose art and the fuselage sashes of the wing squadrons. It was the personal mount of Lieutenant Colonel Frank Rinn, who commanded the 94th FIS at the time.

Armament
The F-86D had no guns fitted, its only armament being 24 'Mighty Mouse' rockets carried in a retractable pack underneath the cockpit. The pack lowered automatically, taking less than half a second to deploy for firing. The rockets were of 2.75-in (7-cm) diameter, and had folding fins which sprung open once out of the launch tube. The 7.5-lb (3.4-kg) high-explosive warhead was devastating, even against a large bomber. The salvo of rockets (either six, 12 or 24 could be chosen by the pilot prior to launch) naturally dispersed after firing, ensuring that a wide area of sky ahead of the Sabre was saturated to guarantee at least one hit on the target.

After years of frustrating development, the F-86D Sabre matured as a capable one-man all-weather interceptor. The 'Dog Sabre' eventually was powered by a J47-GE-33C rated at 7,650 lb (34.03 kN) thrust.

USAF organisation

A confusing picture of US Air Force organisation in the early 1950s was dictated by demands of the Korean War. To spread squadrons around the nation while other units deployed to the Pacific, air defence planners devised new organisational plans to fulfil missions without tying up large numbers of personnel at superfluous command levels. 'Air Defense Wings' replaced operational headquarters to supervise squadrons over a wide geographic area. The 4705th Air Defense Wing was the higher level to which the 94th FIS reported during 1952-55, when the squadron was assigned at Griffiss AFB, New York (together with, during part of this time, the 27th FIS). Squadrons were to an unusual degree independent and autonomous.

With the end of the war in Korea (on 27 July 1953), ADC was able to return to a more traditional command structure. On 20 June 1955, the 1st Fighter Group (Air Defense) was activated and assigned to the 4708th Air Defense Wing, Selfridge AFB, Michigan. The 94th, together with the 71st, was assigned to the group while the 27th remained at Griffiss AFB, New York. Officially, the 94th Fighter-Interceptor Squadron made the move to Selfridge, a familiar location from the squadron's past, on 18 August 1955. At this location, under Project Arrow, the 94th

replaced the 56th FIS. The 1st Fighter Wing (Air Defense) was activated on 18 October 1956 and placed over the group.

In the late autumn of 1956, the 94th converted from the F-86D to the F-86L Sabre. This was a 'rebuild' from the F-86D on-board computer and a datalink to tie the aircraft with the SAGE (Semi-Automatic Ground Environment) defence network. In 1960, the 94th traded in its F-86Ls for the Convair F-106A Delta Dart. The first of 18 aircraft arrived on 3 April 1960. Powered by a 24,500-lb (108.98-kN) thrust afterburning Pratt & Whitney J75-P-17 turbojet engine, the sleek 'Six' proved extremely popular with pilots. This all-weather interceptor is generally considered to be the last of the 'Century Series', USAF fighters with designations in the early 100s.

Soon after taking the F-106A on charge, the 94th Fighter-Interceptor Squadron began to see many of its pilots transferring to other units en route to Vietnam. The squadron did not go to Vietnam but remained in the US, where a reorganisation on 16 January 1967 made the 94th temporarily the only flying squadron in the 1st

Fighter Wing (Air Defense). Equipped with 17 F-106As, two F-106Bs and seven T-33As, the 94th operated at Selfridge until it was deployed to Osan Air Base, Korea, between 20 May and 5 November 1969.

This deployment came in the wake of North Korea's seizure of the intelligence ship USS Pueblo (AGER-2) in 1968 and the shooting down of an EC-121 Super Constellation reconnaissance aircraft on 15 April 1969. It marked the last time the 1st Fighter-Interceptor Wing or the 94th Fighter-Interceptor Squadron carried out an air defence effort.

On 1 December 1969, the 94th was transferred to Wurtsmith AFB, Michigan (the old 1st Pursuit Group's Oscoda training camp) pending the inactivation of the 1st Fighter Wing. The 1st Fighter Wing was barely recognisable as a descendant of the First Pursuit; its three fighter squadrons were now scattered in Maine, Michigan and Montana and its support components were inactive. Moves were underway, however, to restore the 'old' 1st Fighter Wing by the end of 1970. Based on an edict from Tactical Air Command boss General William W. 'Spike' Momyer to "retain illustrious designators for the active tactical forces," the 1st Fighter Wing returned to TAC in October 1970.

In the early 1970s the 94th was a training squadron for Phantom crews, flying from MacDill AFB with 'FE'-coded F-4Es. The 94th number was assigned to the 47th TFS to keep the famous 'Hat in the Ring' unit alive after deactivation as a Delta Dart operator.

The 1st TFW at Langley received F-15A Eagles from 1975, but the 94th TFS was the last of the three constituent units to declare operational readiness, achieving this in December 1977.

This F-15C was one of those assigned to the 'SWA rotation', providing fighters to the detachment in Dhahran, Saudi Arabia for Operation Southern Watch. The aircraft wears the badges of both the 71st and 94th Fighter Squadrons, as both units periodically manned the detachment.

The 1st Tactical Fighter Wing was formed at MacDill AFB, Florida as an RTU (Replacement Training Unit) for the F-4 Phantom. The decision was made to rename existing squadrons (45th, 46th, 47th) using the traditional names associated with the wing (94th, 27th, 71st). The method of assigning the names was determined in a tactical 'shoot-out' held at the Avon Park Gunnery Range on 14 May 1971. Lieutenant Colonel Donald W. Martin, commander of the 47th TFS, scored 113 out of 126 possible points and chose the historic 94th designation. The 27th and 71st designations went to the second- and third-place shooters.

The 94th officially became part of Tactical Air Command on 1 July 1971, still as a fighter-interceptor squadron. By July 1971, the 1st Tactical Fighter Wing was organised so as to evoke memories of the 1st Pursuit Group of earlier days. The wing spent the next four years providing advanced training to F-4 and B-57 crews, most of whom later saw service in Vietnam.

Enter the Eagle

By 1972, discussions were afoot which would have a significant impact on the 94th Tactical Fighter Squadron and its parent wing. On 2 May 1972, General Momyer decided that TAC would base its first F-15 wing at Langley AFB, Virginia. Momyer noted that Langley, the site of TAC headquarters since 1946, was a "traditional home of tactical fighters."

On 14 March 1974, the US Air Force announced its plans to do what Momyer had asked. Neither the Air Force nor TAC had selected a unit to take on this responsibility. TAC's planning staff undertook a major study to "identify and rank fighter wings by historic illustriousness." The 1st TFW ranked first, ahead of the 4th, 31st, 49th, and others. Despite this, a plan existed for some time to make the Langley F-15 wing the 56th. Only after considerable machinations was it decided that the 56th would take over operations at MacDill, releasing the 1st Tactical Fighter Wing and its squadrons (94th, 27th, 71st) to stand up at Langley.

The First TFW, now under the command of Brigadier General Larry D. Welch, worked hard to solve construction, maintenance, operational and training problems associated with the stand-up. The wing's first Eagle arrived on 18 December 1975. The 27th and 71st received the first F-15s, leaving the 94th as the wing's only squadron not yet operationally ready. Belatedly, the 94th built up to operational status by December 1977.

The 94th TFS deployed eight F-15A/B Eagles to Korea, Japan and the Philippines from 21 January to 4 March 1978. Members of the squadron had scarcely unpacked their bags when they were off again, this time on a short-notice, 16-day, 12-aircraft show-the-flag deployment to Saudi Arabia (Prized Eagle, 12-27 January 1979). Further deployments followed thereafter to exercises within the US, and to Europe, the Middle East, Southwest Asia and the Pacific. The 94th TFS was the first squadron in the 1st TFW to convert from F-15A/Bs to F-15C/Ds. They reached IOC on 4 November 1981.

When the US launched Operation Desert Shield on 6 August 1990 – responding to the Iraqi invasion of Kuwait four days earlier – the 'Hat in the Ring' squadron was left behind while the 1st TFW under Colonel John M. 'Boomer' McBroom deployed F-15C/D Eagles of its 27th and 71st TFS from Langley on hours' notice.

A handful of 94th pilots eventually participated in the build-up and in the Gulf War that began on 17 January 1991, but the squadron and its aircraft sat out the conflict at Langley. On 1 October 1991, the US Air Force dropped the word 'Tactical' from the designations of its fighter units. The 94th Fighter Squadron became the new name of the 94th TFS.

The 94th finally got to the war zone with an 'SWA rotation' [Southwest Asia] from 14 June 1992 to 14 September 1992, taking 14 F-15s to Dhahran. 27 August 1992 marked the beginning of Operation Southern Watch, the coalition enforcement of the post-war 'No-Fly Zone' of Iraq. Lieutenant Colonel Dennis G. Krembel, 94th FS commander, led the first wave over Iraqi territory.

In 1996, the 94th was tapped for the first-ever major deployment of US fighters to Jordan in support of Operation Southern Watch. The 1st Fighter Wing, now commanded by Brigadier General William R. Looney, was the host of an Airpower Expeditionary Force (AEF) consisting of about 1,000 people, 34 aircraft, and associated equipment. Looney's *ad hoc* composite wing consisted of not only the 94th but also F-16s from the 347th Wing at Moody AFB, Georgia and the 366th Wing at Mountain Home AFB, Idaho, and KC-135s from the 96th Air Refueling Wing at Fairchild AFB, Washington. **Robert F. Dorr**

Today the 94th Fighter Squadron remains at Langley AFB with the F-15C Eagle and overseas deployments figure prominently in the squadron's activities. It is highly likely that the 1st Fighter Wing will be the first front-line recipient of the F-22 when it enters service early in the next century.

Bertha, Clara, Dora and Emil
Messerschmitt Bf 109
The First Generation

Flying low over the Mediterranean from its base at Ain-el-Gazala in Libya, a Bf 109E-7/Trop of JG 27 displays an exotic camouflage which proved remarkably effective over the arid scrub of the western desert, particularly near the coast where there were pockets of vegetation. By the time the Bf 109 reached North Africa in April 1941 it was past the zenith of its career, but it nevertheless turned the tables in the desert air war.

There will always be long arguments over which really was the greatest fighter of all time, yet to even be considered in the running any contender would have to match the incredible combat record of the Bf 109, in particular the Bf 109E, which was undoubtedly the most successful of the variants. Technically way out in front of its rivals at the time of its debut, the Bf 109 was only really matched in the early days by the Spitfire, and, when the two met head-on over Britain in the late summer of 1940, it was the first and only occasion where the Bf 109E truly met a worthy opponent.

The greatest exponent of the Messerschmitt Bf 109, indeed probably the finest fighter pilot ever, was Werner Mölders, seen here climbing from his cannon-armed Bf 109E-3. Having been top Luftwaffe scorer in the Spanish Civil War, he repeated the feat during the Battle of Britain. He then went to the Russian Front in mid-1941, and had soon passed von Richthofen's 80-kill score., He then became the first ace to pass the magical 100-kill mark on 15 July. After downing his 100th and 101st kills, he was regarded as too valuable to risk losing in combat and was recalled to Germany to take up the post of General der Jagdflieger. Mölders was killed in November, riding as a passenger in an He 111 bomber while on his way to attend the funeral of Ernst Udet, one of Germany's leading aces of World War I.

At the proving centre at Rechlin, the Bf 109 V1 impressed all those who saw it, although Heinkel's He 112 was considered more likely to get the RLM nod as the first monoplane fighter in the new Luftwaffe.

Below right: The Bf 109a (later designated 109 V1) was the first of more than 30,000 Messerschmitt Bf 109s to be built in a period of just under 10 years. Despite many improvements, and a number of different powerplants, the basic outline of the prototype remained recognisable throughout the series.

Right: D-IABI was the only 109 to have an upright (as opposed to inverted) engine. Ironically, this was a Rolls-Royce Kestrel, as used in contemporary RAF fighters such as the Hawker Fury. One perceived advantage of the inverted configuration was improved forward view for the pilot, but in fact all 109s (and all tail-dragger fighters of the era, virtually regardless of engine type) were poor in this respect.

Below: The third B-series aircraft, the Bf 109 V6 D-IHHB, was used to study the stalling characteristics of the design. A pitot tube was mounted on a pole above the cowl so as to be outside the surface airflow, and a ciné camera was attached to the fin.

It has often been said that no war can be won solely in the air: to achieve final victory ground troops must occupy the objective. However, the seizure of total air superiority can make the task of the ground forces much easier by removing the threat of harassment from the air. In recent times, the 1991 Gulf War vividly demonstrated this, but in no conflict was air superiority more vital than in the German Blitzkrieg campaigns that swept through northern Europe in 1939/40. Providing mastery of the air over Poland and France was the Messerschmitt Bf 109, the most enduring image of Hitler's Luftwaffe and in its day the most advanced fighter in the world.

In the early days of the Third Reich, Germany was preparing for war under a veil of secrecy, yet its engineers and scientists were advancing technology far more rapidly than in any other nation. World War I had shown that the aircraft was quickly becoming the major weapon of war, and during the mid-1930s the German aviation industry produced a number of highly advanced world-leading designs. Much of the rush of technological advance of this decade was squandered by internecine politics within the upper echelons of the Reich, but the 1930s laid the foundations for the aircraft that would sweep German forces across virtually all of Europe and part of Africa in just two years. Of these types, none was more crucial than the Bf 109.

Design of the Bf 109 began in March 1934 at the BFW works at Augsburg. The Bayerische Flugzeugwerke had a long history of aircraft manufacture behind it, having taken over the work of the Udet company. Banned from producing military aircraft under the terms of the 1919 Treaty of Versailles, the German aircraft industry produced airliners and mailplanes. Another Bavarian company, Messerschmitt Flugzeugbau, established by Dipl.-Ing. Willy Messerschmitt, was also producing designs, notably the M.18. The Bavarian state government ordained a merger, with Messerschmitt assuming design control while BFW at Augsburg-Haunsletten became the production facility.

Work on the Bf 109 started in answer to an early 1934 requirement for a new fighter issued by the Luftwaffenführungsstab. Arado, Focke-Wulf and Heinkel were the main contenders, as they were established as the principal fighter manufacturers for the new Luftwaffe. Messerschmitt had no experience in designing high-speed aircraft, and he was personally disliked by several Reichsluftfahrtministerium (RLM) officials, notably Erhard Milch. Nevertheless, BFW was allowed to compete for the fighter competition, and was also instructed to produce an aircraft to take part in an international tourist aircraft competition.

Lightplane predecessor

The latter emerged as the Bf 108A, a highly advanced design incorporating fully enclosed cabin, cantilevered monoplane wings with slots and flaps, flush-riveted stressed-skin construction, retractable undercarriage and an excellent performance. Messerschmitt was aided in the design by Dipl.-Ing. Robert Lusser, who had arrived from Heinkel, and Hubert Bauer, both of whom would be highly influential in the design of the Bf 109, as was Ing. Walter Rethel, who joined Messerschmitt from Heinkel. The Bf 108 was not successful in the competition, held in 1934, but it had proved to be the fastest aircraft at the meet. It was subsequently reworked as the four-seat Bf 108B Taifun, which became a standard utility/trainer type for the Luftwaffe and was built in large quantities. More importantly, it provided important spin-off technology for the fighter.

Messerschmitt was painfully aware of the antagonism towards his project, and seemed resigned to the fact that he would not win a production contract. He saw the emerging fighter as a means to incorporate the most modern features available in one airframe rather than address the individual requirements of the customer. Consequently, the design embodied all of the features of the Bf 108, the single spar wings having automatic slots on the outer leading-edge panels and flaps on the trailing edge. The undercarriage was fully retractable and the pilot sat under a hinged canopy. The fuselage was made of light metal, a monocoque structure of roughly oval section, made in two halves joined along the centreline. None of these features was in itself novel, but the Bf 109 was the first to combine all in one fighter design.

From the start, power was intended to come from one of the powerful inverted-Vee 12-cylinder engines under development at Junkers and Daimler-Benz (although a mock-up installation of the BMW 116 was tested). In the event, the Junkers Jumo 210 was selected in the autumn of 1934, with the Daimler-Benz DB 600 as a potential for the future. At a similar time construction of the first prototype, the Bf 109a, began. By May 1935 the aircraft was essentially complete, and the aircraft rechristened Bf 109 V1 (Versuchs) in line with newly adopted German policy. Delivery of the Jumo 210 was delayed so, in a twist of fate to be fully realised five years later, the V1 was hastily fitted with a Rolls-Royce Kestrel VI engine rated at 695 hp (519 kW) for take-off.

With the civil registration D-IABI, the V1 first underwent taxiing trials with the undercarriage locked

Development and training

This aircraft was used as a trials airframe for the DB 600 installation. The unusual tunnel-type supercharger air intake was not adopted. Photographs of aircraft like this were used for propaganda.

Many of the Jumo-powered 'Berthas', 'Claras' and 'Doras' ended their days with fighter training schools. This Bf 109C was assigned to such an establishment at Zagreb in Yugoslavia.

together by means of a horizontal bar. Near the end of May 1935, the exact date unknown, senior test pilot Hans-Dietrich 'Bubi' Knoetzsch lifted the Bf 109 from the Haunstetten runway for the first time. After initial factory trials the aircraft was ferried to the Erprobungsstelle at Rechlin for service trials. These started inauspiciously, for the aircraft suffered an undercarriage collapse on arrival, and was immediately the focus of much criticism on account of its novel configuration. At the time, most fighter pilots still believed in open cockpits and the manoeuvrability of the biplane. However, flight trials soon dispelled any doubts that the test pilots may have harboured, the V1 proving to be considerably faster and better handling than the rival Heinkel He 112 V1 which was also at Rechlin.

Jumo power

At that point, the He 112 was still favourite to win the fighter contract. Its outward-retracting undercarriage gave it much better stability and its lower wing loading was regarded with less suspicion than the faster Bf 109. Nevertheless, the Rechlin trials had made the first inroads into the official antagonism towards the Messerschmitt design. Construction of the next two prototypes proceeded through late 1935, and the Jumo 210A engine became available in October 1935 for fitment to the V2. Wearing civil registration D-IUDE, the V2 joined the flight trials programme in January 1936.

Apart from the Jumo engine, which gave 680 hp (507 kW) for take-off, the V2 differed in only minor detail from the V1, although it was fitted with armament in the form of two 7.9-mm MG 17 machine-guns in the fuselage upper decking, each weapon having 500 rounds. The V3 (D-IOQY) first flew in June, this aircraft having provision for a 20-mm MG FF/M engine-mounted cannon, with corresponding cropped propeller spinner. By this time the Bf 109 was being viewed with increasing favour within the RLM. Across the English Channel the roughly comparable Supermarine Spitfire had been ordered into production, despite having first flown nine months after the Messerschmitt. Continuing trials further eroded the inertia concerning the Bf 109. Both the Bf 109 and rival He 112 were awarded contracts for 10 pre-production aircraft pending the outcome of the official trials.

Any remaining intransigence towards the Bf 109 was virtually wiped away at the official trials held at Travemünde in the autumn of 1936. A remarkable flight demonstration involving flick rolls, tailslides, 21-turn spins, terminal dives and tight turns could not fail to impress the onlookers, and, after the official figures had been pored over, the Bf 109 was announced the winner. Marginally faster in level speed and in the climb, the Bf 109 could outdive the He 112 with ease, and its aerobatic handling

was superb. The leading-edge slots, once viewed with great apprehension, functioned perfectly, giving the Bf 109 the ability to turn much tighter than the Heinkel. Roll rate was also significantly higher. There remained much argument and dissent from various political factions which supported the Heinkel programme, and indeed the He 112 was further developed for export and entered limited Luftwaffe service at the time of the Sudeten crisis.

There were, of course, other competitors in the fighter competition, but these were viewed mainly as back-up designs should both of the main contenders fail to meet specifications. The Arado Ar 80 was a low-wing monoplane which suffered from high drag and too much weight to be a serious contender, while the Focke-Wulf Fw 159 parasol monoplane suffered from undercarriage problems, and was lacking in performance anyway. Thus the field was left clear for the Bf 109, and by the autumn of 1936 some urgency was being attached to the programme as Germany's expansionist plans began to crystallise.

Development proceeded with the 10 pre-production aircraft, which were designated Bf 109B-0. All of these were assigned Versuchs numbers in the range V4 to V13, and were individually known as the Bf 109B-01, B-02 *et seq.* The V4 (D-IALY) took to the air in November 1936, armed with two MG 17 machine-guns and powered by a Jumo 210B providing 640 hp (477 kW) for five minutes

The third prototype was the first to be fitted with armament, the muzzles of the cowl-mounted MG 17s and spinner-mounted MG FF being visible here. This aircraft and its immediate successors, the V4 and V5, were sent to Spain in December 1936 for semi-operational evaluation.

Throughout its career, the Bf 109 was known for its crashworthiness in that the cockpit usually protected its occupant from all but the worst accidents. The V17, fifth of the E-series prototypes, came to grief while wearing Yugoslav fighter codes under its civil registration of D-IWKU.

D-IPKY (above) was one of two DB-powered aircraft at Zürich, immediately distinguishable from the Jumo-powered aircraft (right) by having a three-bladed propeller. The V9 (below) attended in warlike camouflage as a timely warning to the rest of Europe.

Although it was the DB 600-powered aircraft which were the main attractions at Zürich, the three Jumo aircraft won the team trophy. All three had the 210Ga engine, which had fuel injection in place of a float carburettor. The benefits of this system in combat were proven by the few Bf 109Cs which fought in Spain.

Zürich meeting

The fourth International Flying Meeting held at Zurich-Dubendorf in Switzerland between 23 July and 1 August 1937 provided the Luftwaffe with an opportunity to publicise their new capabilities, which they took with both hands. A variety of types were displayed at Zurich, including the Do 17 V8 bomber, like the Bf 109 a type also in service with the less easily publicised Legion Condor. The five Messerschmitts present came away with four of the trophies on offer in the military aircraft category, although one aircraft (the V14) was written off in the course of the competitions. The Propaganda Ministry made great claims for the Bf 109 on the strength of the performance of these unrepresentative pre-production examples, but the rest of Europe was alerted to the threat posed by the resurgent Luftwaffe and its new fighter aircraft.

Above: The Bf 109 V7, V8 and V13 were displayed at Zurich in a high-gloss grey civilian scheme, with the swastika national insignia of the time. The V8 won two trophies – that for fastest individual circuit of the Alps, and for the best time around four laps of a 31-mile (50-km) circuit. The V13, fitted with the DB 600Aa, took the Climb and Dive trophy.

and 540 hp (403 kW) in continuous running. Both the V5 (D-IIGO) and V6 (D-IHHB) had three MG 17s, these aircraft flying in December. The third gun was mounted inside the engine block, firing through the spinner. They differed further by having variable-pitch VDM-Hamilton propellers in place of the Schwarz fixed unit of the early aircraft, and had revised nose contours with three gun cooling slots behind the spinner instead of the single opening, resulting in a marked step.

As a prelude of events to come, the V3, V4 and V5 were dispatched to Spain in December 1936 for an evaluation under operational conditions. These trials were dogged with problems, not least of which was the damage caused to the V3 by an inexperienced pilot during its first post-reassembly test flight. It was not until 14 January 1937 that Leutnant Hannes Trautloft flew the V4 up to the front line. In the ensuing days Trautloft flew the fighter on its first ever combat sorties. Although it achieved no significant success, much operational experience was gained which would smooth the full entry into service a few weeks later of the production Bf 109Bs. At the end of January, the prototypes returned to Germany.

As soon as the fighter competition had been won, BFW began tooling up at Haunstetten for Bf 109 production, the Bf 109B being the production version (the designations Bf 109B-1 and B-2 appear to have been retrospectively applied erroneously to aircraft fitted with the Schwarz and VDM propellers, respectively). The phonetic nickname 'Bertha' was given to the first production version. BFW was also involved in the licence-manufacture of other types, and with the potential of a major fighter contract it had already become obvious that the Haunstetten facilities were not adequate. Accordingly, the Messerschmitt GmbH company was established with a factory at Regensburg, and production of the Bf 109B was soon transferred there. The design offices remained at Augsburg.

First deliveries

Production Bf 109Bs began leaving Augsburg in February 1937, with the famous Richthofen Geschwader, JG 132, earmarked as the first service recipient. However, events in the Civil War in Spain, where the nimble Russian Polikarpov I-15s and I-16s were enjoying superiority over the Heinkel He 51s of the Legion Condor, dictated that the new fighters were needed desperately overseas. A short conversion course completed, II/JG 132 personnel were immediately dispatched to Tablada, near Seville. Sixteen Bf 109Bs were shipped to Spain and reassembled in March 1937.

These 'Berthas' were powered by the uprated Jumo 210Da engine of 720 hp (537 kW), driving the original Schwarz fixed-pitch propeller. Armament was restricted to the two MG 17s with 500 rounds each, aimed using a Carl Zeiss Reflexvisier C/12C reflector sight. A 55-Imp gal (250-litre) fuel tank was fitted behind the pilot's seat, and there was provision for a short-range FuG 7 radio, although this was rarely fitted to aircraft operating in Spain.

2. Staffel der Jagdgruppe 88 was the first unit to get the Bf 109 under the command of Oberleutnant Günther Lützow, who was to achieve ace status in Spain and eventually lose his life in a Me 262 jet in April 1945 with 108 kills to his credit. Conversion to the Bf 109 progressed

remarkably smoothly, despite the considerable differences between the Messerschmitt and the He 51 biplane flown previously. By late April the Staffel was to all intents operational, but it was not until the fighting around Brunete began in July that 2./J 88 got into action.

Assigned to provide escort to Ju 52 bombers and reconnaissance aircraft, the Bf 109Bs soon became entangled with the Polikarpov fighters on the Republican side. Below about 10,000 ft (3050 m) there was little to choose between them, the I-16s enjoying greater manoeuvrability and the Bf 109s better speed and dive performance. At higher altitudes, the Bf 109s were virtually invincible, and it was swiftly learned that the large formations of Republican aircraft could be easily attacked from above and behind, picking off the rear echelons in uncatchable dives. The only recourse available to the Republicans was to lure the Bf 109s down low, but this was far from easy, and the Bf 109 immediately assumed an enviable reputation.

Combat successes

Although the Republicans claimed a Bf 109 kill as early as 8 July (almost impossible, as 2./J 88 was still many miles from the war zone), there were some losses, but there were far more victories, one of the first being credited to Leutnant Rolf Pingel, later commander of I/JG 26. The

Messerschmitt's base at Avila became the subject of increasing Republican bombing raids, so that the Staffel had to mount standing patrols and keep aircraft on alert to meet the intruders. No aircraft were lost on the ground, and by the end of July the battle of Brunete ended, allowing 2./J 88 to return to its previous base at Herrera.

In August 1937 the Nationalists launched an assault on the Santander front, accompanied by the Bf 109Bs which moved almost daily from small strip to small strip. Almost total superiority was enjoyed through this campaign, and this was further heightened by the arrival of more aircraft in September, deliveries of Bf 109Bs eventually totalling 45. Jagdgruppe 88's 1. Staffel converted to the Bf 109 in September with Lützow transferring as commander. The Gruppe itself was commanded by the Olympic gold medal pentathlete Hauptmann Gotthardt Handrick, whose personal Bf 109 wore the Olympic rings on its spinner. The end of the Santander campaign allowed the Nationalists to concentrate on the southern front, with Madrid the eventual prize, and the two Bf 109 units headed south for a period of rest before turning on Guadalajara. Oberleutnant

Above: With the Bf 109B, the Luftwaffe threw off the shackles of the past and began to develop the tactics of Blitzkrieg. This relied on technical superiority to wipe out superior numbers in a short time.

Above left: At the end of 1938, the Swiss government took delivery of the first 10 of what was to become a large number of Bf 109s in service with the Fliegertruppe. These were D models and were accepted pending the delivery of 109Es. Armament and equipment was fitted in Switzerland.

Early Luftwaffe service

Below: Less than 30 Bf 109Bs were produced with the Schwarz fixed-pitch propeller before the VDM-Hamilton was introduced.

Above: Two Staffeln of Bf 109Cs sit at readiness, those in the background being from 2./JGr 102, a heavy fighter unit.

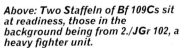

Below: This Bf 109C served with 1./JG 137 at Bernburg. Note the small oil cooler intake under the wing.

Above: Photographs of the Bf 109Bs used for engine development, and fitted with three-bladed propellers were distributed for propaganda.

Below: This line-up shows Bf 109Ds fresh from the Focke-Wulf factory at Bremen. The D was built in parallel with the C during 1938.

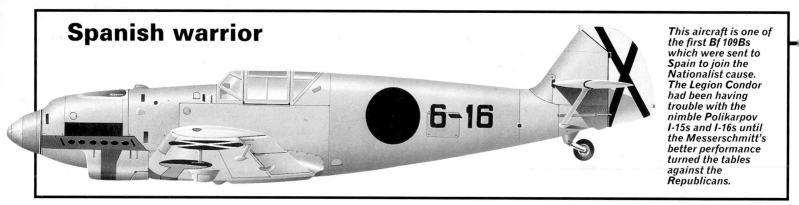

Spanish warrior

This aircraft is one of the first Bf 109Bs which were sent to Spain to join the Nationalist cause. The Legion Condor had been having trouble with the nimble Polikarpov I-15s and I-16s until the Messerschmitt's better performance turned the tables against the Republicans.

Wolfgang Schellmann arrived to take command of 2./J 88, his tally from Spain eventually totalling 12 kills.

Back in Germany, development of the Bf 109 continued. The V3 was fitted with an engine-mounted MG FF/M cannon, but the installation posed vibration problems. In March 1937 the V7 (D-IJHA) first flew, featuring a VDM-Hamilton variable-pitch propeller and a Jumo 210G direct fuel injection engine with two-stage supercharger. The VDM propeller was introduced during the Bf 109B production run, but the fuel injection engine, with the obvious benefits of maintaining full power with the aircraft in any attitude, was not available until the Bf 109C, for which the V7 and V8 (D-IPLU) served effectively as prototypes. Both of these aircraft had repositioned oil cooler intakes, although in the event the C model emerged with a deeper, redesigned radiator bath and oil cooler position as originally fitted to the B. The V8 also tested wing-mounted MG 17 guns, as the fuselage-mounted weapons had proved troublesome. These guns were to become standard on the Bf 109C-1. Both V7 and V8 were subsequently fitted with the Jumo 210Ga engine.

Daimler-Benz into the air

The V10 had started life with a Jumo 210Ga, but in June 1937 had been fitted with a Daimler-Benz DB 600Aa giving 960 hp (716 kW) for take-off and 775 hp (578 kW) in continuous running. This engine also powered the next four pre-production aircraft (V11 to V14). The Benz engine was much longer and heavier, which caused a shift in centre of gravity. This was offset by the redesign of the cooling system, which had a shallow radiator bath under the nose and two underwing radiators behind the centre of gravity. A three-bladed VDM propeller was fitted, and the aircraft had considerable local strengthening, including the undercarriage, to handle the higher weights and loads. The supercharger was aspirated through a prominent port-side intake.

Initial operations in Spain had more than proven the capabilities of the new fighter, and it had come through a

stern test with flying colours, especially given the intensity of operations during the major campaigns and the extremely hot and dusty conditions encountered by ground crews. However, such achievements could not be publicised for political reasons, and so further propaganda opportunities were sought. The 4th International Flying Meeting, held at Zürich-Dübendorf between 23 July and 1 August 1937, was the perfect answer.

Five Bf 109s were dispatched to Dübendorf, comprising three Jumo 210Ga-powered aircraft – the V7, V8 and V9 – and two with the new Daimler-Benz DB 600A, V13 (D-IPKY) and V14 (D-ISLU). Ernst Udet flew the V14 in the 'Circuit of the Alps' race but suffered an engine failure. The event was won by Major Hans Seidemann in the V8, covering the 228-mile (367-km) circuit in 56 minutes 47 seconds at 241 mph (388 km/h). The three Jumo-engined aircraft took the team prize for the fastest trio of aircraft round the same course, while Dipl.-Ing. Carl Francke won the dive and climb competition in the V13 and a four-lap 31-mile (50-km) circuit race in the V8. So impressive were the figures that several competitors dropped out part way through. As a propaganda exercise, Zürich was a total success, the Germans also stating that the fighter was in large-scale service. The name Messerschmitt and the designation Bf 109 were now on the lips of air staff planners the world over.

Of course the aircraft was only in limited service at the time of Zürich. Apart from 1./J 88 (and imminently 2./J 88), the Bf 109B was only in service with I/JG 132 at Döberitz, II/JG 132 at Jüterbog-Damm and I/JG 234 'Schlageter' at Cologne, although none of these was at full strength. In November 1937 II/JG 234 at Düsseldorf began converting to the aircraft, and at the end of the year the first aircraft from a second source – Gerhard Fieseler Werke at Kassel – was delivered. The B model was not built in great quantities and was soon replaced in service by later variants. A few lingered on in Luftwaffe service until the early part of 1940, flying with the fighter schools.

Following the Zürich triumph, the BFW management

This Bf 109B with the Olympic rings symbol on the spinner was the personal aircraft of Oberleutnant Gotthardt Handrick, Gruppenkommandeur of J 88. Handrick was the Modern Pentathlon champion at the 1936 Berlin Olympics, and later went on to command JG 26. In front of the cockpit is the starting handle for the Jumo 210Da engine.

Right: On 4 December 1937 one of the first production Bf 109Bs which had been sent to the Legion Condor (6-15) force-landed out of fuel behind Republican lines. The aircraft was evaluated in Spain by a French mission, and flown by test pilot Capitaine Vladimir Rozanoff. Unfortunately, the (very favourable) report was suppressed for diplomatic reasons and this windfall proved of little practical significance.

strove for further international glory and on 11 November 1937 Dr.-Ing. Hermann Wurster flew the V13 to the world landplane speed record, setting a mark of 379.38 mph (611 km/h) in four runs along a 1.86-mile (3-km) straight course at low level. The aircraft had been specially prepared with a boosted version of the Daimler-Benz DB 601 engine and featured an elongated, streamlined spinner, strengthened cockpit canopy and a polished skin to minimise friction. To capitalise on the successes of the speed record and Zürich, the directors of BFW agreed on 11 July 1938 to the formal renaming of the company as Messerschmitt AG, with by then Dr.-Ing. Willy Messerschmitt as Chairman and Managing Director.

Development after Zürich concentrated on the next production model, the Bf 109C 'Clara'. The V9 was fitted with 20-mm MG FF cannon in the wings in place of the MG 17s. The cannon were mounted further outboard than the MG 17s, and had 60-round drums inboard of the weapons. The breeches were covered by a blister fairing on the lower side of the wing. This armament was not adopted initially for the Bf 109C-1, which had two nose-mounted MG 17s with 500 rounds each, and two in the wings with 420 rounds each. The engine was the Jumo 210Ga with revised exhaust slots and the 'Clara' had the deeper radiator bath. The C-2 was a projected model with a fifth MG 17 mounted in the engine but was not proceeded with. The C-3 was the designation of C-1s retrofitted at the factory with the wing-mounted MG FF cannon originally tested on the V9.

Deliveries began in the early spring of 1938, with I/JG 132 converting during the summer. A small number of C-1s was shipped to Spain, but production was very limited,

the majority of the aircraft produced at the time being the Bf 109D 'Dora', which was built in parallel. This version entered service in early 1938 with I/JG 131 at Jesau, and many served subsequently with the heavy fighter units.

If anything, the 'Dora' was a retrograde step, for it reverted to the Jumo 210Da engine with carburettor. It did, however, have four-gun armament. For many years, the Bf 109D designation was thought to apply to aircraft powered by the DB 600, but no production aircraft had this powerplant. The myth has been perpetuated in many publications to this day, and many photographs which have appeared as being Bf 109Ds were actually early Bf 109Es, while many labelled as 'Claras' were really 'Doras'.

Production Bf 109D-1s were also built at Erla Maschinenwerk in Leipzig and by Focke-Wulf Flugzeugbau at Bremen, second-source production kicking in during early 1938. In August 1938 a batch of five was sent to 3./J 88 in Spain, and the D-1 also attracted export orders from Hungary for three, to be used for evaluation purposes. Most potential customers were far more excited by the prospect of the forthcoming Daimler-Benz-powered version, although Switzerland took delivery of 10 Bf 109Ds for familiarisation prior to receiving the DB-powered Bf 109E. The first of the Swiss 'Doras' was delivered on 17 December 1938, and the batch was fitted with locally-supplied 7.45-mm machine-guns (480 rounds for fuselage guns; 418 for wing guns). The Swiss 'Doras' served alongside the Bf 109Es until finally scrapped in 1949.

Captured in Spain

This account had left the Bf 109Bs of 1. and 2./J 88 having headed south from the Nationalist victories in the north for a recuperation period before the next major phase of the Spanish Civil War. During the late summer and autumn of 1937 there was little activity in the air save for a few bombing raids which were escorted by the Bf 109Bs. This situation lasted until 15 December. However, on 4 December, a significant event occurred. During a raid on a Republican airfield, one Bf 109B, piloted by Feldwebel Polenz, ran out of fuel and had to land on a road behind Republican lines. The aircraft was still fitted with the original Schwarz fixed-pitch propeller, but the Republicans had nevertheless acquired an intact example of the fighter which was causing them so much anguish in the air. At a similar time the Republican forces had also acquired an intact Heinkel He 111 bomber.

Hearing of the Messerschmitt's capture, the French air

Above: Bf 109s were given the type number 6 and numbered consecutively in Nationalist service. 6-52, one of five Ds in Spain, wears the famous 'Zylinder Hut' (top hat) insignia of 3./J 88, subsequently worn on the unit's Bf 109Es, and later adopted by a number of Condor veterans as a personal insignia.

Top left: In order to counter improved versions of the Polikarpov I-16 then entering service, 3./J 88 was re-equipped with Bf 109Cs in April 1938. One of the five aircraft that arrived at that time, marked Luchs (Lynx) is seen here sporting three kill markings.

Above left: Four members of the Legion Condor pose with one of the Bf 109Ds.

Under the nom de guerre of the Legion Condor, the Luftwaffe honed the men, equipment and tactics that were to prove so effective in the wider European conflict to come. The Bf 109D was not vastly superior to the contemporary Republican fighters, but better tactics and formations, such as the four-aircraft Schwarm, meant that the German pilots would usually gain the upper hand against the enthusiastic, but less disciplined government pilots.

Right: Looking very much like a later, Battle of Britain-era machine, the Bf 109 V15 was in fact only the third aircraft to be DB 601 powered. Introduction of the new powerplant bestowed remarkable performance on the 109, and the E was to provide the backbone of the Jagdwaffe for the early, victorious years of the war.

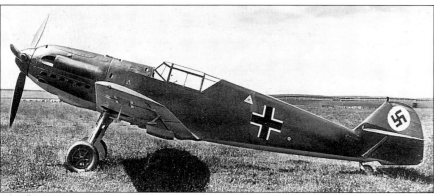

Original plans for the acquisition of the 109 by the Luftwaffe called for production interchangeability between the Jumo 210 and DB 600. In fact, only three machines (including the V11 seen here) were to be DB 600 powered as initial production was slated for bombers. By the time the DB 600 had proved its suitability as a fighter engine, the improved DB 601 was almost available.

The German press made the most of the V13's achievement, the first speed record to be held by a German landplane, and grand claims were made for potential higher speeds at altitude.

attaché signalled Paris and clandestine overtures were made to the Republican forces to seek permission to evaluate the two captured aircraft. As the French had recently sealed the Franco-Spanish border, preventing the flow of Soviet war materiel into Spain, it was in the interests of the Republicans to appease the French in order to reopen the border, so approval was granted.

Arriving in Barcelona on 31 January 1938, the French mission, which included the chief test pilot of the Centre d'Essais en Vol, Capitaine Rozanoff, travelled to Sabadell airfield where an exhaustive study was made of the two types, Rozanoff undertaking many flights. The ensuing reports were very detailed, but were labelled top secret, and were not distributed to the French aviation industry. As would be seen during the Battle of France, the industry had indeed a lot to learn from the Messerschmitt Bf 109.

At the time of Polenz's loss, the Nationalists were preparing for a major offensive, but the Republicans surprised them by opening the battle for Teruél on 15 December. The town was not recaptured by Nationalist forces until 21 February 1938, and the battle involved much air activity. Jagdgruppe 88 deployed from the Guadalajara front to Calamocha, where night-time temperatures were so low that the engines had to be started regularly through the night to prevent them seizing.

In the air, the Bf 109s continued to prove their mastery. On 7 February, a group of J 88 aircraft, led by

Gruppenkommandeur Handrick, waded into an unprotected formation of 22 Tupolev SB bombers. Although a few Polikarpov I-16s arrived later, the rout was completed in five minutes with Bf 109s shooting down 10 bombers and two I-16s for no loss. Also that day, Leutnant Wilhelm Balthasar (later to command JG 2 'Richthofen') was scrambled from Calamocha to intercept a group of SBs attempting to bomb his base. Three bombers and a fighter fell to his guns in just six minutes, the greatest individual success of the conflict. By the end of the Teruél battle, Jagdgruppe 88 had scored 30 kills with no losses.

Soon after, on 9 March, the Nationalists opened their long-planned offensive, which eventually succeeded in cutting Spain in two when ground echelons reached the Mediterranean on 15 April. The Messerschmitts moved with the ground forces but encountered increasingly stiff opposition. The He 51s could hardly operate at all, and the ravages of constant operations in primitive conditions and woeful spares shortages combined to sap considerably the might of the Legion Condor as a whole. Deliveries of fresh aircraft from Germany were small and sporadic.

Battle of the Ebro

In June, 3./J 88 was eventually withdrawn from the battle to begin its re-equipment with the Bf 109. Its commander, Oberleutnant Adolf Galland, returned home after his tour of duty and was replaced by one of the finest fighter pilots of all time: Oberleutnant Werner Mölders. Allowing partial re-equipment for the Staffel was the arrival in April of five Bf 109Cs, with four-gun armament. This coincided with the delivery to the Republicans of the four-gun I-16 Type 10. The air war continued, and, although the Bf 109 still had the upper hand, losses mounted. In early July, 3./J 88 returned to the fray, Mölders scoring his first kill, an I-16, on 15 July. At the end of the month the second Ebro campaign opened, heralding some of the fiercest fighting of the war. The Messerschmitts were heavily tasked with bomber support, the targets in the main being the bridges across the Ebro river which were usually repaired again the night following their daytime destruction.

In early August five Bf 109D-1s arrived, allowing 3./J 88

V13 record-breaker

The Bf 109 V13, which had appeared at Zürich in 1937 with a Jumo engine, was later that year fitted with a special sprint version of the DB 601 for an assault on the world speed record for landplanes, which was rated at around 1,700 hp (1270 kW), the aircraft had a number of aerodynamic refinements, including a streamlined canopy, no pitot tube and all gaps taped over. The aircraft was stripped of paint and the skin was highly polished in preparation for the record attempt in November of 1937. On 11 November Dr.-Ing. Hermann Wurster made six timed runs along a 3-km (1.86-mile) stretch of the Augsburg-Kaufbeuren railway line at an average speed of 610.95 km/h (379.6 mph), breaking the previous record by 44 km/h (27 mph).

'Emil' on the eve of war

Left: *This Bf 109E-3 was operated by II/JG 54 on the outbreak of war. The Bf 109 entered the war with no armour and a lightweight windshield, despite the lessons of Spain.*

Right: *Upon the outbreak of war, many units were redesignated. 2./JG 20's black cat was transferred to 8./JG 51.*

Left: *III/JG 51 was one of the units involved in the Polish campaign and moved to eastern Germany just prior to the outbreak of hostilities.*

Above: Frequent exercises were undertaken in preparation for fast-moving campaigns. Aircraft were regularly serviced in portable canvas hangars.

to reach full strength. The second Ebro campaign lasted through to mid-November, and the Legion Condor had largely achieved air supremacy in early September, although a few losses were still incurred. It was during the second Ebro campaign that Mölders introduced the *vierfingerschwarm* formation. Until this point the Legion had employed a two-ship *rotte* as its main formation, the two aircraft roughly 200 yards apart. By doubling up the formation and adding longitudinal spacing, Mölders at a stroke vastly increased the flexibility of the formation. This was of inestimable value during fighter sweeps, and the 'finger four' became the basic formation of fighter tactics, used to this day.

Mölders had scored his 14th and final kill on 3 November, having shot down 10 I-16s and four I-15s to become the Legion Condor's leading pilot of the war. Wolfgang Schellmann was in second place with 12 and Harro Harder was in third with 11. After the second Ebro campaign there was a period of rest, but the successful outcome had pushed the war irrevocably in favour of the Nationalists. Nevertheless, one more major offensive was required, and the Legion was exhausted and depleted to the point where it could no longer be expected to fight on without fresh supplies of equipment. This was to arrive in the form of the Bf 109E, but too late, as recounted later.

Throughout the year of 1938, the Luftwaffe had undergone a massive expansion in its home forces. On 13 March 1938, the date of the Austrian Anschluss, the following Gruppen had converted or were converting to

the Bf 109: I/JG 131 at Jesau, I/JG 132 at Döberitz, II/JG 132 at Jüterbog-Damm, I/JG 234 at Cologne, II/JG 234 at Düsseldorf and I/JG 334 at Wiesbaden. With the planned annexation of the Sudetenland, after which the Germans feared action from France and Britain, there was a pressing need to boost the domestic air forces. Large numbers of new Gruppen were formed, equipped largely with obsolescent types, and production of the Bf 109 was stepped up. However, the results of this increased production, which now included Arado at Warnemünde in addition to Messerschmitt, Erla, Focke-Wulf and Fieseler, could not be absorbed by the Luftwaffe's operational units. By way of illustration, the Luftwaffe possessed fewer than 300 Bf 109s on 1 August 1938, but by 19 September no fewer than 583 were on strength, although many were not with operational units. All were of the Jumo-powered B, C or D variants, for delays with the Daimler-Benz engine had dented plans for the rapid fielding of the Bf 109E.

On 1 August 1938 a naval Bf 109 unit was also established at Kiel-Holtenau. Equipped with Bf 109Bs, 6. Trägerstaffel/186 was formed to begin the training of pilots destined to serve on the Reich's first aircraft-carrier, the *Graf Zeppelin*, which was launched on 8 December 1938. In mid-1939, 5. Trägerstaffel/186 was formed on the Bf 109B, and both units were to have eventually re-equipped

Above: *As war approached, the tempo of exercises and their realism increased. Here an NCO shouts orders and a 'dead' mechanic lies beneath a Bf 109E-1, as his colleagues carry out field repairs. The devil marking is a personal symbol of a type popular up until the early months of the war.*

Below left: *Yugoslavia was one of the few pre-war export customers of the Bf 109. The 6th Fighter Regiment of the Yugoslav Royal Air Force received its first 109E-3s in late 1939.*

Below: *A pair of JG 51 Bf 109Cs makes a scramble take-off. The dark camouflages of the time were primarily for concealment on the ground.*

Assault on Poland

Above: *Two aircraft of JG 27 are seen at Boenninghard, near Wesel, before the battle for France. The mottling was not common until the latter part of the Battle of Britain.*

Below: *Ground crew reload the wing- and engine-mounted machine-guns on a Bf 109C of III/JG 51. Scrupulous cleanliness was needed for this task.*

Above: *An early war picture of a JG 27 Bf 109E. The oversized wing markings were a recognition aid for German forces, following a number of unfortunate incidents early in the war.*

Left: *As the war approached and then began, individual markings flourished on the predominantly dark green Bf 109s of the Luftwaffe. This E-3 seen in Poland during early September 1939, wore the cartoon character 'Max' of the strip 'Max and Moritz' on the starboard cowl, with 'Moritz' on the other side.*

The first of 40 Bf 109Es to arrive in Spain before the end of the Civil War arrived at the beginning of 1939. 6-91 was the first of these aircraft, whose arrival allowed the Spanish to inherit the older 109s still in service.

with a specialist carrier variant, of which more later. Trägergruppe 186, which also included Ju 87s, was to have been the first of two carrier air groups, the second being earmarked for the carrier *Peter Strasser*.

A major reorganisation of the Luftwaffe took place on 1 November 1938, with the fighter force being divided into *leichten* (light) and *schwere* (heavy) fighter groups, although the latter were rechristened Zerstörergruppen on 1 January 1939. Virtually all of the 14 light groups were flying the Bf 109B or C, although I/JG 130 now also had Bf 109Ds. The seven heavy groups had Bf 109Bs, Cs and Ds, although many subsequently converted to the main Zerstörer type, the Messerschmitt Bf 110.

Enter 'Emil'

At the beginning of 1939 the first Bf 109E 'Emils' began rolling from the production lines with Daimler-Benz engines. The original Luftwaffe requirements that had spawned the Bf 109 had strongly recommended the ability of its new fighter to be powered by either the Jumo or DB 600 engine, and Messerschmitt had designed the Bf 109 accordingly. With the promise of greater power than the Jumo, the DB 600 was always the favoured engine in the early days, but it was at a later stage of development, and could not have been ready by the time that Bf 109 production started.

Daimler-Benz had started work on the DB 600 as far back as 1932, but it was not until June 1937 that one of the DB 600Aa engines had been fitted to a Bf 109. As

recounted earlier, this was the B-07/V10 airframe, which had originally flown under Jumo power. With its new powerplant, it effectively became the prototype for the Bf 109E production series. Subsequent development aircraft were also powered by Daimler-Benz engines, the V11, V12, V13 and V14 all being powered by the DB 600Aa, although a special DB 601 was subsequently fitted to V13 for the speed record attempt.

DB 601s powered the next development aircraft, starting with the V15 (D-IPHR) and V16 (D-IPGS). The DB 601 was very similar to the DB 600 apart from a few vital characteristics. The main one was that it had fuel injection instead of a float carburettor, allowing negative *g* flight and also improving fuel economy. Compression ratio was raised slightly, and there were improvements made to the supercharger. Power output was increased slightly, the engine being rated at 1,175 hp (877 kW) for take-off and 990 hp (739 kW) at 12,140 ft (3700 m). The improvements did themselves throw up some difficulties, which deferred quantity production until late in 1938. This delay consequently postponed production of the Bf 109E, resulting in the much larger than anticipated number of Jumo-powered Bf 109Ds being produced.

Bomber priority

DB 600s could have powered Bf 109s much earlier, but there were three main reasons why this did not occur, the principle reason being that bomber production was accorded priority in the mid-1930s, and the DB 600s were mainly produced for Heinkel He 111 production. When, in 1938, priority moved to fighter aircraft, the DB 601 was nearing maturity, so production of the DB 600 was geared down to concentrate efforts on the DB 601. Lastly, the benefits of the fuel injection system of the DB 601 were seen as great enough to be worth the extra delay. With overall dimensions virtually unchanged, the DB 601 posed no mounting problems in the Bf 109, the hard work of rearranging the cooling system to maintain centre of gravity position having already been undertaken for the DB 600-powered pre-production aircraft.

With the DB 601 fitted, the Bf 109E-1 gained an

The 'Emil' arrived just too late to see action in the Spanish Civil War, although 2. Staffel der Jagdgruppe 88 had just converted when the war ended.

immediate improvement in performance, maintaining its position as the world's most advanced fighter. The extra performance was offset by a degradation in turning circle and high-speed handling caused by the extra wing loading, but in general the Bf 109E retained the superb handling and manoeuvrability of its Jumo-engined predecessors. Take-off and climb performance was exhilarating and, although the stall speed was relatively high, the characteristics were benign, with ample buffet warning of the impending stall. Spin characteristics were exemplary.

The performance of the Bf 109E-1 was outstanding. Company test data compiled in early 1939 revealed a maximum speed of 311 mph (500 km/h) at sea level rising to 354 mph (570 km/h) at 16,405 ft (5000 m). At 19,685 ft (6000 m), the Bf 109's 88-Imp gal (400-litre) tank gave an endurance of over an hour at maximum continuous power. A climb to 3,280 ft (1000 m) could be made in just 60 seconds, while 19,685 ft (6000 m) could be reached in 6.3

minutes. The ceiling was set at 36,090 ft (11 000 m). Take-off run to clear a 66-ft (20-m) obstacle was 1,050 ft (320 m), and landing from the same altitude could be achieved in 2,250 ft (685 m). The fuel injection allowed the Bf 109E-1 to capitalise on the aircraft's already legendary dive performance by making rapid transitions from level to diving flight with no interruption of power.

An unusual feature was the drooping ailerons, which were interconnected with the flaps. When the latter were lowered, the ailerons drooped 20°, with the corresponding pitch change being offset by a change in tailplane incidence.

While the Bf 109 was frequently used in the ground-attack role in Spain, bombs were not carried by the fighter in this war, despite the impression given by this photo which shows bombs awaiting loading into He 111Bs. Bomber and fighter units frequently shared airfields in Spain.

Battle of France

Most of the Bf 109-equipped Jagdgruppen were assembled for the Western Campaign, which swept through much of France and the Low Countries. The Bf 109s maintained air superiority over the defenders with some ease, although attrition was high and fresh supplies of aircraft were virtually non-existent.

Above: These are 'Emils' of III/JG 26 pictured at Villacoublay near Paris, where the Gruppe's rapid advance halted in late June as resistance collapsed.

Below: The Jagdgruppen withdrew from France to make good their losses before the next battle. Here a France-based E-3 awaits the High Command's next move.

The rapid advance across the Low Countries implied operations from airfields with few or damaged facilities. These Bf 109Es of 6./JG 27 were parked in the open, but under camouflage nets, at St Trond in Belgium in May 1940.

Messerschmitt Bf 109

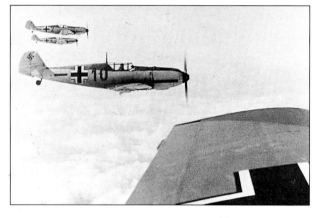

Above: With the RAF on the defensive, the threat of attack on the Luftwaffe bases in the Pas de Calais was limited. Nevertheless, these ground crew are building blast pens for their charges, and thinking of the day soon to come when the war will be over.

Right: Typical early Battle of Britain colours are displayed on these II/JG 27 Bf 109E-3s . At this time, the unit was based at Crepon in western France as part of Luftflotte 3.

Above: This is one of a number of pictures, widely published in Germany, of Luftwaffe aircraft purportedly operating off the coast of England. In fact the scene was more likely in France. The 'finger four' developed in Spain was superior to the RAF formations of the early part of the battle.

Landing speed was 78 mph (125 km/h).

Armament of the E-1 was the same as that of the D-1, comprising two synchronised MG 17 machine-guns in the fuselage upper decking, staggered slightly to accommodate the ammunition feed chutes, and two unsynchronised MG 17s in the wings. The latter each had 500 rounds, while the fuselage guns had 1,000 rounds each. The same Revi C/12C sight was fitted, and the FuG 7 radio was standard, this having a range of about 40 miles (65 km).

Following closely behind the E-1 on the production line was the Bf 109E-3, which retained the fuselage MG 17s but replaced the wing guns with the 20-mm MG FF cannon, each weapon having 60 rounds. Following satisfactory trials with the Bf 109C-3, the Luftwaffe came to favour the heavy throw weight and destructive power of this weapon

despite its slow rate of fire. Dubbed the 'Kanonenmaschine', the E-3 was generally regarded as the best of the early generation Bf 109s – no other variant was to enjoy such a great margin of superiority over its rivals. The E-2 designation was applied to an E-1 with a hub-mounted gun, but this variant was not produced.

Bf 109E deliveries

With the delivery of the first DB 601s in late 1938, production of the Bf 109E-1 got under way. Due to pressing military needs and the political situation, some of the first 'Emils' went to Spain. The Nationalists still urgently required new equipment following the second Ebro campaign. Aircraft such as the Bf 109 had been in short supply as the Luftwaffe needed to build up its home strength in preparation for the Sudeten annexation. However, the urgent needs of the Nationalists could be exploited by Germany to its own advantage, with the Spaniards paying for the re-equipment of the Legion Condor while also securing the supply of strategic materials such as iron ore to fuel the German industries.

The Spaniards themselves also wished to re-equip their fighter units, which had been using the Fiat CR.32 biplane, and to that end they received 17 Heinkel He 112Bs and a promise for the delivery of Bf 109s. In October 1938 three Spanish pilots joined 3./J 88 to gain experience on the

Werner Mölders (below) was given command of JG 51 during the Battle, and he became one of only three pilots to be awarded the Oakleaves to the Knights Cross during this period. Note the head armour fitted to the canopy of Mölders' 'Emil'.

Aces of the Battle of Britain

Below left: Highest-scoring ace of the Battle of France, Wilhelm Balthasar (centre) chats with two other notable pilots, JG 3 Kommandeur Gunther Lutzow (left) and Egon Troha, the Staffelkapitan of 9./JG 3. Balthasar's aircraft, probably an E-4, sports 39 victory bars, 14 of them with downward-pointing arrows, indicating kills achieved against aircraft on the ground.

Horst Tietzen (below) was the Staffelkapitan of 5./JG 51 during the Battle of Britain and had brought his personal score to 18 (including seven victories in Spain) by the time this picture was taken. He had added two further 'kills' by 18 August 1940 when he was shot down into the English Channel by Hurricane Mk Is of No. 501 Squadron and killed.

Adolf Galland (below) was one of the most brilliant fighter leaders of the war, and rose rapidly through the ranks until his differences with Göring finally put a cap on his career. His Bf 109s often had non-standard additions such as a telescopic gunsight and a cigar lighter. During the battle he was promoted from leading III/JG 26 to commanding the Geschwader.

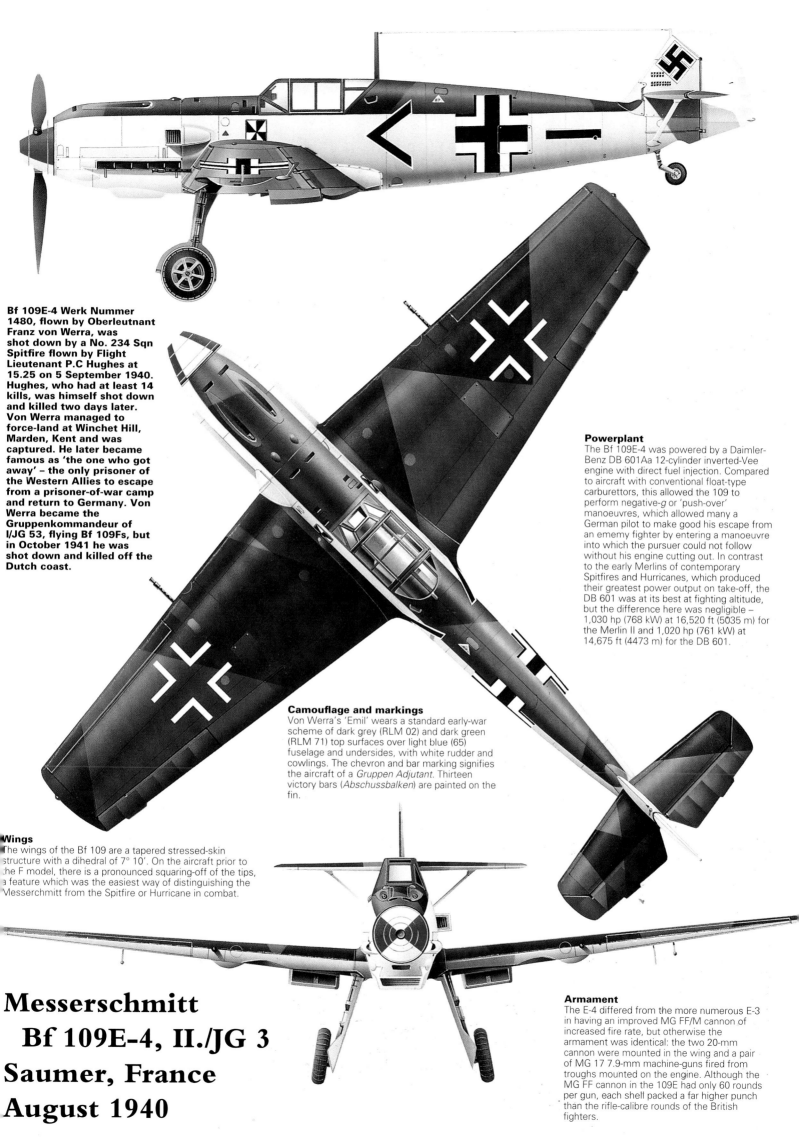

Bf 109E-4 Werk Nummer 1480, flown by Oberleutnant Franz von Werra, was shot down by a No. 234 Sqn Spitfire flown by Flight Lieutenant P.C Hughes at 15.25 on 5 September 1940. Hughes, who had at least 14 kills, was himself shot down and killed two days later. Von Werra managed to force-land at Winchet Hill, Marden, Kent and was captured. He later became famous as 'the one who got away' – the only prisoner of the Western Allies to escape from a prisoner-of-war camp and return to Germany. Von Werra became the Gruppenkommandeur of I/JG 53, flying Bf 109Fs, but in October 1941 he was shot down and killed off the Dutch coast.

Powerplant
The Bf 109E-4 was powered by a Daimler-Benz DB 601Aa 12-cylinder inverted-Vee engine with direct fuel injection. Compared to aircraft with conventional float-type carburettors, this allowed the 109 to perform negative-g or 'push-over' manoeuvres, which allowed many a German pilot to make good his escape from an enemy fighter by entering a manoeuvre into which the pursuer could not follow without his engine cutting out. In contrast to the early Merlins of contemporary Spitfires and Hurricanes, which produced their greatest power output on take-off, the DB 601 was at its best at fighting altitude, but the difference here was negligible – 1,030 hp (768 kW) at 16,520 ft (5035 m) for the Merlin II and 1,020 hp (761 kW) at 14,675 ft (4473 m) for the DB 601.

Camouflage and markings
Von Werra's 'Emil' wears a standard early-war scheme of dark grey (RLM 02) and dark green (RLM 71) top surfaces over light blue (65) fuselage and undersides, with white rudder and cowlings. The chevron and bar marking signifies the aircraft of a *Gruppen Adjutant*. Thirteen victory bars (*Abschussbalken*) are painted on the fin.

Wings
The wings of the Bf 109 are a tapered stressed-skin structure with a dihedral of 7° 10'. On the aircraft prior to the F model, there is a pronounced squaring-off of the tips, a feature which was the easiest way of distinguishing the Messerschmitt from the Spitfire or Hurricane in combat.

Messerschmitt Bf 109E-4, II./JG 3 Saumer, France August 1940

Armament
The E-4 differed from the more numerous E-3 in having an improved MG FF/M cannon of increased fire rate, but otherwise the armament was identical: the two 20-mm cannon were mounted in the wing and a pair of MG 17 7.9-mm machine-guns fired from troughs mounted on the engine. Although the MG FF cannon in the 109E had only 60 rounds per gun, each shell packed a far higher punch than the rifle-calibre rounds of the British fighters.

Messerschmitt Bf 109

Above: Adolf Galland's Bf 109E-3 is one of the best-known fighters of the Battle of Britain. The rudder scoreboard can be seen here, and barely visible are the gothic 'S' badge of JG 26 and Galland's personal 'Mickey Mouse' symbol. By 24 September, Galland's score had reached 40.

Above right: Towards the end of the Battle of Britain, JG 26 carried out sorties in the Jabo (fighter-bomber) role, a tactic which could have been decisive if it had been applied in strength early enough. This Bf 109E-4/B carries a 550-lb (250-kg) bomb.

'Emils' of JG 53 line up for take-off at Dinan for another escort sortie over England. These are II Gruppe aircraft, as distinguished by the horizontal bar aft of the national insignia of each aircraft.

type. Early production Bf 109Es began arriving in Spain in late December, by which time the final offensive of the war had been launched. Fifty-five Bf 109Bs, Cs and Ds had already been sent to Spain, and 37 of these were still in service to support the Catalonian offensive, which opened on 23 December. Barcelona fell on 26 January 1939, after which the Bf 109s were then engaged in preventing Republican aircraft escaping south. The mopping-up campaign claimed its last Bf 109 on 6 February, and the last kill of the Civil War was scored on 5 March, when a Bf 109 downed an I-15. The last combat sortie was flown on 27 March, and on 28 March the Republicans surrendered Valencia and Madrid to end the long, damaging war.

A nucleus of expertise

Around 200 German pilots had flown with Jagdgruppe 88, and the experience they had gained in Spain was to prove of inestimable value in the much larger conflict which loomed months away. Over 30 of these veterans were later to wear the Knight's Cross, and many achieved high rank and lofty positions in the organisation of the Jagdflieger.

Forty Bf 109E-1s and E-3s were shipped to Spain, where the variant was dubbed the 'Tripala' on account of its three-bladed propeller (the Jumo-engined aircraft became 'Bipalas'). The bulk arrived too late to see action, and only about 20 had been reassembled when the war ended, although 2./J 88 officially converted while at Zaragoza before the final surrender. The 20 'Emils', together with

the 27 surviving Jumo-engined aircraft, were then handed over to the Spanish air force. After the reorganisation of the air arm in July 1939, the Bf 109s served with Grupo núm 25 of Regimiento núm 25. Many were subsequently transferred to the Escuela de Caza (fighter school) at Morón de la Frontera, where the last Bf 109E was retired in 1954. One aircraft was used as a testbed for the Hispano-Suiza 12Z 89 in late 1944 as a prelude to the HA1109/1112 derivative series of variants.

Export drive

Another pressing German need was foreign currency to obtain certain strategic materials on the international market. Despite the needs of the home-based fighter units, the export market enjoyed similar priority to the demands of the Legion Condor. The Bf 109 had naturally generated a considerable amount of interest from prospective customers, the two which bore immediate fruition being Yugoslavia and Switzerland. Messerschmitt was authorised to satisfy their orders early in the production run so that payment could be obtained as early as possible.

Yugoslavia had shown interest in the design as early as January 1938, but Reichsmarschall Herman Göring had attempted to dissuade the Yugoslavs from buying such an advanced machine. Using the supply of strategic materials such as iron, copper and chrome ore as a powerful bargaining tool, the Yugoslavs finally got their way and a contract for the supply of 50 Bf 109Es and 25 spare engines was eventually signed on 5 April 1939. On 23 June the Yugoslavs signed for 50 more. The first of these Bf 109E-3s was delivered in the early autumn to the JKRV (Jugoslovensko kraljevsko ratno vazduhoplovstvo – Royal Yugoslav air force) at Zemun, Belgrade.

In Yugoslav service the Bf 109E-3 initially flew with the 6. Vazduhoplovni lovacki pulk (6th Fighter Regiment), but of the 100 ordered only 73 were delivered, and the spares back-up was decidedly inadequate. Many aircraft spent

most of their lives grounded due to lack of parts. In terms of conversion to the new type, Göring had been proven right, for the Yugoslav pilots initially found the Bf 109 a handful after the Hawker Fury, with many landing accidents resulting. An attempt was made to use the Messerschmitt Bf 108B Taifun as a stepping-stone, but in the event the prospective Bf 109 pilot had to first master the Hurricane before converting to the Messerschmitt lightplane. He then stood a chance of surviving the Messerschmitt fighter.

Yugoslav experience with the Bf 109 was not happy: quite apart from the serviceability problems which kept flying hours to a minimum, the pilots never achieved any confidence in the aircraft so that, when the Germans invaded in April 1941, the Yugoslav pilots could do little to defend against the onslaught. They did achieve a handful of kills, however, as recounted later.

Swiss deliveries

On the contrary, Swiss experience was far happier. As recounted earlier, the Fliegertruppe had received an advanced batch of 10 Bf 109D-1s to begin familiarisation with the Messerschmitt. An initial contract covered 30 Bf 109E-3s, although a further 50 were added subsequently. The first 'Emils' reached Switzerland on 14 April 1939, flown in by Swiss pilots. They were delivered without radio or armament, these being fitted locally. On 29 August, the eve of war, the delivery process was altered with German pilots flying to the airfield at Altenrhein on the southern shore of Lake Konstanz, from where the aircraft were collected by Swiss pilots. The last arrived on 27 April 1940.

Unlike the Yugoslavs, the Swiss appear to have had few problems with conversion, despite the fact that their previous fighter was the Dewoitine D 27, a slow, lightly armed parasol. A delay of getting into service was caused by the need to fit radio and armament, but 31 were in service by the time Switzerland mobilised the Fliegertruppen on 30 August. The Bf 109Es initially served with Fliegerkompagnie 6 at Thun and Fliegerkompagnie 21 at Dübendorf, while the Bf 109Ds served with Fliegerkompagnie 15 at Payerne.

Production of the 'Emil' got into its major stride in 1939, so that between 1 January and 1 September, the day of the opening assault on Poland, some 1,091 Bf 109s had been delivered to the Luftwaffe. DB 601 engines were produced by two Daimler-Benz plants at Genshagen and Marienfelde, by the Henschel Flugmotorenbau at Altenbauna and by Büssing-Werke of Braunschweig.

All Messerschmitt Bf 109 production had been transferred to Regensburg by the start of the year, leaving the Augsburg-Haunstetten plant to concentrate on the Bf 110. Focke-Wulf at Bremen was also switched to Bf 110 production, but Erla and Fieseler continued to build Bf 109s, and the production effort was joined by the Wiener-Neustädter Flugzeugbau (WNF) in Austria. Many Bf 109E airframes were built ahead of time pending delivery of the engines.

Rapid build-up

Throughout the spring and summer of 1939 the Jagdgruppen were transitioning to the new variant at fever pitch. During this rapid expansion, on 1 May, the Luftwaffe introduced a more streamlined unit designation system. On 1 September 1939, the Luftwaffe had 1,056 Bf 109s on strength, of which 946 were serviceable. These were assigned to the following units within four Luftflotten:

From initial trials in the Battle of France to a major tasking in the Battle of Britain, the Jabo fighter-bomber role grow enormously in 1940, and continued as a major part of the Bf 109E's repertoire throughout its career. Here the central bomb rack can clearly be seen on this E-4/B.

Despite the widespread adoption of field camouflage during the campaigns of 1940, Bf 109s continued to be delivered with the hard-edged 1940 pattern until much later in the war. This Bf 109E-3 suffered a mishap at De Kooy in Holland in 1941, but the pilot appears to have made his own exit without the aid of the fire crew.

On the Channel Front

Above left: Pilots of Jagdgeschwader 1 rest between missions from De Kooy in Holland in early 1941. The Channel coast was fairly quiet at the time: the Luftwaffe was building up for the massive campaigns in the Balkans and in Russia.

Left: Jagdgeschwader 51 remained in western Europe into early 1941 before heading east for the build-up to Barbarossa. The Geschwader was later named in honour of Werner Mölders, who was killed in November 1941.

When the Germans invaded Yugoslavia, the 6th Fighter Regiment lost all but seven of its 46 serviceable Bf 109Es in the first two days of fighting, although a reasonable amount of damage was done to the attackers in the process. These pilots of the 6th are seen at Zemun prior to the invasion.

Unit	Variant	Number	Serviceable
Luftflotte 1			
I/JG 1	Bf 109E	54	54
I/JG 2	Bf 109E	42	39
10. (Nacht)/JG 2	Bf 109C	9	9
Stab and I/JG 3	Bf 109E	51	45
I/JG 20	Bf 109E	21	20
I/JG 21	Bf 109C/E	29	28
JGr 101 (II/ZG 1)	Bf 109B	36	36
JGr 102 (I/ZG 2)	Bf 109D	44	40
Luftflotte 2			
Stab and I/JG 26	Bf 109E	51	51
II/JG 26	Bf 109E	48	44
10. (Nacht)/JG 26	Bf 109C	10	8
I and II/ZG 26	Bf 109B/D	96	92
JGr 126 (III/ZG 26)	Bf 109B/C	48	44
Luftflotte 3			
I/JG 51	Bf 109E	47	39
I/JG 52	Bf 109E	39	34
JGr 152 (I/ZG 52)	Bf 109B	44	43
I/JG 53	Bf 109E	51	39
II/JG 53	Bf 109E	43	41
1. and 2./JG 70	Bf 109E	24	24
1. and 2./JG 71	Bf 109C/E	39	18
Luftflotte 4			
I/JG 76	Bf 109E	49	45
I/JG 77	Bf 109E	50	43
II/JG 77	Bf 109E	50	36
JGr 176 (II/ZG 76)	Bf 109B/C	40	39
Luftwaffe-Lehrdivision			
Stab and I (Jagd)/LG 2	Bf 109E	39	37
11. (Nacht)/LG 2	Bf 109E	10	9
Oberkommando der Marine			
II/JG 186	Bf 109B	24	24

As can be seen, many of the Zerstörergruppen were temporarily given Jagdgruppen titles, and there were also night-fighter units mainly operating the Bf 109C. The Lehrdivision was an organisation involved in the development of operational tactics, but also had an operational tasking. The naval unit comprised two Staffeln of Bf 109s which were training crews for the forthcoming carrier force.

Polish campaign

Despite this good strength, the Bf 109 was employed in only small numbers during the Polish campaign. This was due in part to a reluctance by the German high command to commit large numbers of aircraft to the campaign in case the attack brought about instant military reaction from Britain and France. Indeed, the whole Polish invasion was a big risk, for the Luftwaffe had insufficient reserves of fuel and ammunition to undertake any major action in the West should the occasion arise. Of course, the British and French were no more prepared for major war than were the Germans, and a mutual lack of intelligence prevented any escalation in the West until the following year.

At the start of the campaign, Bf 109 units assigned to the fighting comprised JGr 101 with Bf 109Bs, I/JG 21 flying Bf 109Cs, JGr 102 with Bf 109Ds, and Bf 109Es flying with I (Jagd)/LG 2, I/JG 1 and I/JG 21. In the air the Poles put up little resistance, and what was provided by the hopelessly outclassed PZL P.7 and P.11 fighters was easily quashed by the Bf 109s. The immediate establishment of aerial supremacy allowed two of the Gruppen, I/JG 1 and I/JG 21, to be withdrawn back to the West soon after the start of the fighting, while the remaining Bf 109s largely turned to

Right: This Bf 109E-1 of JG 77 was brought down during the Balkans Campaign. In Yugoslavia, 'Emil' faced 'Emil' for a few days of fighting, and a number of defending aircraft were brought down by 'friendly' anti-aircraft fire.

ground-strafing missions. There were a few losses to fighters, but the majority of the 67 losses recorded between 1 and 28 September were to groundfire.

Owing to the numerical state of the Jagdgruppen, this was serious, but due to the relative inactivity of the next few months, this attrition was easily remedied. Activity by the RAF in the West was largely confined to tentative coastal reconnaissance and bombing missions, and the Bf 109s were on alert to intercept such attempts. The first kill in the West was a Wellington of No. 9 Squadron, downed on 4 September by a Bf 109E-1 of II/JG 77. On the last day of the month JG 53 Messerschmitts dispatched four out of five Fairey Battles engaged on a daylight mission, relegating the light bomber to nocturnal missions thereafter. The largest air battle of 1939 was played out on 18 December, when Bf 109Bs, Cs and Es, together with Bf 110s, from a variety of units took on 24 Wellingtons near Wilhelmshaven. Twelve of the bombers were shot down, and another three crash-landed back in England. Two Bf 109s were lost, but RAF Bomber Command had suffered a severe blow, one which was to change its future tactics.

Phoney War

These early months of the war, known in England as the 'Phoney War' and in Germany as the 'Sitzkrieg', provided few opportunities for fighter versus fighter combat, but on the few occasions that the Bf 109E met either M.S.406s or the Hurricanes of the advanced RAF force in France, the Messerschmitt proved far superior. Conversion to the Bf 109E from the earlier models continued, with Bs and Cs passing mainly to Jagdfliegerschulen. The 'Doras' were mainly passed to the hastily-formed night-fighter force.

The first element of this force had been established in the summer of 1939 as 10. (Nacht)/JG 26, under the command of Oberleutnant Johannes Steinhof. The unit was tasked with developing night-fighting tactics, and was initially equipped with Arado Ar 68s and Bf 109Bs. These gave way to Bf 109Cs, and a second C night unit was formed, 10. (Nacht)/JG 2. A third unit, 11. (Nacht)/JG 2, formed in late 1939 with Bf 109D-1s, and this took up residence in the Helgoland region, where it was joined by the other two Staffeln to form IV/JG 2. By now all three units were operating the 'Dora', and continued in service defending northern Germany at night until the summer of 1940, when the last Jumo-powered Bf 109s were finally phased out of the Luftwaffe front line.

During the 'Sitzkrieg' the Allies were presented with two golden opportunities to study the Bf 109 exhaustively. The first occurred as early as 24 September 1939, when an aircraft of II/JG 51 landed at Strasbourg-Neuhof airfield. After only limited test flying, a French pilot damaged the aircraft during a heavy landing at Nancy on 6 September. Following repair, the 'Emil' was flown again, but on 28 November it was lost in a mid-air collision with a Curtiss Hawk 75A being flown by Capitaine Rozanoff, the pilot who had originally evaluated the Bf 109 captured in Spain.

The fighters of 7./JG 52 are seen lined up on a former civil airfied during the Balkans campaign. The yellow nose, wingtips, rudder and fuselage band on these Bf 109E-1s were theatre markings.

Just days before, another 'Emil' (of I/JG 76) had landed by mistake on the wrong side of the Franco-German border. Promptly ferried by road to the Centre d'Essais en Vol at Orléans-Bricy, the Bf 109 was tested by several pilots before being flown to Boscombe Down in England on 4 May 1940. On 14 May it transferred to the Royal Aircraft Establishment at Farnborough and, assigned RAF serial AE479, was thoroughly assessed by the Aerodynamic Flight.

These flights confirmed that the Bf 109 was superior in almost all respects to the Hurricane, except for low-altitude manoeuvrability and turning circle. Dependent on the type of propeller fitted, the Spitfire Mk I fared much better. The Bf 109 was in most respects superior to the Spitfire fitted with the two-pitch propeller then in widespread service with RAF squadrons, but with the Rotol three-bladed variable-pitch propeller, the Spitfire was faster. Above 20,000 ft (6096 m) the Spitfire was untouchable, but the Bf 109 could outclimb the RAF aircraft to that height. Nothing could out-dive the Messerschmitt, and the benefits of the fuel injection engine in such a manoeuvre were not lost on the British pilots.

Staged fighting

Mock combats were staged between the Bf 109 and the Hurricane and Spitfire. In low-speed turns the RAF fighters had no trouble staying with the Messerschmitt, and at high speeds aileron forces became too heavy for rapid manoeuvres. An interesting point was that the cockpit of the Bf 109 was so cramped that the pilot could only apply two-thirds of the sideways pressure on the stick achievable in the Spitfire.

In conclusion, the RAF pilots judged that the best escape manoeuvres for the Bf 109 were a steep-angle climb, which the Hurricane and Spitfire could not match, and a bunt manoeuvre which utilised the dive prowess and fuel

The two-bladed propellers immediately identify these aircraft as Jumo-powered. They are 'Claras', seen in the service of one of several Jagdfliegerschulen which operated the older types into 1941.

injection of the Bf 109 to increase spacing. On the other hand, both Hurricane and Spitfire could evade a pursuing Messerschmitt using any number of violent manoeuvres, such as a half-roll followed by a rapid pull-out of the ensuing dive. If the Messerschmitt attempted to follow these it would either encounter too-heavy control forces at high speeds or stall out at lower speeds. In either case, around 2,000 to 3,000 ft (600 to 900 m) of altitude would be lost, fatal when fighting near the ground. Indeed, several Messerschmitts were noted to have been downed in this way without a shot having been fired.

AE479 was transferred to the Air Fighting Development Unit at Northolt on 20 September 1940, with whom it flew until being damaged in a crash landing on 5 January 1941. It was then flown by No. 1426 (Enemy Aircraft) Flight at Duxford until being crated and shipped to Wright Field, Ohio, in April 1942 for evaluation by the US Army Air Forces. Another Bf 109E was assembled out of parts from various aircraft and was flown by the RAF on 25 February 1941. With registration DG200, this aircraft was used for calibration trials by Rolls-Royce, and was later

Bf 109 in Greece

Although it still wears the badge of JG 52, this aircraft served with I (Jagd)/LG 2 during the Greece campaign. The pilot was the Gruppen-kommandeur, Hauptmann Herbert Ihlefeld, who had already scored seven kills in Spain when the war started. Ihlefeld became the Kommodore of several Geschwaders, surviving the war with 130 victories.

Messerschmitt Bf 109

Far right: Despite their activities in the arid conditions of the Mediterranean, the Bf 109Es of 7./JG 26 retained their north-European colour scheme of mottled greys and yellow extremities. This is the E-7 of Ernst Laube at Gela, Sicily.

Right: Only about a dozen pilots served on JG 26's Mediterranean sojourn. Their undoubted star was their Kommandeur, Joachim Müncheberg, who added a number of RAF aircraft to his eventual tally of 135 during this period. This could be Müncheberg's Bf 109E-7 'white 12'.

something of a celebrity with several public appearances. Today the aircraft resides in the RAF Museum at Hendon, returned to Luftwaffe camouflage.

Bf 109s played little part in Operation Weserübung, the invasion of Denmark and Norway, where there was little fighter opposition and the ranges too great to be covered by the Bf 109. The main unit involved was II/JG 77, which occupied several bases in Denmark during April. The main effort in early 1940 was to gear up for the assault in the West, Operation Fall Gelb, which abruptly brought to an end the 'Sitzkrieg' on 10 May. To say the French were unprepared for the shock of meeting the Bf 109 in combat is an understatement: despite the bad weather in the winter of 1939-40, there had been sufficient aerial skirmishes for the French to see just how inferior their aircraft were. The margin of superiority could not be bridged by the acknowledged skill and bravery of the French pilots. Indeed, in many ways the Germans were better trained and flew with far superior tactics thanks to the experiences of the Spanish Civil War.

The assault in the West was as much a gamble as that on Poland, for the Luftwaffe still did not have sufficient depth of spares and supplies to sustain a long campaign. Production of aircraft had barely risen during the early

months of 1940, so that just over 1,000 Bf 109s were available to the vast majority of the Jagdgruppen which prepared for the attack. A greater determination in production was later to take hold, especially as it was realised that a successful French campaign did not automatically mean the end of the war.

Air superiority

From the outset, the Bf 109E fighters of JGs 1, 2, 3, 21, 26, 27, 51, 52, 53 and 54 established total air superiority over the Dutch, Belgian, British and French air forces, allowing the Stukagruppen and Kampfgruppen to devastate the Allied forces. Only the Dewoitine D.520, available in small numbers, posed any serious threat to the Bf 109. Holland capitulated on 14 May, and on 21 May the RAF pulled its tattered British Expeditionary Force Air Component out of France and Belgium, and the British AASF (Advanced Air Strike Force) moved way back into France. The Bf 109s followed closely on the heels of the rapidly advancing Wehrmacht, moving bases often. On the other side of the lines, the constant retreat of Allied air units and the continuous bombing their fields received turned maintenance and spares supply into a nightmare. Many Allied fighters were destroyed on the ground, and those

Sicily and Malta

In February 1941 the first German single-seat fighter unit arrived in Sicily to help the Italian forces who were unable to subdue the Allied units defending Malta. This was 7./JG 26 who detatched from the parent unit on the

Channel Front, and under Oberleutnant Joachim Müncheberg. They sorely tested the RAF on and around Malta until late May when the Staffel was ordered to Greece, and then Libya, returning to France in August.

These three photos depict E-4/Bs of 9./JG 27 bombing up for a mission over Malta. Of note is the presentation of tactical numbers on the cowls of the Messerschmitts peculiar to this unit. The aircraft flying a metal pennant from the radio mast is that of Staffelkapitan Erbo Graf von Kageneck who was JG 27's highest-scoring pilot at the time of his death from wounds in January 1942.

Aces in Sicily

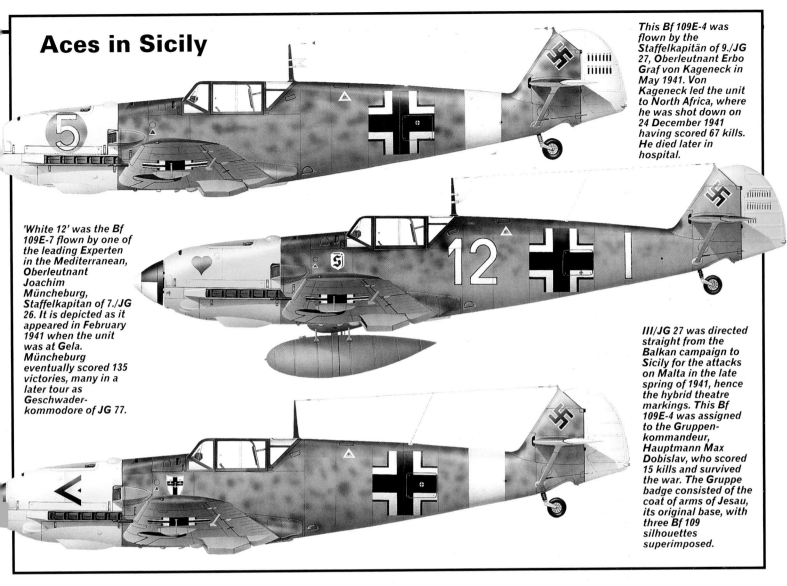

This Bf 109E-4 was flown by the Staffelkapitän of 9./JG 27, Oberleutnant Erbo Graf von Kageneck in May 1941. Von Kageneck led the unit to North Africa, where he was shot down on 24 December 1941 having scored 67 kills. He died later in hospital.

'White 12' was the Bf 109E-7 flown by one of the leading Experten in the Mediterranean, Oberleutnant Joachim Müncheburg, Staffelkapitan of 7./JG 26. It is depicted as it appeared in February 1941 when the unit was at Gela. Müncheburg eventually scored 135 victories, many in a later tour as Geschwader-kommodore of JG 77.

III/JG 27 was directed straight from the Balkan campaign to Sicily for the attacks on Malta in the late spring of 1941, hence the hybrid theatre markings. This Bf 109E-4 was assigned to the Gruppen-kommandeur, Hauptmann Max Dobislav, who scored 15 kills and survived the war. The Gruppe badge consisted of the coat of arms of Jesau, its original base, with three Bf 109 silhouettes superimposed.

that did engage the enemy made little impact on the air battle.

The major enemy of the Jagdgruppen was the speed of the advance itself, which lengthened supply lines to almost breaking point. The light attrition suffered by the force throughout May and June nevertheless proved difficult to atone given the parlous state of the reserves back in Germany. The final evacuation of the Allies from Dunkirk was not quite the military disaster that it is often painted, for it was the Germans' intention to prevent any such evacuation to Britain. That they failed to do so was largely due to the long distances the Bf 109s had to fly to cover the bombers attacking the Allies, which in turn meant they suffered heavy losses. Another factor which was to have much greater bearing a few weeks later was the first encounters with the Supermarine Spitfire, which began to cover Allied forces from bases in England.

From 3 June, the Western campaign took less than three weeks to complete, ending in a French armistice. During this time the Bf 109s had little trouble against the French, despite the depleted numbers within the Jagdgruppen. Units were progressively withdrawn to Germany for re-equipment and recuperation, although this process was exacerbated by the low rate of production and the fact that export contracts were still being fulfilled. Among these was the delivery to the Soviet Union of five Bf 109E-3s for evaluation purposes in return for raw materials. Like the French earlier, the Soviets concluded that they had nothing to learn from the Bf 109 – how expensive that conclusion was to become the following year!

Sights on Britain

Militarily, the campaigns of early 1940 were an outstanding success for the Germans: all of mainland Europe was now either under their control or neutral. Only Britain remained. While the German forces were in no state to tackle Albion just yet, the German High Command's sights were set firmly across the Channel. Following a month's lull in activity, during which only the three Gruppen of JG 51 Bf 109s remained in France to face the RAF, a slow but deliberate build-up of forces began on 12 July with the return of III/JG 3. At the end of July, JGs 26, 27 and 52 returned to France. Other Gruppen followed.

Although the Bf 109s had enjoyed air superiority over France, combat losses were still high, and one of the chief concerns was the lack of armour protection. In the summer of 1940 Bf 109E-3s began to appear with a heavily-framed canopy and 8-mm seat armour. A further armour plate was

Left: The first Luftwaffe fighter unit to be sent as a Gruppe to the Middle East was I/JG 27. The pilots were all seasoned veterans of the western campaigns and in some cases, Spain. The officer at left with papers is Hauptmann Karl-Wolfgang Redlich, here briefing pilots of the Gruppe for the final Sicily-Libya leg of their journey to the war.

Above: The desert imposed harsh conditions on man and machine. The inevitable sand storms whipped up by aircraft necessitated wide spacing on take-off. The first unit in the desert, I/JG 26, left all its aircraft behind when it left due to unservicabilty brought about by the dust and unforgiving landing strips.

The mission of the 'Emil' in the desert ranged from pure fighter interception to ground attack to long-range escort. Here, the E-7/Trop of I/JG 27's adjutant Oberleutnant Ludwig Franzisket escorts a Ju 87B Stuka with empty bomb cradle over Libya in April 1941.

Far right: The greatest ace of the desert was Hans-Joachim Marseille, who had only seven victories on arrival in Africa – relatively few compared to some of the Experten already serving with JG 27. Early in his career he had a lucky escape when his Bf 109E-4/Trop. suffered combat damage close to the engine, as seen here.

The perfect matching of camouflage with environment is rare in wartime, but the sand with brownish-green topsides of this I/JG 27 Bf 109E-4/Trop blends in perfectly with the scrubby terrain of North Africa, at least at low level.

provided over the pilot's head, attached to the canopy. The Bf 109E-4 rapidly replaced the E-3 on the production line, this variant differing by having the MG FF/M cannon in the wings. Essentially similar to the first 20-mm weapon, the new gun had an improved rate of fire. Ikaria-Werke studied a belt-feed for the MG FF, but in the event the trial installation was not flown until early 1941, and was cancelled. The Bf 109 retained the capability for an engine-mounted weapon, although problems with cooling and vibration had meant they were not fitted. The hollow spinner was nevertheless retained in the fighter variants.

In late August 1940 the Bf 109E-7 began to arrive at fighter units. This differed from the Bf 109E-4 by having the capability to carry a 66-Imp gal (300-litre) jettisonable plywood fuel tank. The lack of range had been one of the main disadvantages of the Bf 109 during the French campaign, and would further embarrass the Jagdgruppen over England, limiting combat time to just a few minutes. In practice, the tank was prone to terrible leaks and suspected of a tendency to ignite. It was rarely used in action due to the suspicions of the pilots. The rack could also carry a single SC 250 bomb.

Other more radical approaches were being made to address the range problem in the summer of 1940. The most novel involved the use of bombers literally towing the fighters to the target area before they were cast off and went about defending their erstwhile tugs. At Augsburg,

Desert Experten

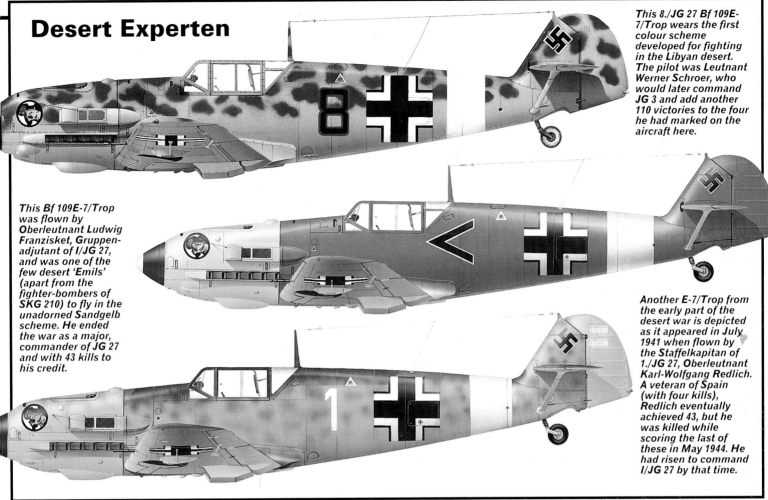

This 8./JG 27 Bf 109E-7/Trop wears the first colour scheme developed for fighting in the Libyan desert. The pilot was Leutnant Werner Schroer, who would later command JG 3 and add another 110 victories to the four he had marked on the aircraft here.

This Bf 109E-7/Trop was flown by Oberleutnant Ludwig Franzisket, Gruppen-adjutant of I/JG 27, and was one of the few desert 'Emils' (apart from the fighter-bombers of SKG 210) to fly in the unadorned Sandgelb scheme. He ended the war as a major, commander of JG 27 and with 43 kills to his credit.

Another E-7/Trop from the early part of the desert war is depicted as it appeared in July 1941 when flown by the Staffelkapitan of 1./JG 27, Oberleutnant Karl-Wolfgang Redlich. A veteran of Spain (with four kills), Redlich eventually achieved 43, but he was killed while scoring the last of these in May 1944. He had risen to command I/JG 27 by that time.

Karl Baur tested the concept using a Bf 110 towing a Bf 109, attaching the towline in the hollow spinner. Both aircraft took off under their own power, attached by the tow cable. Once at altitude, the 109's engine was cut and the propeller fully-feathered. The trials showed some promise, but the idea was not adopted.

With the benefits of experience from France, the summer months of 1940 saw a flurry of development activity, the most important being the development of the Bf 109 as a Jagdbomber, or Jabo, type. Under the command of Hauptmann Walter Rubensdörffer,

Left: The French obtained two examples of the Bf 109E before the end of 1939, both of which landed in error in French territory. The first was written off in a collision. The second aircraft shown here, an E-3 of I/JG 76, was flown by a number of test pilots and then sent to Britain at the start of the Battle of France.

Captured aircraft

The few intact Bf 109s that fell into Allied hands in the early part of the war were thoroughly evaluated to determine the strengths and weaknesses of the type. Flown against Allied fighters, the 109 was found to be about equal to the Spitfire, but superior to the Hurricane in most respects except low-altitude turning circle. The experienced operational pilots who flew the 'Emil' were impressed by its low-speed handling, high top speed and climb rate, and its fuel-injected engine that did not cut out when inverted. On the other hand, the heaviness of the controls at high speed was criticised, as was the high wing loading and consequent poor turning circle. Other faults were seen as the lack of a rudder trimmer and the cramped cockpit that prevented the pilot getting full movement from the controls in combat. Unfortunately, and partly due to a series of mishaps, the French were again unable to

make much use of the data from the captured Messerschmitts in time to counter them when they appeared in force in May 1940. The British evaluations of airworthy examples were of more benefit, although they were not completed in time to be of use during the Battle of Britain.

Below: The ex-French Bf 109E-3 was tested in the summer of 1940 at Farnborough and Boscombe Down with the RAF serial of AE479. It wore a standard RAF scheme of dark earth and dark green.

Above: The second Bf 109E to be flown in evaluations by the RAF was E-3/B Wk Nr 4101 of 2./JG 51, which crash-landed at Manston after combat with Spitfires on 27 November 1940. Refurbished by Rolls-Royce, the aircraft was given the serial DG200 and operated mainly from Hatfield, where the canopy was removed in order to accommodate test-pilot Harvey Heyworth who was over 6 ft (1.83 m) tall.

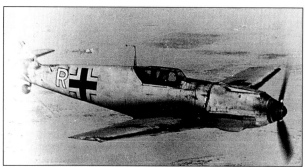

Erprobungsgruppe 210 was established to evaluate fighter-bomber tactics, using Bf 109s equipped with a rudimentary centreline rack for a single bomb from 110 to 550 lb (50 to 250 kg) weight. The unit went into action against coastal shipping in July 1940.

No specialist bombing systems were added to these aircraft, but it was soon discovered that the Revi gunsight could be used with some accuracy for 45° diving attacks. To set up the attack, a line was painted at 45° on the cockpit glazing for alignment. Such were the successes of Rubensdorffer's unit that an immediate order was issued for each Jagdgeschwader to establish a Jabo unit. At first the Bf 109E-1 was hastily converted to Bf 109E-1/B status by the addition of a rack for a single SC 50 (110-lb/50-kg) bomb, although the Bf 109E-4/B was also introduced on the factory production line, this having a better rack capable of lifting a single SC 250 bomb or four SC 50s. The E-4/B finally dispensed with the hollow spinner in favour of a streamlined unit, and in later months the weapon repertoire of the Jabo variants grew considerably.

Reconnaissance

Small numbers were also produced in parallel with the E-4 of tactical reconnaissance aircraft. The Bf 109E-5 variant had the wing cannon removed, and a single vertical Rb 21/18 camera mounted in the rear fuselage immediately behind the cockpit. The Bf 109E-6 retained its wing cannon, but featured an Rb 50/30 camera. The final variant to reach the Luftwaffe before the launch of the attack on Britain was the Bf 109E-4/N. This aircraft had a DB 601N engine, which was a result of major tinkering with the DB 601A. By using 96 octane C3 fuel in place of

the standard 87 octane B4, and by raising the compression ratio considerably, the DB 601N could put out 1,200 hp (895 kW) for take-off and 1,270 hp (947 kW) at 16,400 ft (5000 m), although both output figures could only be maintained for a maximum of one minute.

Adlerangriff (attack of the eagles) was the grand name bestowed on the operation aimed at Britain, and 13 August was Adlertag (day of the eagles), the date of the major opening bombing assault. Prior to this there were a growing number of exploratory missions along the coast and several skirmishes ensued. The Jagdgruppen were still at about 80 per cent of their strength when they had launched the Western campaign, and on Adlertag their numbers comprised 805 serviceable Bf 109Es. They were divided between Luftflotte 2 in Belgium and the Netherlands, with the full Geschwaders JGs 3, 26, 51 and 52, together with the Stab and I./JG 54 fighter-bombers of 3./Erprobungsgruppe 210, and Luftflotte 3 in France, which boasted JGs 2, 27 and 53.

Tactical freedom

In the initial onslaught on Britain, the Bf 109s enjoyed great success, largely because they were entrusted with an anti-fighter role which allowed the 'Emil' to fight in its best environment. Complete tactical freedom in the *freie Jagd* role allowed the Luftwaffe to exploit the dive and climb characteristics in picking off RAF fighters almost at will, and the fluid tactical formations devised in Spain by Mölders proved to be so much better than the rigid and predictable tight formations based on three-ship vics flown by the RAF. Begrudgingly, the RAF began to adopt the finger-four formation, with dramatically improved results.

Where the Luftwaffe was at a real disadvantage was in the poor performance of the much-vaunted Messerschmitt Bf 110, which was supposed to be escorting the bombers. The Zerstörer forces were cut to ribbons, and it became painfully obvious to the Luftwaffe commanders that the Bf 110 could no longer provide adequate protection for the bombers. Accordingly, the Bf 109 was switched from its fighter sweep role to close escort around the beginning of September, immediately denying the tactical freedoms enjoyed by the Messerschmitt pilots during the opening weeks of the battle. With its limited range, the Bf 109 could reach no further than London, while combat over the southern coast of England could rarely be maintained

Jagdbomber

Production of the Bf 109E had been phased out by the summer of 1941, and the numbers in service dwindled until the type disappeared from the fighter role in the Luftwaffe altogether. In one role, however, that of ground attack, the 'Emil' lingered on until well into 1943 in the Middle East and particularly in Russia. The last units operating the 'Emil' in action were the Schlacht (literally: Slaughter) Gruppen, mainly with E-7/B aircraft.

for more than 20 minutes at the most.

This situation severely hampered the attempts of the Luftwaffe to defeat the RAF in the air, and, coupled with the decision to leave the bombing of RAF airfields and begin attacking the cities, marked a turning point in the battle. Hurricanes and Spitfires began to exploit the situation to the full, introducing more advanced tactics themselves to keep the rampant Bf 109s in check. Tied closely to the bombers, the Bf 109s could be easily out-turned by both Spitfires and Hurricanes, and, instead of being the hunters who struck at large formations in slashing manoeuvres from altitude, the German aircraft found themselves on the receiving end. Losses began to escalate.

Of course, the Bf 109 was still a most feared opponent, especially in the hands of experienced pilots of the Jagdgruppen who, under the tutelage of Spanish veterans such as Galland and Mölders, built upon their experiences over France to rack up impressive victory tallies. Mölders himself was the leading ace of the Battle of Britain, becoming the first pilot to pass 50 victories while serving with JG 51. Galland, flying with JG 26, was not far behind. Apart from its performance characteristics and experienced pilots, a key advantage enjoyed by the Bf 109E was the 20-mm MG FF cannon, which proved to be devastating against the British fighters.

Establishment of the Jabostaffeln

As the battle progressed, the Bf 109 units were reorganised to reflect their new-found encumberment. The fighter-bomber unit had been joined by I (Jagd)/Lehrgeschwader 2 with new Bf 109E-7s, and the Bf 109E-4/Bs of II (Schlacht)/LG 2. These units mounted several effective raids, although of little destructive effect.

31 October is recognised as the last day of the Battle of Britain. Since July the Luftwaffe had lost 610 Bf 109s, while RAF Fighter Command lost 631 Hurricanes and 403 Spitfires. Drained of energy by the bloody daytime battle of attrition, both sides withdrew from the fighter battle to attempt to recover their strengths, both in numbers of aircraft and from an emotional standpoint. Looked at from an objective, strategic standpoint, the battle ended inconclusively, although from the British perspective the fact that it, alone in Europe, had not succumbed to the might of the German military machine was seen as a great victory. From a German point of view, the fact that it had not completely crushed the RAF was conversely seen as defeat. A vitally important corner in the course of the war had been turned.

Two important lessons had been learned by the Luftwaffe. One was that the need to reverse the dwindling trend in fighter production was paramount, and the other was that the Bf 109E needed considerable development to stay ahead of its opponents. By February 1941 the decrease in production was turned around dramatically, a fact helped by the addition of the AGO Flugzeugwerke at Oschersleben to the Bf 109 manufacturing complex. The parent company also hastened the development of the next major variant, the Bf 109F 'Friedrich', although the 'Emil' stayed in production a while longer. There was still much fighting for it to do before later models completely replaced it in front-line service.

An interesting sideline was the Bf 109T 'Toni', the carrier version of the Bf 109. As described earlier, the nucleus of a Trägergruppe (carrier air group) had been laid down in 1939 with the establishment of Ju 87 and Bf 109B squadrons at Kiel-Holtenau, and Messerschmitt had been asked to develop a special carrierborne version. The resulting Bf 109T was a simple modification of the Bf 109E-1 with each wing extended by a 21.25-in (0.54-m) panel and corresponding increases in leading-edge slot and ailerons. Flap travel was increased to further reduce landing speed. The wings were provided with a manual folding point although this required that the flaps be removed first. Folded span was 15 ft 0.75 in (4.59 m). Catapult points and an arrester hook were fitted to the fuselage with local strengthening. Armament remained the same at four MG 17s, although it was envisaged that production aircraft would have the MG FF cannon in the wings.

Fieseler was responsible for finalising the design and production, and a 10-aircraft batch of Bf 109T-0 pre-production aircraft was built. They were powered by the DB 601A and featured retractable spoilers on the upper wing surfaces to steepen the glide angle. A strengthened

Above: The introduction of the ETC 50/VIIID rack with capacity for four SC 50 bombs greatly increased the versatility of the Bf 109E as a ground attack platform. With a liquid-cooled engine and limited armour protection, the Messerschmitt was not an ideal aircraft in the close-support role.

Left: Ground crew load an SC 500 500-kg (1,100-lb) fragmentation bomb on a Bf 109E-4/B of II (schlacht)/LG 2. In addition to conventional bombs, the 109 could drop up to 96 SD-2 'butterfly bombs', which were devastating against troops or soft-skinned transport.

A Hauptmann of 15. (span)/JG 51 inspects the cannon of a Bf 109E/Trop somewhere on the central Eastern Front in August 1942. This unit was formed as the 'Blue Squadron' (Escuadron Azul) with Spanish volunteers in March 1942, and was rotated with new pilots from Spain every six months.

Messerschmitt Bf 109E-7
3. Staffel
Lehrgeschwader 2
Calais-Marck, September 1940

Lehrgeschwader 2
The two Lehrgeschwader (operational development groups) in the Battle of Britain – LG 1 and LG 2 – were equipped with a variety of types including Ju 88 bombers, Ju 87 Stukas, Bf 110 Zerstörers and Bf 109E fighters. Manned largely by former instructors and personnel of the pre-war Development Flying Unit, they undertook a number of roles including reconnaissance and the testing of new tactics and weapons. LG 2 was the smaller of the two, with one Staffel flying Bf 110C-5s and two with Bf 109s.

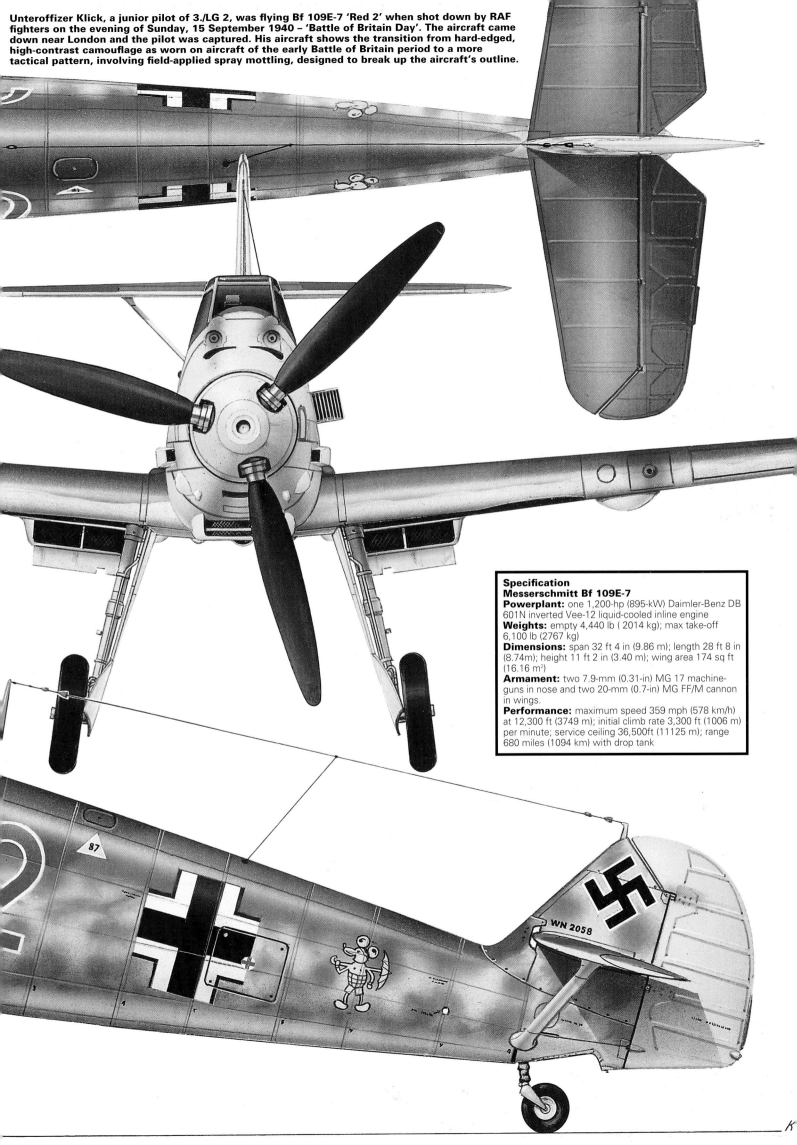

Unteroffizer Klick, a junior pilot of 3./LG 2, was flying Bf 109E-7 'Red 2' when shot down by RAF fighters on the evening of Sunday, 15 September 1940 – 'Battle of Britain Day'. The aircraft came down near London and the pilot was captured. His aircraft shows the transition from hard-edged, high-contrast camouflage as worn on aircraft of the early Battle of Britain period to a more tactical pattern, involving field-applied spray mottling, designed to break up the aircraft's outline.

Specification
Messerschmitt Bf 109E-7
Powerplant: one 1,200-hp (895-kW) Daimler-Benz DB 601N inverted Vee-12 liquid-cooled inline engine
Weights: empty 4,440 lb (2014 kg); max take-off 6,100 lb (2767 kg)
Dimensions: span 32 ft 4 in (9.86 m); length 28 ft 8 in (8.74m); height 11 ft 2 in (3.40 m); wing area 174 sq ft (16.16 m²)
Armament: two 7.9-mm (0.31-in) MG 17 machine-guns in nose and two 20-mm (0.7-in) MG FF/M cannon in wings.
Performance: maximum speed 359 mph (578 km/h) at 12,300 ft (3749 m); initial climb rate 3,300 ft (1006 m) per minute; service ceiling 36,500ft (11125 m); range 680 miles (1094 km) with drop tank

One of the lesser-known recipients of the Bf 109 was Japan, which was sent five unarmed Bf 109E-7s for evaluation in 1941. The aircraft were tested by the Army and Kawasaki, who did not think much of the aircraft but adopted the DB 601 for use in the Ki-61 'Tony'. Russia also received a small number of Bf 109Es prior to the German invasion.

Below right: One Bf 109E-1 was fitted with a ski undercarriage or Schneekufen in January 1941 to explore the suitability of the Bf 109 for operations on snow-bound airfields. A three-wheeled jettisonable trolley was used for some trial flights, as seen here. After more than 80 test flights, the aircraft crashed on landing.

Below: After the official dismissal of proposals for piggy-back fighters delivering explosive-packed bombers to high-value targets, Fritz Stamer of DFS undertook trials of the concept for transporting small troop gliders. A Bf 109E was one of a series of aircraft flown joined to a DFS 230 glider in the 1942 experiments. The Messerschmitt had a retracting tailwheel as well as attachment points for the joining structure.

undercarriage was fitted. During the winter of 1939/40, the Bf 109T-0s underwent extensive evaluation at Travemünde, but work on the aircraft-carrier and its aircraft had already been curtailed, and was stopped completely in May 1940. The prospective carrier Staffeln, meanwhile, had become II/JG 186, and had fought in the Netherlands with Bf 109E-1s. In June it moved to Norway, and became III/JG 77 on 6 July.

Fieseler had an outstanding order for 60 Bf 109T-1s when work halted. The stoppage was brief, for in November 1940, following the British attack on Taranto, the Germans renewed their interest in the aircraft-carrier, and Fieseler resumed the construction of the 'Tonis'. These were to be completed as Bf 109T-2 landplanes, stripped of carrier equipment but retaining the high-lift features for operations from short land strips. A ventral rack was provided for carrying a 66-Imp gal (300-litre) drop tank or bombs and the aircraft had the MG FF wing cannon. Powered by the high-octane DB 601N engine, the Bf 109T-2 was found to lose little in performance compared to a standard-span Bf 109E-4/N. Unsticking at 74.5 mph (120 km/h), the 'Toni' could clear an 80-ft (25-m) obstacle in just 550 yd (500 m), while landing from the same altitude could be accomplished in 765 yd (700 m).

Land-based career

T-2s were to enjoy a long career. The original carrier unit, III/JG 77, had been replaced in Norway by I/JG 77 with Bf 109E-3s, and it was to this unit that the aircraft were delivered in June 1941. They operated primarily from Stavanger-Sola, equipping all three Staffeln. The 'Einsatzstaffel Drontheim' was a detachment at Trondheim. In January 1942 the unit was redesignated I/JG 5, and soon after 3. Staffel was relocated to the island of Herdla, near Bergen, where it operated from a wooden-planked airstrip of tiny dimensions. I/JG 5 re-equipped with Fw 190As in the summer, and the displaced Bf 109T-2s returned to Germany. In April 1943 the Jagdstaffel Helgoland was formed to defend the tiny island, and this used the 'Tonis'. In November the unit became 11./JG 11, and then 8./JG 4. In the summer of 1944 the few T-2s remaining returned

to Norway, where they survived in operations until the end of the year.

For the mainstream Jagdgruppen, the winter of 1940/41 was a time for recovering the strength lost during the epic fighting over Britain. The Bf 109F became available in early 1941, the élite units on the Channel coast getting the first examples, although III/JG 26 with Bf 109E-4s was dispatched to Gela in Sicily to bolster the Italian and German forces attacking Malta. Many units were in the process of conversion to the 'Friedrich' when the Wehrmacht launched its next major attack: Operation Marita. This thrust into the Balkans was a logical step after Romania and Bulgaria had joined the Axis Tripartite Pact in November 1940 and March 1941, respectively. Access to bases in both countries allowed the Germans to virtually encircle Yugoslavia, which had repudiated the Pact, and provide a jump-off point into Greece. Bf 109Es would provide the fighter cover, units moving south into Romania and Bulgaria to prepare for the onslaught, these comprising the Stab, I and II/JG 27, I (Jagd) and II (Schlacht)/LG 2 and Stab, II and III/JG 77.

Blitz on Belgrade

A major bombing raid on Belgrade on 6 April 1941 signalled the opening of Operation Marita, and the Luftwaffe found itself in the unusual position of fighting against other Messerschmitts. Despite their problems, the Yugoslavs still had 32 Bf 109Es serviceable with the 6th Fighter Regiment, split between the 32. Lovacka grupa (fighter group) at Prnjavor and the 51. Lovacka grupa at Zemun. Both of these units had the defence of Belgrade as their task, while the 31. Lovacka grupa of the 2nd Fighter Regiment, with a further 11 Bf 109Es, was assigned the defence of the major industrial areas. Three more Bf 109Es were with the training unit at Mostar for a serviceable total of 46.

On the first day the Yugoslavs put up a stout defence, downing at least 10 bombers, but their inexperienced pilots, who lacked confidence in the Bf 109, were no match for the Luftwaffe. The 6th Fighter Regiment lost 13 Messerschmitts on the first day, and a 2nd Regiment aircraft was also shot down. Yugoslav anti-aircraft gunners occasionally fired on friendly Bf 109s to further add to the misery. The next day, 7 April, a further 12 6th Regiment aircraft were lost, leaving just seven. These were flown out to Veliki Radinci where on 11 April they were burned to prevent them falling into German hands. The 2nd Regiment had burned its Messerschmitts the day before.

Operation Marita also included the invasion of Greece, which the Italians had been trying unsuccessfully to take for some months. JG 27 and JG 77 soon became involved in major air battles with the RAF forces, losing several aircraft to Hurricane Mk IAs. On the other hand, the Bf 109s made short work of the Blenheim squadrons, shooting down six during one raid and destroying an entire squadron

The Royal Bulgarian air force was a late recipient of the Bf 109E, obtaining 19 E-4s in 1942. Like a number of eastern European air forces, the Bulgarians found themselves switching allegiances during the war, and they adopted the colourful red, white and green insignia shown here at the time they joined with Soviet forces in September 1944.

on the ground in another. During 19 and 20 April air battles raged over Athens, the Hurricanes putting up a stout defence led by No. 33 Squadron's commander, Squadron Leader Marmaduke 'Pat' Pattle. In the end, the Luftwaffe numbers prevailed, and the RAF pulled back. Bf 109s destroyed 13 of the priceless Hurricanes on the ground during a massive strafing raid, and the remaining aircraft were quickly evacuated to Crete. Athens fell on 27 April.

Following their success in the Balkans, the Germans pushed into the Mediterranean. On 20 May the Luftwaffe turned on Crete, with fighter cover coming from Stab, II and III/JG 77 and I (Jagd)/LG 2. These units operated from Molaoi in the Peloponnese and had been employed during the previous weeks on a massive softening-up campaign of strafing. After appalling losses on the ground, the Wehrmacht eventually took Crete at the end of the month.

Messerschmitts to the desert

The Italians were also having a hard time in the deserts of North Africa and forces were dispatched to Libya to help, under the command of Generalleutnant Erwin Rommel, who arrived in Tripoli on 12 February 1941. In early April, Stab and I/JG 27 passed through the Balkans on their way to Sicily, where the aircraft were tropicalised with the addition of a dust filter over the supercharger air intake. The resulting aircraft were designated Bf 109E-4/N Trop and E-5/Trop for the reconnaissance version, and they were immediately dispatched to North Africa, where they arrived to begin combat operations from Ain-el-Gazala on 19 April 1941. A forward base was established for daytime operations at Gambut. The Bf 109E-7/Trop was supplied soon after, this having a centreline rack for fuel tank or bomb.

The arrival of the Bf 109s provided a rapid turnaround in the fortunes of the Axis air forces in the desert. In June III/JG 26 arrived to bolster the forces. Among the pilots of these 'Emils' in the desert was I/JG 27's Hans-Joachim Marseille, who had already scored seven kills in the Battle of Britain, and who soon achieved more victories in his E-7. He, of course, would gain fame as the 'Star of Afrika', the highest-scoring Luftwaffe pilot in the West. In

September 1941 II/JG 27 arrived, bringing Bf 109F-2s with it. This was a major worry for the Allies, and signified the beginning of the end of the Bf 109Es, which were soon replaced with the existing units. By the beginning of 1942, the desert fighter force had standardised on the 'Friedrich'.

The last major offensive in which the 'Emil' took part was Operation Barbarossa, the invasion of the Soviet Union, for which most of the Jagdgruppen were assembled. Many of these were by now flying the Bf 109F, but those still operating the 'Emil' were largely the units which had been involved in the Balkans operations. These comprised II and III/JG 27, I and II/JG 52, II and III/JG 77 and I (Jagd)/LG 2.

Barbarossa began at 04.15 on 22 June 1941, and the following day saw the Luftwaffe unleash the most savage pre-emptive strike ever witnessed in modern warfare, despite the fact that the Soviets had adequate intelligence to warn them of impending events. Sixty-six Soviet airfields were hit on the first day, with the result that over 1,000 aircraft were destroyed on the ground, and a further 322 claimed in the air by the Jagdgruppen.

Like the Polish, French and British campaigns, Barbarossa was a great gamble for the Germans. The attack would only work if the conflict ended in a matter of weeks for, yet again, there had been insufficient time to establish a worthwhile stock of reserves with which to fight a sustained campaign. With 830 Bf 109s at their disposal, the Jagdgruppen had less aircraft than it had taken into battle during the Western offensive.

There was no doubting the aggression and spirit of the Soviet fighter pilots, but, equipped mostly with the Polikarpov fighters (I-15, I-15bis, I-153 and I-16), they did not have the machinery or the tactics to seriously affect the outcome of the air battles. As in the Spanish Civil War, the

About 60 of the Bf 109T series carrier fighter were built, although none was to see service at sea, as Hitler's ambitious aircraft-carrier programme never came to fruition. The T-1 carrier aircraft were completed as T-2 land-based fighters, without the folding wings and other naval equipment. They were basically equivalent to Bf 109E-4/Ns, including armament. RB+OP was not to join the majority of 'Tonis' built, which served in Norway and the Helgoland, for it crashed while under test.

Two units of the Slovakian air force were equipped with the Bf 109E. One of these was the volunteer 13. (slowak) Staffel of JG 52 operating in the southern part of the Eastern Front, and the other, whose pilots are seen here at Piestany, was the home-based 11.stihaci letka with Bf 109E-7s.

Romanian allies

Romania became an Bf 109 operator in 1942, when it received 69 Bf 109E-4s. These were assigned to the Grupul 1 Vinatoare (1st Fighter Group), which had three squadrons. The basic splinter was all but hidden by the national insignia, fin-flash, codes and Russian Front theatre markings. The aircraft fought alongside the Luftwaffe on the southern sector of the front.

At the end of the Spanish Civil War around 20 Bf 109Es had been assembled for the Legion Condor, and these were handed over to the new Spanish air force. The aircraft were initially assigned to fighter group 6-G-6, but in July 1939 a Spanish air force reorganisation resulted in them being flown by Grupo núm 25. Later still they were operated by Escuadron 23 of Ala de Caza 2.

Polikarpovs did pose some problems due to their extreme agility, but the Bf 109s were little threatened and during June, July and August the Experten scored prolifically. Six or seven sorties were flown a day, and most of the fighting was at low altitude. Werner Mölders became the first ever pilot to pass the 100-kill mark on 16 July, whereupon he was immediately recalled to Germany. In November he died as a passenger in an He 111. The Jagdflieger had been robbed of their spiritual leader.

During the year of 1941 the Bf 109E all but vanished from the front-line fighter units, which converted to the Bf 109F and, from July, the Focke-Wulf Fw 190. Nevertheless, a few 'Emils' issued from the production line throughout the year, the last being delivered in early 1942. Throughout the year the aircraft was still operated in some numbers by the Jabo units, flying a mix of E-4/Bs and E-7s. The Jabo Staffeln were taken out of the Jagdgeschwader organisations and grouped into specialist Schnell-kampfgeschwaders or Schlachtgeschwaders. Among the notable units to fly Jabo Bf 109Es were SKG 210, operating in the desert, and SchG 1, which flew Jabo 'Emils' on the Russian front into the early part of 1943. In addition to standard bombs, the SchG 1 Bf 109Es dropped the SD-2 'butterfly bomb' cluster weapon.

Boosted 'Emil'

There was little development of the Bf 109E beyond the E-7. The Bf 109E-7/U2 was a version with 5-mm armour beneath the radiator, oil cooler and fuel pumps to increase survivability in the close support role, while the Bf 109E-7/Z was fitted with a GM 1 nitrous oxide booster. The tank for this was situated behind the pilot, feeding pressurised nitrous oxide liquid to the engine by compressed air. The GM 1 provided extra oxygen for the engine above its rated altitude and acted as an anti-detonant. The GM 1 worked well, and was used by many later variants, but unfortunately the positioning of the nitrous oxide tank had a detrimental effect on the centre of gravity, resulting in the aircraft having a tendency to yaw when pulled out of a dive. Unless corrected immediately,

the aircraft would stall and spin.

Among the last 'Emil' variants was the Bf 109E-8, similar to the E-7 but powered by a DB 601E engine and with improved back armour. The Bf 109E-9 was a reconnaissance equivalent with an Rb 50/30 camera in the rear fuselage. By careful 'tweaking', Daimler-Benz had coaxed a few more horsepower out of the DB 601E, which was rated at 1,350 hp (1007 kW) for take-off. These last variants were built in small numbers.

Among the many tests carried out by Bf 109Es was the Wurzelsepp overwing tank configuration, in which two jettisonable slipper tanks of 66-Imp gal (300-litre) capacity were carried above the wings. There was little appreciable difference in performance and handling, but the idea was not adopted. However, experience with this led to a more unusual scheme using the same principle. The attachment points for the tanks were used to carry personnel container pods for either agent-dropping or casualty evacuation. These were test-flown in the summer of 1943, and again impaired performance marginally. Testing of the concept was continued with later variants. One Bf 109E-1 was tested with a fixed ski undercarriage, which proved to be stable when taking off from either the skis or a three-wheel trolley, but the standard undercarriage had minor problems with compacted snow so there was little need for skis.

Piggyback fighter

Perhaps the most unusual test programme was the *Huckepack* (piggy-back). This originated with Siegfried Holzbauer, who proposed using a manned fighter carried piggy-back on an explosives-packed unmanned bomber. The pilot would guide the bomber to its target, release it and then fly away. Such a scheme was seen as too unorthodox in the early part of the war, but the concept did have some validity as a means of transporting assault gliders. Following trials with a Klemm Kl 35 and Focke-Wulf Fw 56 carried above a DFS 230 glider, a Bf 109E was substituted during trials in 1942. The scheme showed promise, and Holzbauer's original plan was resurrected to become the Mistel programme.

As the war progressed several other nations began using the Bf 109E. Three E-4s were supplied to Japan in mid-1941 for evaluation against its Kawasaki Ki-61 fighter, which had been heavily influenced by the Messerschmitt design. Romania acquired 69 Bf 109E-4s in early 1942 to equip the three squadrons of the Grupul 1 Vinatoare (1st Fighter Group), and 19 were received by the 6th Royal Bulgarian Fighter Regiment. Some of these aircraft were later used in anger against the Luftwaffe when Bulgaria began flying with the Soviets.

Slovakia had a squadron (11. stihaci letka) of Bf 109E-7s based at Piestany from late 1942, and another group of Slovakian volunteers equipped a Bf 109E-7 Staffel on the Russian Front (13. (slowak)/JG 52). Two other volunteer units equipped with the Bf 109E-7 were the Croatian 15. (kroat)/JG 52 and the Spanish Escuadron Azul, which fought first as 15. (span)/JG 27 and from March 1942 as 15. (span)/JG 51.

Spanish survivors

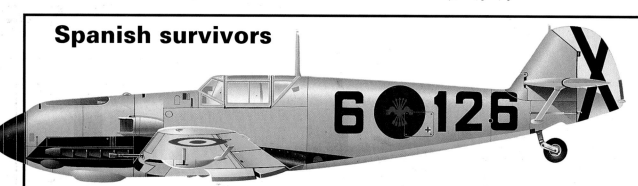

After they had been left behind by the departing Legion Condor, the Spanish Bf 109Es were to serve for well over a decade more, some lasting on fighter schools into the 1950s. The basic type was also developed with Hispano and Merlin engines after the war.

Swiss neutrals

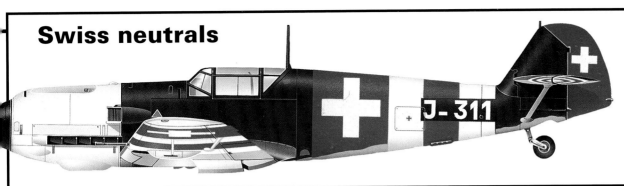

Despite the country's neutrality, the Swiss Bf 109s had a very active war, including the downing of several German aircraft. From September 1944 they were painted in this very conspicuous neutrality scheme to avoid being shot down by USAAF fighters operating from Italy.

Throughout the war the Swiss Bf 109s had been on constant alert. Three more units had formed on the type, so that Fliegerkompagnie 6, 7, 8, 9, 15 and 21 all operated the Messerschmitt, FlK 15 flying the 'Dora'. When the Western offensive began in May 1940, there were numerous incursions by Luftwaffe aircraft into Swiss airspace, resulting in several skirmishes with Swiss Bf 109s. After several meetings had resulted in shots being fired, an He 111 was downed, followed by two more. Tensions were rising quickly, and the next time the Luftwaffe appeared on 4 June they had Bf 110 fighter cover. The ensuing tangle cost the Swiss one Bf 109D for the destruction of two He 111s and a Bf 110. On 8 June over 30 Bf 110s appeared in a highly provocative move. The Swiss responded and a single Bf 109E was lost in the tangle, which cost the Luftwaffe three more Bf 110s. Such actions ended when France fell, but later in the war Swiss Bf 109s regularly intercepted USAAF bombers, forcing them to land and be interned. These flights were largely uneventful, although on one occasion a P-51 shot down one Bf 109 and damaged another while they were escorting a B-24, its pilot probably thinking the Messerschmitts were German.

Post-war Swiss service

As in Spain, the Bf 109E was to enjoy a long and productive career in Swiss hands. Dornier-Werke at Altenrhein even completed a batch of eight new-build aircraft, with another airframe made up from spares. The final delivery of the extra batch was not made until 19 March 1946. These aircraft utilised spare DB 601Aa engines and retained the original light-framed canopy. Instead of the standard VDM propeller, the nine aircraft had Escher-Wyss EW-V6 variable-pitch propellers, and could be readily identified by the pointed spinner. They also had a Saurer fuel injection system and other local components. These aircraft did not leave service until 28 December 1949

Development of the Bf 109 of course continued throughout the war, with the Bf 109F, G and K series, but these never enjoyed the complete mastery over their opponents of the early 'Emils'. Like most fighters, the ever-spiralling weight and power provided its own problems,

Above: The Swiss operated the 109 in a variety of forms from 1939 until 1949, even building a small batch under licence after the war's end. J-318 was delivered in 1940 and flew with a number of Fliegerkompanien until being lost in a collision in 1946.

Left: The eight Bf 109Es built post-war under a licence agreement signed when Messerschmitt was still in the fighter business can be distinguished by their pointed spinners. J-398 was the second-to-last Bf 109 to enter service and had a career of just under three years before being struck off in December 1949.

and the basic Bf 109 airframe seemed to run out of solutions long before that of the tractable Spitfire. Other superb fighters came along, such as the Fw 190, the middle-mark Spitfires and the P-51, each adding their claim to be the best fighter of the war. Yet none achieved such successes, and none achieved the degree of supremacy over its peers, as the Bf 109E of the early-war period. The frightening vision of a Europe under total Nazi dominance almost became reality – in no small way due to the Bf 109E. **David Donald**

Preserved Bf 109Es

Of the many thousands of 109Bs, Cs, Ds and Es built (no accurate production figures have survived), only a tiny handful remain, and all are E models. The most famous of these is E-4 Wk Nr 4101, the former DG200, now at the Battle of Britain Hall of the Royal Air Force Museum. Although it has a number of missing and non-standard parts, it is the most representative of an operational 'Emil' on display today. When the Swiss phased out their Messerschmitts in 1949, only E-3 J-355 (Wk Nr 2422) was preserved, and is now at the museum at

Dübendorf. In Germany itself, an E-3, Wk Nr 790, formerly 6-106 with the Spanish air force, is displayed at the Deutsches Museum, Munich. An unidentified Bf 109E has recently appeared at the Central Museum of the Great Patriotic War in Moscow, and it is not impossible that further such aircraft exist in the former Soviet Union. A small number of 'Emils' exist in private hands, including the former C4E-88 of the Spanish air force, now under restoration with Robs Lamplough near Hungerford, UK; and Wk Nr 1190, a genuine Battle of

Britain aircraft stored for many years at Bournemouth Airport in southern England. Craig Charleston in Essex is working on a pair of aircraft: 109E-1 3579 for David Price in California, and E-4 1342 for Sir Tim Wallis in New Zealand. These two aircraft should fly within the next two years, reviving a sight and sound not seen for approaching half a century.

These are British (above) and Swiss (below) preserved examples of Bf 109Es.

The continuation of the Messerschmitt Bf 109 story, covering the Bf 109F, G and K, together with the Spanish and Czech post-war derivatives, will be featured in a forthcoming volume of *Wings of Fame.*

Early Bf 109 colours

Prototypes

Bf 109 V1
The Kestrel-powered V1 first prototype, also known as the Bf 109a, was finished in 63 Hellgrau with powder blue undersides. The civil registration D-IABI was applied under the wings, although is not visible on all photographs of the prototype.

Bf 109 V7
D-IJHA was the seventh prototype (V7) and wore an all-over grey-green scheme with civilian registration and national insignia on the fin only. This was one of three Jumo 210Ga-powered aircraft entered in the 1937 Zürich competition.

Bf 109 V13

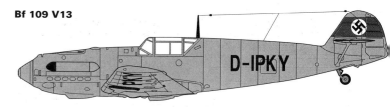

Two of the Messerschmitts which were at Zürich were powered by the Daimler-Benz DB 600 engine, comprising the V13 D-IPKY (above) finished in 63 Hellgrau, and the V14 D-ISLU (below) which was in all-over red. Ernst Udet flew the red aircraft in the prestige 'Circuit of the Alps' race but force-landed due to engine failure. The DB 600 installation featured an unusual ducted supercharger intake on the port side of the cowling, this later giving rise to the erroneous belief that the Bf 109D was a DB 600-powered aircraft. Only a few of the prototype series featured this engine, the 'Dora' being powered by Jumo 210Da with carburettor.

Bf 109 V14

Luftwaffe

Luftwaffe aircraft were initially delivered in all-over dark green, followed by a hard-edged splinter pattern on the top and side surfaces. In the winter of 1939/40 the pale blue was extended up the fuselage sides, radically altering the appearance of the aircraft. Mottling was applied at unit level over the top of this basic scheme. Later schemes were more arbitrarily applied at unit level, although using the splinter as a basis.

Bf 109B, 1937
The hard-edged splinter pattern was adopted from February 1937, and was applicable to many of the B, C and D series fighters. The splinter was in 70 Schwarzgrün/71 Dunkelgrün, with 65 Hellblau undersides. Spinners were usually in 70, but occasionally in 02 RLM-Grau. Aircraft with metal propellers had the blades in 70 also, while wooden blades were painted in 02. The red fin-flash was worn into 1938.

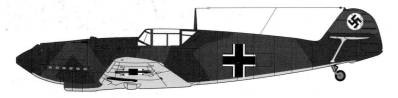

Bf 109D-1, 1938/39
In addition to the splinter scheme, many aircraft had a single green colour scheme, in this case 71 Schwarzgrün. The swastika was applied in black only, although the fuselage cross was outlined in white. The overall drab effect was rescued by the bright codes applied by many units, this aircraft being assigned to JG 71.

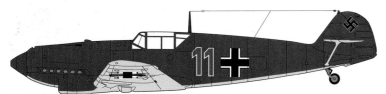

Bf 109E-1, November 1939
A variation on the single green scheme used 71 Dunkelgrün in place of 70. The undersides remained 65 Hellblau. This aircraft was in service with JG 53 during this period. The gun troughs and supercharger intake grille were in 02 RLM-Grau.

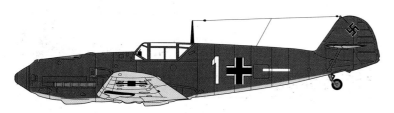

Splinter camouflage
The splinter pattern was standard from aircraft to aircraft, the design having been produced centrally. The original 70/71 colours were very close in tone, and in many photographs the aircraft appear to be overall green. Units often applied 75 Grau to the wing leading edges to tone down the harsh demarcation between the splinter and the 65 Hellblau undersides.

Grey/green splinter
From early 1940 the 70/71 splinter mix was changed to a mix of 71 Dunkelgrün and 02 RLM-Grau, which gave far more demarcation between the two colours. The pattern of the splinter remained essentially unchanged, and many aircraft had the colours altered at unit level by simply overpainting the original areas of 71 Schwarzgrün.

Bf 109E-3, up to early 1940
The hard-edged splinter pattern of 70 Schwarzgrün and 71 Dunkelgrün along the fuselage sides was continued until early 1940, when the 65 Hellblau was extended up the fuselage sides, leaving just the top surfaces in 70/71.

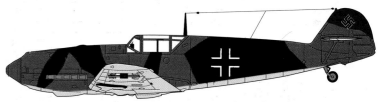

Aircraft from I Gruppe of JG 3 carried a Tatzelwurm (a dragon resembling a crested or spiked worm) on the nose. This insignia was applied in green to Stab (staff) aircraft, in white to aircraft of 1 Geschwader, in red to aircraft of 2 Geschwader, and in yellow to aircraft of 3 Geschwader. The foremost part of the spinner was painted in the same colour. JG 3's II Gruppe used a gyrone shield as their badge, while III Gruppe had a tilted shield containing a fearsome looking axe.

Camouflage

The Luftwaffe's Messerschmitt Bf 109s originally wore dark green upper surfaces with light blue-grey (Hellblau) undersides, but these colours were replaced by a disruptive two-tone green splinter camouflage on the top surfaces. The two shades of green were so close to one another in tone that they looked almost like a single colour, and weathering further reduced the differentiation between the shades. In the winter of 1939, the top surface colours were limited to the upper surfaces of the wings and tailplanes, plus the top decking of the fuselage. The fuselage sides and fin were painted Hellblau. On most aircraft the top surface camouflage was repainted, with 71 Dunkelgrün (the lighter of the two tones used previously) and 02 Grau (a pale grey-green). These had a greater tonal variation than the previous colours. The basic new camouflage scheme was modified at unit level during the Battle of Britain. Some aircraft had a neutral grey area painted along the wing leading edge to soften the demarcation between the dark topsides and light undersurfaces. Fuselage sides were often overpainted with a mottled 02 Grau, as seen on this aircraft.

Powerplant

The Bf 109D had been designed to be compatible with either the Junkers Jumo 210 or the Daimler-Benz DB 600, and it had been intended that the Daimler-Benz engine would power the definitive production 'Dora'. Unfortunately, the engine was not considered reliable enough for installation in a single-engined front-line fighter and, although a number of Bf 109Ds may have been fitted with DB 600s and photographed for propaganda purposes, the series production Bf 109D retained the Jumo engine. The Bf 109E was designed around the improved DB 601 engine, which offered major improvements in reliability and performance. A liquid-cooled inverted V-12 engine (like an upside-down Rolls-Royce Merlin in configuration), the DB 601Aa was rated at 1,175 hp (875 kW) for take-off. Delivery rates of the new engine were initially very slow, and engineless airframes were stockpiled so that, when engine production did get into its rhythm, a large number of Bf 109Es were delivered very quickly. Some of these aircraft went to the Legion Condor in Spain, and others were delivered to home-based Jagdgruppen. Thirty were delivered to the Swiss Fliegertruppen from 14 April 1939, providing the Reich with much-needed hard currency.

Although the Jumo 210Da-powered Bf 109D-1 retained a two-bladed VDM propeller (a licence-built Hamilton variable-pitch prop), the Bf 109E-1 introduced a new three-bladed prop. The spinner still had the hollow centre designed to allow carriage of the engine-mounted 20-mm cannon, but this was still far from being reliable enough to be adopted for use. Early Bf 109E-3s had the troublesome cannons fitted, but they again proved unsuccessful, and the Bf 109E-4 had no provision for the cannon, although the 'holed' spinner was often fitted. Some Bf 109Es even had a new spinner, in which case the former cannon port was faired over. The nose contours of the Bf 109E were completely changed, with the small oil cooler (fitted below the port inner wing of Jumo-powered '109s) moved to a position below the nose, while the much larger 'chin' radiator was replaced by a pair of underwing glycol radiators, just aft of the main undercarriage bays. Aft of the engine firewall, the Bf 109E was little different to the Bf 109D-1, which had been strengthened in anticipation of the higher weights which would have been possible with the DB 600 engine. When it first appeared, the Bf 109E enjoyed a marked performance advantage over the contemporary Spitfire Mk I, which at the time had a two-pitch, twin-bladed propeller. By the time the Bf 109E-4 was in service, Spitfires all had constant-speed three-bladed propellers and the performance advantage was eroded.

Armament

During the early part of its career, the Bf 109 was given progressively heavier armament. The prototype was originally specified with two cowling-mounted 7.92-mm MG 17 machine-guns (each with 500 rounds of ammunition), with a third later added between the banks of cylinders to fire through the propeller hub. This provided a useful concentration of fire, while the central gun did not need to be harmonised. Unfortunately, Messerschmitt were never able to make the centre-mounted gun work properly: it produced too much vibration for the engine, while the engine produced too much heat for the gun. The Russians and Americans produced more successful 'through-the-hub' cannon installations on the P-39 Airacobra and Yak-3/-9 series. A heavier 20-mm MG FF cannon was tested in the central position by the Bf 109C-1, but proved no more successful than the engine-mounted MG 17. The C-3 model instead received an extra pair of 7.92-mm MG 17 machine-guns in the wings, just outboard of each mainwheel bay, each with 420 rounds of ammunition. Accuracy was improved in the Bf 109D through addition of a Revi C/12D gunsight. The Bf 109E-1 standardised on the armament of four MG 17s, while the E-2 and E-3 tried to re-introduce the engine-mounted cannon (with 200 rounds). Some E-3s were delivered with the cannon, but these were soon removed. Most E-3s had a revised armament wherein wing-mounted MG FF cannon (with 60 rpg) replaced the MG 17 machine-guns but the cowling-mounted pair of MG 17s was retained, albeit with ammunition capacity for these guns doubled. Aircraft with the wing-mounted cannon had small bulges on the underside of the wings, covering the weapon's larger breech blocks, and the cannon muzzles projected slightly from the leading edge. The Bf 109E-5 was a tactical reconnaissance version and had the wing cannon removed, with an RB 21/18 cannon in the fuselage adjacent to the trailing edge. The Bf 109E-6 was another recce version, with four MG 17s. The Bf 109E-4 was the first variant of the 109 to see service in the fighter-bomber (Jabo) role. The Bf 109E-4/B used a rudimentary ETC 500 bomb rack between the mainwheels, capable of carrying a single 250-kg or 500-kg bomb. Trials by Erprobungsgruppe 210's 3. Staffel proved very successful, and each Bf 109 Gruppe was ordered to convert some of its Staffeln to the Jabo role, while Lehrgeschwader 2's II Gruppe traded its ageing Henschel 123s for Bf 109E-4/Bs. The /B designation suffix was applied to all Bf 109Es used as fighter-bombers, resulting in Bf 109E-1/Bs and Bf 109E-3/B designations. The Bf 109E-7 differed from earlier versions of the 'Emil' in that it could carry a 300-litre (66-Imp gal) fuel tank in place of the underfuselage bomb. The E-7/U2 had extra armour on the oil cooler, radiators and fuel pump. The Bf 109E-9 was a reconnaissance aircraft, based on the re-engined Bf 109E-8; it lacked wing cannon and but did have an Rb 50/30 camera in the rear fuselage.

Up-engined 'Emils'

The Bf 109E-4/N was powered by a DB 601N engine, whose flattened (instead of concave) piston heads gave a higher compression ratio, and which used higher octane fuel. The Bf 109E-7 was similarly powered, and the Bf 109E-7/Z introduced a nitrous oxide (GM1) supercharger injection system, which boosted altitude performance and was known as the 'Ha-Ha' system. A similar performance increase was provided in the Bf 109E-8 and the recce-roled Bf 109E-9 by the new DB 601E engine, with increased maximum rpm, improved supercharging and take-off power of 1,350 hp 1006 kW). The down side was that the new engine was considerably less economical, and even with a 100-litre (22-Imp gal) increase in fuel capacity (to 400 litres/88 Imp gal) the Bf 109E's already inadequate reach was not greatly improved.

Messerschmitt Bf 109E-4
Gruppenkommandeur's aircraft
I Gruppe, Jagdgeschwader 3
Grandvilliers, France, August 1940

Bf 109s in the Battle of Britain

After supporting the Wehrmacht in its Blitzkrieg through the Low Countries and France (to say nothing of the offensives in Poland and Norway), the Jagdflieger pilots were experienced, battle-hardened and confident. After the fall of France, Britain refused to make peace, and an aerial offensive against Britain became inevitable. Adlerangriff (the attack of the eagles) was to be launched on 10 August (Adlertag, or eagle day), although fierce attacks began even earlier, with a major air battle on 8 August. Adlertag itself was delayed until 13 August by bad weather. Thus started the Battle of Britain. While the RAF's Spitfire and Hurricane squadrons contained relatively few pilots with combat experience, the pilots were quick learners, and inadequate pre-war tactics were soon modified or abandoned. The Bf 109 squadrons started the battle below establishment, depleted by attrition. Furthermore, while the RAF was equipped with Spitfires and Hurricanes, which were in many respects equal to or better than the Bf 109E, and enjoyed the great advantage of being controlled by radar. The Luftwaffe soon found itself confronting its most formidable foe to date. While the Luftwaffe's Bf 109Es were fighting at the very limit of their range, the RAF fighters had fuel to linger and fight, and even to pursue their retreating enemies. When a Bf 109 was shot down, its pilot was inevitably killed or captured, while downed RAF pilots were usually recovered to fly and fight again – sometimes the same day. The battle was closely fought until the Luftwaffe was ordered to switch from attacks against RAF airfields to attacks against Britain's cities, and until the Bf 109s were ordered to stick close to the bombers they were escorting. For the first time, the Luftwaffe's Bf 109Es were assigned what was essentially a strategic role (the destruction of the RAF) and, as the battle progressed, the Luftwaffe began to find itself getting the worst of it – an unfamiliar and alarming experience. The Luftwaffe lost 610 of its Bf 109s (and 235 Bf 110s) on operations, while the RAF lost 631 Hurricanes and 403 Spitfires (272 and 219 to the Bf 109, respectively). The honours in single-seat fighter combat were as near to even as made no difference; this represented an RAF victory, since it lost far fewer pilots, and since the British industry was able to make up attrition more rapidly than was the German.

Bf 109E, Poland 1939
The Bf 109s assembled for the opening assault of World War II wore either the standard splinter or single-green schemes. Outsize crosses were applied to the wings for identification purposes.

Bf 109E-1, 1939
Among the many different schemes which began appearing in the winter of 1939 was this three-tone pattern. It used 71 Schwarzgrün upper surfaces and 65 Hellblau lower, with large areas of 02 RLM-Grau and 71 Dunkelgrün oversprayed. The aircraft served with JG 53.

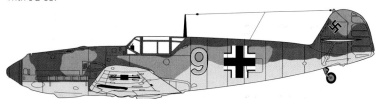

Bf 109C, early 1940
A major new scheme was introduced in early 1940, consisting of 70/71 or 70/02 topsides with the 65 Hellblau extending up the fuselage sides. This aircraft has the 70/71 top splinter. This scheme was standard through 1940, although the majority of units applied varying degrees of mottling (usually in 02 RLM-Grau).

Bf 109E-4, Eastern Front 1941
Yellow theatre markings were applied to nose, wingtips and rear fuselage for the Russian campaign. From late 1940 onwards there was virtually nothing visible of the standard pattern camouflage on any front-line Bf 109s, so heavy was the mottling, although the original 65 undersides and 70/71 top can still be made out here. An alternative scheme used 75 Grau topsides and 76 Weissblau lower surfaces.

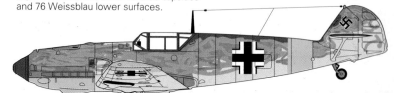

This group of Bf 109Es on an airfield in Norway in 1940 shows just how radically the unit-applied mottling could alter the appearance of the aircraft. In the background the aircraft are in standard 71 Dunkelgrün/02 RLM-Grau splinter camouflage upper sides with 65 Hellblau undersurfaces and fuselage sides. The aircraft in the foreground has undergone a heavy mottling process along the fuselage sides and tail, the painter having carefully gone round the fuselage codes, swastika and cross. This practice first appeared during the Battle of France, became prevalent during the Battle of Britain and almost standard for operations in the East. Units developed more sophisticated overpainting processes as the war developed, including wavy lines, weave patterns and rough diagonal crosses. The standard splinter pattern on the upper surfaces was usually left untouched.

Spain

Bf 109B, Legion Condor, 1937
Aircraft destined for the Spanish Civil War were usually painted in 63 Hellgrau upper surfaces with 65 Hellblau undersides, all other markings being in white or black. The upper wing and tailplane surfaces were sometimes painted in brown.

Bf 109B, 2./J 88, spring 1937
A variation on the standard light grey scheme involved at least three of the later B aircraft, delivered in 70 Schwarzgrün with 65 undersides. The light grey scheme was more effective over the Spanish countryside than the northern Europe schemes.

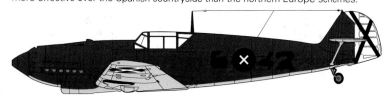

Bf 109E-1, Legion Condor, 1939
The 'Emils' were sent to Spain with the same 63/65 scheme as most of the Jumo-powered aircraft. The black streak was added to the lower fuselage sides and wing roots to hide the dirt from the exhausts. The white cross had disappeared from the national insignia by this time.

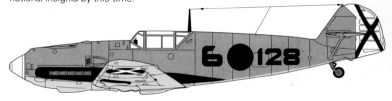

Bf 109E-3, Escuadrón 23, circa 1950
Throughout the war and into the 1950s the Spanish survivors retained the basic 63/65 scheme with black exhaust panel. All that changed was the adoption of the roundel in place of the black circle and the addition of new unit codes.

Bf 109E-4/B, North Africa, 1941
The standard desert scheme comprised 79 Sandgelb upper surfaces and 78 Himmelblau lower surfaces, with a white band round the rear fuselage as a theatre identification marking. Several early aircraft retained the yellow nose which was applied for the Balkans campaign.

Switzerland

The first Swiss Bf 109s, the batch of 10 'Doras', arrived in standard Luftwaffe finish of dark green upper and side surfaces and pale blue undersides. Some of the 'Emils' had a disruptive two-tone Schwarzgrun/Dunkelgrün pattern, but reverted to a single-tone side surfaces with the darker tone on top.

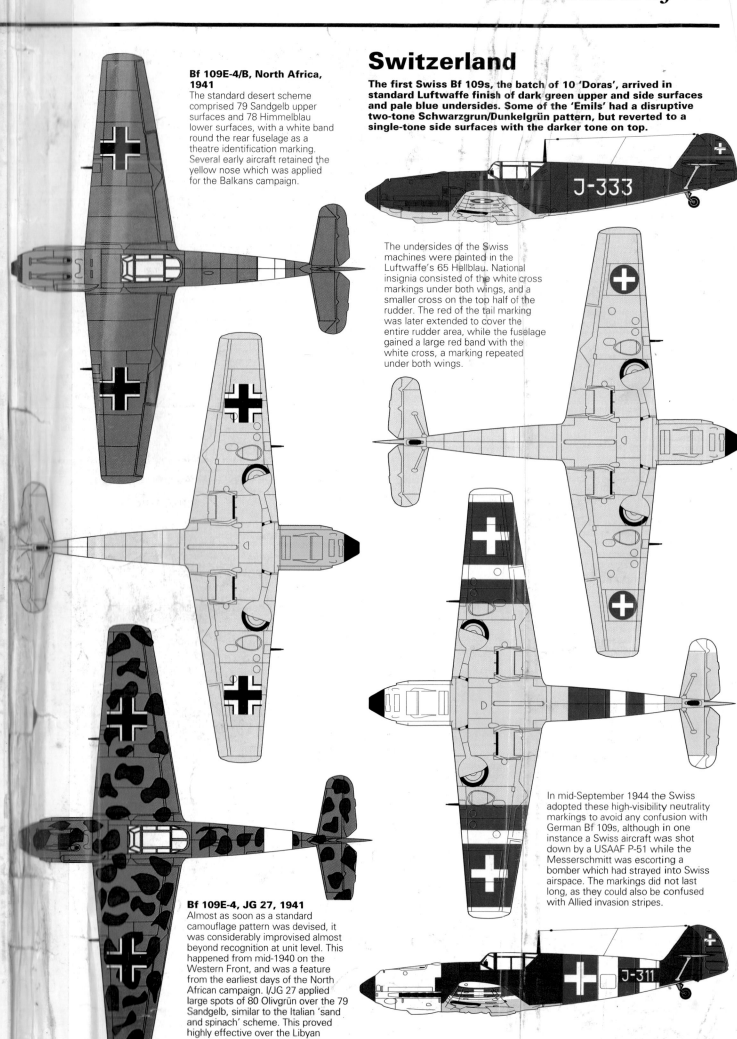

The undersides of the Swiss machines were painted in the Luftwaffe's 65 Hellblau. National insignia consisted of the white cross markings under both wings, and a smaller cross on the top half of the rudder. The red of the tail marking was later extended to cover the entire rudder area, while the fuselage gained a large red band with the white cross, a marking repeated under both wings.

Bf 109E-4, JG 27, 1941
Almost as soon as a standard camouflage pattern was devised, it was considerably improvised almost beyond recognition at unit level. This happened from mid-1940 on the Western Front, and was a feature from the earliest days of the North African campaign. I./JG 27 applied large spots of 80 Olivgrün over the 79 Sandgelb, similar to the Italian 'sand and spinach' scheme. This proved highly effective over the Libyan desert.

In mid-September 1944 the Swiss adopted these high-visibility neutrality markings to avoid any confusion with German Bf 109s, although in one instance a Swiss aircraft was shot down by a USAAF P-51 while the Messerschmitt was escorting a bomber which had strayed into Swiss airspace. The markings did not last long, as they could also be confused with Allied invasion stripes.

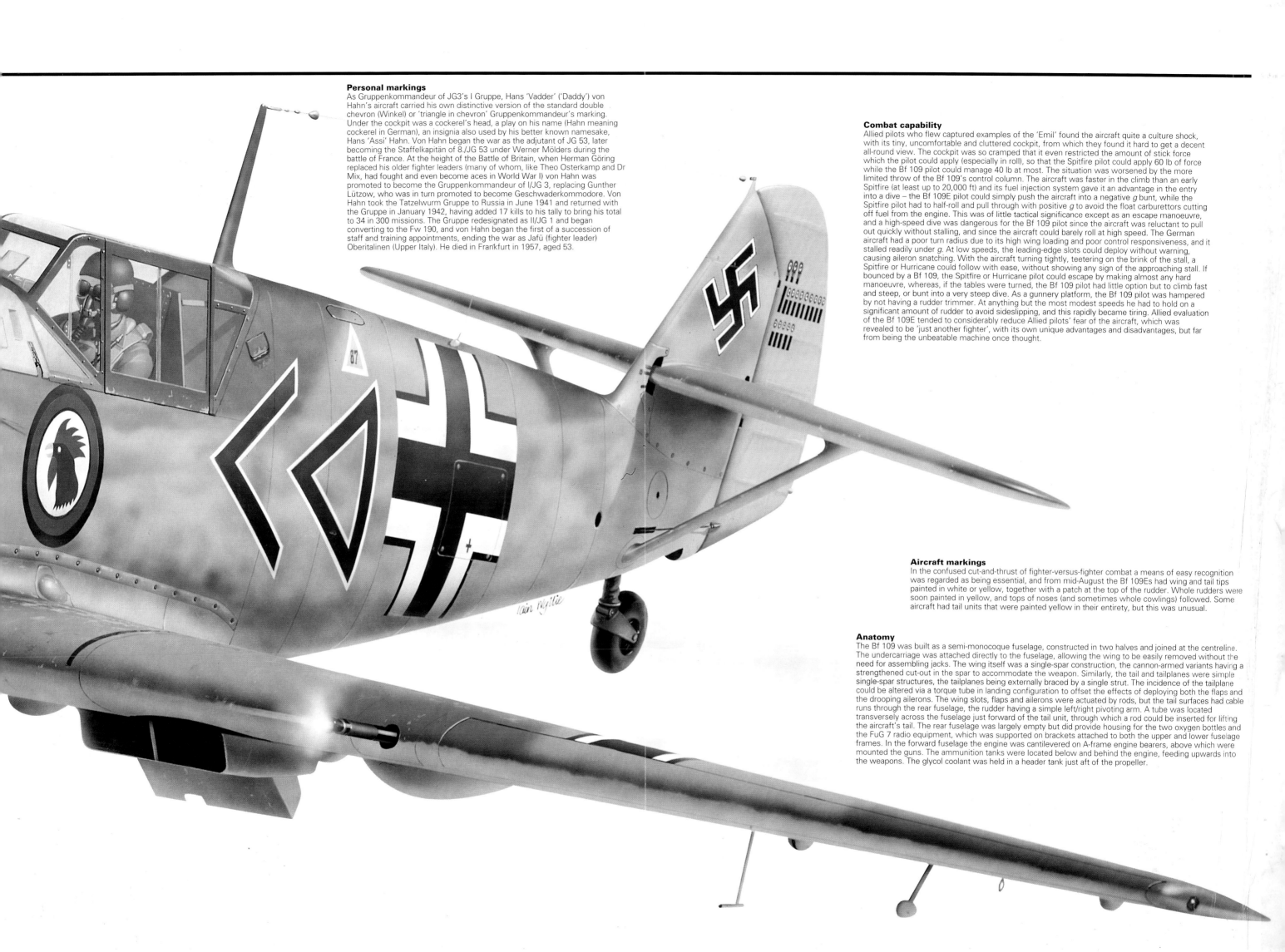

Personal markings

As Gruppenkommandeur of JG3's I Gruppe, Hans 'Vadder' ('Daddy') von Hahn's aircraft carried his own distinctive version of the standard double chevron (Winkel) or 'triangle in chevron' Gruppenkommandeur's marking. Under the cockpit was a cockerel's head, a play on his name (Hahn meaning cockerel in German), an insignia also used by his better known namesake, Hans 'Assi' Hahn. Von Hahn began the war as the adjutant of JG 53, later becoming the Staffelkapitän of 8./JG 53 under Werner Mölders during the battle of France. At the height of the Battle of Britain, when Herman Göring replaced his older fighter leaders (many of whom, like Theo Osterkamp and Dr Mix, had fought and even become aces in World War I) von Hahn was promoted to become the Gruppenkommandeur of I/JG 3, replacing Gunther Lützow, who was in turn promoted to become Geschwaderkommodore. Von Hahn took the Tatzelwurm Gruppe to Russia in June 1941 and returned with the Gruppe in January 1942, having added 17 kills to his tally to bring his total to 34 in 300 missions. The Gruppe redesignated as II/JG 1 and began converting to the Fw 190, and von Hahn began the first of a succession of staff and training appointments, ending the war as Jafü (fighter leader) Oberitalinen (Upper Italy). He died in Frankfurt in 1957, aged 53.

Combat capability

Allied pilots who flew captured examples of the 'Emil' found the aircraft quite a culture shock, with its tiny, uncomfortable and cluttered cockpit, from which they found it hard to get a decent all-round view. The cockpit was so cramped that it even restricted the amount of stick force which the pilot could apply (especially in roll), so that the Spitfire pilot could apply 60 lb of force while the Bf 109 pilot could manage 40 lb at most. The situation was worsened by the more limited throw of the Bf 109's control column. The aircraft was faster in the climb than an early Spitfire (at least up to 20,000 ft) and its fuel injection system gave it an advantage in the entry into a dive – the Bf 109E pilot could simply push the aircraft into a negative g bunt, while the Spitfire pilot had to half-roll and pull through with positive g to avoid the float carburettors cutting off fuel from the engine. This was of little tactical significance except as an escape manoeuvre, and a high-speed dive was dangerous for the Bf 109 pilot since the aircraft was reluctant to pull out quickly under g. At low speeds, the leading-edge slots could deploy without warning, causing aileron snatching. With the aircraft turning tightly, teetering on the brink of the stall, a Spitfire or Hurricane could follow with ease, without showing any sign of the approaching stall. If bounced by a Bf 109, the Spitfire or Hurricane pilot could escape by making almost any hard manoeuvre, whereas, if the tables were turned, the Bf 109 pilot had little option but to climb fast and steep, or bunt into a very steep dive. As a gunnery platform, the Bf 109 was hampered by not having a rudder trimmer. At anything but the most modest speeds he had to hold on a significant amount of rudder to avoid sideslipping, and this rapidly became tiring. Allied evaluation of the Bf 109E tended to considerably reduce Allied pilots' fear of the aircraft, which was revealed to be 'just another fighter', with its own unique advantages and disadvantages, but far from being the unbeatable machine once thought.

Aircraft markings

In the confused cut-and-thrust of fighter-versus-fighter combat a means of easy recognition was regarded as being essential, and from mid-August the Bf 109Es had wing and tail tips painted in white or yellow, together with a patch at the top of the rudder. Whole rudders were soon painted in yellow, and tops of noses (and sometimes whole cowlings) followed. Some aircraft had tail units that were painted yellow in their entirety, but this was unusual.

Anatomy

The Bf 109 was built as a semi-monocoque fuselage, constructed in two halves and joined at the centreline. The undercarriage was attached directly to the fuselage, allowing the wing to be easily removed without the need for assembling jacks. The wing itself was a single-spar construction, the cannon-armed variants having a strengthened cut-out in the spar to accommodate the weapon. Similarly, the tail and tailplanes were simple single-spar structures, the tailplanes being externally braced by a single strut. The incidence of the tailplane could be altered via a torque tube in landing configuration to offset the effects of deploying both the flaps and the drooping ailerons. The wing slots, flaps and ailerons were actuated by rods, but the tail surfaces had cable runs through the rear fuselage, the rudder having a simple left/right pivoting arm. A tube was located transversely across the fuselage just forward of the tail unit, through which a rod could be inserted for lifting the aircraft's tail. The rear fuselage was largely empty but did provide housing for the two oxygen bottles and the FuG 7 radio equipment, which was supported on brackets attached to both the upper and lower fuselage frames. In the forward fuselage the engine was cantilevered on A-frame engine bearers, above which were mounted the guns. The ammunition tanks were located below and behind the engine, feeding upwards into the weapons. The glycol coolant was held in a header tank just aft of the propeller.

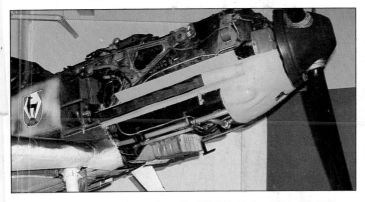

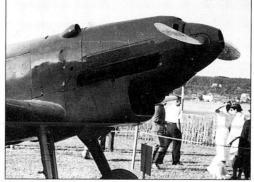

Above and right: Two views show the DB 601 engine of the Bf 109E on its cantilevered engine bearers. The supercharger was on the port side, its position marked by the louvred air intake on the exterior.

The Jumo 210Da installation of the Bf 109B had a deep chin inlet with auxiliary ejector flap. Note the Schwarz fixed-pitch propeller.

The V7 and V8 were both powered by the Jumo 210Ga with VDM propeller, and uniquely had the oil cooler intake ahead of the radiator intake.

The DB 600 installation of the V10 to V13 tested the intake arrangement for the Bf 109E, the radiators being moved back under the wings.

Messerschmitt Bf 109E-4

1 Hollow propeller hub
2 Spinner
3 Three-bladed VDM variable-pitch propeller
4 Propeller pitch-change mechanism
5 Spinner back plate
6 Glycol coolant header tank
7 Glycol filler cap
8 Cowling fastener
9 Chin intake
10 Coolant pipe fairing
11 Exhaust forward fairing
12 Additional (long-range) oil tank
13 Daimler-Benz DB 601A engine
14 Supplementary intakes
15 Fuselage machine-gun troughs
16 Anti-vibration engine mounting pads
17 Exhaust ejector stubs
18 Coolant pipes (to underwing radiators)
19 Oil cooler intake
20 Coolant radiator
21 Radiator outlet flap
22 Cowling frame
23 Engine mounting support strut
24 Spent cartridge collector compartment
25 Ammunition boxes (starboard loading)
26 Engine supercharger
27 Supercharger air intake fairing
28 Forged magnesium alloy cantilever engine mounting
29 Engine mounting/forward bulkhead attachment
30 Ammunition feed chutes
31 Engine accessories
32 Two fuselage-mounted MG17 machine-guns
33 Blast tube muzzles
34 Wing skinning
35 Starboard cannon access
36 20-mm MG FF wing cannon
37 Leading-edge automatic slot
38 Slot tracks
39 Slot actuating linkage
40 Wing main spar
41 Intermediate rib station
42 Wing end rib
43 Starboard navigation light
44 Aileron outer hinge
45 Aileron metal trim tab
46 Starboard aileron
47 Aileron/flap link connection
48 Combined control linkage
49 Starboard flap frame
50 Cannon ammunition drum access
51 Fuselage machine-gun cooling slots
52 Gun mounting frame
53 Firewall/bulkhead
54 Instrument panel near face (fabric covered)
55 Oil dipstick cover
56 Control column
57 Oil filler cap (tank omitted for clarity)
58 Rudder pedal assembly
59 Aircraft identity data plate (external)
60 Mainspar centre-section carry-through
61 Underfloor control linkage
62 Oxygen regulator
63 Harness adjustment lever
64 Engine priming pump
65 Circuit breaker panel
66 Hood catch
67 Starboard-hinged cockpit canopy
68 Revi gunsight (offset to starboard)
69 Windscreen panel frame
70 Canopy section frame
71 Pilot's head armour
72 Pilot's back armour
73 Seat harness
74 Pilot's seat
75 Seat adjustment lever
76 Tailplane incidence handwheel
77 Cockpit floor diaphragm
78 Landing flaps control hand wheel
79 Seat support frame
80 Contoured ('L' shape) fuel tank
81 Tailplane incidence cables
82 Fuselage frame
83 Rudder cable
84 Oxygen cylinders (2)
85 Fuel filler/overspill pipes
86 Baggage compartment
87 Entry handhold (spring loaded)
88 Canopy fixed aft section
89 Aerial mast
90 Aerial
91 Fuel filler cap
92 Fuel vent line
93 Radio pack support brackets
94 Anti-vibration bungee supports
95 FuG VII transmitter/receiver radio pack
96 Aerial lead-in
97 Tailplane incidence cable pulley
98 Rudder control cable
99 Monocoque fuselage structure
100 Radio access/first aid kit panel
101 Elevator control cables
102 Fuselage frame
103 Lifting tube
104 Tailfin root fillet
105 Tailplane incidence gauge (external)
106 Tailplane support strut
107 Starboard tailplane
108 Elevator outer hinge
109 Elevator balance
110 Starboard elevator
111 Tailfin structure
112 Aerial stub
113 Rudder balance
114 Rudder upper hinge
115 Rudder frame
116 Rudder trim tab
117 Tail navigation light
118 Port elevator frame
119 Elevator balance
120 Rudder control quadrant
121 Tailplane structure
122 Elevator torque tube sleeve
123 Tailplane end rib attachment
124 Fuselage end post
125 Elevator control rod
126 Port tailplane support strut
127 Non-retractable tailwheel
128 Tailwheel leg
129 Elevator control cable rod link
130 Tail wheel leg shock-absorber
131 Rudder control cable
132 Fuselage stringer
133 Accumulator
134 Fuselage half ventral join
135 Electrical leads
136 Fuselage panel
137 Radio pack lower support frames
138 Entry foothold (spring loaded)
139 Wingroot fillet
140 Flap profile
141 Port flap frame
142 Port aileron frame
143 Aileron metal trim tab
144 Rear spar
145 Port wingtip
146 Port navigation light
147 Wing main spar outer section
148 Solid ribs
149 Leading-edge automatic slot
150 Rib cut-outs
151 Control link access plate
152 Wing rib stations
153 Port wing 20-mm MG FF cannon installation
154 Ammunition drum access panel
155 Inboard rib cut-outs
156 Flap visual position indicator
157 Control access panel
158 Main spar/fuselage attachment fairing
159 Wing control surface cable pulleys
160 Port mainwheel well
161 Wheel well (zipped) fabric shield
162 20-mm MG FF wing cannon
163 Wing front spar
164 Undercarriage leg tunnel rib cut-outs
165 Undercarriage lock mechanism
166 Wing/fuselage end rib
167 Undercarriage actuating cylinder
168 Mainwheel leg/fuselage attachment bracket
169 Leg pivot point
170 Mainwheel oleo leg
171 Mainwheel leg door
172 Brake lines
173 Torque links
174 Mainwheel hub
175 Axle
176 Port main wheel
177 Mainwheel half-door
178 Ventral ETC centre-line stores pylon, possible loads include:
179 Early-type (wooden) drop tank
180 66-Imp gal (300-litre) (Junkers) metal drop tank
181 551-lb (250-kg) HE bomb, or
182 551-lb (250-kg) SAP bomb

This is the definitive installation of the DB 601 of a Bf 109E-3. The main undercowling intake fed the oil cooler, and there were additional cooling intake just behind the spinner, two on top and one underneath. The exhaust ejector stubs were partially sunk into a trough. The bulge just below the front of the exhaust fairing covered coolant pipes.

Above and below: Two views show the VDM three-bladed propeller of the Bf 109E. Most aircraft retained the hollow shaft for the engine-mounted cannon, but this was rarely fitted.

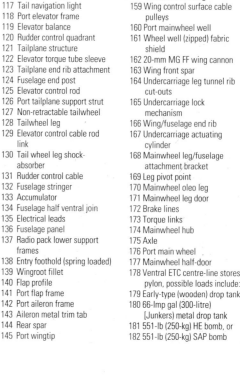

The upper and lower cowlings were easily removed for access to the engine for maintenance, while the propeller had a standard Revel fixing. The small tank immediately to port of the propeller shaft was the header tank for the glycol coolant.

The centre section of the heavily-framed canopy hinged to starboard for access. Noticeable inside is the armour plate around the pilot's head which was attached to the canopy itself.

The single-strut main undercarriage units were attached directly to the fuselage structure and had oleo suspension with a small scissors-type torque link at the bottom of the strut. The brake cables ran down the front of the strut.

Below: Owing to the single-spar wing construction, incorporation of the wheel well posed few structural problems. Visible behind is the wing-mounted radiator.

Above: Due to the Bf 109's narrow fuselage, the cockpit was very cramped compared to other wartime fighters. This, combined with the short length of the control column, made control inputs difficult to make. The dashboard was topped by the Reflexvisier reflecting sight, offset to starboard. A circuit breaker panel was on the starboard side of the cockpit.

Right: The Bf 109's tail control surfaces were aerodynamically balanced. A key omission was a rudder trimmer, which made gunnery and long-distance flying tiring. Note the strut-braced, variable-incidence tailplane and the lifting tube forward of the tailwheel.

Two underwing views show the DB 600-powered V13 (above) and the Bf 109E (right), providing details of the aileron linkages, radiator ejector flaps and the aileron horn balances, the latter differing between the two aircraft. The bulge under the wing of the 'Emil' housed the breech of the wing-mounted MG FF cannon.

Fighter Combat over Korea

PART 4

THE FINAL YEAR

As the United Nations faced its 31st month of combat in Korea, the peace talks were making no progress and the end of the war was not in sight. This regional war, which should have ended in 1950, had become a commander's nightmare.

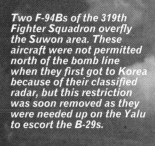

Two F-94Bs of the 319th Fighter Squadron overfly the Suwon area. These aircraft were not permitted north of the bomb line when they first got to Korea because of their classified radar, but this restriction was soon removed as they were needed up on the Yalu to escort the B-29s.

B y the beginning of 1953, the front lines had stabilised at approximately the same place they were when the war began. The manpower provided by the Chinese was still as impressive as it had been in late 1950. Numerically, the United Nations air arm, its ground forces, and the number of Chinese MiG-15s were greater than ever before. To the naked eye, it appeared to be a stand-off, but this was not the case.

Beneath the surface, there was a massive 'board game' being played by the Chinese and the UN Forces. The trump card that was always in the hands of the United Nations was their fighter-bomber operation. They contained the amount of supplies flowing to the south, thus preventing the Chinese from mounting an effective offensive and driving the MLR further south. Taking the game to a higher level was the fact that the decisive advantages for either side were determined during the hours of darkness, putting tremendous

Below: This USAF Lockheed C-121 Constellation has brought a load of high-ranking Air Force personnel and visiting South Korean dignitaries to Pusan Air Base (K-9) just a few weeks before the war ended. This was the home of the 17th Bomb Wing and its Douglas B-26 Invaders.

Below: The use of the Curtiss C-46 for the entire duration of the Korean War was very significant. Considering the heavy payload they could carry, they did very little damage to the PSP compared to the C-54s and C-119s. This aircraft was seen at Pusan in the spring of 1953.

pressure on the B-26s and the Marine night-fighters. The F-80s, F-84s, F4Us, F9Fs etc. would prowl during the early daylight hours to look for stragglers and any road traffic jammed up by night attacks. They would also make their rail cuts, bomb repaired bridges, and crater road intersections to slow up the following night's movement of troops and supplies by the Communists.

The old 'Dollar Nineteen' was all over South Korea, from the early days through all of the post-war era. The C-119 shown here has been helping the 18th Fighter Bomber Wing make the move to its new 'super base' at Osan (K-55), photographed in late January 1953. Shortly after this the 18th began receiving their new F-86F fighter-bombers.

As long as the Chinese were able to get enough supplies through to hold the line, it was very difficult to negotiate with them. When the peace talks broke down in October 1952, the FEAF Staff and General Glenn Barcus of 5th Air Force held meetings to determine what might be done from their end to get the talks back on course. General Barcus was worried as to what an enemy air offensive would do to his capability to keep the Chinese ground forces in check.

January 1953
THE 'BEAGLE' THREAT

Intelligence reports had shown that in early January 1953, the Chinese had received about 100 Il-28 jet bombers into their inventory. These bombers were determined to be the greatest single threat to FEAF. Of the 1,485 total combat aircraft that the Communists had grouped at Manchurian bases, 950 of them were MiG-15s. These could be handled by the F-86 squadrons, but the Il-28s presented a problem to all of the United Nations ground forces that were on the MLR.

The Il-28 was known to be able to carry a bombload of 4,000 lb (1815 kg) at a speed of 400 kt (460 mph; 740 km/h) and a combat radius of 690 miles (1110 km). They would not be very effective during daylight hours and the F-86s would have no trouble with them or their MiG escorts, if they tried to penetrate down to the front-line area. The real threat was in its night-attack potential. On 17 December 1952, the Communists flew two Il-28s along the Yalu opposite a flight of F-86s that was patrolling 'MiG Alley'. The distance was such that the Sabres could not go after them but, nevertheless, the enemy had made a bold statement.

The Il-28 'Beagle' entered production in 1950, and a few reached Korea late in the conflict. Just as in Vietnam more than a decade later, it represented the only real airborne threat posed by the Communists to ground forces. In neither conflict was it used in anger, but the threat was sufficient to divert US fighter forces away from other tasks.

Lockheed F-94B-5-LO, 51-5449, Captain Ben L. Fithian/Lieutenant Sam R. Lyons

The F-94 arrived in-theatre in mid-1951, and was intended as a replacement for the F-82 Twin Mustang. However, the type was generally too fast to counter the nocturnal nuisance raiders. It was not until 30 January 1953 that it scored its first kill, when Captain Ben L. Fithian (pilot) and Lieutenant Sam R. Lyons (radar operator) flew this aircraft to victory against an unidentified 'Bedcheck Charlie'. Their squadron was the 319th FIS, the second of two F-94 units to arrive in Korea, having previously served at Moses Lake AFB, Washington, prior to arriving at Suwon on 10 March 1952. The F-94 was credited with three further kills, including one MiG-15 and an unidentified jet. Another prop 'victory' resulted from a mid-air collision which also destroyed the F-94, with the loss of its crew.

January 1953
BOTTLENECK CAMPAIGN

While the presence of the Il-28 had been incorporated into the FEAF 'Worry List', there were far more pressing issues to attend. At this rate, the war could last for years, so something had to be done about bringing the Communists back to the peace talks and putting an end to a very unpleasant conflict. General Barcus suggested that they put the current air interdiction of Communist supply lines under scrutiny. The previous tactics of 'delay and disruption' had been successful, but now it was time to make some changes. Until now, when the UN aircraft made a series of critical rail cuts, the Chinese would recklessly throw countless numbers of trucks on the road to get the supplies through. Now, this tactic would be altered.

Barcus ordered his fighter-bombers to concentrate on sealing everything at the bottlenecks.

Lt Wesley Jacobsen flies the 474th Wing commander's F-84 on a rescue attempt into North Korea. The big centreline tank gave sufficient loiter time over the area. The fuselage badge is that of the 430th FBS.

Right: The business end of a Thunderjet: it has been loaded with ordnance, serviced and readied for the next mission out of Taegu AB near the end of the war. This F-84 was assigned to the 428th FBS and its pilot was Lt Randy Presley.

When this was accomplished, several maximum efforts would be sent into the areas to completely destroy anything caught in the jams. The workhorse in this campaign would be the Republic F-84. This aircraft was numerically superior to any other in theatre; 218 Thunderjets were available in 1953, and they were flown by exceptionally experienced pilots. These crews received very little publicity for their mission, but they achieved outstanding daytime results. General Barcus was so impressed with the results attained by his F-84s that he was looking into the possibility of using some of them for night work.

The biggest 'choke' point in the north/south rail system was in the Chongshon estuary northwest of Sinanju. That would be a logical place to start this intense campaign, but there was one drawback: at this

Right: Captain Malcolm R. Pearson prepares to fly his 125th combat mission of the war on 25 June 1953. Pearson was commander of 'C' Flight, 430th FBS, and is seen in the wing CO's (Colonel Joe Davis) aircraft.

late period in the war, the Chinese had become masters at setting up AA emplacements around key targets. The first wave of fighter-bombers to hit these targets might have the element of surprise, but the second waves caught hell. The fire was so intense that the chances of administering the lethal blow was greatly reduced. Some of this was bypassed by sending in Shoran B-29s at night, to drop some of the bridge spans.

On orders from 5th Air Force, a few F-84 pilots were selected to begin working the roads at night. In reality, there was no choice in the matter. The B-26s were overworked and spread thin with the change in the Marine night-fighter's mission. In the past, the B-26s had shared this nocturnal mission with the F4U-5Ns and the F7F-3Ns of VMF(N)-513. When '513 received its full complement of F3Ds, its mission changed to escorting the B-29s and keeping the night-flying MiG-15s on the north side of the river. The older, close support Corsairs and Tigercats were retired from combat.

334th FIS – 'Pigeons'

F-86F-1-NA
Captain Manuel J. 'Pete' Fernandez

For a while in May 1953 Fernandez was the top scorer in the Korean War, before being overtaken by McConnell and Jabara. He was officially credited with 14½ kills. Although assigned to Fernandez, this aircraft was also regularly used by Jabara.

F-86F-30-NA
Captain Ralph S. Parr

Parr was one of the best-known pilots of the Korean War. In 1950-51 he compiled 185 combat missions with the 7th FBS, and then returned in 1953 with the 334th FIS flying Sabre fighters, becoming a double ace with 10 kills. During his time with the 334th he flew at least three Sabres, the best-known being this aircraft, (*Barb/Vent de Morte*). Another, 51-12955, was christened *Barbara*.

January 1953
NIGHT ATTACK

Lieutenant Ralph Ritteman, a Thunderjet pilot in the 8th Fighter Bomber Squadron recalls, "There were about eight of us selected to test the feasibility of night strafing and dive bombing. This also included developing the tactics to make it as effective and safe as possible. A schedule of practice missions was set up on the gunnery range and lighted targets were provided. After a couple of weeks, we began to feel at home in the dark. Sometime in January of 1953, we flew our first night missions into North Korea. To avoid running into the B-26s, our missions had to be co-ordinated with theirs. Sometimes, we were assigned an area that was north of where the '26s would be working. We took

Lts Kopf, Armstrong and Walker pose by a 429th FBS F-84G at Taegu in July 1953. Thunderjets were airborne intensively in the last weeks of the war.

off individually, spaced about an hour apart, so that we would have one F-84 over the supply routes all night. The effectiveness of these missions was not measured solely in the number of trucks or trains destroyed, but also in the number of hours that the enemy's supply lines could be shut down. As we made our presence known in an area, you could see lights being turned off for miles and the traffic coming to a standstill. It would be very difficult to convey the magnitude of the enemy supply

effort at night. During the day, you could fly for hours and not see any sign of vehicles on the roads, but at night, from 30,000 ft, you could see all of the major supply routes, in North Korea, lit up with thousands of truck lights. It was a very impressive sight."

Lieutenant Milton Riggs, an F-84 pilot from the 69th Fighter Bomber Squadron, also did some night work. He spent most of his time harassing labour crews that

Above: 1st Lt Ralph Ritteman poses in heavy winter flying gear by his F-84, right after a mission during which the Thunderjet had sustained some hits from groundfire.

Left: A 430th FBS F-84 undergoes an engine change at Taegu in 1953. Even at this late stage facilities were very crude at the Korean bases.

were repairing rail cuts and damaged bridges. Riggs recalls, "Each of our aircraft carried two 1,000-lb bombs, with proximity fuses timed to explode between 50 and 100 ft above the target. This prevented the workers from effectively doing their jobs. Flak wasn't a serious problem, because we moved so fast that the gunners would be firing at our sound several hundred yards behind us. My biggest fear was having a searchlight hit in the cockpit, blinding me. With the rugged terrain on either side of us and the low altitude, without our eyesight, we would have been goners for sure."

335th FIS – 'Chiefs'

F-86F-30-NA
Captain Clyde A. Curtin

Curtin scored his first two kills in October and December 1952. It was not until the last weeks of the war, in July 1953, that he rapidly added three more to join the ranks of Sabre aces. The 335th was notable for the consistent skill of all its pilots, rather than the heroics of a few experts, and it emerged as the highest-scoring squadron of the war by a considerable margin.

F-86F-10-NA
Captain Lonnie R. Moore

Lonnie Moore was one of three double aces within the ranks of the 335th (along with Lt Col Vermont Garrison and Col James Johnson), all of whom scored 10 kills. Moore's aircraft wore the name *Billie* on the port side, and *Margie* on the other. Moore had been involved in the Gun Val project.

Early 1953
'HONCHOS' AND BOMBERS

While the efforts of the interdiction planners increased, the F-86s continued their dominance over 'MiG Alley', with very little sign that any of the MiGs were going to stray further south than Pyongyang. January, February and March statistics show that the Sabres generated a total of 9,702 combat sorties and lost nine of their aircraft to the MiGs. During this same period, the Sabres had confirmed 96 kills, all but one of which were MiG-15s. For some reason, the MiGs were not as active during the early months and inclement weather did not seem to be a factor. The enemy fighters definitely had the numerical advantage, as they had since the early months of 1951. They flew in large formations above the Sabre's ceiling. However, there

Seen here taxiing the aircraft assigned to Captain R.T. Dewey is 'Pete' Fernandez, one of the Sabre force's leading 'honchos'.

was a certain element that did choose to fight and knew exactly what they were doing. To the F-86 pilots they were known as 'honchos', and their experience level and aggressiveness put them on a level playing field with any fighter pilots who flew the Sabre.

The B-29s that were operating out of bases in Japan and Okinawa started 1953 with some of their

most effective missions since the war started. Much of this had to do with the number of aircraft that could be put over any designated target. In the autumn of 1952, the 19th Bomb Group had an in-commission rate of less than 70 per cent. The aircraft were all veterans of World War II fights

Right: Apache was one of the 19th Bomb Group B-29s which ran into bad luck over the target, but made it back safely to the nearest friendly base. After minor repairs it flew back to its Okinawa base.

Below: The 'Y' on the tail marks this B-29 as from the 307th BG, seen here taxiing out of its parking space at Kadena. The long night missions left in the afternoon.

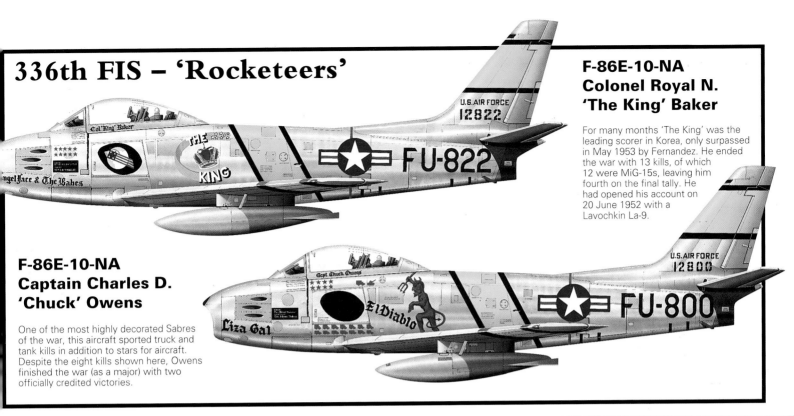

336th FIS – 'Rocketeers'

F-86E-10-NA Captain Charles D. 'Chuck' Owens

One of the most highly decorated Sabres of the war, this aircraft sported truck and tank kills in addition to stars for aircraft. Despite the eight kills shown here, Owens finished the war (as a major) with two officially credited victories.

F-86E-10-NA Colonel Royal N. 'The King' Baker

For many months 'The King' was the leading scorer in Korea, only surpassed in May 1953 by Fernandez. He ended the war with 13 kills, of which 12 were MiG-15s, leaving him fourth on the final tally. He had opened his account on 20 June 1952 with a Lavochkin La-9.

---

against Japan and they had been up almost constantly for over two years since the Korean War started. SAC, which controlled all the other bomb groups in-theatre, had moved away from the old 'crew chief' system of servicing aircraft. By forming a separate maintenance squadron, their B-29s had an outstanding mission rate. The 19th, under the leadership of Colonel H. C. Dorney, abandoned the old system on 13 January 1953 and organised a provisional periodic maintenance squadron. Not long after this went into effect, the in-commission rate exceeded the desired 70 per cent and there were more B-29s putting their bomb loads on North Korean targets. As logistical support improved from the States, each of the three B-29 bomb groups that were involved in the war were programmed to fly 1,800 hours per month. This gave Far East Bomber Command a capacity of 20 combat sorties each day. However, during the January-July period of 1953, the B-29s were only able to average 1,307

Right: Only the aircrews that had been shot down over water could ever realise what a beautiful sight the Albatross was. This UF-2 served with the US Navy.

hours per month, which netted 16 combat sorties per day.

The bombing results of the B-29's efforts at night were excellent, and due in part to being threatened only by AAA and not by the MiGs. The Marine night-fighters and their F3Ds had dented the nocturnal success of the MiG-15. The number of MiGs that were using ground control to fly at night had greatly increased during the final three months of 1952, and the quality of the pilots was exceptional in 1953. UN intelligence had no way of knowing, at the time, but the Soviets were writing a fighter doctrine that would make the ground radar controller and the pilot act as one. These tactics would be used by the Soviet Union and all of the Soviet Bloc until the demise of the system in the early 1990s.

Early 1953
NIGHT FIGHTING

Major Jack Dunn, an F3D pilot, and his R/O Sergeant Larry Fortin can attest to just how skilled these pilots were. Dunn tells about an encounter they had with a MiG-15 on the night of 12 January 1953. It was the first kill for VMF(N)-513 in 1953.

"This one night, the MiGs were all over the place. They attempted to lure us out and away from the

bomber stream, by flying right up to the edge of the formations and then turning quickly back towards the Yalu. We stayed right with the '29s and all were able to hit their targets at Sinanju. After they had turned back south, our F3Ds remained in the area with ground control vectoring us in various directions toward any 'bandit' activity. All of a sudden, this aircraft flew right in front of us

Right: The North American LT-6G was used for 'Mosquito' forward air control missions, assigned to the 6147th Tactical Control Group. Their operations were instrumental in the success of the close support campaign.

Several Douglas F3D Skyknights from VMF(N)-513 are seen in formation over their base in South Korea in late July 1953. The war had just ended, and most of their flying time in the coming months would be during the day over friendly territory.

with his wing lights on. Fortin had him on the screen and began giving me vectors to follow, while at the same time I was telling our ground control at Chodo what we were experiencing. They came

back and said there were no friendlies in the area we were in and for us to try and nail him. It took the better part of five minutes to get a 'lock on', and as we were getting closer and closer it seemed

Early 1953

The plunder by MiG-15s of the B-29 night formations over North Korea came to an abrupt end when Marine F3Ds started mingling in the bomber streams. The night-fighters achieved several kills over the MiGs.

strange that an F3D could close the gap on a much faster MiG. Because of this fact, I can only guess that the MiG pilot was 'dogging' it to enable me to stay close enough to follow, but still just out of firing range. Chodo ground control told me we were now directly over the earlier B-29 target of Sinanju. The enemy fighter commenced circling to the left, with his wing lights still on. At that moment, about six searchlights from the ground switched on and caught us broadside. It was just like bright sunlight, with a blinding effect that was instant. The AA cut loose and bounced us around a bit, but we were fortunate and didn't take any hits.

"I was able to keep turning inside the MiG more and more. This was one characteristic that the F3D had over it. Finally, when we had him in range, I opened up with three bursts, but nothing seemed to happen. Suddenly, he started in a dive with me right on his tail. I gave him a couple of more bursts on the way down. Fire was now coming from the enemy aircraft and we followed until he hit the ground in a fiery explosion. Looking back on this, when we made a pass through the searchlights the MiG would turn off his wing lights, and I could only assume that at that point he would accelerate, make a 180° turn and head back toward us, at which

time he would turn his wing lights back on. We went through the searchlights three times, and on the fourth time we got him."

Less than a week after Dunn's kill, another '513 pilot, Captain George Kross, had a spectacular night encounter with a MiG-15. He was jumped from behind by a MiG-15 that had been given the advantage by a good radar controller. Kross took numerous hits and dove straight down from his altitude of 30,000 ft (9144 m). The MiG followed and, at one point, Kross said that an IAS of 750 mph (1.02 Mach) was achieved in the vertical dive. When he tried to pull out, there was no elevator response; the F3D was past the limiting Mach number and the shock wave was

The RO's equipment on the right-hand side of the F3D had displays for the APQ-35, which was the first track-while-scan system. The top scope is for the APS-28 tail warning radar, the left scope is a plan position indicator for azimuth/range, while the right scope is a 'C' scope for azimuth/elevation.

Below: All F3Ds in-theatre were flown by VMF(N)-513, the 'Flying Nightmares'. After dark they were much more than a match for the MiG-15.

Lt G. E. Scott, radar operator on this 319th FIS F-94B, makes a few last-minute checks to the radar equipment prior to attending the briefing for the night's mission. Although it had good radar, the F-94B was too fast to catch nuisance raiders, and had insufficient range to escort bombers.

blanking out the tail surfaces. He was able to pull out at a very low altitude above the Yellow Sea. The next morning, it was revealed that Kross's aircraft had taken several hits, including one that went through 19 fuselage stringers and finally impacted on the escape hatch door. Later, military experts determined that the MiG would not have been able to follow Kross's evasive action unless it had been equipped with airborne radar. This explained why the night-flying MiG-15s had become so effective.

Individual aircraft
This F3D-2 was used by Major
Jack Dunn (pilot) and Sergeant
Larry Porton (radar operator) to
score a MiG-15 kill on 12 January
1953, achieved during a routine
bomber escort mission over North
Korea. VMF(N)-513 scored a total
of six victories, comprising four
MiG-15s, one Yak-15 (type not
confirmed) and a Po-2 'Bedcheck
Charlie'.

dar system
F3D was the first aircraft to
oduce a track-while-scan system. It
prised two sets, the APS-21 search
ar and the APG-26 gun-laying radar.
APS-21 could acquire fighter-sized
ets at about 20 miles (32 km) range,
wing the R/O to vector the aircraft
lose range. At about two miles (3.2
the target was handed off to the
-laying radar, allowing the APS-21 to
tinue searching for other targets. In
ition to the R/O's displays, the
em generated steering information
range for the pilot.

Accommodation
The two-man crew sat side-by-
side. There were no ejection
seats, which would have added
too much weight, so the crew
had a vaulting bar and an escape
chute leading to the underside of
the fuselage.

Douglas F3D-2
Skyknight
VMF(N)-513

**Despite its portly looks, the Skyknight ruled
the airspace at night over Korea in the latter
part of the war. Whereas the Corsair and
Tigercat which it replaced were largely tasked
against ground targets, the F3D was used in
the main to escort the Boeing B-29 bomber
streams, a role it performed excellently. The
F3D was the most successful of the
Navy/Marine types during the conflict, also
scoring history's first jet versus jet night kill.**

Powerplant
The F3D-2 was designed around the 4,600-lb (20.47-
kN) thrust Westinghouse J46 engine, and featured
larger intakes to cater for the great mass flow.
However, the aircraft were completed with the
Westinghouse J34-WE-36 turbojets of the F3D-1,
each offering 3,400 lb (15.13 kN) thrust. This left
them relatively underpowered, although the top
speed of 600 mph (966 km/h) and rate of climb of
4,500 ft (1370 m) per minute were highly respectable,
and the large, straight wing allowed the F3D to out-
turn a MiG at most speeds. The engines dropped out
of their bays for maintenance, and could be changed
in about one hour.

rmament
he standard armament of the Skyknight
as four 20-mm cannon with 800 rounds
ammunition in the lower forward
selage. The underwing pylons carried
el tanks, although later the F3D-2M
riant became the first aircraft to carry
e Sparrow missile operationally.

Spring 1953
CARRIER
OPERATIONS

As the spring of 1953 arrived, the intensity of naval air activity off the coasts of North Korea was at an all-time high. When the US Navy put one of its carriers on station far to the north, there were no targets in hostile territory that were safe. The large number of Navy AD Skyraiders were able to get in close, giving them much more time to work the targets. One day (2 June 1953), USS *Boxer* sent its ADs to bomb the big Hamhung West airfield. They made 55 craters in the runway and put it out of business for several days. On that day, the *Boxer*'s aircraft flew 102 sorties. They easily averaged that many each day, and on 15 June they put 147 in their log. This trend continued until the war ended on 27 July. It was the Air Force that got the lion's share of the publicity during this period, because the land-based aircraft were more accessible to the press. One can only imagine the number of fighter-bomber types that were over North Korean airfields during the final 48 hours of the war. The Communists wanted to get as many aircraft into North Korea as they could by the final day, and they were not very successful in accomplishing this.

Generally speaking, the carriers conceded the night time to the Air Force, Marine night-fighters and the enemy. They were not in the business of conducting operations after dark. However, one heckler mission that was flown from USS

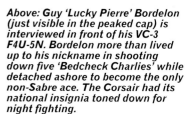

Below: A land-based F2H-2P Banshee of Marine squadron VMJ-1 prepares to launch from Suwon. It will be escorted by USAF Sabres. The camera-nosed Banshee was widely used by both Navy and Marine Corps for reconnaissance.

Above: Guy 'Lucky Pierre' Bordelon (just visible in the peaked cap) is interviewed in front of his VC-3 F4U-5N. Bordelon more than lived up to his nickname in shooting down five 'Bedcheck Charlies' while detached ashore to become the only non-Sabre ace. The Corsair had its national insignia toned down for night fighting.

Valley Forge on 3 May 1953 does deserve some overdue recognition.

The mission was to hit the Chosin No. 1 power plant. This was one of the most heavily defended targets in North Korea, with about 30 37-mm AA guns and at least a dozen more of larger calibre. This made any low-level daytime attacks extremely risky. Three Skyraiders launched at 03.00. The lead ship went in over the plant and dropped an illuminating flare. Immediately behind the lead were two ADs carrying two 1,000-lb (454-kg) bombs each. The bombs impacted on target. As the ADs began their flight back to the carrier, they verified that the plant was spewing sparks, which was evidence that

they had done some serious damage. This mission was flown by aircraft from VC-35 and was led by Lieutenant Commander W. C. Griese.

Final figures published by the US Navy after the war revealed that they had lost 312 F4U Corsairs during the conflict. This was followed by the loss of 124 Skyraiders. These two aircraft carried the bulk of the responsibility for close air support over heavily defended targets.

They were both prop types, which made them slow and therefore more exposed to ground fire for a longer period on each bomb run. The faster F9F Panther also did outstanding close support, but they only lost 64 aircraft.

Of course, all of these figures are directly proportional to the numbers of the aircraft that were in-theatre. On the other end of the spectrum is the fact that only one F3D was lost to enemy action, and that was on a rare close support sortie flown by the Marine squadron commander right after the unit had received the night-fighters. Then, only one squadron flew this particular aircraft during the hostilities.

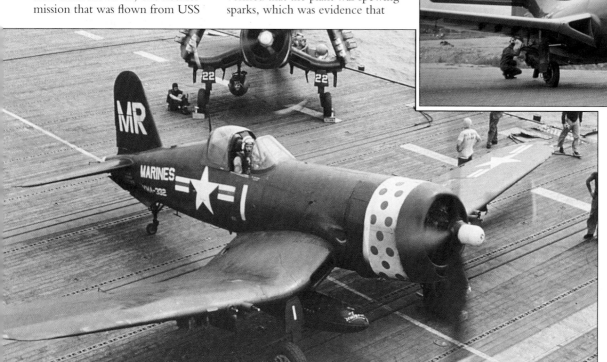

Above: This VMF-115 Panther ran into major problems over its target in North Korea. Suffering battle damage, it landed at Taegu, which was one of the first friendly bases south of the bomb line. Two Marine squadrons flew the F9F under the control of the 1st Marine Air Wing.

Left: An F4U Corsair from VMA-332 'Polka Dots' moves into position to launch from the USS Bairoko in early July 1953. VMA-332 took over VMA-312's Corsairs and got into combat about six weeks before the end of the war.

Mikoyan-Gurevich MiG-15, Colonel Yevgeni Pepelyaev, 196th IAP

Even after the US revised its initial Korean War kill/loss lists to more believable proportions, there remain large discrepancies between the figures presented by either side. Despite this, it is most credible that the highest-scoring aces of the war were both Russians: Pepelyaev with 23 kills and Nikolai Sutyagin with 21. Far from denigrating the UN achievements in the air, the Russian figures (if true) further underline the outstanding successes of the Sabre pilots, who were often flying against seasoned combat veterans with arguably better equipment, and not against the third-rate opposition as has often been portrayed. Pepalyaev flew this aircraft as commander of the élite 196th IAP, which made up half of the 324th IAD which was commanded by World War II ace Ivan Kozhedub.

April 1953
NOCTURNAL THUNDERJET

The use of the F-84, at night, had increased somewhat. They stayed away from the B-26s and flew reconnaissance of the roads in the extreme northern sectors. These missions were usually flown at altitude, which made them very visible to ground control radar around the Communist airfields in Manchuria. First Lieutenant Wesley Jacobson, a pilot in the 430th Fighter Bomber Squadron, remembers one of those missions. "Our mission on this night was to recce a segment of highway northwest of Kaesong towards Sariwon and Pyongyang. This road was heavily travelled by trucks coming in from Manchuria and heading straight down to the major North Korean supply centres right above the front lines. Our stretch of road was about 50 miles long. We were a two-ship and we would be working different areas.

"We would fly a line about 15 miles offset from the highway and when we spotted a long convoy of trucks coming, we would power

*This is the 429th **FBS** flight line at Taegu in the summer of 1953. The F-84 tail markings were highly confusing, as different squadrons took over a departing unit's aircraft without changing the markings.*

back to idle power and glide on down to the road to line up with the columns of vehicles at about 5,000 ft. We would make the bomb drop at about 3,000 ft. It seems that their early warning system for aircraft consisted of army troops stationed in the nearby hills armed with shotguns. When they heard approaching aircraft, they would fire the guns in the air. This worked pretty well with the B-26s, but with the F-84s gliding in with engines at idle it gave them no warning. We added power after the drop and they fired their shotguns about the time the bombs were impacting on the columns."

It was a very rare mission when an F-84 had to tangle with a MiG-15 at night. On one of these night reconnaissance missions, Lieutenant Jacobson had a very close call and the other '84 that was working the same sector with him was shot down by the MiG. He recalls the night of 12 April.

"On this evening, Lieutenant Leonard DeLuna took off first and I launched 20 minutes later. When I crossed the bomb line and entered North Korean airspace, the radar controller who worked this area told me that they had tracked an enemy aircraft that had come down from China, closed in behind

*The ordnance crews are heavily involved in their jobs on the flight line as they prepare these 429th **FBS** F-84Gs for the next strike.*

DeLuna (callsign BLOODSTONE 45) and that he had disappeared off the scope. They asked me to go into the area and verify any signs that the F-84 had been shot down. They gave me a quick vector to a suspected enemy supply area, so I could drop the bombs, and after that they put me into the last-known area of where BLOODSTONE 45 had been. It didn't take long to spot a fire burning on the ground, and that was probably the remains of the F-84. I gave them the co-ordinates and was immediately sent up to

22,500 ft, which was the altitude that the MiG-15 was maintaining. I was directed in behind the bogie at 300 mph IAS and was told by the controller that if I got a visual, I was clear to fire. It wasn't long before I had a lock-on on the A-4 gunsight ranging dial, and I watched it crank down to 500 ft distance to target, at which point it gave me a red flashing warning light for being too close. I looked through the gunsight and saw an object that looked like the fire coming through the turbine section of a jet engine, at night. From the short tailpipe, I knew it had to be a MiG. There was no moon so the night was totally black. I had heard from other pilots that if you fired the guns at night, the flash caused by the incendiaries could make you lose your night vision for at least 15 minutes. If this happened and I missed the MiG, then he would have an easy job in shooting me down. I decided that the best thing to do was to slow down, and ease my way out and back to base. Both myself and the ground controller that I was working with had decided the MiG definitely had some type of airborne radar because he had got DeLuna rather easily."

16th Fighter-Interceptor Squadron

F-86E-10-NA
Major Edwin L. Heller

Heller was a veteran 8th Air Force ace with 5½ kills from World War II. He added another 3½ to his score during the Korean conflict. He flew a succession of Sabres, all named *Hell-er Bust* and, as a lieutenant colonel, commanded the 16th FIS during the latter part of the war. He was regarded as a controversial leader, eager to push the rules by heading north across the Yalu.

F-86E-1-NA
Captain Dolphin D. Overton III

Having earlier flown a 102-mission tour in F-84s with the 8th FBS, 'Dolph' Overton returned to Korea with the 16th FIS. He made ace during the course of four days right at the end of his Sabre tour, downing two MiGs on 21 January 1953, followed by single victories on the next three days.

Above: This is the rather cramped cockpit of a veteran F-86F, photographed in the summer of 1953 at Suwon AB. Note the kill markings. This aircraft was assigned to the 39th FIS of the 51st FIW. This squadron produced the war's top Sabre ace – Captain Joe McConnell (16 kills).

Below: Prolonged rains turned much of Korea into a mudbath, as can be seen from the landscape beneath this 335th FIS F-86F flying on a test hop in the Seoul area. This was one of the last F models built before the introduction of the '6-3' wing with extended wing leading edges.

Early 1953
THE BENEFITS OF EXPERIENCE

It will probably never be known just how many errors and bad decisions were made by Soviet air commanders in control of Communist air operations in Korea. Mistakes happened on both sides. One glaring mistake that has been recently brought to light was the Soviet policy of pulling entire units out of combat and replacing them with all-new units that had no previous jet combat experience. If you were to ask any combat commander in any war what he would most like to have going for his troops, the answer would be 'Experience'. The USAF worked this to absolute perfection.

Whether a pilot flew a fighter-bomber or an air superiority type, he was always under the wing of an experienced veteran. Many of the 4th and 51st Wing F-86 pilots would not have had much of a chance of being an element lead until he had flown about 50 missions; to become a flight leader would require close to 75+ missions, unless the pilot was exceptional. It was this philosophy that contributed to the significant kill ratio of the Sabre and also to the survival rate among Sabre pilots, many of whom rotated back to the US after their 100 missions and became flight instructors at Nellis AFB.

Most pilots who flew in the Korean War remember their first few missions and they will admit that they were scared, even with experienced people with them. Second Lieutenant Robert D. Carter was a new F-86 pilot assigned to the 335th Fighter Squadron in late 1952, and he was thrown into a tight situation with an experienced MiG-15 pilot on his second mission. Carter relates: "My first few missions were flown on the wing of a very experienced RAF exchange pilot named Flight Lieutenant John Nicholls. Nick was a great fighter pilot and he later went on to become Air Vice Marshall in the RAF and commanded their Tactical Air Command. It was my second

25th Fighter-Interceptor Squadron

U.S. AIR FORCE
24584
FU-584

F-86F-30
Major John H. Glenn Jr

Several exchange pilots flew with the 25th FIS, the best-known being Glenn, the 'MiG Mad Marine' who scored three kills while with the squadron. He went on to greater fame, first as the pilot during a transcontinental record run in a Crusader, then as the first American in space, and more recently as an Ohio state Senator.

F-86F-1-NA
1st Lieutenant Henry 'Hank' Buttelmann

Buttelmann's aircraft was one of the few Sabres to have received the 'US Air Force' titles before the war's end. At 23, the pilot was the youngest of the 40 aces in Korea, his final score standing at seven. Buttelmann was one of only four lieutenant aces, the others being Becker, Low and Kasler, all of the 335th FIS.

U.S. AIR FORCE
12890
U.S. AIR FORCE FU-890

mission and Nicholls was my flight leader. While directly over the Yalu, we encountered a lone MiG and Nick went after him immediately. He was flying one of the new 'F' models and I was in one of the older 'Es' that had the slat wing. In the two minutes that it took him to close the gap, I was left quite a distance in trail. I called out that his six o'clock was clear and he should go ahead and shoot. He did and was getting hits all over the MiG. At that moment, I caught a flash of light out of the corner of my eye. It was another MiG and it was coming down on me right out of the sun. I called out to Nick that I might have somewhat of a problem and that when the MiG got about 2,000 ft out, I would call a break; when I did, the MiG stayed right on me. I was plenty scared.

"In an effort to shake him, I was pulling as many gs as I could without snapping the aircraft. Seconds later, two F-86s came out of nowhere and shot enough holes in the MiG to get him off my tail. I was drenched in sweat. I found

out later that one of those pilots was Captain 'Black Dan' Druen who later went on to become a lieutenant general in the Air Force."

Above: To look up and see this VMA-121 AD bearing down would have been an unforgettable experience if one had lived through it. The aircraft is loaded with 2,000-lb and 250-lb bombs, and has sunk considerably in the dirt.

This was just one example of how experienced combat veterans contributed to the safety and education of the future combat veterans. It takes little imagination to visualise just how a very young, inexperienced MiG-15 pilot must have felt with a 90-mission F-86 'honcho' locked onto his tail.

Below: Used by Marines and Navy alike, the Douglas AD Skyraider was one of the most deadly close support aircraft operating during the Korean War. This example, seen resting at the 'Mosquito' base at Chunchon (K-47) in 1953, was assigned to Marine Squadron VMA-121. This unit was the Corps' principal AD unit throughout the war.

Left: Sometimes the winter weather severely restricted flying or even halted it altogether. This snowstorm hit Suwon, giving these 16th FIS pilots a welcome day off. The storm had come down out of Manchuria – the Communist airfields would have been even harder hit.

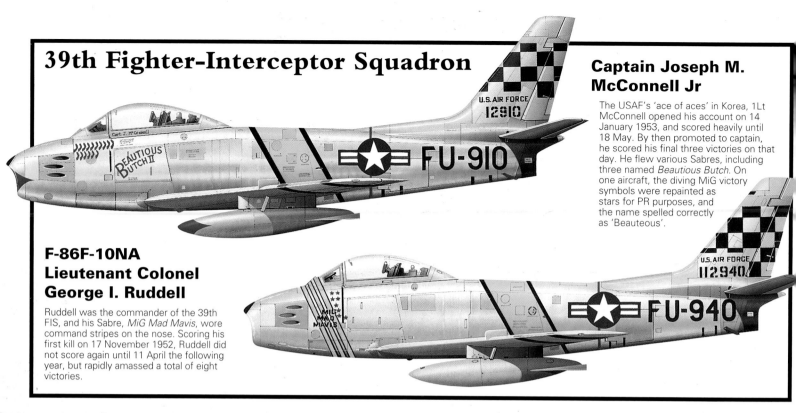

39th Fighter-Interceptor Squadron

U.S. AIR FORCE 12910

FU-910

Captain Joseph M. McConnell Jr

The USAF's 'ace of aces' in Korea, 1Lt McConnell opened his account on 14 January 1953, and scored heavily until 18 May. By then promoted to captain, he scored his final three victories on that day. He flew various Sabres, including three named *Beautious Butch*. On one aircraft, the diving MiG victory symbols were repainted as stars for PR purposes, and the name spelled correctly as 'Beauteous'.

F-86F-10NA
Lieutenant Colonel
George I. Ruddell

Ruddell was the commander of the 39th FIS, and his Sabre, *MiG Mad Mavis*, wore command stripes on the nose. Scoring his first kill on 17 November 1952, Ruddell did not score again until 11 April the following year, but rapidly amassed a total of eight victories.

U.S. AIR FORCE 112940

FU-940

18 April 1953
MiG IN A SPOT

Above: 2Lt Robert Carter, Capt Vince Stacy and 2Lt Harry Jones of the 335th FIS celebrate their joint downing of a MiG on 15 April. The official credit was shared by the junior lieutenants.

Below: A pair of 4th FIW Sabres clambers skywards, heading north to patrol along 'MiG Alley'.

First Lieutenant Sam Jackson was a young F-86 pilot in the 336th Fighter Squadron. He had just got 15 missions in his log book when he had an opportunity to see just how a young MiG pilot did react in a tight situation, on an occasion when the 336th CO had him in his gunsight at a very close range. "It was 18 April, and I was launched out of Kimpo as a lone Sabre. My job was to orbit over Chodo Island as a spare, in case one of the F-86s that were on a sweep had to abort. This was my 15th combat mission and my first as a spare. It didn't take long to get the call from mission control and I was vectored in to fill in for an aircraft that had to return to Kimpo due to a drop tank that had hung up. I was to fill in on Lieutenant Colonel Louis Green's

wing. He was my squadron commander and one of the best fighter pilots in the 4th Wing.

"We immediately kicked into a combat spread formation and saw four MiGs slightly above and ahead. They were evidently confused because they were gradually descending and they were not moving fast enough to be in a combat zone. They were at 33,000 ft and spreading out in a strange line-abreast. Colonel Green called out for the MiG on the right and I covered his rear. After a couple of short bursts, Green's MiG started smoking and exploded. We had been separated from the other element in the flight, so we formed up to continue our patrol. Minutes later, Colonel Green called out a lone MiG at 10 o'clock. It was a mottled green camouflage colour, but it had the same markings as the other we had seen earlier. Evidently they were all from the same unit. Radio chatter confirmed that the other element lead had shot down his MiG, so this one probably was a confused survivor of the flight of four. It was obvious he was trying to escape, as he took no notice of us and was in a high-speed shallow dive to get back into Manchuria. Colonel Green called a hard, diving, heavy-*g* to the left, and as the turn rounded 270° I was having real problems in staying with the colonel. We rolled out of the dive about 200 ft apart at a very high Mach (0.9) and the MiG still was not aware of us. We were both in excellent position to make the

kill, depending on which way the MiG turned.

"Suddenly, the MiG started to sway a bit as its pilot became aware of the precarious position we had him in. He moved slightly to the left and then the right, looking over at me as he straightened up. He evidently panicked, held his MiG straight and level and ejected. It was at 30,000 ft and his chute opened. We circled back around for a close look and he was hanging limp, so he was either dead or unconscious. It was impossible to tell much about his facial features, but he was dressed in a black leather flying suit and helmet. It had been Colonel Green's 3rd and 4th kills."

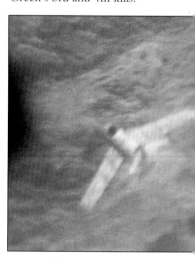

A MiG-15 with a camouflage scheme takes his pursuer down on the deck under a low overcast. This gun camera film was taken by the 39th FIS while the pilot was firing at close range. The MiG was some distance from the Yalu River, well inside North Korea.

North American F-86F-30-NA, 52-4341, Major James P. Hagerstrom

When the attack-dedicated 67th Fighter Bomber Squadron (of the 18th FBW) converted from the F-51D to the F-86F, several experienced Sabre pilots were drafted in from the 4th and 51st Wings to ease the conversion process. Major James P. Hagerstrom was one of these pilots, already the conqueror of two MiGs with the 4th FIW during the latter part of 1952. He added a further 6½ victories while with the 67th, including two on 27 March 1953. The red intake lip was common to most 67th FBS Sabres.

Early 1953
ARRIVAL OF THE F-86F

When 1952 came to a close, 23 pilots had achieved the status of ace. That meant that there were 16 pilots, in-theatre, that would bag their fifth or higher before 27 July. The sharpshooters were out in force when the new year started. Both First Lieutenant Harold Fischer and Captain Dolph Overton got their fifth kill on 24 January. In February, it heated up a little. Captain Joe McConnell, Captain Manuel Fernandez and Major James Hagerstrom all became aces.

These kills were all significant, but Hagerstrom's was a harbinger of the type of problems that the Communist's air power would be facing in the months to come. In the early weeks of 1953, two fighter-bomber types that had been an easy adversary for the MiGs had been retired. The 18th Fighter Bomber Wing had traded its F-51 Mustangs, and the 8th Fighter Bomber Wing gave up its ageing F-80Cs, in both cases for the new F-86F. This meant that if the MiGs were to break through the F-86 fighter screens up on the Yalu and get a shot at the fighter-bombers, they could be in for a lot of trouble. Major Hagerstrom was the commanding officer of the 67th Fighter Bomber Squadron and, after he had dropped his bombs, he flew quickly up to where the MiGs were and bagged one. In the past, all the fighter-bomber pilots wanted to do was put their ordnance on target and get home safely. The thought of getting a crack at a MiG just did not cross their mind. Now, all that changed. It was a hungry bunch of fighter-bomber jocks flying up north in those F-86Fs.

The 8th Wing's transition to the F-86F could not have gone better. The 36th Squadron was the first to change over, on 22 February, followed by the 35th Squadron on 14 March. The 80th Squadron 'Headhunters' was the final squadron to change over; the delay was due to their new F-86s arriving in-theatre with ultra-high-frequency radio sets, necessitating a retrofit with a communications system that would work. This staggered transition allowed all of the top timers in the F-80C to finish their tours by flying with whichever

Above: In early 1953 the 8th FBW turned in its fatigued F-80Cs for F-86Fs. This 35th FBS Sabre, My Sweetie, was assigned to Lt James Carter.

Above: Dennis Clark was operations officer for the 67th Fighter Bomber Squadron, and was assigned this suitably-named F-86F. The aircraft was one of the first built with the '6-3' wing.

squadron still had the F-80. The 80th flew the last sorties in the Shooting Star and it went out in a very impressive blaze of glory. On 24 April, the 80th, using 20 aircraft and 29 pilots, flew 120 effective sorties, dropping 228,000 lb of bombs on enemy targets. Four pilots flew four missions that day, 10 pilots flew five missions and two had six missions. The latter two tied the record for combat missions flown in the Korean War in a single day. The final F-80 sortie was flown by the 80th on 30 April.

In the early weeks of 1953, the 12th Fighter Bomber Squadron converted from the F-51D Mustang to the F-86F, adorned with yellow intakes. The F models ranged deep into North Korea, delivered their 1,000-lb bombs on enemy supply lines and then waited in the hope of being jumped by MiGs.

Lt Lloyd Irish prepares to take off on a close support mission with two 1,000-lb bombs loaded on his new F-86F Irish's Shillelagh. *The red sunburst tail markings indicated that this was a 36th Fighter Bomber Squadron aircraft, the unit having only recently been flying the F-80C.*

26 May 1953
FOUR-KILL SORTIE

Many of the wingmen who flew with the aces on their kills say that it was an experience they will never forget. Lieutenant Richard Frailey, a pilot in the 334th Squadron, remembers one in which he was wingman for Major James Jabara, the first jet ace in history. "This mission was on 26 May 1953 and it was to be my 76th, all of which were flown as a wingman. At this time, Jabara was a soon-to-be triple ace. I had flown with him several times and it was always exciting because group always gave him the best flight times, when the MiGs were more likely to be up. It was a favourite tactic of the MiGs to catch the Sabres low on fuel and heading home. This time, we would be timing it to catch the MiGs in the same situation. We climbed to 35,000 ft, dropped our empty external tanks, test fired our guns and listened to the radio chatter that indicated the MiGs were coming across the river in large-formation 'trains'. As we approached the area we moved into combat formation, which placed me slightly behind Jabara and off his right wing about 1,800 ft. My job, as usual, was to keep the leader's six o'clock clear.

"We reached the Yalu and I spotted a large flight of MiGs ahead of us, making a slow turn to the north. Jabara set up an intercept and, in a few minutes, pulled up behind two of them. They took no evasive action and I figured they had to be students or slightly dumb. In seconds, Jabara fired on one of them, set it on fire, and it exploded. He kicked in a little rudder, and fired on the second one. Large pieces flew off of the MiG, then a long column of fire and smoke, followed by a steep descent into the ground. I was so intent on what Jabara was doing that when I finally scanned the area, I noticed that a lone MiG was flying off of my right wing. He was so close I could see the pilot with his leather helmet. We watched each other while I called to Jabara to tell him what was happening. He replied, 'shoot the bastard!' I immediately started a slow turn into the MiG. Instead of him turning into me, he turned away in a slow descending turn. I followed him and fired a short burst which went above his canopy. At that point, he ejected. I fired another burst into the MiG, then turned sharply to avoid a collision. Jabara joined up and congratulated me. A third member of the flight, Lieutenant Bill Mailloux, also had a kill, giving the flight a total of four kills on a single mission. This was probably a record for the 334th Squadron. It had lasted one hour and 45 minutes."

Congratulations for the three 334th FIS pilots who scored four kills between them on the same mission. On the left is Major James Jabara, in the centre is Lt Bill Mailloux and on the right is Lt Richard Frailey. Jabara ended the war with 15 kills.

June 1953
MORE ACES

June 1953 proved to be the 'ball buster' month for the Sabre's epic combat history. Numerically, the quantity of aircraft that were involved in combat must have set a record for all time. The F-86s had 77 confirmed kills for the month, and lost 14 of their own to the MiGs. Another nine Sabres were lost to operational losses other than enemy fire. This netted down to a record 7,696 sorties for the '86. There were five more aces to be put in the record books in June. These included Lieutenant Colonel Vermont Garrison, Captain Lonnie Moore, Captain Ralph Parr, Colonel Robert Baldwin and Lieutenant Henry Buttelmann. In the final month of the war (July), the kill total was only 31, and one can only assume that the Communist losses in June caused them to cut back on sorties the following month. They also knew that the war would be over in a matter of days.

With the recent fall in our time of the Soviet Union, there have been some details published about their participation in the Korean War. It was much more extensive than anyone had imagined. When the war ended, the official air force records showed that over

All bases in Korea were protected by anti-aircraft emplacements, but since the Communists never mounted any kind of day air attack, the gunners had an uneventful life. This 40-mm gun is at the new Osan AB (K-55), seen soon after the 18th FBW had moved in with its F-86Fs.

Gloster Meteor F.Mk 8, A77-851, Sergeant George Hale, No. 77 Sqn, RAAF

Although not recorded on the official list, Sgt Hale shot down a MiG-15 on 27 March 1953 during the course of a ground strafing mission along the Pyongyang-Singosan road. Hale and his wingman went to the aid of two RF-80s which were being pursued by MiGs, but while chasing off the Communist jets were themselves attacked from out of the sun by further MiG-15s, causing much damage to the wingman's aircraft. Hale shot down one MiG attempting to get behind his wingman, and caused damage to another. In addition to the nickname *Halestorm*, the words 'MiG killer' appeared scrawled in the carbon deposits around the 20-mm cannon ports after the mission.

Right: No. 2 Squadron, South African Air Force (the 'Flying Cheetahs') flew F-51Ds as part of the 18th FBW for most of the war, but also converted to the F-86F in early 1953, beginning operations on 16 March. They flew 2,032 combat sorties with the Sabre after over 10,000 with the Mustang. Ground attack was the main tasking.

Below: A Meteor F.Mk 8 from the Australian No. 77 Squadron (attached to the 4th FIW) rests between missions at Kunsan. The 'Meatbox' was outclassed by the MiG-15, and was used mainly for close support missions. The four 20-mm cannon were usually augmented by underwing rockets.

800 MiGs had been damaged in combat with the F-86. It is unclear how many of these damaged aircraft made it back safely to their bases. During 1951, many of the fighter pilots that had seen their tracers walk all over some of the MiGs could not understand why they continued to fly and get away. They could only get credit for a damage.

Now, the former Soviet pilots are telling how some of their aircraft got back to Antung with numerous 0.50-in (1.27-cm) holes in them. They were patched up and were back in combat within a day or so. Had this been reversed, several hits from cannon fire would have disintegrated a Sabre.

Early 1953
PROJECT GUN VAL

Comments from F-86 pilots helped formulate a top secret project that sent eight E and F model Sabres to Korea, armed with four 20-mm cannon. The project was known as Gun Val. The tests began in early 1953 and lasted about 16 weeks, including combat flights by some of the most experienced pilots in the Air Force. While in Korea, all of these '86s were assigned to and flown by the 335th Fighter Squadron/4th Wing at Kimpo. Of the 41 MiG-15s that were fired on, six were destroyed, three were probables and 13 were damaged. The test was successful enough for the cannons to be installed later in the F-86Hs and the F-100s. While the Gun Val tests were in progress, one of the F-86 pilots from the 334th Squadron avoided what could have been a major tragedy with one of the cannon-equipped F-86s. It took a good eye and fast reflexes.

Lieutenant Bruno Giordano recalls this mission. "It was very late in the war. The weather was clear and it was a beautiful day. We were a little late in taking off, so we pushed it and arrived in our patrol area at a high rate of speed,

full internal tanks and plenty of altitude. Up ahead, I could see the fight with quite a few MiGs ahead and below. It was very unusual to see them at a lower altitude than us. As a flight leader, I came screaming down into the fight with my wingman right behind me. There were so many swept-wing aircraft in the area that it was hard to pick out the enemy. Suddenly, I saw one of them firing and there were the tell-tale intermittent puffs coming out of the gun ports. When the Sabre fired, the puffs were very close together because of the rapid-fire machine-guns. But, when the MiG-15s fired, the puffs were spaced because of the slow-firing cannon. I immediately locked onto this one and told my wingman to stay with me. I had the speed advantage and it was going to be a broadside shot. I put the pipper on him, moved in a little closer and, as I got ready to

Lt Bruno Giordano stands in the cockpit of his F-86E parked in its revetment at Kimpo AB. Giordano had a MiG kill on 16 May 1953 while flying with the 334th FIS. During the month F-86s shot down 56 MiGs, the third highest monthly total of the war.

pull the trigger, I saw the yellow i.d. bands on the wings. It was an F-86! I don't know how I could have made the mistake, so I pulled around to find a MiG and the sky was empty. Years later, I was in a bar in Tripoli discussing strange things that had happened during the war and that subject came up.

That is when I found out that specific F-86 was on a secret project and was equipped with four 20-mm cannon. That explained the MiG-like puffs. I also found out that the pilot had been the Korean War ace Captain Lonnie Moore, who had shot down 10 MiG-15s in Korea."

Spring 1953
FIGHTING AGAINST THE ODDS

There were very few times that the F-86s were in a situation where they had the numerical advantage. Sometimes the odds were 10:1, although it did not seem to make much difference to the Sabre pilots. A flight of four on patrol over the Yalu could count the contrails of 40-50 MiGs coming their way. The four would turn into them, with no fear showing. It was just the way they had to

fight and they accepted it. One of the most unusual stories to come out of the war involved an F-86 pilot who had been shot down in 1952 and was being held in a POW compound just north of the river. On one occasion, he told about a cold, clear day in the spring of 1953 when he was looking out of the small window in his cell, and saw a huge gaggle of contrails forming up and heading south. It was another

bandit train. As they crossed into North Korea, he noticed two contrails coming up slowly under and behind the huge formation. He knew that they had to be F-86s. As the two contrails converged on the large group, all hell broke loose as the MiGs

This F-86 saw plenty of action with the 51st at Suwon. It was the mount of the 51st Group commander Colonel Malcolm Norton. The legend on the side says it all.

scattered in every direction. It was a memorable sight.

The pilot of one of those F-86s was Second Lieutenant Tom Vogel of the 39th Fighter Squadron. He recalls that mission. "We started out in a flight of four F-86Fs on a high-altitude reconnaissance mission looking for MiGs. As we were on our way to the patrol area, one of our aircraft had problems, so he and his wingman turned around and went back to Suwon. Our flight of two continued north at about 35,000 ft. As we approached the river, I counted 26 contrails of MiG-15s at about 45,000 ft, flying westbound, following the Yalu. Our fuel was marginal, but we decided to intercept them. This took some calculation because we had to climb

This spectacular photograph was taken by Lt Robert Niklaus, flying on the far right of the flight. It shows a typical combat formation at high altitude, the other three Sabres being highlighted by their vapour trails. The flight consisted of F-86Fs from the 67th FBS.

Kills list 1953

Date	Pilot	Aircraft/Unit	Enemy
2.1.53	2nd Lt William R. Bowman	F-86, 39 FIS	MiG-15
7.1.53	Capt. Charles C. Carr	F-86, 25 FIS	MiG-15
12.1.53	Maj. Elswin P. Dunn, USMC	F3D, VMF(N)-513	MiG-15
13.1.53	Col Royal N. Baker	F-86, 336 FIS	MiG-15
13.1.53	Col James K. Johnson	F-86, 335 FIS	MiG-15 (½)
13.1.53	Lt Col George L. Jones	F-86, 335 FIS	MiG-15 (½)
14.1.53	Capt. Charles C. Carr	F-86, 25 FIS	MiG-15 (½)
14.1.53	2nd Lt Robert G. Cooke	F-86, 39 FIS	MiG-15
14.1.53	Capt. Van C. Eisenhut	F-86, 335 FIS	MiG-15
14.1.53	Capt. Manuel J. Fernandez Jr	F-86, 334 FIS	MiG-15
14.1.53	1st Lt. Fred W. Gray	F-86, 25 FIS	MiG-15 (½)
14.1.53	Capt. Leonard W. Lilley	F-86, 334 FIS	MiG-15
14.1.53	Capt. Jack E. Mass	F-86, 335 FIS	MiG-15
14.1.53	1st Lt Joseph M. McConnell Jr	F-86, 39 FIS	MiG-15
14.1.53	Capt. Murray A. Winslow	F-86, 335 FIS	MiG-15
15.1.53	Capt. David T. Davidson	F-86, 334 FIS	MiG-15
16.1.53	1st Lt Peter J. Frederick	F-86, 336 FIS	MiG-15
17.1.53	Capt. Vincent E. Stacy	F-86, 335 FIS	MiG-15
20.1.53	Capt. Richard J. Condrick	F-86, 39 FIS	MiG-15
20.1.53	Capt. Robert Wade, USMC	F-86, 16 FIS	MiG-15
21.1.53	2nd Lt Frank H. M. Arbuckle	F-86, 336 FIS	MiG-15
21.1.53	Col Royal N. Baker	F-86, 335 FIS	MiG-15
21.1.53	1st Lt Joseph M. McConnell Jr	F-86, 39 FIS	MiG-15
21.1.53	Col John W. Mitchell	F-86, 39 FIS	MiG-15
21.1.53	Capt. Dolphin D. Overton III	F-86, 16 FIS	MiG-15
21.1.53	Capt. Dolphin D. Overton III	F-86, 16 FIS	MiG-15
21.1.53	Maj. Robinson Risner	F-86, 336 FIS	MiG-15
22.1.53	2nd Lt William R. Bowman	F-86, 39 FIS	MiG-15
22.1.53	Capt. Cecil G. Foster	F-86, 16 FIS	MiG-15
22.1.53	Lt Col Edwin L. Heller	F-86, 16 FIS	MiG-15
22.1.53	Lt Col Edwin L. Heller	F-86, 16 FIS	MiG-15
22.1.53	Capt. Dolphin D. Overton III	F-86, 16 FIS	MiG-15
23.1.53	1st Lt Harold E. Fischer	F-86, 39 FIS	MiG-15
23.1.53	Maj. Harold J. Herrick	F-86, 16 FIS	MiG-15
23.1.53	Capt. Dolphin D. Overton III	F-86, 16 FIS	MiG-15
24.1.53	1st Lt Harold E. Fischer	F-86, 39 FIS	MiG-15
24.1.53	Capt. Cecil G. Foster	F-86, 16 FIS	MiG-15
24.1.53	Capt. Cecil G. Foster	F-86, 16 FIS	MiG-15
24.1.53	Capt. Dolphin D. Overton III	F-86, 16 FIS	MiG-15

Date	Pilot	Aircraft/Unit	Enemy
28.1.53	Capt. J. R. Weaver, USMC	F3D, VMF(N)-513	MiG-15
30.1.53	Capt. Ben L. Fithian	F-94, 319 FIS	Prop.
30.1.53	1st Lt Raymond Kinsey	F-86, 335 FIS	Tu-2
30.1.53	1st Lt Joseph M. McConnell Jr	F-86, 39 FIS	MiG-15
31.1.53	1st Lt Joseph M. McConnell Jr	F-86, 39 FIS	MiG-15
31.1.53	Lt Col Robert F. Conley, USMC	F3D, VMF(N)-513	MiG-15
2.2.53	Col James K. Johnson	F-86, 335 FIS	MiG-15
2.2.53	Maj. Foster L. Smith	F-86, 334 FIS	MiG-15
7.2.53	Capt. Ryland T. Dewey	F-86, 334 FIS	MiG-15
7.2.53	1st Lt Merton E. Ricker	F-86, 335 FIS	MiG-15
14.2.53	Col Royal N. Baker	F-86, 335 FIS	MiG-15
15.2.53	1st Lt Lester A. Erikson	F-86, 16 FIS	MiG-15
15.2.53	1st Lt Harold E. Fischer	F-86, 39 FIS	MiG-15
15.2.53	Col James K. Johnson	F-86, 335 FIS	MiG-15
15.2.53	Capt. Howard P. Mann	F-86, 39 FIS	MiG-15
16.2.53	1st Lt Harold .E Fischer	F-86, 39 FIS	MiG-15
16.2.53	1st Lt Harold E. Fischer	F-86, 39 FIS	MiG-15
16.2.53	1st Lt Joseph M. McConnell Jr	F-86, 39 FIS	MiG-15
17.2.53	2nd Lt John L. McKee	F-86, 335 FIS	MiG-15
18.2.53	1st Lt Ivan J. Ely Jr	F-86, 334 FIS	MiG-15
18.2.53	Capt. Manuel J. Fernandez Jr	F-86, 334 FIS	MiG-15
18.2.53	Capt. Manuel J. Fernandez Jr	F-86, 334 FIS	MiG-15
18.2.53	1st Lt Peter J. Frederick	F-86, 336 FIS	MiG-15
18.2.53	1st Lt Donald H. Hooten	F-86, 334 FIS	MiG-15
18.2.53	Col James K. Johnson	F-86, 335 FIS	MiG-15
18.2.53	2nd Lt John L. McKee	F-86, 335 FIS	MiG-15 (½)
18.2.53	2nd Lt Robert J. Strozier	F-86, 335 FIS	MiG-15 (½)
19.2.53	Col Royal N. Baker	F-86, 335 FIS	MiG-15
19.2.53	Col James K. Johnson	F-86, 335 FIS	MiG-15
21.2.53	1st Lt Robert D. Carter	F-86, 335 FIS	MiG-15
21.2.53	Maj. Vermont Garrison	F-86, 335 FIS	MiG-15
21.2.53	Capt. Vincent E. Stacy	F-86, 335 FIS	MiG-15 (½)
25.2.53	1st Lt Harold E. Fischer	F-86, 39 FIS	MiG-15
25.2.53	Maj. James P. Hagerstrom	F-86, 67 FBS	MiG-15
8.3.53	Col Royal N. Baker	F-86, 335 FIS	MiG-15
8.3.53	Maj. Harold J. Herrick	F-86, 16 FIS	MiG-15
8.3.53	1st Lt Joseph M. McConnell Jr	F-86, 39 FIS	MiG-15
9.3.53	1st Lt Leon B. Perkins Jr	F-86, 16 FIS	MiG-15
9.3.53	Capt. Manuel J. Fernandez Jr	F-86, 334 FIS	MiG-15
9.3.53	1st Lt John W. Goodwill	F-86, 16 FIS	MiG-15
9.3.53	Col John W. Mitchell	F-86, 39 FIS	MiG-15
13.3.53	Col Royal N. Baker	F-86, 335 FIS	MiG-15
13.3.53	Capt. Elmer N. Dunlap	F-86, 67 FBS	MiG-15 (½)

Right: An F9F of VMF-311 stops for fuel at Suwon in 1953. The Marine Panthers were based at Pohang.

Below: Marine Sgt Ralph Reed poses by the MAG-33 sign at Pohang. The group controlled both USMC Panther squadrons in Korea.

about 10,000 ft and not lose too much airspeed at the same time. As it turned out, we flew into position below the rear end of their formation and we had our engines

at 100 per cent RPM. We gradually slipped up toward their formation without losing too much distance horizontally. As we pulled up to within 1,000 ft, enjoying this magnificent spectacle of 26 contrails just above us, someone spotted our two cons below them. They broke, turned, dove and split-essed in all directions. We started firing at all moving targets. One passed within 100 ft of me. They all headed north across the river. We followed a short distance, still firing at long range. We did not want to go down too low for fear we would use too much fuel climbing back up to go home. We turned south and climbed back to about 35,000 ft, throttled back and headed back to base. We both landed on fumes, but did manage to taxi back to our parking area. We were both sure that we had got in some good hits (black smoke), but nothing was confirmed. It had been a great mission!"

Left: Lt Ken Koon's new F-86F The Princess sits on the ramp at the 67th FBS base at Osan. All of the 67th's aircraft wore their 'Fighting Cocks' badge on the fuselage, and had the 18th FBW's large red, white and blue fin stripe.

Lt Col Robert J. Dixon of the 4th FIW examines the remains of the tail of his F-86F. He had been positioning himself on the tail of a MiG when AAA shot away most of the rudder.

Date	Pilot	Aircraft/Unit	Enemy	Date	Pilot	Aircraft/Unit	Enemy
13.3.53	Maj. Raymond E. Evans	F-86, 335 FIS	MiG-15 (½)	12.4.53	Maj. Roy L. Reed, USMC	F-86, 39 FIS	MiG-15
13.3.53	Maj. James P. Hagerstrom	F-86, 67 FBS	MiG-15	13.4.53	Maj. James P. Hagerstrom	F-86, 67 FBS	MiG-15
13.3.53	Maj. James P. Hagerstrom	F-86, 67 FBS	MiG-15 (½)	15.4.53	1st Lt Robert D. Carter	F-86, 335 FIS	MiG-15 (½)
13.3.53	1st Lt William F. Loyd	F-86, 336 FIS	MiG-15	15.4.53	2nd Lt Harry A. Jones Jr	F-86, 335 FIS	MiG-15 (½)
13.3.53	Col Maurice L. Martin	F-86, 67 FBS	MiG-15	16.4.53	Col James K. Johnson	F-86, 335 FIS	MiG-15
13.3.53	Capt. Lonnie R. Moore	F-86, 335 FIS	MiG-15 (½)	16.4.53	Capt. Joseph M. McConnell Jr	F-86, 39 FIS	MiG-15
13.3.53	Maj. Eugene M. Sommerich	F-86, 336 FIS	MiG-15 (½)	17.4.53	1st Lt Philip C. Davis	F-86, 16 FIS	MiG-15 (½)
13.3.53	Sqn Ldr Graham S. Hulse, RAF	F-86, 336 FIS	MiG-15 (½)	17.4.53	Capt. Manuel J. Fernandez Jr	F-86, 334 FIS	MiG-15
14.3.53	Col Robert P. Baldwin	F-86, 39 FIS	MiG-15	17.4.53	1st Lt John W. Goodwill	F-86, 334 FIS	MiG-15 (½)
14.3.53	1st Lt Walter W. Fellman Jr	F-86, 336 FIS	MiG-15	17.4.53	1st Lt Frederick E. W. Mamerow	F-86, 16 FIS	MiG-15
14.3.53	Capt. Manuel J. Fernandez Jr	F-86, 334 FIS	MiG-15	17.4.53	Lt Col George I. Ruddell	F-86, 25 FIS	MiG-15
14.3.53	1st Lt Joseph M. McConnell Jr	F-86, 39 FIS	MiG-15	17.4.53	Capt. Floyd W. Salze	F-86, 39 FIS	MiG-15
21.3.53	Maj. Raymond E. Evans	F-86, 335 FIS	MiG-15 (½)	22.4.53	1st Lt Walter W. Fellman Jr	F-86, 336 FIS	MiG-15
21.3.53	2nd Lt Joe B. Farris	F-86, 335 FIS	MiG-15 (½)	24.4.53	Capt. Joseph M. McConnell Jr	F-86, 39 FIS	MiG-15
21.3.53	Capt. Manuel J. Fernandez Jr	F-86, 334 FIS	MiG-15	30.4.53	Capt. George P. Kelley III	F-86, 39 FIS	MiG-15
21.3.53	Capt. Manuel J. Fernandez Jr	F-86, 334 FIS	MiG-15	30.4.53	Maj. Clyde L. Wade	F-86, 39 FIS	MiG-15
21.3.53	Capt. Harold E. Fischer	F-86, 39 FIS	MiG-15	3.5.53	2nd Lt Stanton G. Wilcox	F-94, 319 FIS	Prop
21.3.53	2nd Lt Richard P. Guidroz	F-86, 335 FIS	MiG-15	8.5.53	Capt. Manuel J. Fernandez Jr	F-86, 334 FIS	MiG-15
21.3.53	Lt Col George L. Jones	F-86, 335 FIS	MiG-15 (½)	9.5.53	Col James K. Johnson	F-86, 335 FIS	MiG-15
21.3.53	Maj. Jack E. Mass	F-86, 335 FIS	MiG-15 (½)	9.5.53	2nd Lt Samuel J. Reeder	F-86, 335 FIS	MiG-15
21.3.53	Capt. Houston N. Tuel	F-86, 336 FIS	MiG-15	10.5.53	Capt. Manuel J. Fernandez Jr	F-86, 334 FIS	MiG-15
21.3.53	Capt. Murray A. Winslow	F-86, 335 FIS	MiG-15	10.5.53	Capt. Manuel J. Fernandez Jr	F-86, 334 FIS	MiG-15 (½)
26.3.53	Maj. Vermont Garrison	F-86, 335 FIS	MiG-15	10.5.53	Capt. John R. Phillips	F-94, 319 FIS	JET
27.3.53	Maj. James P. Hagerstrom	F-86, 67 FBS	MiG-15	10.5.53	Maj. Foster L. Smith	F-86, 335 FIS	MiG-15 (½)
27.3.53	Maj. James P. Hagerstrom	F-86, 67 FBS	MiG-15	13.5.53	Maj. John C. Giraudo	F-86, 25 FIS	MiG-15
27.3.53	1st Lt John L. Metten	F-86, 67 FBS	MiG-15	13.5.53	Capt. Joseph M. McConnell Jr	F-86, 39 FIS	MiG-15
28.3.53	Col James K. Johnson	F-86, 335 FIS	MiG-15	14.5.53	2nd Lt Edwin E. Aldrin	F-86, 16 FIS	MiG-15
29.3.53	Col James K. Johnson	F-86, 335 FIS	MiG-15	14.5.53	2nd Lt Al B. Cox	F-86, 335 FIS	MiG-15
29.3.53	Lt Col George L. Jones	F-86, 335 FIS	MiG-15	14.5.53	Maj. John C. Giraudo	F-86, 25 FIS	MiG-15
29.3.53	Capt. Maynard E. Stogdill	F-86, 334 FIS	MiG-15	15.5.53	Maj. Lowell K. Brueland	F-86, 39 FIS	MiG-15
29.3.53	Capt. Murray A. Winslow	F-86, 335 FIS	MiG-15	15.5.53	Capt. Joseph M. McConnell Jr	F-86, 39 FIS	MiG-15
7.4.53	Col Robert P. Baldwin	F-86, 16 FIS	MiG-15	15.5.53	Col John W. Mitchell	F-86, 39 FIS	MiG-15
7.4.53	Lt Col George L. Jones	F-86, 335 FIS	MiG-15	16.5.53	1st Lt Forist G. Dupree	F-86, 336 FIS	MiG-15
7.4.53	Maj. Roy L. Reed, USMC	F-86, 39 FIS	MiG-15	16.5.53	1st Lt Walter W. Fellman Jr	F-86, 336 FIS	MiG-15
11.4.53	1st Lt Thomas F. Kozak	F-86, 39 FIS	MiG-15	16.5.53	Capt. Manuel J. Fernandez Jr	F-86, 334 FIS	MiG-15
11.4.53	Col John W. Mitchell	F-86, 39 FIS	MiG-15	16.5.53	Capt. Peter J. Frederick	F-86, 336 FIS	MiG-15
11.4.53	Lt Col George I. Ruddell	F-86, 39 FIS	MiG-15	16.5.53	1st Lt Bruno A. Giordano	F-86, 334 FIS	MiG-15
12.4.53	Maj. William L. Cosby Jr	F-86, 334 FIS	MiG-15	16.5.53	Maj. James P. Hagerstrom	F-86, 67 FBS	MiG-15
12.4.53	1st Lt George D. Matthews	F-86, 25 FIS	MiG-15	16.5.53	Maj. James Jabara	F-86, 334 FIS	MiG-15
12.4.53	Capt. Joseph M. McConnell Jr	F-86, 39 FIS	MiG-15	16.5.53	Capt. Joseph M. McConnell Jr	F-86, 39 FIS	MiG-15
12.4.53	Capt. Lonnie R. Moore	F-86, 335 FIS	MiG-15	16.5.53	2nd Lt Philip A. Redpath	F-86, 335 FIS	MiG-15
12.4.53	Lt Col George I. Ruddell	F-86, 39 FIS	MiG-15	16.5.53	1st Lt Merton E. Ricker	F-86, 335 FIS	MiG-15
12.4.53	2nd Lt Len C. Russell	F-86, 334 FIS	MiG-15	16.5.53	Maj. John F. Bolt, USMC	F-86, 39 FIS	MiG-15

27 July 1953
THE FINAL MISSION

The war had lasted a long 37 months, much longer than anyone would have thought. As that last night before the ceasefire rolled around, it only seemed appropriate that the 8th Bomb Squadron would fly the final bomb sortie, especially since the 8th was the first unit to fly a bombing mission against the invading North Korean army. The pilot would be First Lieutenant Donald W. Mansfield, the navigator was First Lieutenant Billy Ralston, and the gunner was Airman Second Class D. J. Judd. They would be flying a B-26C named *Bye Bye Bluebird* and their call sign was TYPHOON 73.

Lieutenant Mansfield remembers the details well. "The briefing for the mission was held in the afternoon, followed by a standard pre-take-off briefing later that evening. Our target was to be a suspected supply dump just north of the bomb line. The Chinese were doing everything they could to stockpile supplies. There was a lot of activity going on all over North Korea because all movement of troops, supplies and equipment was supposed to cease at 22.00 that night. UN truce teams would be dispatched in the morning to inventory the level of supplies, etc. This inspection was supposed to freeze it where nothing more could be brought in. The one thing I remember about the Colonel LeBailly's briefing was that 5th Air Force did not want us crossing over into North Korea after 21.30.

"We took off from Kunsan around 20.15 hours. We had experienced some delay due to a VHF radio malfunction and had a rough-running right engine during our climb out. Also, a member of the Press was flying with us. We checked in with our TACC, but the controller assigned to work with us was experiencing problems with his radar. We were to make our bomb drop from an altitude of 8,000 ft with the TACC vectoring us over the Initial Point (IP) and down the bomb run, and giving us a countdown to the bomb release point. The TACC finally got us in positive radar contact at 21.25 hours and we were still 12 miles south of the bomb line. In compliance with our wing commander's orders, I requested TACC to notify 5th AF and get their permission to proceed. At 21.30, we received word that the Joint Operations Center had cleared the drop. We were immediately vectored across the bomb line and at 21.33 the bomb release countdown was completed; both Lieutenant Ralston and myself pressed our bomb release switches, and we headed south. There was still sporadic shelling across the line, some ground fire, but only occasional ground-to-air firing. We were impressed by how little chatter there was on the radio. Several controllers called us to wish us well. I heard the RB-26 from the 12th Tactical Reconnaissance Squadron check in as he crossed the bomb line behind us. Fifteen minutes later, we were back at Kunsan and there were over 200 guys waiting for us in the de-arming area. It was an experience I will never forget."

B-26C *Dennis the Menace was one of the 8th BS Invaders, the photo being taken by Lt Mansfield who flew the last mission of the war. The impressive tally of 135 missions was typical.*

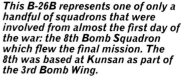

This B-26B represents one of only a handful of squadrons that were involved from almost the first day of the war: the 8th Bomb Squadron which flew the final mission. The 8th was based at Kunsan as part of the 3rd Bomb Wing.

Date	Pilot	Aircraft/Unit	Enemy	Date	Pilot	Aircraft/Unit	Enemy
17.5.53	Maj. David T. Davidson	F-86, 334 FIS	MiG-15	5.6.53	Maj. Vermont Garrison	F-86, 335 FIS	MiG-15
17.5.53	Maj. Vermont Garrison	F-86, 335 FIS	MiG-15	5.6.53	Lt Col Julian A. Harvey	F-86, 336 FIS	MiG-15 (½)
17.5.53	Col James K. Johnson	F-86, 335 FIS	MiG-15 (½)	5.6.53	1st Lt Harry A. Jones Jr	F-86, 335 FIS	MiG-15
17.5.53	Maj. John H. Jones	F-86, 16 FIS	MiG-15	5.6.53	Capt. Lonnie R. Moore	F-86, 335 FIS	MiG-15
17.5.53	1st Lt Cleve B. Watson	F-86, 39 FIS	MiG-15	5.6.53	Capt. Lonnie R. Moore	F-86, 335 FIS	MiG-15 (½)
17.5.53	Capt. Dewey F. Durnford, USMC	F-86, 335 FIS	MiG-15 (½)	5.6.53	Capt. Floyd W. Salze	F-86, 25 FIS	MiG-15
18.5.53	1st Lt Leland W. Carter	F-86, 16 FIS	MiG-15	5.6.53	2nd Lt William E. Schrimsher	F-86, 335 FIS	MiG-15 (½)
18.5.53	Lt Col Louis A. Green	F-86, 336 FIS	MiG-15	5.6.53	1st Lt Thomas W. Seuffert	F-86, 25 FIS	MiG-15
18.5.53	Lt Col Louis A. Green	F-86, 336 FIS	MiG-15	7.6.53	1st Lt Edwin E. Aldrin	F-86, 16 FIS	MiG-15
18.5.53	Capt. George W. Love	F-86, 336 FIS	MiG-15	7.6.53	1st Lt Walter W. Fellman Jr	F-86, 336 FIS	MiG-15
18.5.53	Capt. Joseph M. McConnell Jr	F-86, 39 FIS	MiG-15	7.6.53	2nd Lt James M. Howerton Jr	F-86, 336 FIS	MiG-15
18.5.53	Capt. Joseph M. McConnell Jr	F-86, 39 FIS	MiG-15	7.6.53	Lt Col Robert V. McHale	F-94, 319 FIS	MiG-15
18.5.53	Capt. Joseph M. McConnell Jr	F-86, 39 FIS	MiG-15	7.6.53	Capt. Ralph S. Parr Jr	F-86, 335 FIS	MiG-15
18.5.53	1st Lt Robert E. Perdue	F-86, 336 FIS	MiG-15 (½)	7.6.53	Capt. Ralph S. Parr Jr	F-86, 335 FIS	MiG-15
18.5.53	Lt Col George I. Ruddell	F-86, 39 FIS	MiG-15	10.6.53	Maj. James Jabara	F-86, 334 FIS	MiG-15
18.5.53	1st Lt Harold B. Schmidt	F-86, 336 FIS	MiG-15 (½)	10.6.53	Maj. James Jabara	F-86, 334 FIS	MiG-15
18.5.53	2nd Lt James L. Thompson	F-86, 39 FIS	MiG-15	10.6.53	Capt. Ralph S. Parr Jr	F-86, 335 FIS	MiG-15
18.5.53	1st Lt Walter G. Zistte	F-86, 39 FIS	MiG-15	13.6.53	1st Lt Don R. Forbes	F-86, 12 FBS	MiG-15
18.5.53	Capt. Harvey L. Jensen, USMC	F-86, 25 FIS	MiG-15	15.6.53	Maj. George H. Linnemein, USMC	AD-4, VMC-1	Po-2
23.5.53	Maj. Vermont Garrison	F-86, 335 FIS	MiG-15	16.6.53	Col Robert P. Baldwin	F-86, 25 FIS	MiG-15
23.5.53	1st Lt Samuel R. Johnson	F-86, 16 FIS	MiG-15	16.6.53	Maj. Stephen L. Bettinger	F-86, 336 FIS	MiG-15
26.5.53	Capt. Ryland T. Dewey	F-86, 334 FIS	MiG-15	16.6.53	Maj. George W. Howell Jr	F-86, 25 FIS	MiG-15
26.5.53	1st Lt Richard W. Frailey	F-86, 334 FIS	MiG-15	16.6.53	Capt. Duncan M. Morton	F-86, 25 FIS	MiG-15
26.5.53	Maj. James Jabara	F-86, 334 FIS	MiG-15	16.6.53	1st Lt James L. Thompson	F-86, 39 FIS	MiG-15
26.5.53	Maj. James Jabara	F-86, 334 FIS	MiG-15	18.6.53	Col Robert P. Baldwin	F-86, 25 FIS	MiG-15
26.5.53	1st Lt William P. Mailloux	F-86, 334 FIS	MiG-15	18.6.53	Maj. James Jabara	F-86, 334 FIS	MiG-15
26.5.53	Maj. Jack E. Mass	F-86, 335 FIS	MiG-15	18.6.53	Capt. Lonnie R. Moore	F-86, 335 FIS	MiG-15
26.5.53	Maj. Jack E. Mass	F-86, 335 FIS	MiG-15	18.6.53	Capt. Ralph S. Parr Jr	F-86, 335 FIS	MiG-15
26.5.53	1st Lt Robert H. McIntosh	F-86, 334 FIS	MiG-15	18.6.53	Capt. Ralph S. Parr Jr	F-86, 335 FIS	MiG-15
26.5.53	1st Lt Thomas H. McQuade	F-86, 336 FIS	MiG-15	18.6.53	Flt Lt R. T. F. Dickinson, RAF	F-86, 25 FIS	MiG-15
26.5.53	1st Lt Merton E. Ricker	F-86, 335 FIS	MiG-15	19.6.53	2nd Lt Alvin R. Bouchard	F-86, 16 FIS	MiG-15
26.5.53	Lt Col George I. Ruddell	F-86, 39 FIS	MiG-15	19.6.53	1st Lt Henry Buttelmann	F-86, 25 FIS	MiG-15
26.5.53	2nd Lt George Spataro	F-86, 334 FIS	MiG-15	19.6.53	1st Lt Ivan J. Ely Jr	F-86, 334 FIS	MiG-15
29.5.53	2nd Lt Robert H. Erdmann	F-86, 16 FIS	MiG-15	19.6.53	Capt. Ralph S. Parr Jr	F-86, 335 FIS	MiG-15
29.5.53	Lt Col George I. Ruddell	F-86, 39 FIS	MiG-15	19.6.53	1st Lt Lawrence Roesler	F-86, 335 FIS	MiG-15
1.6.53	Capt. Lonnie R. Moore	F-86, 335 FIS	MiG-15	19.6.53	Lt Col George I. Ruddell	F-86, 39 FIS	MiG-15
5.6.53	Maj. Stephen L. Bettinger	F-86, 336 FIS	MiG-15	22.6.53	Col Robert P. Baldwin	F-86, 25 FIS	MiG-15
5.6.53	1st Lt Frank D. Frazier	F-86, 336 FIS	MiG-15 (½)	22.6.53	2nd Lt Alvin R. Bouchard	F-86, 16 FIS	MiG-15
5.6.53	Maj. Vermont Garrison	F-86, 335 FIS	MiG-15	22.6.53	1st Lt Henry Buttelmann	F-86, 25 FIS	MiG-15

Vought F4U-5N, BuNo 24453, Lieutenant Guy Bordelon, VC-3

Bordelon was the only non-Sabre ace of the war, and lived up to his nickname of 'Lucky Pierre' by shooting down five 'Bedcheck Charlies' in the last two months of the war, his victims comprising four Yaks and a Lavochkin. VC-3 was normally based aboard USS *Princeton*, but following the failure of the USAF's F-94 to effectively catch the nocturnal nuisance raiders, a request was made for the slower and more manoeuvrable night-fighter Corsairs to be based ashore. Bordelon was one of the lucky pilots manning the two-aircraft 'Detachment Dog' at K-6. The normally white markings were rapidly oversprayed to reduce conspicuity in the dark.

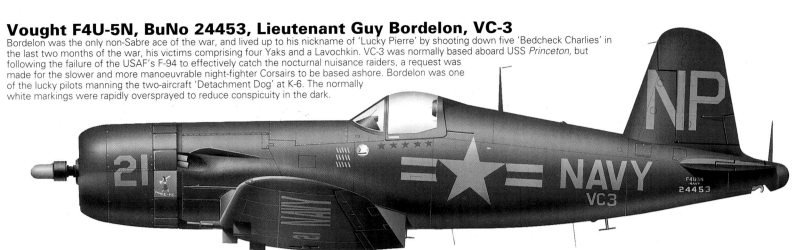

27 July 1953
THE END OF THE FORGOTTEN WAR

On 31 July 1953, four days after the war ended, the inventory for 5th Air Force in Korea consisted of 128 B-26s, 218 F-84s, 165 F-86 fighter interceptors, and 132 F-86F fighter-bombers. When the war ended, 5th AF was capable of putting up 85 B-26 sorties, 181 F-84 sorties, 171 F-86 fighter interceptor and 143 F-86 fighter-bomber sorties. This was considered more than enough to have kept the Chinese army in complete check, prevent any major offensive, cut supplies coming south to an unacceptable level and to keep the Communist air threat bottled up in 'MiG Alley', with no threat to the UN ground forces. It was undoubtedly air power that had broken the back of the North Koreans and Chinese.

Korea has been labelled the 'Forgotten War', and this is very apt. The impact that it made on the military community, however, was tremendous. It moulded a new post-World War II combat doctrine, both on the ground and in the air. The tactics that were proven over North Korea remained valid until after the Vietnam War, 20 years later. It was a time when the old prop types came out of their 'retirement' to lend a hand to the new jets, and together they worked a magic that may never be seen again. **Warren Thompson**

Above: An RB-45C is prepared for a fast photo-run along the North Korean coast just weeks after the end of the war. The Tornadoes became the prime target for the North's MiGs, and a couple of kills were recorded by Sabres escorting the RB-45s.

Left: Sabres remained in Korea long after the end of the war to deter further Communist aggression. This 4th FIW aircraft was seen in December 1953.

Date	Pilot	Aircraft/Unit	Enemy	Date	Pilot	Aircraft/Unit	Enemy
22.6.53	1st Lt Homer J. Carlile	F-86, 39 FIS	MiG-15	30.6.53	Maj. John F. Bolt, USMC	F-86, 39 FIS	MiG-15
22.6.53	Capt. Philip C. Davis	F-86, 16 FIS	MiG-15	30.6.53	Sqn Ldr John McKay, RCAF	F-86, 39 FIS	MiG-15
22.6.53	Capt. James G. Nichols	F-86, 335 FIS	MiG-15	7.53	Lt Guy P. Bordelon, USN	F4U-5N, VC-3	Yak-18
22.6.53	Maj. John F. Bolt, USMC	F-86, 39 FIS	MiG-15	7.53	Lt Guy P. Bordelon, USN	F4U-5N, VC-3	Yak-18
24.6.53	1st Lt Roscoe E. Anderson	F-86, 25 FIS	MiG-15	11.7.53	Maj. John F. Bolt, USMC	F-86, 39 FIS	MiG-15
24.6.53	Maj. Vermont Garrison	F-86, 335 FIS	MiG-15	11.7.53	Maj. John F. Bolt, USMC	F-86, 39 FIS	MiG-15
24.6.53	Capt. James G. Nichols	F-86, 335 FIS	MiG-15	12.7.53	Maj. Stephen L. Bettinger	F-86, 336 FIS	MiG-15
24.6.53	1t Lt George W. Ober	F-86, 335 FIS	MiG-15	12.7.53	1st Lt Curtis N. Carley	F-86, 335 FIS	MiG-15
24.6.53	Capt. Dean A. Pogreba	F-86, 336 FIS	MiG-15	12.7.53	Capt. Lonnie R. Moore	F-86, 335 FIS	MiG-15
24.6.53	Maj. Foster L. Smith	F-86, 335 FIS	MiG-15	12.7.53	Capt. Lonnie R. Moore	F-86, 335 FIS	MiG-15
24.6.53	Maj. Foster L. Smith	F-86, 335 FIS	MiG-15	12.7.53	Capt. Ralph S. Parr Jr	F-86, 335 FIS	MiG-15
24.6.53	Maj. John F. Bolt, USMC	F-86, 39 FIS	MiG-15	12.7.53	1st Lt John D. Winters	F-86, 25 FIS	MiG-15
26.6.53	Lt Col Vermont Garrison	F-86, 335 FIS	MiG-15	12.7.53	Maj. John J. Glenn, USMC	F-86, 25 FIS	MiG-15
26.6.53	1st Lt Thomas H. McQuade	F-86, 336 FIS	MiG-15	15.7.53	Capt. Clyde A. Curtin	F-86, 335 FIS	MiG-15
27.6.53	1st Lt Henry Buttelmann	F-86, 25 FIS	MiG-15	15.7.53	Maj. James Jabara	F-86, 334 FIS	MiG-15
27.6.53	Flt Lt John H. J. Lovell, RAF	F-86, 25 FIS	MiG-15	16.7.53	Maj. Stephen L. Bettinger	F-86, 336 FIS	MiG-15
29.6.53	1st Lt Henry Buttelmann	F-86, 25 FIS	MiG-15	16.7.53	Maj. Lowell K. Brueland	F-86, 39 FIS	MiG-15
29.6.53	1st Lt Roland B. Howell Jr	F-86, 16 FIS	MiG-15	16.7.53	Lt Col Harold C. Gibson	F-86, 39 FIS	MiG-15
29.6.53	1st Lt George W. Jensen	F-86, 16 FIS	MiG-15	16.7.53	1st Lt Lawrence Roesler	F-86, 335 FIS	MiG-15
29.6.53	1st Lt Thomas E. Nott	F-86, 16 FIS	MiG-15	17.7.53	Lt Guy P. Bordelon, USN	F4U-5N, VC-3	Lavochkin
29.6.53	1st Lt Kenneth L. Palmer	F-86, 25 FIS	MiG-15	18.7.53	Capt. Lonnie R. Moore	F-86, 335 FIS	MiG-15
29.6.53	Lt Guy P. Bordelon, USN	F4U-5N, VC-3	Yak	18.7.53	Maj. Foster L. Smith	F-86, 335 FIS	MiG-15
29.6.53	Lt Guy P. Bordelon, USN	F4U-5N, VC-3	Yak	19.7.53	Lt Col Jack R. Best	F-86, 336 FIS	MiG-15
29.6.53	Flt Lt John H. Granville-White, RAF	F-86, 39 FIS	MiG-15	19.7.53	1st Lt Henry Buttelmann	F-86, 25 FIS	MiG-15
30.6.53	1st Lt Henry Buttelmann	F-86, 25 FIS	MiG-15	19.7.53	Capt. Clyde A. Curtin	F-86, 335 FIS	MiG-15
30.6.53	Lt Col William L. Cosby Jr	F-86, 334 FIS	MiG-15	19.7.53	Capt. Clyde A.Curtin	F-86, 335 FIS	MiG-15
30.6.53	Lt Col Vermont Garrison	F-86, 335 FIS	MiG-15	19.7.53	1st Lt Frank D. Frazier	F-86, 336 FIS	MiG-15
30.6.53	Maj. James Jabara	F-86, 334 FIS	MiG-15	19.7.53	Lt Col Vermont Garrison	F-86, 335 FIS	MiG-15
30.6.53	Maj. James Jabara	F-86, 334 FIS	MiG-15	19.7.53	Capt. Lonnie R. Moore	F-86, 335 FIS	MiG-15
30.6.53	Col James K. Johnson	F-86, 335 FIS	MiG-15	19.7.53	1st Lt Jerald D. Parker	F-86, 25 FIS	MiG-15
30.6.53	2nd Lt Cecil E. Lefevers	F-86, 336 FIS	MiG-15 (½)	19.7.53	1st Lt Robert J. Strozier	F-86, 335 FIS	MiG-15
30.6.53	Capt. George W. Love	F-86, 336 FIS	MiG-15 (½)	19.7.53	Maj. John H. Glenn Jr, USMC	F-86, 25 FIS	MiG-15
30.6.53	Lt Col Earle P. Maxwell	F-86, 16 FIS	MiG-15	20.7.53	Maj. Stephen L. Bettinger	F-86, 336 FIS	MiG-15
30.6.53	Capt Lonnie R. Moore	F-86, 335 FIS	MiG-15	20.7.53	Maj. Thomas M. Sellers, USMC	F-86, 336 FIS	MiG-15
30.6.53	1st Lt Waymond C. Nutt	F-86, 334 FIS	MiG-15	20.7.53	Maj. Thomas M. Sellers, USMC	F-86, 336 FIS	MiG-15
30.6.53	Capt. Ralph S. Parr Jr	F-86, 335 FIS	MiG-15	22.7.53	1st Lt Henry Buttelmann	F-86, 25 FIS	MiG-15
30.6.53	Capt. Ralph S. Parr Jr	F-86, 335 FIS	MiG-15	22.7.53	2nd Lt Sam P. Young	F-86, 25 FIS	MiG-15
30.6.53	1st Lt Jimmie Pierce	F-86, 334 FIS	MiG-15	22.7.53	Maj. John H. Glenn Jr, USMC	F-86, 25 FIS	MiG-15
30.6.53	1st Lt George J. Spataro	F-86, 334 FIS	MiG-15	27.7.53	Capt. Ralph S. Parr Jr	F-86, 335 FIS	Il-12

Douglas A-4 Skyhawk Variants

The A-4 Skyhawk is truly one of the classics of the aircraft designers' art. Delivered below weight and budget, but above specification, the 'Scooter' proved reliable, durable and 'fun to fly'. The vast majority of aircraft delivered went to the US Navy and Marines, some of whose units operated the type for more than 30 years. From a 'one-trip' nuclear striker to a fast forward air controller and dogfighting aggressor, the A-4 evolved into a well-loved and widely exported fighter and light attacker. Expected to still be in US Navy service on the type's golden anniversary, 'Heinemann's Hotrod' has proved the adage that good things come in small packages.

T he initial impetus for the introduction of the Skyhawk into the US Navy and Marine Corps arose from two separate sources: the stringent requirements of long-range carrier strike missions, and the increasing weight, complexity and expense of combat aircraft.

In the early 1950s, the fleet was facing the challenges of the Cold War; this dictated the necessity of launching low-level flights from the decks of aircraft-carriers and penetrating the Iron Curtain, then popping up and sending a nuclear weapon at a specified target and – hopefully – egressing safely back to the carrier. With the aircraft of that day, the flight would have lasted eight to 12 hours, a fatiguing mission for the pilot. As such, a requirement existed for a faster, turbine-powered aircraft to accomplish this important mission.

At the El Segundo Division of the Douglas Aircraft Company, Chief Engineer Ed Heinemann was preoccupied with an old problem that persisted in the design of aircraft: that of excessive growth in the weight and complexity of a vehicle in order to meet the customer's spiralling requirements. He had some experience in this, as Douglas had just built two wartime aircraft, the SB2D and the TB2D, that were not put into production because of the

The Skyhawk was very much designed around the single mission of delivering a nuclear bomb from the deck of an aircraft-carrier, a task previously given to large multi-engined bombers such as the AJ Savage and A3D Skywarrior. However, the A-4 design was versatile enough for adaptation to conventional missions and armaments such as the 'slick' bombs and Bullpup guided missiles seen here.

degraded performance brought about by such developments. With these failures in mind, Heinemann submitted his AD Skyraider design at a weight 5,000 lb (2268 kg) lighter than its competition, the Martin AM Mauler. In 1951, Heinemann and his associates saw that the continuing rise in weight, cost and complexity was a worrying trend that had to be stopped. They prepared an engineering report showing that some items could be reduced and the costs of aircraft brought back to an affordable amount. These findings were shown to various representatives of the Department of Defense during their frequent visits to the factory. This view-

point was passed up the chain of command and Ed Heinemann was asked to formally present this position to the Chief of the Bureau of Aeronautics and his staff in January 1952.

Heinemann's proposal was based on achieving lower cost, weight and simplicity by better engineering, and used as its theme the factor by which an aircraft must be increased in size as

Above: Although it was the 'Blue Angels' who made the Skyhawk famous as a demonstration aircraft, a number of other units and nations have displayed the A-4 in close formation. These are the 'Air Barons' of VA-209, an Illinois-based Reserve unit showing off six of the 100 A-4Ls that were reworked from the A-4C.

Despite the lack of electronic countermeasures (ECM) equipment or radar that was fitted to later versions, the A4D-2 or A-4B saw much action over Vietnam. The early Skyhawks had only three weapons pylons, used here on this VA-95 example for two 1,000-lb bombs and a 300-US gal (1136-litre) fuel tank, and this limited the usefulness of the design in a conventional war scenario.

weight and equipment are added if performance and combat radius were to be held constant. This factor for the average jet aircraft at that time was approximately 10, meaning that for every pound of equipment weight added, the gross weight had to be increased 10 lb to maintain the desired performance. To prove his point, Heinemann submitted a design to the Bureau for an interceptor fighter which weighed only 7,000 lb (3175 kg). The members were impressed, as many had resigned themselves to this growth and complexity trend which presented severe procurement, operational and maintenance problems, as well as headaches for the designers of aircraft-carriers. Since there was, at that time, no requirement for a new interceptor in the Navy, Heinemann was asked if this philosophy could be applied to the pressing requirement of a new attack aircraft. The requirements stipulated a gross weight not exceeding 30,000 lb (13610 kg) and that the primary payload was to be an atomic bomb.

One month later, the Douglas Aircraft Company submitted an attack proposal to the US Navy that specified, among other things, that the aircraft's gross weight would be 12,000 lb (5443 kg) and that it would meet all of the desired performance criteria. During the submission's evaluation the range requirements were increased, accounting for the raising of the design gross weight to 14,000 lb (6350 kg).

Douglas Aircraft Company was given a contract for one aircraft on 12 June 1952, designated as the XA4D-1 and allocated the bureau number (BuNo.) of 137812. (This was financed by shifting funds from the cancelled A2D Skyshark contract.) That specification called for a "lightweight, single-engined, single-place, high-performance, carrier-based, day-attack land plane, capable of performing dive bombing, interdiction and close air support missions." It further stated that, "The airplane shall be capable of the delivery of conventional or special weapons and it is intended to be capable of attacking sea and land targets with or without fighter escort where control of the air has not been established." The specified empty weight was 8,136 lb (3690 kg). This compared with 13,790 lb (6255 kg) for the North American FJ-4B Fury, a contemporary aircraft that had the same engine and the same internal fuel volume.

Tailed delta

The A4D could be described as having a delta-wing configuration with a normal tail, a conventional control system, carrying a crew of one and powered by a single Wright J65-W-2 axial flow turbine engine (the Bristol Siddeley Sapphire licence-built by Curtiss-Wright). Rather than the normal folding-wing configuration to allow the aircraft to be placed on the carrier elevators for transportation between decks, the wing span was limited to 27 ft (8.2 m) to accommodate the elevator size. This structural design also saved considerable weight in hydraulics and actuators that are normally required on folding-wing designs. It also helped in the installation of a 568-US gal (2150-litre) fuel tank within the wing. A large variety of weapons or external fuel tanks could be carried externally on three underwing locations: the centreline station was capable of carrying up to 3,575 lb (1622 kg), and the outer wing racks were stressed for 1,000 lb (454 kg) each. Design gross weight with one Mk 12 weapon was 14,250 lb (6464 kg), and the combat radius with this weapon with internal fuel only was 400 miles (643 km). The design catapult weight was 19,760 lb (8963 kg). Maximum speed in the clean condition at sea level was 596 kt (Mach 0.9), while the combat ceiling at combat weight was 50,000 ft (15240 m).

The weight of the aircraft was one-half that of contemporary fighters and bombers, with one-third fewer parts than required for a 30,000-lb (13608-kg) aircraft. The target cost was $1,000,000, and the A4D-1 came in at $860,000. Maintenance was reduced 40 per cent, and overhaul time was one-half that for contemporary aircraft. The aircraft was 100 kt (185 km/h) faster than, and its radar signature 1/100th of, the specification requirements. Fuel consumption was approximately one-half of other jet aircraft.

The diminutive aircraft was officially named the Skyhawk in February 1954, while some members of the fleet called it 'the Scooter'. In deference to the designer it was also known as 'Heinemann's Hotrod'.

Although the Skyhawk was initially designed for a nuclear delivery mission, it was never used as an A-bomber. Its introduction to conventional combat occurred during the 1958 Lebanon crisis, when A-4s from US Navy Air Task Force 201 and the aircraft-carrier USS *Essex* supported troops attempting to stabilise that Middle Eastern country's civil war. The continuing possibility of US involvement in these small, contained conflicts resulted in the development efforts of the Skyhawk being redirected toward improvement of its conventional warfare capability. This process was accelerated by Communist actions in Southeast Asia.

The A4D-1 could carry up to 5,500 lb (2495 kg) of bombs or external fuel tanks on three stations. Mines, rockets or other weapons could be substituted, including a nuclear weapon weighing up to 3,500 lb (1588 kg) on the centreline station. In comparison, the last major configuration, the A-4M, has an external weight capability raised to 9,195 lb (4170 kg), an increase of 67 per cent, with stores including such guided missiles as Shrike, Maverick, Bullpup and Sidewinder.

While acknowledged as the supreme attack aircraft of its day, the Skyhawk also performed other roles in an equally outstanding manner.

Douglas had suggested almost from the initial conception that a two-place version of the A-4 was viable. However, budget limitations of the US Navy precluded the funding of the development until the realities brought on by the losses incurred in Vietnam forced an allocation of funds. One way in which to re-equip the fleet was to release the single-place A-4s from the training mission in the RAG

The conflict in Vietnam provided the spur for new, more capable versions of the Skyhawk design able to make repeated forays into heavily defended airspace. This A-4E, ready for launch from USS Hancock in the Gulf of Tonkin, does not yet have the avionics 'hump' fitted but the elongated nose carries air-to-ground radar and defensive ECM antennas, giving some measure of all-weather and self-defence capability.

A-4 Skyhawk Variants

Thousands of naval aviators have gained their wings of gold on the TA-4J in 25 years of service with Training Command. The venerable Skyhawks are being slowly phased out in favour of the McDonnell Douglas/BAe T-45A Goshawk, but are expected to soldier on until the first part of next century. This VT-24 'T-bird' is on the downwind leg for Lexington (CVT-16).

(Replacement Air Group) squadrons where pilots were brought up to speed in the use of A-4s in combat. These squadrons were tasked with teaching battle tactics and the intricacies of the aircraft systems to pilots from the training command or pilots reassigned from other duties. To release these Skyhawks for combat, it was decided to replace them with a new two-seat version that would be more effective in this type of instruction. The initial configuration of the dual-seat version retained the full ordnance capability and suffered only from the reduction in range when a 230-US gal (870-litre) fuselage tank was removed to allow space for the second crewman. Later, when it became necessary to replace the worn-out Grumman TF-9J Cougar advanced trainers in the Navy Training Command, the twin-seat A-4 was selected. That version, first delivered to the advanced training squadrons in 1969, is still in use today, although it is being replaced by the T-45 Goshawk.

The US Marine Corps also developed a special use for the two-place Skyhawks in addition to type training. The combat-equipped OA-4M version was assigned to the Marine Headquarters and Maintenance Squadrons (H&MS), acting as battlefield spotters and co-ordinators for Marine ground units, selecting and marking targets with smoke rockets. This mission was known as Fast FAC (Fast Forward Air Control).

An additional mission undertaken by the A-4

was that of aggressor aircraft. To bring the kill ratio during the Vietnam War to an acceptable figure, a special unit was formed within the US Navy in 1969. The Navy Fighter Weapons School (NFWS), better known as 'Topgun', drew on the A-4 inventory to provide a vehicle that could simulate the performance and tactics of MiG-17 aircraft used by the Soviet Bloc nations. A-4Es were used initially, configured to remove the normal bomb racks and pylons and other drag-producing elements such as the aft avionics pod. This resulted in an aircraft that could provide performance almost equal to the Navy's first-line fighter, especially at the lower altitudes. Later versions were also used in this manner, as were the TA-4s. Most of these aircraft had a distinctive colour pattern applied to provide trainees with examples of what they might meet in combat. Eventually, many other regular and reserve squadrons were assigned the task of providing the operational squadrons with aggressor training to keep their skill level high and to supplement the 'Topgun' instructions.

These A-4s also featured the special non-standard markings and colours. The result of this training was dramatic: the kill ratio of 3.5:1 in 1968 subsequently raised to 12.5:1.

'Blue Angels'

Another role that the Skyhawks filled admirably was that of flight demonstration. The most famous example of this is the Naval Flight Demonstration Squadron, better known as the 'Blue Angels', who used the A-4 for 17 years, entertaining the public in an effort to recruit new members for the US Navy and Marine Corps. Their spectacular manoeuvres flown by the ever-capable A-4F Skyhawk were seen by millions of spectators. Other units also found that the A-4 could be used in this manner. The 'Air Barons' of the US Navy Air Reserve flew A-4C and then A-4L Skyhawks for three years. Singapore's air force has also used its A-4S aircraft in a demonstration group known as the 'Black Knights', as has 'Kiwi Red' of the Royal New Zealand Air Force with its A-4Ks.

The ability of the A-4 to continually perform its missions is illustrated by the quantity of aircraft delivered. In a production run that lasted 27 years, 2,960 Skyhawks were built and delivered, mainly to the US Navy and Marine Corps. The two-seater accounted for 555 of that total. Four foreign nations also procured new aircraft from Douglas, and four others used the refurbished aircraft from US surplus stock. The export versions of the A-4 series will be covered in the next volume of *Wings of Fame*.
Harry S.Gann

In October 1962 the US Department of Defense changed the US Navy aircraft designation system to one similar to that of the USAF. This affected the Skyhawk model designations as follows:

System prior to 1962	System after 1962
A4D-1	A-4A
A4D-2	A-4B
A4D-2N	A-4C
A4D-3	not built
A4D-4	not built
A4D-5	A-4E

Note: A-4D not used in new system, A-4F and later did not have prior designations.

During production and in service, the Marine Corps' A-4M received a variety of upgrades. This early A-4M with the original fin-tip is dropping an AGM-62 Walleye TV-guided bomb.

THE TEAM LEADER: EDWARD H. HEINEMANN

Edward H. Heinemann, who was responsible for the concept and design of the A-4 Skyhawk, was a gifted, self-taught engineer who took a hands-on approach to all phases of the development of his creations, including the marketing. He had the rare ability to predict the services' requirements and then sell them on his designs. Some of this ability, no doubt, was acquired from his boss of the early 1930s, the legendary John K. Northrop (who was also a non-degree-holding engineer). Northrop recognised the abilities of Heinemann and assigned him to responsible positions within his company, which became a subsidiary of the Douglas Aircraft Corporation. At an early age of 25, Heinemann was directed to develop the XFT-1, 3A fighters and the BT-1 divebomber. In 1937, he was promoted to Chief Engineer of the Northrop division. In 1938 Douglas restructured the division and renamed it the El Segundo Division of Douglas Aircraft. The development of the BT-1 continued as the SBD Dauntless. Almost 6,000 of these dive-bombers were built and are credited with a major share of stopping the Japanese forces in the Pacific during World War II. Heinemann's other World War II designs that followed the SBD were the DB-7/A-20 and the A-26 twin-engined attack bombers. Ten thousand of these attack aircraft were built and used by all of the Allied forces. The A-26 continued its service through the Vietnam conflict. After World War II, Heinemann was directed by Douglas to concentrate his efforts at El Segundo on products for the US Navy and the Marine Corps; other Douglas facilities at Long Beach and Santa Monica, California concentrated on USAF-directed products or on transports.

The AD Skyraider was the first of Heinemann's designs to follow this direction, and it further enhanced his reputation for simplified construction in order to meet the rigid requirements of the US Navy and successfully accomplish its missions. The Skyraider served in many roles, but its primary one was that of attack aircraft. Of the 3,180 built, many were modified to be used in all-weather attack, airborne early warning, electronic countermeasures, and carrier replenishment roles. The US Air Force obtained some examples from the Navy and used them in its 'Sandy' operations, where they escorted rescue helicopters picking up downed aircrew. With their relatively long endurance, the ADs could stay on station while the helicopters accomplished their retrieval efforts and could provide protection from the enemy by expending some of the bombs and rockets carried on the external wing stations.

Heinemann's first production jet was the F3D Skyknight, an all-weather, two-seat, twin-jet fighter. Initially used in Korea, the Skyknight was used successfully by shore-based US Marines to detect and rid the skies of night raiders. Its versatility was enhanced when the F3D airframe was modified for use as an ECM aircraft; it was the Marines' first-line platform in this mission until replaced by the Grumman EA-6 aircraft in the late 1960s.

One of the more innovative carrier-based

The Skyhawk was in service for 10 years before a two-seat version arrived, and the development of the TA-4F increased its versatility and marketability. Prior to this the export market had been dormant, partly due to the lack of a variant for training and operational conversion.

aircraft was also the design of Heinemann. This was the A3D Skywarrior, intended to provide the US Navy with the capability for world-wide nuclear strike. The Skywarrior proposal was submitted in response to a specification that listed the maximum gross weight as 100,000 lb (45360 kg). Heinemann brought the design in at 70,000 lb (31750 kg) and met all of the specified performance criteria. In addition to performing as a heavy attacker, the aircraft functioned as long-range reconnaissance and ECM platforms, systems trainers, inflight tankers and VIP transports. The A3D and the A4D gave Douglas the distinction of providing the US Navy with both the largest and the smallest carrier-based jet aircraft.

Heinemann's F4D Skyray carrier-based interceptor-fighter was the first-line Navy and US Marine fighter during the late 1950s, and shared some of the systems installed in the Skyhawk. It set the world absolute speed record and many time-to-climb records.

Heinemann was also responsible for a series of high-speed research aircraft, the D-558 Skystreak and the D-558-II Skyrocket. In a joint NACA-US Navy programme, they were used to explore the outer edges of aircraft speed and altitude performance. The Skystreak also set an official world absolute speed record on two occasions, while the Skyrocket was the first aircraft to attain Mach 2, as well as reaching previously unattainable altitudes.

He also designed ancillary products including ejection seats, special external stores such as refuelling (buddy system) pods, streamlined shapes for a family of fuel tanks, and many low-drag bomb racks. Heinemann had a far-reaching influence on the progression of aircraft technology. He was awarded many pres-

tigious honours, including the Collier Trophy. One of his personal delights was the fact that most naval aviators from World War II until the present have flown Heinemann-designed aircraft. During the 1950s and 1960s, there were instances of carrier deployments where all the aircraft (with the exception of the light photo and carrier resupply aircraft) were designed by Heinemann.

Edward H. Heinemann passed away on 26 November 1991, at the age of 83. He was the last of the first generation of super aircraft designers.

Ed Heinemann stands with the last of nearly 3,000 A-4s built, in 1979. The A-4's designer made only one Skyhawk flight, from Miramar over Catalina Island in 1974.

XA4D-1

The first Skyhawk was initially designated as XA4D-1. As a result of the mock-up board meeting in October 1952 to review the proposed design, it was decided to order an additional 19 aircraft. These were to be built with production tooling rather than the 'soft tooling' normally used in experimental aircraft. The initial aircraft had the benefit of this production system and, after some flights, the 'X' was quietly dropped from the designation. The first 20 aircraft were essentially identical.

The initial configuration of the Skyhawk fuselage had a shortened tail pipe resembling that of the Grumman F9F Panther. This was changed to the extended configuration prior to production. The wing design was unique in that it did not fold, although that was a typical feature of carrier-based aircraft. The length of the wing span was dictated by the size of the elevators that carry the aircraft from below deck to the launching deck. The 27-ft (8.2-m) overall span of the A-4 eliminated the need for the folding mechanism, thus saving valuable weight both in mechanisms and hydraulics. The delta-shaped wing formed a single box with integral fuel tankage, and the upper and lower skins were single pieces measuring 27 ft x 8 ft x 0.064 in (8.2 m x 2.4 m x 0.16 cm) each. The spars and stringers are continuous from tip to tip, with the spar machined from 2-in (5-cm) thick plate.

The XA4D-1 was fabricated and assembled at El Segundo, California and trucked to Edwards AFB, 100 miles (160 km) north of the factory for first flight by Douglas engineering test pilot Bob Rahn. 137812 was flown from the Edwards dry lake bed on 22 June 1954, just two years after the go-ahead was given.

US Navy/Marines Bureau Number:
137812

Above: When the XA4D-1 first flew, on 22 June 1954, it had gained a ventral blade aerial. The test boom measured static pressure as well as pitch and yaw.

Top: The XA4D-1 is seen in front of the Douglas plant at El Segundo, which was still building piston-engined Skyraiders in 1954. The aircraft is so well finished that the fuselage-mounted airbrake is virtually invisible. Brown paper covers the designation/Bureau Number panel for 'security reasons'.

Right: By late in the XA4D-1's career, most production features had been fitted: the tailhook, jetpipe fairing, vortex generators and all three weapons pylons.

Douglas XA4D-1

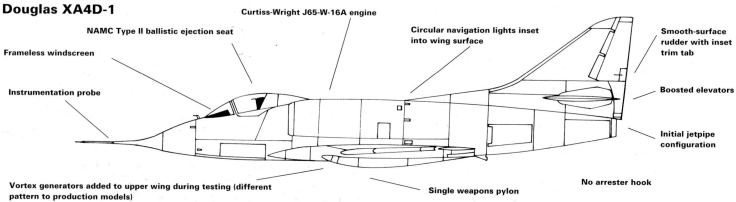

NAMC Type II ballistic ejection seat

Curtiss-Wright J65-W-16A engine

Circular navigation lights inset into wing surface

Smooth-surface rudder with inset trim tab

Frameless windscreen

Instrumentation probe

Boosted elevators

Initial jetpipe configuration

Vortex generators added to upper wing during testing (different pattern to production models)

Single weapons pylon

No arrester hook

A4D-1 (A-4A)

The first A4D-1 (BuNo. 137813) flew on 14 August 1954, just two months after the prototype's first flight. It became a mainstay in the flight test programme to prove the aircraft could meet the objectives of the US Navy and the Marine Corps. 137813 subsequently accumulated 319 test hours in 326 flights, demonstrating aerodynamic features as well as aircraft systems. At the completion of its service life, the aircraft was put on display at the National Museum of Naval Aviation at Pensacola, Florida. Of the first 19 A4D-1 aircraft, nine were used in the extensive flight test programme.

During the two years of this testing, it was decided that one way to demonstrate the Skyhawk's capability was to break one of the international airspeed records. The 500-km (310-mile) closed-course record was chosen, then held by the USAF in a North American F-86H Sabre at a speed of 649.46 mph (1045.18 km/h). Navy test pilot Lieutenant Gordon Gray was selected to pilot A4D-1 BuNo. 137820 on the speed run. A 12-pylon course of 100-km (62-mile) circumference was set up on the California desert near Edwards AFB, and on 15 October 1955 Gray flew five laps at an altitude of 100 m (328 ft) at a certified speed of 695.163 mph (1118.73 km/h). Thus, the Skyhawk became the first attack aircraft to hold this record.

The first factory-to-fleet delivery of the A4D was made in October 1956 to the 'Blue Hawks' of US Navy Attack Squadron 72 (VA-72). US Marine Attack Squadron 224 (VMA-224) also received A4D-1s in 1956, to initiate the new aircraft into the Corps. Soon, many other units began receiving the A4D-1; VA-93, the 'Blue Blazers', became the first fleet squadron to operate A4Ds on the West Coast and to deploy to the western Pacific Ocean aboard the carrier USS *Ticonderoga* (CVA-14) in September 1957.

Eventually, 18 US Navy and Marine Corps attack squadrons operated A4D-1s, of which 165 were built. As this version was phased out of the fleet operational units, they were assigned to Navy and Marine Reserve squadrons. Some of these aircraft were redesignated as TA-4A during the Vietnam conflict. There were no changes to the aircraft. The redesignation was made to reflect the lack of added capability of later versions and to reduce the apparent attack inventory in an effort to procure more aircraft for Vietnam action.

US Navy/Marines Bureau Numbers:
Some redesignated as TA-4A

Amount	from	to
19	137813	137831
52	139919	139970
94	142142	142235
TOTAL: 165		

Marine Attack Squadron 224, the 'Bengals', was the first of dozens of A-4 units in nine countries. Notable here are the original smooth rudder, and the characteristic overflow oil stain from the J65.

Some of the conventional and 'special' weapons available to the A4D-1 are shown here (left to right): 150-US gal (568-litre) fuel tank, Mk 84 bomb, Mk 82, Mk 83, Mk 12 'Brok' nuclear bomb, Mk8 (TX-8-X2) nuclear bomb, 300-US gal (1136-litre) fuel tank, Mk 7 nuclear bomb, possibly Mk 91 nuclear bomb, RCPP-105 external power unit, AERO 6A rocket pod, 150-US gal fuel tank.

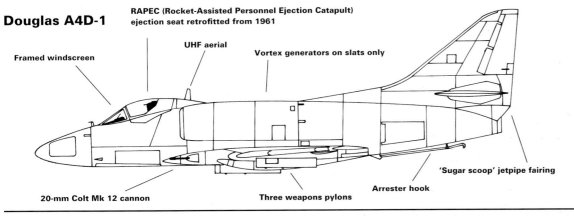

Douglas A4D-1

RAPEC (Rocket-Assisted Personnel Ejection Catapult) ejection seat retrofitted from 1961

UHF aerial

Vortex generators on slats only

Framed windscreen

20-mm Colt Mk 12 cannon

Three weapons pylons

Arrester hook

'Sugar scoop' jetpipe fairing

The third A4D broke the 500-km closed-course speed record in October 1955. At this time, it had no hook, wing pylons or 'sugar scoop'.

A4D-2 (A-4B)

Before initial deliveries of the A4D-1 were made to the fleet, an improved version had already been ordered into production. Developed to meet more demanding requirements regarding range and navigational capability, the A4D-2 was first flown on 26 March 1956 by Douglas test pilot Drury Wood. Twenty-eight per cent of the structure had been modified to incorporate desired improvements. The most notable external additions were the inflight-refuelling probe added to the right side of the fuselage, and stiffening of the rudder by building it 'inside out' with the ribs showing and bonding it together, rather than by rivetting. This arrangement, known as a tadpole rudder, reduced the tendency of the trailing edge of the rudder to vibrate like a tuning fork at high speeds, thus creating fatigue cracks.

Additional navigational equipment, coupled with provisions for carrying 300-US gal (1136-litre) external tanks and a refuelling probe, provided for longer-range flights on special weapon and strike missions. The ordnance delivery system was improved by addition of the Bullpup air-to-ground, piloted guided missile capability, in addition to an improved bomb delivery system. Additional improvements were made to the flight control systems. The landing gear was strengthened and a pressure fuelling system was added. A4D-2 production totalled 542 aircraft. Fleet introduction of the new Skyhawk model began with VMA-211 in September 1957.

As was the A4D-1, some A4D-2 Skyhawks were redesignated as TA-4B after assignment to the US Navy and Marine Corps Reserve units to reflect their training mission. No physical changes were made to the aircraft. Some A4D-2 aircraft were made available for use by the

An A4D-2 'belonging' to the CAG of USS Essex sits on the ramp at El Centro at an air gunnery meet with its fighter counterpart, the (Heinemann-designed) Douglas F4D Skyray. The Skyray was about 20 per cent larger than the Skyhawk but had almost twice the empty weight.

Argentine air force and naval air units (see the A-4P and A-4Q).

US Navy/Marines Bureau Numbers:
Some to TA-4B, A-4P and A-4Q

Amount	from	to
60	142082	142141
8	142416	142423
280	142674	142953
194	144868	145061
TOTAL: 542		

The A-4B was the first version with the familiar 'inside-out' rudder and the first with refuelling (dispensing as well as receiving) capability.

Douglas A4D-2

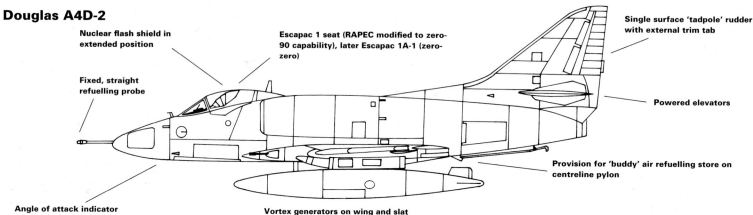

Nuclear flash shield in extended position

Escapac 1 seat (RAPEC modified to zero-90 capability), later Escapac 1A-1 (zero-zero)

Single surface 'tadpole' rudder with external trim tab

Fixed, straight refuelling probe

Powered elevators

Provision for 'buddy' air refuelling store on centreline pylon

Angle of attack indicator

Vortex generators on wing and slat

Left: The raison d'être of the Skyhawk's design was the carriage of the new class of small nuclear weapons. The A4D-1 could carry a bomb of up to 3,375 lb (1531kg) on the centreline station. Delivery methods ranged from high-altitude dive bombing to loft (or 'toss') bombing in a pull-up from low altitude, to lay-down bombing from very low level with a delayed action bomb. Naturally, most of the mission plans involved carrier launch, but the Naval Air Test Center trialled jet-assisted take-off (JATO) rockets as a means of launching from land bases quickly.

As the A-4C replaced the A-4B in the fleet, the earlier models were sent to reserve and training units, and often redesignated as TA-4Bs.

A4D-2N (A-4C)

The Douglas engineering staff constantly worked to improve the performance of the Skyhawk. New requirements were being generated by users and passed through channels to the Bureau of Weapons (formerly BuAer). One specific addition requested to the capability of the Skyhawk was greater range through foul weather and shrouded terrain. Radar was needed to penetrate beyond mountainous areas, and improved instrumentation – as well as an autopilot – were needed for increased instrument flight capability.

The Navy had developed an all-attitude bombing and navigational system which appeared to be an improvement. Douglas submitted a proposal for the A4D-3 to meet these requirements. It was to be powered with a new engine being developed for the Grumman A-6A: the Pratt & Whitney J52. The specific fuel consumption of the J52 was less than the Curtiss-Wright J65 of the earlier Skyhawks, while the maximum thrust generated was increased from 7,700 to 8,500 lb (34.25 to 37.81 kN). Orders for four aircraft were let on a development contract; however, development costs of the engine and the avionics could not be fitted into the austerity of the Navy

This test A4D-2N carries three AGM-12 Bullpup command-guidance air-to-surface missiles, a weapon used widely by A-4s in Vietnam.

procurement budget, and the A4D-3 was cancelled before production was initiated.

To fulfil the requirements for additional aircraft within the framework of the budget restrictions, a compromise aircraft was developed. Designated A4D-2N (A-4C), it retained the J65 engine but added a fairly sophisticated aircraft autopilot, a low-altitude bombing, all-attitude indicating gyro system, a terrain-clearance radar and an angle-of-attack indicating system. The aircraft was flown on 21 August 1958 and became operational in February 1960 with VMA-225. By December 1962, the last of the 638 A4D-2Ns had been delivered to the fleet. To fulfil a requirement for the US Navy and Marine Reserves, 100 A-4Cs were altered to the A-4L configuration. Some A-4C and A-4L Skyhawks were also transferred to foreign air units (Argentina, Singapore and Malaysia).

US Navy/Marines Bureau Numbers:
See also A-4L, A-4P, A-4Q, A-4S and A-4PTM

Amount	from	to
85	145062	145146
0	146460	146693
	CANCELLED	
181	147669	147849
14	148304	148317
178	148435	148612
160	149487	148646
20	150581	150600
TOTAL: 638		

The changing role of the Skyhawk is illustrated by the weapons loadout on this VA-46 'Clansmen' A-4C. All these weapons are conventional, with bombs from 250 lb (113 kg) to 2,000 lb (907 kg), three types of rocket pod, Bullpup AGMs and a pair of AIM-9 Sidewinder air-to-air missiles.

Douglas A4D-2N

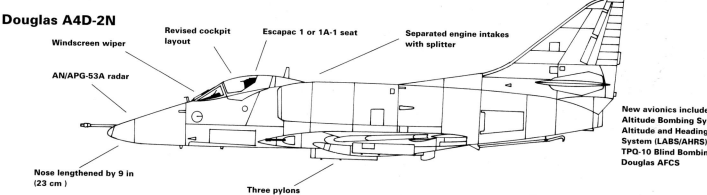

Windscreen wiper

AN/APG-53A radar

Revised cockpit layout

Escapac 1 or 1A-1 seat

Separated engine intakes with splitter

New avionics include: AJE-3 Low Altitude Bombing System/ Altitude and Heading Reference System (LABS/AHRS); TPQ-10 Blind Bombing System; Douglas AFCS

Nose lengthened by 9 in (23 cm)

Three pylons

Relatively few single-seat Skyhawks flew with training units. This A-4C of VT-86 in 1973 has no guns and an A-4E/F-type antenna under the nose. Also seen is the A-4's distinctive boarding ladder – TA-4s often used one with a longer platform.

The stalky undercarriage of the A-4 caused tricky crosswind handling. Nosewheel steering was not introduced until the TA-4F model.

The last A-4Cs in US service were used by the private company Flight Systems Inc. on a variety of government contracts.

In addition to the attack role, the **A-4C** served briefly as a dedicated fighter in a small number of VSF (anti-submarine fighter) squadrons. This VSF-1 A-4C is seen on USS Independence prior to a Vietnam deployment in 1967.

Many A-4s received the 'N' prefix to their designation signifying an aircraft so modified for test purposes that it could not be practically returned to the active inventory. This is a Naval Air Development Center NA-4C.

A4D-5 (A-4E)

Again, even before the A4D-2N flew, new requirements were being generated by the fleet. It appeared that the tactics of putting all the eggs in the single 'A-bomb basket' may have been premature. Iron bombs and guns were still necessary in the environment created by the world-wide brush fires. The basic A-4 design was flexible enough that its capability as a conventional weapons carrier could be greatly enhanced. Discussion between Douglas and Navy personnel turned into specifics and a formal proposal was submitted in February 1959. Authority to proceed was given on 30 July 1959 and the existing A4D-2N contract was altered to allow the delivery of two aircraft as A4D-5s.

The changes agreed upon consisted of the substitution of the Pratt & Whitney J52 for the Curtiss-Wright J65, as proposed in the cancelled A4D-3. In addition to its 800 lb (3.5 kN) of additional thrust, the J52-P6A was 770 lb (350 kg) lighter and used less fuel. More importantly, the J52 was a new design and its growth potential was much greater than the older J65, which was out of production. Installation of the J52 in the airframe required a redesign of the centre fuselage and inlet ducting.

Above right: This is the second A-4E, one of only eight aircraft to actually carry the A4D-5 designation. The extra wing stations on the E allowed for a wide range of weapons and fuel options.

Below: As delivered, the A-4E was still a simple aircraft, not that much better equipped than its big brother, the R4D-8 Super Dakota. The A-4 may well exceed the Dakota's longevity in world military service.

Below right: The Marines flew many close support missions in Vietnam from the limited facilities at Chu Lai. Here they perfected operation of SATS (Short Airfield for Tactical Support), a ground catapult system.

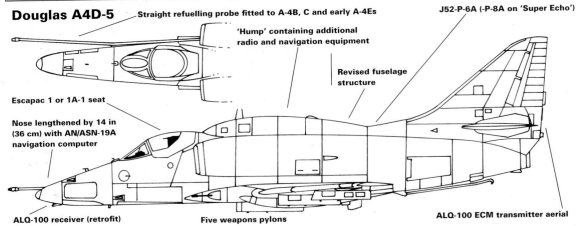

Douglas A4D-5

Straight refuelling probe fitted to A-4B, C and early A-4Es

J52-P-6A (-P-8A on 'Super Echo')

'Hump' containing additional radio and navigation equipment

Revised fuselage structure

Escapac 1 or 1A-1 seat

Nose lengthened by 14 in (36 cm) with AN/ASN-19A navigation computer

ALQ-100 receiver (retrofit)

Five weapons pylons

ALQ-100 ECM transmitter aerial

To increase the armament-carrying capability, two additional external hardpoints were added to the existing three stations on the delta-winged Skyhawk. The airframe structure was strengthened to increase the catapult gross weight to 24,500 lb (11113 kg). New equipment installed included TACAN, Doppler navigation, Mk 9 toss-bombing system, radio altimeter and the AJB-3A low-altitude bombing system.

First flight of this version was on 12 July 1961. By this time, the order for modification of two A4D-2Ns had been augmented by a production contract. When the last aircraft left the factory, 500 A-4E Skyhawks had joined the units of the US Navy and Marine Corps.

When the Pratt & Whitney J52-P8A with 9,300 lb (41.37 kN) of thrust became available, some A-4Es were equipped with this engine in place of the P6A. Although no official letter designator was applied to this

version, they were unofficially referred to as 'Super Echos'. Another item later installed on the fleet A-4Es was the upper avionics pod developed initially for the A-4F. This also did not carry a designation update.

The A-4E entered service with the 'Black Knights' of VA-23 in January 1963.

US Navy/Marines Bureau Numbers:

Some were transferred to Israel and then to Indonesia

Amount	from	to
2	148613	148614
20	149647	149666
180	149959	150138
180	151022	151201
0	151202	151261
	CANCELLED	
118	151984	152101
	152101	
	converted to prototype A-4F	

TOTAL: 500

Top: Early A-4Es like this VA-55 aircraft were distinguishable from the C model by the nose profile, intake splitter plate and lack of a windscreen wiper. Later, the aircraft were retrofitted with avionics humps and bent refuelling probes.

Left: Jet-Assisted Take-Off (JATO) equipment could be fitted to production A-4s from the A-4C on. The large bottles attached to clips on the airbrakes and significantly reduced the (already short) take-off run.

Above: The A-4E was the first Skyhawk to be used as adversary aircraft by the Navy Fighter Weapons School ('Topgun'). Those aircraft fitted with the P-408 engine were unofficially called 'Super Echoes'.

Below: The A-4E incorporated more changes from the previous model than any other variant. The long nose, dorsal hump and cranked refuelling probe were the main visible differences, but the new engine was the most significant.

Douglas A-4E Skyhawk VA-72 'Blue Hawks' USS *Independence* South China Sea May 1965

Armament

In addition to the fixed armament of a pair of Colt 20-mm Mk 12 cannon mounted in the wingroots and staggered to provide clearance for the magazines, this A-4E carries six 500-lb Snakeye bombs. They allowed the aircraft to outpace the blast, thus permitting delivery from lower level than with normal 'slick' bombs. The A-4 could carry conventional bombs as large as 3,000 lb (1361 kg), but only on the centreline pylon. The total warload of the A-4E was in the order of 9,900 lb (4500 kg), although fuel tanks of (typically) 150-US gal (568-litre) and 400-US gal (1514-litre) capacity were often carried on the centreline and inboard pylons respectively.

The 'Blue Hawks'

VA-72 was the first Navy unit to operate the A-4, receiving A4D-1s in September 1956. The squadron nickname at the time was 'Skyhawks', but this was changed to 'Blue Hawks' when the A-4 adopted the name. The A-4Es of VA-72 undertook two Vietnam deployments: on *Independence* from May to December 1965, and from June 1966 to February 1967 on the *Franklin D. Roosevelt*, after which the squadron traded down to the A-4B. VA-72 had transitioned to the A-7B Corsair II by September 1970 and was the last fleet users of the A-7 when disestablished in June 1991 following the Gulf War.

Undercarriage

To Ed Heinemann's annoyance, the Navy, concerned about swept-wing jets dragging their tails, insisted on a tall spindly undercarriage for the A-4. This arrangement adversely affected the Skyhawk's crosswind handling but provided a greater ground angle of attack and thus better take-off performance. To maintain the integrity of the wing structure, the main gear legs retracted into fairings with the wheels lying forwards of the fuel tank box. Forward-retracting gear would lock into the extended position with gravity and airflow, which reduced the demands on the hydraulic system and saved weight and complexity.

A-4E

The A-4E was the first Skyhawk variant to be powered by the Pratt & Whitney J52, which provided another 700 lb (3.1 kN) static thrust compared to the Wright J65. The higher-thrust but lower-weight J52 increased the maximum take-off weight by 2,000 lb (907 kg), which allowed the provision of two extra outboard pylons, found on all subsequent new-build models except the TA-4J. The main recognition features for the early A-4E without avionics hump compared to the A-4C are the longer nose with ECM receiver antenna, and the separated engine intakes.

Wing

The Skyhawk's wing is essentially a cropped delta only 27 ft 6 in (8.38 m), the A-4's wingspan was le than that of a Sopwith Camel, and, more importan less than the aperture of the deck elevators on US carriers. The wing was immensely strong, being b as a one piece unit tip-to-tip and serving as a giant integral fuel tank. The oval panels allowed access the tank interior during strip-down maintenance. Spoilers to dump lift on landing were added inboard of the ailerons from the A-4F model onwards.

A-4F

Continued usage of the A-4 as the prime Navy and Marine attack aircraft in Vietnam resulted in operational losses. To replace these aircraft, the A-4F was ordered in 1965. The A-4F was similar to the A-4E except that it incorporated the nosewheel steering, lift spoilers, Escapac 1C-3 ejection seat and the uprated J52-P8A engine introduced in the TA-4F. The A-4F (which was revised from the last A-4E airframe, BuNo. 152101) first flew on 31 August 1966.

One improvement later added to the 'Foxtrot' was an upper avionics pod. Kits were supplied for aircraft already delivered to the fleet, and those aircraft not delivered were modified at the plant. The pod consisted of a compartment added to the top of the fuselage aft of the canopy which provided for the installation of special electronics gear dictated by the requirements of the Vietnam War. This location was selected because the internal space of the compact Skyhawk was so completely occupied that the addition of any more equipment would have been nearly impossible, as would its access for maintenance.

This pod was also retrofitted to all operational A-4E and some A-4C aircraft. This A-4C installation was a part of the A-4L modification.

Another revision to the A-4F was made in the form of an engine change. Douglas supplied 100 kits to enable the Navy's rework facility to replace the Pratt & Whitney J52-P8A engine with the J52-P408, thus increasing the thrust to 11,200 lb (49.82 kN). The performance of the already nimble A-4 was appreciably increased. After seeing combat, this configured A-4 was used by the 'Blue Angels' demonstration team, and performed some adversary duties as well as joining the USMC Reserve forces.

Production aircraft were initially delivered to the 'Black Knights' of VA-23 and the 'Blue Blazers' of VA-93, assigned to Carrier Air Wing 19 (CVW-19) which deployed to WESTPAC and the Southeast Asia area in late 1967 on the USS *Ticonderoga* (CVA-14). Including one aircraft revised as an A-4E, the production run of the A-4F totalled 147. Two of these airframes were later converted to A-4Ms (BuNos 155042 and 155049).

US Navy/Marines Bureau Numbers:
(1) 152101 Converted from A-4E

Amount	from	to
46	154172	154217
100	154970	155069
	155042,	155049

Converted to prototype A-4Ms
155051, 52, 55, and 60 through 155064 delivered to Royal Australian Navy as A-4G
TOTAL: 146

Stripped of combat equipment such as guns and ECM kit, and fitted with the J52-P-408 engine, the A-4F 'Super Fox' made an extremely nimble adversary aircraft. This aircraft was from VF-43, based at Oceana.

This A-4F belonging to Reserve unit VFC-13 'Saints' retained the ALR-45 antenna on the fin, while losing its hump. Note the false canopy on the nosewheel door, designed to confuse opponents in ACM training.

Douglas A-4F

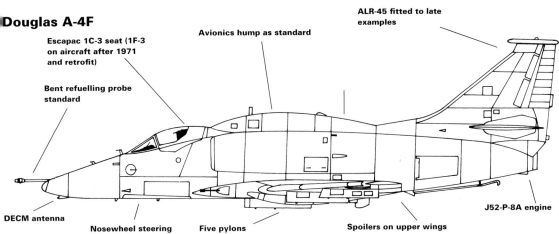

- **Escapac 1C-3 seat** (1F-3 on aircraft after 1971 and retrofit)
- **Bent refuelling probe standard**
- **Avionics hump as standard**
- **ALR-45 fitted to late examples**
- **DECM antenna**
- **Nosewheel steering**
- **Five pylons**
- **Spoilers on upper wings**
- **J52-P-8A engine**

Above: As delivered, the A-4F carried the avionics hump and chin antenna as seen on this anti-radar configured aircraft during the Vietnam War.

VMA-142 'Flying Gators' operated the A-4F and the A-4M before transitioning to the F/A-18 in 1990. The markings and camouflage seen here are unusual for a regular attack unit. This aircraft represents the ultimate configuration of the A-4F.

Above: The pilot of this VA-22 A-4F is wearing a full pressure helmet. Note the cannon and the shield to prevent gun gases entering the intake.

Below: This NA-4F is fitted with a variety of non-standard aerials. Test units continued to use early A-4s long after phase-out by the Fleet.

A-4F 'Blue Angels'

During the 'Blue Angels' 1973 show season, a decision was made to re-equip with the A-4F Skyhawk aircraft. This was predicated on the need to reduce the funds required to sustain the operation of the flight demonstration team. Expected savings were to be made in maintenance and operational cost, especially in fuel usage. In addition, a tragic accident had taken the lives of three of the team members in a mid-air collision of two of the McDonnell Douglas F-4J Phantom II aircraft that had been the assigned aircraft since 1969. This accident hastened the change to the lighter, more easily maintained A-4.

The timing was just right for the switch. McDonnell Douglas had supplied 147 A-4Fs to the Navy and had provided 100 kits to replace the Pratt & Whitney J52-P8 engines with the J52-P408 powerplant, which resulted in a thrust gain of about 2,000 lb (8.9 kN). This power increase was obtained without the use of a fuel-guzzling afterburner. At this time, the US Navy was replacing the last of the A-4s in the carrier air wings with the LTV A-7, which made the A-4Fs available to the 'Blue Angels'.

Airframes were identified and eight were sent to the Douglas plant in Long Beach in late 1973 for modification to meet the 'Blue Angel' requirements. The changes were of a minor nature and consisted of: deletion of the aft avionics package (this was an add-on to the A-4F after initial fleet deliveries); addition of a drag chute, additional load feel bungees to provide demonstration flight stick force, a smoke system, an inverted fuel system, and a foldable ladder for crew entry at left gun position; alterations to the pilot's restraint harness, and to the horizontal stabiliser actuator to provide 3° nose-down trim; and bolting wing slats in the closed position.

A new TA-4J aircraft (BuNo. 158722) was also delivered to the team to provide for the narrator's flight programme and various logistical duties. Other than the drag chute, the foldable ladder and the 'Blue Angel' markings, this two-seat A-4 was similar to that used in training command aircraft.

The A-4s provided yeoman service for the squadron (the team was officially designated a squadron in early 1974 under the leadership of then-Commander Tony Less). The Skyhawks were not relieved until the season of 1987 after 13 years of operation, when they were replaced by the F/A-18 Hornet, another McDonnell Douglas product.

During the 13 years that the A-4s served the 'Blue Angels', 18 different single-seat Skyhawk II aircraft were used. One TA-4J was assigned to the team, and three other two-seat Skyhawks were used temporarily during heavy maintenance of the prime aircraft. At the completion of their tour with

Below: The leading edge slats of the 'Blues' Skyhawks were fixed shut to prevent asymmetric operation whilst flying tight formations such as this. The aircraft were sometimes known as 'Skyhawk IIs'.

the NFDS, four single-seat A-4s were reassigned to adversary squadrons and the trainer was reassigned to Training Command. One aircraft went to the Museum of Flight at Seattle, Washington for display. Three of the aircraft are on display at the National Museum of Naval Aviation at Pensacola, Florida. In addition, there are many A-4s painted to represent the 'Blue Angels' that are on display in various locations in the United States.

US Navy Bureau Numbers of Aircraft Assigned to the 'Blue Angels':
A-4F INITIAL
154176, 154177, 154179, 154975, 154983, 154984,

Above: Differences to the 'Blue Angels' A-4Fs were relatively minor, but this version introduced several features to Skyhawk production, such as the P-408 engine and the braking parachute.

154986 and 155029.
A-4F REPLACEMENTS
154202, 155056, 155033, 154180, 154172, 154217, 154992, 154211, 155000, and 154973
TA-4J PERMANENT
158722
TA-4J TEMPORARY ASSIGNED
158107, 153477 and 153667

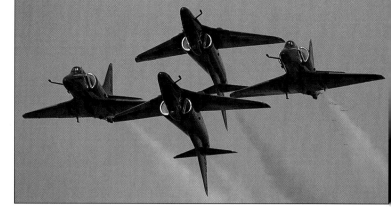

TA-4E/TA-4F

During the continual discussions between Douglas and the Navy, the subject of a two-seat model (referred to as the A4D-5T in correspondence) of the Skyhawk was constantly being raised. It was suggested that this configuration would be ideal for advanced navigational, type training or familiarisation, or some combat missions where an additional pilot or eyes might be advantageous. However, budget limitations precluded any orders for such an aircraft until 1964, when the Navy convinced the Department of Defense that money should be allotted for buying a two-seat version. The convincing argument, in addition to these obvious training advantages, was that single-seat Skyhawks used in training could be released for combat duty in Vietnam, where they were sorely needed at that time. As a result, the existing A-4E contract was altered to specify that the last two

single-seat Skyhawks, BuNos 152102 and 152103, would be taken off the production line and modified into two-seat aircraft and designated as TA-4E.

In addition to the 28-in (71-cm) fuselage plug added for the second seat and the necessary dual controls and instruments, it was decided to add a few other improvements at the same time. Probably one of the more important alterations was the installation of the new Douglas-designed ejection seat, the Escapac 1C-3. The rocket-driven seat allowed either one or both of the two crewman to eject from a disabled aircraft while at ground altitude and with zero forward velocity. This feature greatly improved the chances of a safe egress.

Another improvement added to this version was the installation of wing lift spoilers on the upper trailing edge of the wing. Because of the geometry of the Skyhawk landing gear arrangement, the crosswind characteristics could be a

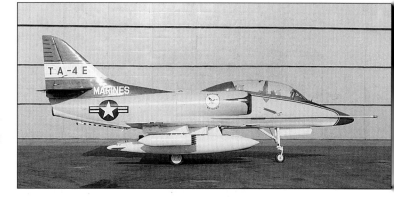

The first 'two-holer' A-4 was in fact a wooden forward fuselage mounted on a surplus single-seat airframe. The aircraft was exhibited at the Paris air show and helped drum up interest in the A-4 in potential export markets.

Douglas TA-4F

Escapac 1C-3 seats (1F-3 retrofit)

Two-seat cockpit with dual controls and enlarged canopy

Straight-framed windscreen

Fuselage lengthened by 28 in (71 cm)

J52-P8-A engine

Five weapons pylons

Spoilers above flaps

The actual two-seat prototype was TA-4E 152102, seen here with an unusual load of four AIM-9 Sidewinders. Only the first two aircraft were designated TA-4E.

Below left: Each of the four marine air wings had a unit tasked with fast FAC. In MAW-3 this was H&MS-13, three of whose TA-4Fs are shown in experimental colours in 1977, together with an example in the standard USN/USMC scheme.

Bottom: The TA-4F (or NTA-4F) was popular with test units such as the Naval Weapons Center (NWC), one of whose aircraft is seen here with a HARM missile seeker fitted into the nose.

problem to neophyte pilots when forced to use runways not aligned with the direction of the prevailing wind. The use of the lift spoiler allowed the pilot to remove the lift component which provided greater effectiveness of the brakes. As a bonus, the added drag of the spoilers in the airflow reduced the landing rollout. Nosewheel steering by the pilots was also added to allow for better control during crosswind taxiing and ramp or carrier deck manoeuvring.

The latest version of the Pratt & Whitney J52, developing 9,300 lb (41.37 kN) of static thrust, an increase of 800 lb (3.56 kN) over the P6A, was selected to power the aircraft.

BuNo. 152102 first flew 30 June 1965 and was designated as TA-4E. However, the designation was shortly afterwards changed to TA-4F in view of the many improvement to the basic A-4E airframe. The TA-4F became operational in May 1966 with the 'Roughriders' of VA-125 at NAS Lemoore in California. VA-125 was a squadron within Replacement Carrier Wing 12 (RCVW-12) and its function was to train combat pilots in the A-4. These pilots were just out of Training Command, veteran pilots being reassigned from other types of aircraft, or A-4 squadrons or ex-A-4 drivers who needed to requalify in the Skyhawk.

The production run of the TA-4Fs totalled 241, including the two aircraft originally ordered as TA-4Es. Many of the TA-4Fs were later converted to the TA-4J configuration during an overhaul cycle and reassigned to the Training Command to supplement the advanced trainer Skyhawks.

One of the many uses of the TA-4F was in a fast forward air control mission (Fast FAC) for the USMC. This was to serve as the 'eyes' to direct the Marine pilots and aircraft in pinpointing targets. They served with Marine Headquarters and Maintenance Squadrons (H&MS), later to be changed to Marine Aviation Logistics Squadrons (MALS). Twenty-three of these aircraft were also modified to the OA-4M configuration.

Another modification was redesignated as the EA-4F. These aircraft were used by Navy squadrons such as VAQ-33 to help 'exercise' the radar operators assigned to the surface fleet.

US Navy/Marines Bureau Numbers:

Amount	from	to
TA-4E		
2	152102	153103
Redesignated as TA-4F		

TA-4F
Most TA-4F converted to TA-4J, 23 TA-4F converted to OA-4M, 4 aircraft redesignated as EA-4F

33	152846	152878
31	153660	153690
73	153459	153531
57	154287	154343
44	154614	154657

154647 and 154648 delivered to Royal Australian Navy as TA-4G

1	155071	

TOTAL: 241

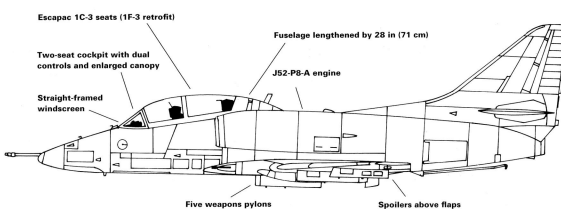

A-4 Skyhawk Variants

EA-4F

The success of the Naval Fighter Weapons School (NFWS) – popularly know as 'Topgun' – to teach combat tactics to Navy and Marine fighter pilots initiated during the Vietnam conflict prompted the naval surface fleet to adapt a similar approach. To support this concept, VAQ-33 was organised at Norfolk, Virginia, later moving to NAS Key West, Florida. It had a mixed bag of aircraft assigned to the squadron, consisting of R7V Constellation, A3D Skywarriors, F4H Phantom II, EA-4Fs and later EA-6As.

The EA-4F Skyhawks were TA-4F aircraft modified to carry external stores that could electronically simulate the signals of incoming Russian missiles and aircraft. Thus, VAQ-33 could 'exercise' the surface Navy, helping to develop the tactics necessary to reduce that threat.

US Navy Bureau Numbers:
EA-4F
152852, 152869, 153481 and 154655

Only four EA-4Fs were built and all served with VAQ-33 of FEWSG (Fleet Electronic Warfare Support Group). Modifications included adding target missile launching capability and deletion of the guns.

TA-4J

The US Navy Advance Training Command's requirement for a replacement for its ageing Grumman TF-9J Cougars resulted in the purchase of the TA-4J in 1968 to provide advanced training for pilots for the Navy and Marine Corps. Because the TA-4F combat trainer had been operational since 1966, it was relatively simple and inexpensive to tailor the two-seat Skyhawk design for the advanced training role.

The adaptation consisted of deleting tactical weapon systems such as the air-to-air and the ground missile launching equipment, low-altitude bombing system, radar and associated gear, plus removing the inflight-refuelling tanker capability but retaining the receiver capability. The resulting deletion reduced the aircraft's empty weight by 230 lb (104 kg). The lower-rated J52-P6 engine rated at 8,500 lb (37.81 kN) was installed in place of the J52-P8A with 9,300 lb (41.37 kN) thrust. A red-and-white paint scheme inline with Navy specifications was substituted for the gull grey and white of the fleet Skyhawks.

The TA-4J first flew on 17 December 1968 (the 65th anniversary of the Wright Brothers' initial heaver-than-air flight) and entered service with VT-21 in mid-1969. A mass delivery of 50 aircraft to NAS Kingsville, Texas was made from the final assembly plant at Palmdale, California. Factory to training command deliveries of the TA-4J versions amounted to 226 aircraft. This number was later supplemented with many TA-4F airframes that were converted by the deletion of certain ordnance equipment.

Of the total of 2,960 Skyhawks built, 555 were two-seaters; this total also includes some foreign deliveries.

US Navy/Marines Bureau Numbers:
In addition, most TA-4Fs were converted to TA-4Js

Amount	from	to
1	155070	
48	155072	155119
60	156891	156950
75	158073	158147
75	158453	158527
12	158712	158723
6	159090	159104
TOTAL: 277		

Right: The 'Blue Angels' TA-4J was used to transport the team's commentator and give flights to lucky VIPs. The main external difference to standard TA-4s was the probe-like fairing in the left gun bay for the crew entry ladder.

Above: Tucked in close to a pair of VF-31 F-4J Phantoms, this VF-43 TA-4J served in a variety of roles supporting Oceana fighter squadrons. Navy A-4s flew with VA, VAQ, VC, VF, VT, VX, VSF and even RVAH units – a distinction which must be unique for a single type. The USMC found nearly as many uses for the Skyhawk.

Above: Wearing one of a variety of Soviet-style camouflage schemes adopted by adversary units, this is a TA-4J of VF-126 'Bandits', the Pacific Fleet adversary squadron based at Miramar.

Above: The main role of the TA-4J is to train carrier pilots, a task which it has carried out since 1969. This aircraft, wearing the 'C' code of Training Wing Three, also wears the titles of the Chief of Naval Air Training (CNATRA).

Left: A small number of TA-4Js appeared with an ILS aerial on the fin and a large dorsal blade aerial, as seen on this VC-10 aircraft at El Libertador, Venezuela in 1990. The unit's TA-4s were designated Js but retained five pylons.

Below: This TraWing One TA-4J is one of a small number to retain at least one 20-mm cannon. Training Command is the last major US user of the A-4.

Above: The only reliable guide to whether a TA-4 is an F or a J is the number of wing pylons. Many TA-4Fs were converted to Js, mainly by removing unnecessary internal equipment.

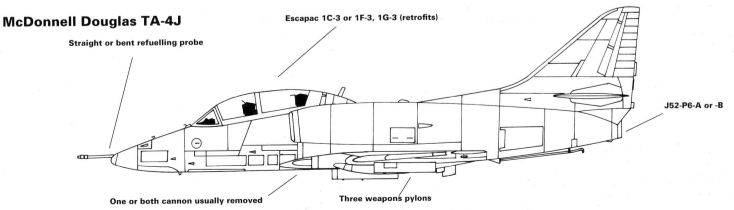

McDonnell Douglas TA-4J

Escapac 1C-3 or 1F-3, 1G-3 (retrofits)

Straight or bent refuelling probe

J52-P6-A or -B

One or both cannon usually removed

Three weapons pylons

A-4L

Because of the Vietnam conflict, the US Naval Air Reserve pushed for an upgrading of their Skyhawks to include tactical and ECM equipment similar to that installed in the fleet aircraft. When plans were finalised in 1970 to form two Reserve carrier air wings that would be fully combat ready, approval was given to Douglas to flight test one modified A-4C (BuNo. 148307) and to fabricate 99 kits to enable A-4Cs to be modified at Navy Aviation Repair Facilities (NARF). The first of the reworked A-4Cs came off the Navy line in December 1969 and were delivered to the Naval Reserve Training Unit (NARTU) at Jacksonville, FL.

The A-4L, as the modified A-4C was designated, had an uprated J65 engine and relocated electronic gear in the newly installed upper avionics pod located on the upper centre fuselage. Wing lift spoilers, first introduced on the TA-4F, were included in the modification package.

The initial A-4L was flown on 21 August 1969 and was the first of 100 aircraft so modified. Surplus A-4L aircraft were reworked to A-4PTM for Malaysia

US Navy/Marines Bureau Numbers:
145065, 145076, 145077, 145078, 145092, 145101, 145103, 145114, 145117, 145119, 145121, 145122, 145128, 145133, 145141, 147669, 147671, 147690, 147703, 147706, 147708 ,147717, 147723, 147727, 147736, 147750, 147754, 147761, 147768, 147772, 147780, 147782, 147787, 147793, 147796, 147798, 147802, 147807, 147815, 147825, 147827, 147836, 147843, 148306, 148307, 148316, 148436, 148446, 148453, 148479, 148487, 148490, 148498, 148505, 148530, 148538, 148555, 148578, 148581, 148586, 148588, 148600, 148602, 148611, 149497, 149500, 149502, 149506, 149508, 149516, 149518, 149531, 149532, 149536, 149539, 149540, 149551, 149555, 149556, 149569, 149573, 149579, 149583, 149591, 149593, 149595, 149604, 149607, 149608, 149620, 149623, 149626, 149630, 149633, 149635, 149640, 149646, 150586, 150593, 150598.
TOTAL:100

Above: The A-4L was basically an A-4C with hump and spoilers, retaining the J65 engine and other features of early Skyhawks such as three pylons and early pattern mainwheel hubs.

As with the A-4C, the last outpost of the A-4L in the US was the civilian support contractors Flight Systems Inc., which operated a number of A-4s on the US civil register. N402FS now resides in the RNZAF Museum.

Above: The A-4L was a relatively little-known variant, operated mainly by USN and USMC Reserve squadrons such as VMA-112, seen here in Bicentennial markings in 1976.

A-4M Skyhawk II

In 1968, an engine development by Pratt & Whitney was to be instrumental in extending the already long life of the Skyhawk. In production for 14 years at that time, the versatile A-4 had remained equal to the task imposed on it by constantly upgrading the detail features of a basic airframe that reflected its excellent design. But how far could you stretch a good design?

Pratt & Whitney provided the answer when they developed a new version of their J52 engine with a rating of 11,200 lb (49.82 kN) static thrust, a 20 per cent increase over its J52-P8A predecessor. The cost of this thrust increase was a one per cent weight raise and no significant change in specific fuel consumption. Smokeless burner cans were also installed to reduce the level of visible exhaust. This engine was designated as the J52-P408.

Other changes added to the A-4M included a larger canopy to improve pilot visibility, especially in the rearward direction. This was accomplished by using a windscreen similar to those installed on the trainer versions and increasing the width of the canopy by 3 in (7.62 cm).

To complement the added short-field capability provided by the increased engine thrust, a ribbon-type drag chute similar to that installed on the A-4H and A-4K was added to slow the aircraft after touchdown. Thus, routine operations from relatively short 4,000-ft (1219-m) runways were possible, a feature matching the Marines' requirement for operations on short strips in close air support of ground troops.

Two other recognition differences were the squared-off tip of the vertical tail and the repositioning of the inflight-refuelling probe. Installation of an IFF antenna was the reason for the tail geometry, while the refuelling boom was canted to allow the installation of a wider-angle target acquisition system.

Douglas gave the name Skyhawk II to this version of the 'Scooter' to reflect the added capability.

To accomplish the A-4M flight tests, two A-4Fs (BuNos 155042 and 155049) were returned to the factory and reworked into the A-4M configuration after authority to proceed was given in May 1969. Test pilot Walt Smith flew the first aircraft on 10 April 1970 before many eager Marine officials at the Douglas assembly and flight test facility at Palmdale, California. Fleet deliveries began on 26 February 1971 to VMA-324, normally based at MCAS Beaufort, South Carolina but on deployment to MCAS Yuma, Arizona.

During the 10-year production run of this version, significant improvements made to the basic A-4M resulted in some recognition differences. Incorporated in the Fiscal Year 1974 procurement was (1) a new head-up cockpit arrangement designed to improve pilot efficiency, function and comfort; (2) an improved weapons display delivery system integrated with an Elliott head-up display (HUD) which included both air-to-air and air-to-ground modes; (3) laser spot tracker system to provide for acquisition and tracking of laser designated targets; (4) Advanced ECM and DECM systems; and (5) a new aircraft generator system, the variable-speed constant-frequency system developed by General Electric.

Approval was granted to proceed with additional developments such as the angle rate bombing system (ARBS) and a new landing gear (which increased the catapult take-off weight to 25,500 lb/11567 kg) for installation in FY 1977 aircraft.

As a result of these many improvements, some thought was given to the redesignation of the aircraft as the A-4Y. However, this redesignation was not adopted and the A-4M designation was retained with the eventual upgrading of the majority of the early A-4M-configured aircraft.

Including the two revised A-4F aircraft, a total of 160 A-4Ms was procured. The final A-4M was also the last A-4 built (number 2960) and was delivered on 27 February 1979, making it (at that time) the longest production run of any American tactical aircraft: 27 years.

The 'Mikes' served the active-duty Marines until 27 February 1990, when VMA-211 transferred its last Skyhawk (BuNo. 158428) to MAG-42, a reserve group at NAS Alameda, California. This ended the operational career of the A-4 as an attack aircraft with the US Marine and Navy regular squadrons. The A-4M served with these reserve squadrons until 1994, when VMA-131 became the last US unit to operate the Skyhawk as an attack aircraft.

US Navy/Marines Bureau Numbers:

36 surplus A-4M aircraft sent to Argentina		
Amount	from	to
(2)	155042,	155049
From A-4F airframes		
49	158148	158196
24	158412	158435
20	159470	159489
4	159490	159493
13	159778	159790
24	160022	160045
24	160241	160264
TOTAL: 158		

As first delivered, A-4Ms had few of the excrescences later to become associated with the variant. This VMA-331 aircraft, making a rare carrier launch from Kennedy in 1975, has the original squared-off fin tip.

This A-4M was used as the prototype for fitting of the Angle Rate Bombing System (ARBS) and wore the title 'Smart Hawk'. By this time, ECM upgrades and a HUD had been added to the basic A-4M.

Above: The nose antenna grouping on the A-4M is dominated by the window of the ARBS TV sensor and LST (Laser Spot Tracker). To either side are antennas for the ALR-45 radar warning system, while the devices below are the ALQ-126 active jamming system antennas.

Above right: A VMA-211 A-4M flies with its eventual replacement, an AV-8B Harrier II. The variety of antennas on the tail of the A-4M can be seen, as can the 'inside-out' rudder, added as a 'temporary' fix after the A-4A, and fitted to all 2,794 later aircraft.

Below: Even the A-4M found its way into 'Topgun', although such aircraft were rare. Unusually for an adversary aircraft, this 'Mike' retains its hump and fin fairing. The different canopy profile of the 'Skyhawk II' can be clearly seen.

McDonnell Douglas A-4M

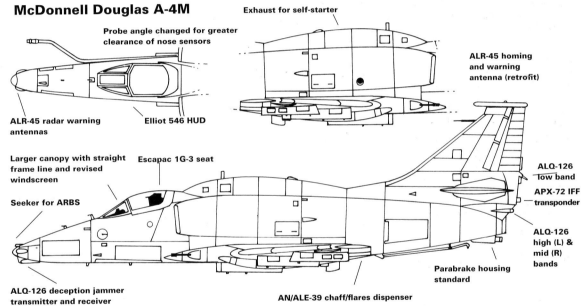

Probe angle changed for greater clearance of nose sensors

Exhaust for self-starter

ALR-45 homing and warning antenna (retrofit)

ALR-45 radar warning antennas

Elliot 546 HUD

Larger canopy with straight frame line and revised windscreen

Escapac 1G-3 seat

Seeker for ARBS

ALQ-126 low band

APX-72 IFF transponder

ALQ-126 high (L) & mid (R) bands

ALQ-126 deception jammer transmitter and receiver

AN/ALE-39 chaff/flares dispenser

Parabrake housing standard

OA-4M

With the incorporation of the A-4M Skyhawk II into the USMC inventory in 1971, a requirement also developed for the upgrading of the capability of the Fast FAC A-4s that directed the close air support efforts of the Marine Corps against the land targets in Vietnam.

The Naval Air Rework Facility (NARF) at NAS Pensacola was authorised to rework 23 TA-4Fs to incorporate AFC-542 for use in a high-speed reconnaissance and tactical air control, airborne mission. The modifications incorporated a ground control bombing system, KY-28 secure voice, armour plate, modified inflight-refuelling probe, APN-194 altimeter, ARC-159 radio and ARC-114 VHF radio. These were initially installed in TA-4F BuNo. 152856. An upper avionics pod was also installed, similar to that fitted to the single-seat

Skyhawks. Some consideration was also given to installing the Pratt & Whitney J52-P408 engine with its 11,200-lb (49.82-kN) thrust capability; however, this proved impractical and the 9,300-lb (41.37-kN) thrust J52-P8A engine was retained.

The initial OA-4M aircraft, BuNo. 154294, was outfitted and flight tested at NATC Patuxent River, Maryland in July 1978. The first squadron to receive these reworked, two-seat Skyhawks was US Marine Corps Squadron H&MS-32, located at MCAS Cherry Point, Virginia.

US Navy/Marines Bureau Numbers:

152856, 152874, 153507, 153510, 153527, 153529, 153531, 154294, 154306, 154307, 154328, 154333, 154335, 154338, 154340, 154623, 154624, 154628, 154630, 154633, 154638, 154645, 154651
TOTAL: 23

The main role of the OA-4M was down among the terrain, marking targets selected by the 'mud Marines' with rockets, and calling in the heavier firepower. The OA-4Ms were basically TA-4Fs modified with the electronics of the A-4M, the main USMC close-support aircraft.

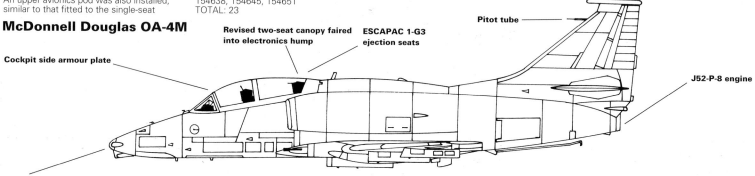

McDonnell Douglas OA-4M

Cockpit side armour plate

Revised two-seat canopy faired into electronics hump

ESCAPAC 1-G3 ejection seats

Pitot tube

J52-P-8 engine

ARBS not fitted, LST window faired over

Left: The nose sensor group of the OA-4M was basically the same as that of the A-4M, with the exception of ARBS, which was not needed on aircraft which were not employed in the pure bombing role.

Above: The H&MS (Headquarters and Maintenance Squadrons) carried out a variety of missions with the OA-4M other than fast FAC. Typical of these was target towing, as shown by this H&MS-32 aircraft carrying a TDU-10 target.

Above: Only 23 OA-4Ms were converted from TA-4Fs, but they served with four Marine units including H&MS-12, seen here. These units were later redesignated MALS (Marine Aviation Logistics Squadrons).

A4D-2N (A-4C) for US Army

In 1961, two A4D-2Ns (BuNos 148490 and 148483) were modified for a US Army evaluation along with the Northrop N-156 (F-5) and the Fiat G-91. To enhance its performance on a sod field, the Skyhawk was equipped with a revised landing gear in which dual mainwheels and an A3D Skywarrior drag chute were incorporated. To save time and money for the test, a 'quick and dirty' fairing for the landing gear was installed. Despite a 9.5-week testing session, no production contracts were awarded after these Army-sponsored test. The US Army decided to put its aerial emphasis on helicopters, and the USAF agreed to look into close air support.

US Navy/Marines Bureau Numbers

148490, 148483

Top: One of the least-known A-4 variants was the modified A4D-2N which competed for an Army close air support contract in 1961. In this view of one of the two aircraft so modified, the revised fairings for the new undercarriage, and the drag chute borrowed from an A3D Skywarrior, can be seen clearly.

Douglas' entry in the evaluation was modified from a standard A4D-2N in only two weeks (the other entrants were unmodified designs). In addition to the drag chute and double mainwheels, the test aircraft carried a variety of underwing camera pods.

Folding-wing A4D-1 (A-4A)

One Skyhawk variant that has not previously been documented, but which has puzzled many who have seen it, is the A-4A with folding wings and fin statically displayed at air shows in the US in the early 1970s. The A-4 is, famously, one of the very few carrierborne jets not to require folding wings, due to its diminutive size. A closer inspection of these (by then obsolete) early-model A-4s reveals that there is no proper wing-fold mechanism and that there are unusual external brackets each side of the fold point on the wing. These aircraft were in fact redundant A-4As used as a recruiting tools by the Navy. The folding surfaces were simply a means of transporting them by standard road vehicle between exhibition sites .Nonetheless, the two aircraft so modified, one belonging to NAS Lemoore and the other to NAS Jacksonville, were frequently displayed and photographed with wings and tail in the folded position, leading to much speculation over the years.

The sole A-4A Skyhawk fitted with folding wings and tail is seen here in 1971 at an air show at NAS Lemoore. In practice, folding wings would have saved a little space, but at the cost of increased weight and complexity and a reduction in wing structural integrity.

Commonwealth
CA-15
The 'Kangaroo' Fighter

There are several contenders for the title of 'ultimate piston-engined fighter', but few have the credentials presented by the Commonwealth CA-15. Only the second fighter design to be produced in Australia, the CA-15 combined state-of-the-art aerodynamic and structural refinements with a hugely powerful and superbly installed Griffon engine to produce a fighter of outstanding speed, climb and range performance. It was also to be the last all-new piston-engined fighter design to fly.

In 1942 Australia found itself at war in its own backyard. Its nascent aerospace industry had produced the Boomerang fighter which, during the year, had surprised many with its performance. Success during the Boomerang trials had convinced the RAAF to issue a further requirement (2/42) for a much more ambitious fighter with high speed and long range.

Initially, the Commonwealth Aircraft Corporation looked at improving the existing design, but after brief studies it became readily apparent that the Boomerang's airframe could not handle the extra weight and power, and that an all-new design would be needed. The programme, by now designated CA-15, was temporarily shelved while the more pressing demands of the war situation forced Commonwealth to prepare for licence-construction of the North American Mustang at its Fishermen's Bend factory. In the event, the numbers of CA-17/18 Mustangs produced was small (200), and they were not delivered until 1946, although the RAAF did take delivery of US-built aircraft earlier.

The CA-15 taxis at CAC's Fishermen's Bend factory. In the background is a Mustang, the type which the CA-15 was intended to replace. In the event, the Mustang went on to serve in Korea, and was eventually replaced by the Vampire and Meteor in the fighter role.

Following the initial discussions regarding Mustang production, CAC resumed work on the CA-15 in 1943, although this progressed slowly. It was not until 1944 that the RAAF issued a revised set of specifications, requiring an aircraft with considerably greater performance than the Mustang which would, in effect, be its successor. Key areas of the requirements were a high rate of climb and good acceleration, maximum performance in the 20,000-ft (6096-m) region and good manoeuvrability, especially in the rolling plane. No official name was ever bestowed on the CA-15, although unofficially 'Kangaroo' was considered.

Powerplant choices

At the outset of design, the Pratt & Whitney R-2800-10W Double Wasp was the intended powerplant, but, when the production line closed down, CAC had to find a replacement engine. The R-2800-57W with General Electric C2 was the favoured choice, with the Bristol Centaurus CE-12S.M. as an alternative. Turbochargers were tested during 1942 by a modified Boomerang, the CA-14, and data from these flights was later used to verify calculations for the CA-15. Drawings of the R-2800-powered CA-15 show an aircraft with a deep forward fuselage with a lower trunking leading to a rear-facing exhaust, through which engine exhaust gases and spent intercooler air was ejected to gain additional jet thrust.

As time went on there was increasing doubt as to the availability of the Double Wasp in sufficient numbers, so discussions switched to an inline engine, the Rolls-Royce Griffon 125 with three-speed supercharger being the choice. This offered a potential top speed of 495 mph (797 km/h), but had yet to be developed. In 1945, the decision was taken to power the prototype CA-15 with a Griffon 61 (as used by the Spitfire Mk 20 series) while the more powerful engine was developed. Two Griffon 61s were obtained from the United Kingdom under a Lend-Lease agreement.

Overall, the CA-15 showed some similarity to the P-51 Mustang. The fuselage was a

This remarkable photograph of the sole CA-15 fighter over Melbourne was captured from the rear turret of a Lincoln bomber, using only a standard lens on the camera. The face of pilot Flight Lieutenant Lee Archer is plainly visible, and some idea of the excellent view from the cockpit can be gathered. Archer was the unfortunate pilot who suffered a total hydraulic failure and had to land the aircraft with no flaps and partially deployed undercarriage. Despite the experience of the ensuing crash, he was back flying the CA-15 as soon as it had been rebuilt.

stressed skin semi-monocoque structure built around four longerons, with flush rivetting. The engine cowling rose steeply to the small aft-sliding canopy, giving the pilot an excellent view forwards. The cockpit was laid out in traditional RAF manner, with three main columns of instruments, the Sperry artificial horizon being in the centre. On the left side of the cockpit were grouped the throttle, propeller controls, flap selector, trim wheels, undercarriage and fuel controls. Electric and hydraulic controls

The CA-15 left much to be desired in the beauty stakes, yet its bulky and angular looks were the key to its outstanding performance. The canopy seemed far too small, but in fact offered an unrivalled view with 8° downward vision along the cowling line and superb vision to the rear.

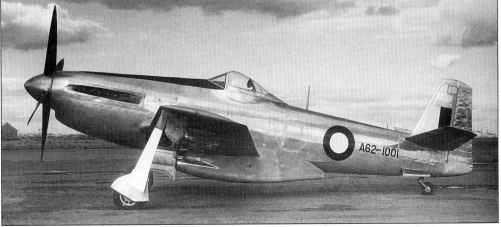

Above: From most angles the CA-15 bore a superficial resemblance to the Mustang, thanks in part to the underslung fairing for the cooling radiators. Visible at the rear of the fairing is the variable ejector flap for exhausting hot air from the system.

Left: With cowlings removed the CA-15 displays its flexible sheet-metal mounts for the Griffon engine, with turbocharger installation behind. The engine bearers were mounted directly to the main fuselage structure longerons.

were on the right side. A three-piece armoured windscreen was provided, and, together with the 229 lb (104 kg) of armour plating, gave the pilot much better protection than the P-51, including proof against 20-mm cannon hits from the rear quarter. The canopy, headrest and rear armourplate could be jettisoned in an emergency.

The wings were made in two sections, joined on the centreline, and were of a NACA 66 low-drag laminar flow cross-section similar to that of the Mustang, with 5° dihedral and an aspect ratio of 5.12. The thickest part of the wing was at 45 per cent of the chord. The tailplanes had 9° dihedral and an aspect ratio of 4.2. Conventional controls were fitted, including 48 per cent span ailerons with shrouded nose balances and fabric seals. While the ailerons had electric trimming, operated by a toggle switch, the rudder and elevators had standard wheel-controlled mechanical trimming. Single-slotted flaps were fitted, with a 20° setting for take-off and 50° for landing.

At 14 ft (4.27 m) track, the main undercarriage gave good stability on the ground. The gear retracted into the inner section of the wings between the main spars. The tailwheel retracted forwards and was covered in flight by double doors. A Dowty engine-driven pump provided hydraulic power for the flaps and undercarriage. Fuel was mainly held in the wings (220 Imp gal/1000 litres), with a 30-Imp gal (136-litre) tank in the fuselage.

Engine installation

The Griffon was mounted flexibly on sheet-metal bearers, and encased in a close-fitting cowling. Lord Hives, head of Rolls-Royce, later commented it was the best Griffon installation of any. The engine drove a Dowty compressed-wood four-bladed propeller of 12 ft 6 in (3.81 m) diameter, unusually rotating anti-clockwise. A cartridge starter was fitted. The cooling system consisted of a Morris single-row intercooler and a three-row main radiator with a total matrix area of 5.8 sq ft (0.54 m²). A heat exchanger was provided to cool the oil in the intercooler system. The cooling system was packaged in a large fairing under the central fuselage, with a large scoop at the front and a variable ejection flap at the rear, controlled by thermostat. Exhaust from the engine was ejected through rear-facing stubs set into a trough.

There was some discussion as to what the aircraft should carry in the way of armament, various combinations of 20-mm cannon and 0.50-in (12.7-mm) machine-guns being mooted. In the interim a fixed armament of six 50-cals was chosen, mounted just outboard of the main undercarriage, each weapon having 250 rounds carried inboard of the gun. Hardpoints were provided under each wing to allow the carriage of two 500-lb (227-kg) or 1,000-lb (454-kg) bombs. Alternatively, 10 rockets could be carried, or six with two drop tanks. The latter could be of either 40-Imp gal (182-litre) or 100-Imp gal (454-litre) capacity.

Construction of the prototype (c/n 1074) and production tooling had progressed slowly during 1944/45, and with one of the Griffon 61s fitted, the CA-15 began taxiing trials on 12 February 1946. A few minor problems were swiftly rectified, and at 6:10 p.m. on 4 March, Jim Schofield lifted the CA-15 from Fishermen's Bend for a 15-minute first flight. The aircraft wore the RAAF serial A62-1001. Apart from strong propeller torque on take-off, there were no problems. The next few flights were aimed at harmonising the controls, and most were accomplished by Schofield, although RAAF pilots Wing Commander J. E. Harper, and Squadron Leaders D. R. Cuming and G. C. Brunner from No. 1 Aircraft Performance Unit also flew the aircraft.

Above: The CA-15 initially flew with wartime-style blue/white roundels and fin-flash. Later in its career it acquired the post-war three-colour roundels, the red centre having been deleted from the national insignia to avoid confusion with the Japanese 'meatball'.

Right: Thanks to attention to detail and flush rivetting, the surface of the CA-15 was exceptionally clean. The exhaust stubs were located in a low-drag trough.

All reported no major difficulties apart from some aileron and elevator heaviness, and problems with overtrimming the rudder. The CA-15 also proved somewhat difficult to get into. The pilot had to climb up one of the undercarriage legs and walk along the wing to the cockpit. On the plus side, all were impressed by the aircraft's performance, and its excellent view over the nose, which was much better than that from the Mustang.

After 16 hours 35 minutes airborne in 23 flights, the CA-15 was handed over to the RAAF's No. 1 APU at Point Cook on 27 June 1946 to begin calibration and performance testing. As well as Harper, Cuming and Brunner, the CA-15 was also flown by Wing Commander G. D. Marshall, Squadron Leaders C. W. Stark and G. H. Shiells, and Flight Lieutenant J. A. Lee Archer. Performance measurements showed a top speed of 448 mph (721 km/h) at 26,400 ft (8045 m) and a climb rate at low altitude of 4,900 ft (1494 m) per minute. The range on internal fuel was 1,150 miles (1850 km), although this could be extended to 2,540 miles (4088 km) through the use of external tanks, making the type ideal for long-range escort missions. Stall speed was shown to be a perfectly manageable 90 mph (145 km/h) with flaps and undercarriage down.

The performance was nothing short of excellent, and would have been considerably better had the original Double Wasp or three-speed Griffon engines been available.

Forced landing

These RAAF proving flights came to an abrupt end on 10 December 1946 when Lee Archer suffered a hydraulic failure on approach to Point Cook caused by a leaking ground test gauge. The main gear locked half way down, and despite numerous attempts to lower the gear further by emergency systems and shaking, Archer had no option but to burn off most of the fuel before attempting a flapless forced landing on the grass. The tailwheel had locked down, and this hit the ground first, whereupon the aircraft stalled. The airscoop dug into the ground, causing the machine to pitch forward and then fall back. Thankfully Archer was unhurt, but the CA-15 was badly damaged. It had flown 43 hours 25 minutes during the RAAF test phase.

It was not until June 1947 that the CA-15 was returned to CAC for rebuilding, and this work proceeded slowly. By that time it was obvious to all that jet power was the future, and plans were afoot to produce the Vampire and Meteor. Nevertheless, it was felt that the

CA-15 could still perform some useful trials work. Nearly a year passed before the CA-15 was officially handed back to the RAF, delivered to No. 1 Aircraft Depot at Laverton for inspection on 19 May 1948. On 26 May it was handed over to the Aircraft Research and Development Unit. The day before, 25 May, had seen the CA-15 with Archer again at the controls clock its highest ever speed in level flight – 502.2 mph (808.2 km/h), achieved after a 4,000-ft (1220-m) dive.

Limited flying continued but by early 1950 the writing was on the wall for the aircraft. The CA-15 was becoming increasingly difficult to support in terms of spare parts, and calls were being made to return the loaned Griffon engines to the UK. Finally, on 1 May 1950, the CA-15 was switched from ARDU to No. 1 Aircraft Depot for what was officially termed 'conversion to components'. Australia had been quietly robbed of a lasting monument to its finest hour in aircraft development.

David Donald

Had more urgency been attached to the CA-15 programme, the RAAF may have had an excellent long-range fighter, ideal for the Pacific theatre, before the war with Japan ended. Like so many other projects of the period, the 'Kangaroo' was finally submerged in the technological surge of the turbine revolution.

Specification

Powerplant: one Rolls-Royce Griffon 61 rated at 1,540 hp (1149 kW) for take-off and 2,035 hp (1518 kW) at 7,000 ft (2134 m); fitted with two-speed, two-stage turbocharger providing up to 18 lb/in² (124 kPa) boost

Weights: empty 7540 lb (3420 kg); normal combat 9,500 lb (4309 kg); maximum take-off 12,340 lb (5597 kg); normal wing loading 37.5 lb/sq in (183 kg/m²)

Dimensions: wing span 36 ft 0 in (10.97 m); tailplane span 13 ft 10 in (4.22 m); length 36 ft 2½ in (11.04 m); height 14 ft 2 in (4.32 m); wing area 253 sq ft (23.50 m²)

Performance: maximum speed 448 mph (721 km/h) at 26,400 ft (8047 m), 432 mph (695 km/h) at 37,000 ft (11278 m), 368 mph (592 km/h) at sea level; initial rate of climb 4,900 ft (1493 m) per minute; climb to 20,000 ft (6096 m) in 5 minutes 30 seconds; service ceiling 39,000 ft (11887 m); range 1,150 miles (1850 km) on internal fuel, 2,540 miles (4088 km) with drop tanks

Armament: six 0.50-in (12.7-mm) Browning machine-guns with 250 rounds per gun; underwing hardpoints for two bombs of up to 1,000 lb (454 kg), or up to 10 rocket projectiles

Beyond the Frontiers
BAC TSR.2

The brief designation TSR.2 is likely to be remembered for all time as a textbook lesson in how not to arm an air force. The very mention of it arouses passions, some thinking that this aircraft should never have been cancelled and others that it should never have been started. Like so much of Britain's aerospace history, it was an amalgam of indecisiveness by the customer, massive and chaotic bureaucracy and disastrous involvement by the politicians. What made this programme unique was that it was used to help win a general election by pouring venom on the harassed and dedicated engineers who were trying to create it.

The TSR.2 project is one of the most significant milestones in British aviation history. It was a triumph for the nation's aerospace industry but a shameful failure for those whose task it was to protect that industry and its future.

It all began 40 years ago. In 1956 the needs of the RAF were met by issuing sets of requirements to the British aircraft industry. Admittedly, in 1938 American aircraft had been purchased because of the desperate need for numbers, and in the early 1950s such types as the Sabre, Superfortress, Skyraider, Avenger, Neptune and Whirlwind had filled gaps left because the post-war Labour government had failed to order British aircraft in time. These were seen as exceptions to the basic principle that the Ministry of Supply issued a GOR (General Operational Requirement), for which up to 20 companies then competed. These companies were so famous that they had become 'household words'.

One of these, A. V. Roe, was busy with an incredible supersonic bomber, the Type 730, a stainless-steel tail-first design with eight engines on the wingtips. During 1956 the Air Staff had increasingly doubted that this was what they wanted. Ideas of warfare were changing. Instead of Mach 3 at 65,000 ft (19812 m), the call was for the highest possible speed – possibly Mach 1.2 – at the lowest possible height, such as 200 ft (61 m), in order to avoid detection by hostile radars. Instead of a 10,000-ft (32808-m) runway, future aircraft were going to have to operate from perhaps 3,000 ft (914 m) of dirt, in order

to disperse away from enemy airfield-destroying missiles. There was also a general consensus that the Avro 730 was too large, and by the end of 1956 opinion had hardened on the concept of a more conventional aircraft not much larger than the Canberra, to replace that machine in the tactical strike and reconnaissance (TSR) roles.

The revised ideas were encapsulated in GOR.339, issued in March 1957. It called for an aircraft to replace the Canberra, able to operate from the shortest possible unpaved runway and to fly to a target 1,000 nm (1853 km; 1,152 miles) distant and attack in any weather, delivering a Red Beard tactical nuclear bomb in an 'over the shoulder' toss from low level. It was also to carry the latest reconnaissance cameras and SLAR (sideways-looking airborne radar), which was one of a host of items which had to be specially designed.

Unfortunately, the waters, never crystal clear, were muddied by a number of factors. One, which possibly influenced the programme less than the media thought, was that at the very time GOR.339 was being issued, the Minister of Defence was putting finishing touches to a document called 'Statement on Defence: an Outline of Future Policy'. The Minister was Duncan Sandys, who during World War II had organised the Z-batteries of unguided anti-

aircraft missiles. These almost useless weapons had so captivated his attention that by 1956 he was convinced that very soon all fighters and bombers would be swept away and replaced by missiles. Accordingly, on 4 April 1957 – the day on which the RAF's next fighter, the Lightning, first flew – Statement on Defence announced that the RAF was "unlikely to require" any more fighters or bombers, and that "work on such projects will therefore stop." Of the Lightning, it was said "This has unfortunately proceeded too far to cancel."

Today such a view can be seen to be stark lunacy, but at the time not many observers – and certainly no serving officer – was disposed to question it. Its immediate effect was to make the launch of any new project for a military aircraft much more difficult, and to unite Her Majesty's Treasury in implacable opposition against it.

The Buccaneer factor

The second water-muddying factor was that back in 1952 a specification called NA.39 had been issued for a carrier-based attack aircraft, specifically planned with startling foresight to fly at low level. The contract was won by Blackburn, whose first NA.39 prototype flew in April 1958, leading to the production Buccaneer. Not unreasonably, the Treasury asked whether this might perhaps also meet the needs of the RAF. Sadly, instead of actually considering this suggestion, the RAF saw it as a possibly dangerous challenge to the GOR.339 aircraft. Accordingly, it spared no effort to prove why the naval aircraft would be utterly useless. The main shortcomings were: it was not super-

sonic, it needed a long runway, its combat radius was too short, and its navigation and blind attack avionics were primitive.

The fact that Blackburn had answers to all these shortcomings was ignored. In the RAF's view, "If we show the slightest interest in NA.39 we might not get the GOR.339 aircraft." By the simple process of cancelling the glittering alternatives, the RAF began operating this aircraft in 1969. It was then gradually realised that the 'Bucc' was a first-rate aircraft, until in the late 1980s the RAF's opinion was "The only thing that can replace the Buccaneer is another Buccaneer, with next-generation avionics." But from 1957 the official RAF view was that the Buccaneer was totally inadequate. As late as December 1966, long after TSR.2 had been consigned to history, Air Cdre 'Teddy' Donaldson, air correspondent of the *Daily Telegraph*, followed the official line with "Mr Healey, Minister of Defence, may try to force on the RAF an obsolete subsonic bomber... Acceptance of the Buccaneer would make the RAF the world's only air force operating a subsonic bomber." Apart from the grotesque nonsense of the latter statement, it gives a flavour of the times. This attitude was to cost the RAF and the country dearly.

Yet another complicating factor was that the government had decided there were too many British aircraft manufacturers. This was probably true, but the government loved to flex its muscles in the procurement of not only military aircraft but also equipment for the nation's airlines. It blandly decreed that, in order to be considered for either the GOR.339 aircraft or its engines, or a new short-haul jet airliner

The Vickers Supermarine Type 571 and English Electric P.17A proposals were merged (as were the two companies) to arrive at the final TSR.2 design. Its futuristic shape was unlike that of any contemporary, or current, aircraft.

wanted by British European Airways, several companies would have to collaborate and, if possible, effect complete mergers. This was in line with a "policy of rationalisation" suggested by the Minister of Supply (Aubrey Jones), which month by month became ever harsher and irreversible, just as the RAF requirement itself became ever more demanding.

Arguments continued through 1958. In August the Air Ministry Deputy Under Secretary (R. H. Melville), after 'knocking' the NA.39 and explaining why the GOR.339 aircraft was absolutely essential, added "For RAF purposes the NA.39 will be obsolescent by the time it is produced... neither it nor the suggested derivative would meet the military requirement, nor survive in the operational

Avro Vulcan engine testbed

Left: With 1,900 hours of ground running behind it, the TSR.2's Rolls-Royce Olympus 320-22R engine began air tests aboard a (surplus) Vulcan B.Mk 1, XA894, on 23 February 1962.

Right: XA894 undertook 35 flights and such was the performance of the new Olympus 22R engine that the Vulcan could fly on its power alone – with its own Olympus 101s throttled back to provide only electrical and hydraulic power.

Left: In November 1963 the Vulcan testbed, with Roland Beamont at the controls, took the 22R to full three-stage reheat. It was at these high-power settings that disaster would later strike XA894.

conditions that OR.339 is designed to meet."

Bidders for the GOR.339 aircraft had been told to respond by 31 January 1958. By that date replies had been received from Armstrong Whitworth, Avro, Blackburn, Bristol, de Havilland, English Electric, Fairey, Handley Page, Hawker, Short Brothers and Vickers-Armstrongs (prepared by the subsidiary design office formerly called Supermarine Aviation). In the course of 1958 some of these proposals were modified or merged, one of the more unconventional ideas being to mount the outstanding English Electric P.17A on Short's P.17D VTOL (vertical take-off and landing) platform powered by 44 vertical RB.108 lift engines, 16 tilting RB.108 engines and 10 RB.145 lift/propulsion engines set at 60°.

In fact, by July 1958 the Air Staff had decided that the P.17A was the best aircraft, but it was run very close by the Supermarine 571 proposed by Vickers-Armstrongs. The latter astonished them by the depth with which it embraced the 'Weapon-System Concept' in which the air vehicle is just part of a total system centred on avionics, weapons and ground equipment for training and servicing. It was soon decided to award the contract to English Electric and Vickers-Armstrongs, with the latter

firm leading, despite the former company's written agreement to collaborate with Short Brothers if either was awarded the contract. The Belfast company was cunningly eliminated by redrafting the requirement around the EE-Vickers merged design, calling it OR.343, and then following with a tight specification called RB.192D.

On 11 November 1958 the Air Minister (George Ward) and Chief of the Air Staff (Sir Dermot Boyle) discussed the matter with Minister of Defence Sandys, who two days later stated, "I am satisfied that you have made out the case for replacing... the Canberra with an aircraft which would comply with... OR.339. The way is therefore clear for you to ask the Minister of Supply [Jones] to approach the Treasury for authority to place a development contract." On 15 December the Treasury reluctantly sanctioned an initial design contract at an estimated cost of £150,000. This figure was just the first of a succession of supposed costs which, even at the time, could be seen to be underestimated to the point of absurdity. This merely guaranteed grave difficulty in the future.

TSR go-ahead

On 17 December Air Minister Ward made the first public statement: "It has been decided to develop a new strike/reconnaissance aircraft as a Canberra replacement. This will be capable of operating from small airfields with rudimentary surfaces." On 1 January 1959 Supply Minister Jones announced, "Subject to satisfactory negotiations, development of the new aircraft, TSR.2, will be undertaken by Vickers-Armstrong and English Electric, the work being shared on a 50-50 basis. A joint project team drawn from both companies is being established at the Vickers works at Weybridge. The engine will be undertaken by Bristol Siddeley Engines, the new company formed out of Bristol Aero-Engines and Armstrong Siddeley Motors. TSR.2 will be a Tactical Support [sic] and Reconnaissance aircraft."

Even at this time the project was the subject of bitter and growing controversy. The design of the aircraft was based on the English Electric P.17A project, created at Warton in Lancashire by a team led by Teddy Petter and Freddie Page. Now it had to be merged and extended on a 50-50 basis with the prime contract placed not with them but with Vickers at Weybridge, 200 miles (322 km) to the south, where the project team was led by Sir George Edwards (who was busy on the VC10), Henry Gardner, and George Henson of the former Supermarine design team.

At one time Sir George Edwards had thought that the Vickers STOL study and the P.17 with its tiny wing seemed "irreconcilable". Eventually Vickers took on the nose, forward fuselage and centre fuselage (which housed virtually all the avionics, sensors, fuel and internal weapons, and much more than half the cost) and English Electric the wings, rear fuselage and tail. The splice came halfway along the wing torsion box, which sat on top of the joined centre and rear fuselages.

While the ground crew checked and rechecked the fuel and hydraulics in anticipation of XR219's maiden flight at Boscombe Down, engineers at BAC were toiling to solve the worrisome engine vibration problems and tailchute hitches.

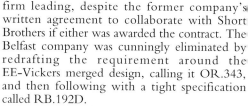

XR219 has the distinction of being the only TSR.2 to fly and on many of these sorties it was accompanied by company photographer John Whittacker in a Lightning T.Mk 4. Sadly, many TSR.2 photos were subsequently destroyed.

Very gradually, the 'us and them' attitude between Lancashire and Surrey was overcome, and in January 1960 it was announced that a wholly new company, British Aircraft Corporation (BAC), was to be formed from English Electric Aviation, Vickers-Armstrong (Aircraft), Bristol Aircraft and, from September 1960, Hunting Aircraft. Obvious problems arise when you have four technical directors, four chief designers, four chief test pilots and four design offices each with a proud heritage of doing things 'their way'.

Assaults from all comers

From the outset the new aircraft received intractable hostility from the Treasury, which doubted the need for it and was increasingly horrified at its escalating costs. The situation was exacerbated by the recent unequivocal statement of the Minister of Defence that the RAF was unlikely to require any new fighter or bomber.

TSR.2 also encapsulated all the opposition of the Royal Navy, whose antagonism to the upstart Royal Air Force had simmered not far below the surface from 1918. The conflict was now brought into sharp focus by the excellence of Blackburn's NA.39, and by the determination of the Air Staff to write figures into their specification which appeared to have been selected in order to disqualify the naval aircraft. Once plucked from thin air, these figures were then regarded as if they were carved in stone.

Yet another source of discontent was that the specially formed OR.343 project team at Weybridge – half of whose members either had to move house or commute 200 miles (322 km) to meetings – evaluated engine proposals from Bristol Siddeley and Rolls-Royce and unanimously selected the latter. This cut no ice with Aubrey Jones (whose ministry had in October 1959 been renamed not Supply but Aviation), who said the contract had to go to Bristol Siddeley because they had obeyed the government's instructions and were the result of a merger. The engine thus had to be the Olympus 22R Mk 320, which was an uprated version of the Vulcan B.Mk 2 engine with an added afterburner, rated at 19,610 lb (87.2 kN) dry and 30,610 lb (136.2 kN) with reheat.

This thrust was greater than that of any previous jet engine. Moreover, as it was a derivative of an extremely mature turbojet, it was expected to pose few problems and quickly to become very reliable. Its main shortcoming was that for maximum range the engine should have been a bypass turbojet, or turbofan, with afterburning when necessary in both core and bypass flows. Such an engine was the RB.14213, which had been proposed by Rolls-Royce, but disqualified politically.

Development wrangle

One more cause for aggravation was that TSR.2 was essentially the only new combat aircraft for the RAF, and thus the object of undivided attention not only by the air marshals but also by the vast army of scientific civil servants. The 1957 decree of "No more manned aircraft" might have been expected to slash their numbers drastically; instead, this army had never ceased to grow. To give a flavour of the situation, TSR.2 chief test pilot Roland P. 'Bee' Beamont later recalled, "I held monthly meetings to progress the design of cockpit layout and aspects of control and systems operation raised as a result of day, night and weekend work on the avalanche of design appreciations, technical specifications and test notes which poured in relentlessly. Often the recommendations made were turned down subsequently at the Ministry Cockpit Co-ordination Committee, at which about 30 three-year-tour personnel

Right: The TSR.2's lengthy forward fuselage had the advantage of minimising boundary-layer air flow into the engine intakes. As a result the aircraft featured quite simple splitter plates. The much-vaunted F-111 was not nearly so lucky.

Below: The TSR.2's four airbrakes were mounted above and below the fuselage. They were driven by hydraulically-powered screw-jacks, in much the same fashion as the wing flaps. Each engine had its own hydraulic system to guard against failure and an accumulator was also fitted.

would debate for half a day the position of a switch and the label to put under it, and then get it wrong, as demonstrated subsequently by flight experience."

Quite apart from the intense scrutiny of hordes of officials, TSR.2 suffered from requiring a vast range of items of equipment for all its airborne systems which were right at the leading edge of technology and did not previously exist. Over 1,000 firms were marshalled to provide these items, some of the largest being entirely new to Britain. These included the multi-mode forward-looking radar, a terrain-following radar linked to a flight-control and autopilot system of unprecedented complexity, inertial navigation, a new advanced Doppler system, a pilot's HUD (head-up display), an analog/digital converter, fully variable engine inlets and nozzles, and full-span flaps with high-energy blowing from the engines. In the USA

such equipment was either available off the shelf or was being developed for many aircraft. In Britain, the bill had to be charged to TSR.2.

As if all these problems were not enough, the entire programme happened inside a goldfish bowl of media attention. Having been told that no more fighters or bombers would be required, this expensive new wonderplane gradually began to make headlines – virtually all of them highly unfavourable – on a weekly if not daily basis. A further twist to the tale was that the Labour Party, after years in opposition, suddenly saw that TSR.2 just might provide a ticket back to power. Labour politicians, led by Denis Healey and Roy Jenkins (respectively spokesmen on defence and aviation), gradually built up a rapport with the media which never missed an opportunity to rubbish the aircraft itself, the competence of those developing it and the underlying need for it, while assuring possible foreign customers that, should they be elected, the whole programme would be cancelled. From this distance it is impossible to judge whether they stopped to consider whether this might actually be desirable.

BAC signs the contract

On 7 October 1960 the newly formed BAC received the development contract. Of course, the amount (£90 million) was kept secret, as was the fact that, in addition to the R&D and production tooling, it covered nine development aircraft, XR219-227. Later an additional 11 were added. Over the next three years TSR.2 was translated from paper into hardware.

The programme repeatedly attracted the attention of the media, particularly when politicians opened their mouths. In 1959 Supply

Minister Jones had announced, "TSR.2 is not a deterrent weapon. It is not a bomber in the conventional sense of the word, but an aircraft intended to give strike support to ground forces. The reason for the delay in deciding on it was the redesign of the aircraft to make it suitable for limited-war contingencies overseas." One marvelled at how it could need to be redesigned in order to meet such an obvious requirement, and how it could give strike support carrying no weapons except bombs and yet not be a bomber. As for not being a deterrent weapon, the central requirement from Day 1 had been the ability to deliver a nuclear weapon. In February 1963 new Air Minister Hugh Fraser stated, "TSR.2 will operate in the strategic role, both before and after the introduction of Polaris submarines."

TSR.2 transformed

By this time the basic design of the aircraft had long been settled. Many parts of the English Electric P.17A remained, including of course the overall configuration of a long and almost untapered fuselage with pilot and navigator seated in tandem in the nose, a broad delta wing mounted on top, delta tailerons (tailplanes used also as ailerons), a single fin, and main gears with two wheels in tandem retracting into the fuselage. On the other hand, much had changed.

TSR.2 became a big aircraft, in no sense a close relative of supersonic fighters. It was 20 ft (6.1 m) longer than a Lancaster, and nearly twice as heavy. On the other hand, its wing was relatively small, the span being kept to the absolute minimum (similar to the span of most Spitfires) to meet the demand of Mach 1.2 at sea level without 'shaking the crew's eyeballs out'.

There were, and to this day remain, two ways of meeting this demand. One is to use a fixed-geometry wing of minimum span, fitted with exceedingly powerful blown flaps to generate adequate lift for take-off and landing. The other is to use a variable-geometry 'swing wing', with the outer sections mounted on pivots. TSR.2 was designed just as the latter answer was coming into fashion, which was yet another source of trouble. In fact, the prime contractor, Vickers-Armstrong, had pioneered the swing-wing concept. In 1958, following the proclamation that there would be no more British manned combat aircraft, the Ministry of Supply sent all the company's test data on pivoting wings to NACA (which was in the process of becoming NASA). This materially assisted the design of the F-111, which (as explained later) was to be ironic.

A most remarkable wing

In fact, the fixed-geometry wing was an excellent answer. Like that of the P.17A, the wing was a 60° delta, with an aspect ratio of only 1.96. Cross area was 700 sq ft (65 m²). The leading edge was fixed, and devoid of fences or sawcuts. The trailing edge was at 90° to the fuselage, and the main part of the wing was horizontal. Mounting it above the fuselage avoided the problem of undesirable airflow over the tail, especially at high angles of attack. Instead of the whole wing having anhedral, only the tips (the outermost 4 ft/1.2 m on each side) were tilted down sharply, at 30°.

Inboard of these downturned sections were very powerful flaps, blown with hot high-pressure air from the engines. Such a system had been pioneered in Britain by Supermarine on the 525 and Scimitar, and it enabled the TSR.2 to meet the demands of short field length. Even at maximum weight the take-off run in temperate conditions was a mere 2,400 ft (732 m), and at the weights for most missions it would have been about 1,600 ft (488 m). Bearing in mind the wing's thin (3.7 per cent) supersonic profile

Right: The first 13 TSR.2 flights were all conducted from Boscombe Down. In this photo the open engine relief intake doors, deployed at low speed, are clearly visible. Throughout its career XR219 never carried anything approaching the definitive TSR.2 avionics suite, relying instead on standard TACAN and a single UHF radio.

Below: During XR219's maiden flight the chase aircraft crew were alarmed to see what they took to be fuel venting from the wing tanks. This soon proved to be substantial – and spectacular – condensation vortices flowing off the wing leading edge at the wingtip join.

to the target and back was 1,000 nm (1853 km). If necessary, 450-Imp gal (2046-litre) drop tanks could be hung on four wing pylons, increasing typical combat radius to 1,500 nm (2780 km). For ferrying, a 570-Imp gal (2591-litre) tank could be plumbed into the weapons bay, giving a range of 3,700 nm (6856 km). It was intended also to provide for a jettisonable tank of 1,000-Imp gal (4546-litre) capacity to be scabbed under the fuselage. The theoretical maximum fuel capacity was 8,188 Imp gal (37223 litres), weighing appreciably more than the empty weight of the aircraft, which was typically 44,850 lb (20344 kg).

Alloy construction

Structurally, the aircraft was conventional, with most of the airframe assembled from machined planks or extrusions of L.65 aluminium/copper alloy. In some areas subjected to mild heating, Al-Li (aluminium-lithium) structure was used, this alloy being imported from the USA. Much of the rear fuselage was RR.5B, a substance invented by High Duty Alloys for engine pistons and retaining almost full strength to 300°C. Several ICI titanium alloys were used for the engine bays and other hot parts. TSR.2 experience enabled these alloys and, especially, RR.58 to be used later with confidence for most of the airframe of Concorde.

Among the small proportion of special materials was ultra-strong vacuum-melted nickel/chromium/molybdenum/vanadium steel supplied by

On Flight 14, XR219 travelled to Warton for a new phase of flight tests. The transit from Boscombe Down included a supersonic leg along the Irish Sea. Engaging afterburner on one engine only, the TSR.2 left Jimmy Dell's accompanying Lightning T.Mk 4 'standing'.

– which for optimum efficiency varied, especially towards the root – this was a truly remarkable achievement.

A feature of TSR.2 was the care with which the wing/fuselage joint was designed. The main torque box of the wing, which was also an integral fuel tank, had no fewer than seven spars. Each of these was joined on each side of the aircraft to the top of a fuselage frame, but not one of the 14 connections was rigid. Each one was made via a two-pin swinging link, free to rock either longitudinally or transversely, or able to slide through a distance of about 0.25 in (6 mm). Thus, though lacking nothing in strength, the wing and fuselage could each flex and distort individually during supersonic flight through turbulent air, without increasing stress at any location. This significantly increased fatigue life, and a by-product was reduced transmission of vertical and lateral accelerations to the fuselage. The cockpit, carefully located at a nodal point of flexure, was given a particularly smooth ride.

As noted, almost the entire wing formed an integral fuel tank, although its shallow depth restricted capacity to about one-quarter of the total. This total, almost three times that of a Lancaster, was housed mainly in very large integral cells in the front and rear fuselage, the skin of which was made up of machined integrally stiffened panels. It was the intention that the aircraft would be cleared to use any standard turbine fuel, including Avtur, Avtag (petrol), Avcat or diesel.

Advanced fuel system

The Lucas fuel system automatically managed the feed to the engines so as to maintain longitudinal trim. The system could be replenished at a rate of 450 Imp gal (2046 litres) per minute by twin pressure connections under the forward fuselage, or via a neat folding inflight-refuelling probe on the left side of the nose. Without using inflight refuelling, combat radius allowing for a 200-nm (371-km) dash at minimum level

TSR.2 cockpits

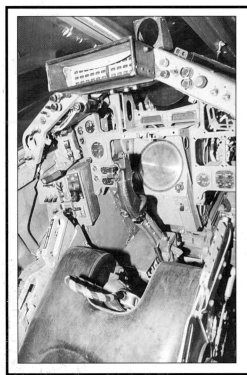

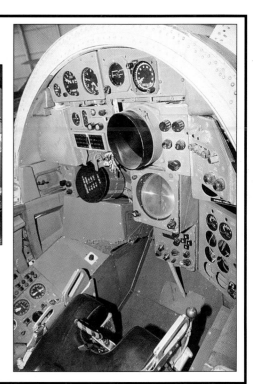

Above: The TSR.2 was fitted with Martin-Baker Mk 8VA rocket-powered ejection seats. These were a zero-zero design, intended for use at heights up to 56,000 ft (17068 m) and speeds of up to Mach 2.

Left: XR220's actual cockpit bore little resemblance to Ferranti's production design, which featured three of what would now be termed Multi-Function Displays.

Right: The navigator's position in XR220 was more representative and was dominated by the radar display, SLAR, linescan and other recce systems controls.

English Steel Corporation for the landing gears. Of basically Vickers design, as was the landing gear of the Valiant, but produced by Electro-Hydraulics Ltd, the main units resembled those of the earlier bomber in having two wheels in tandem. The difference was that they were mounted on a beam pivoted at the centre to a single leg, with an exceptionally long-stroke shock strut. The entire unit retracted forwards (the opposite of the P.17A) into compartments on each side of the fuselage under the intake ducts. The tubeless tyres were large, because their inflation pressure was low enough for emergency landings at maximum weight on an unpaved strip, if necessary bulldozed from the jungle. They were supplied by both Dunlop and Goodyear, but in full production probably one supplier would have been chosen.

For minimum-length take-off the nose leg, with twin hydraulically-steered wheels, could be hydraulically extended by 42 in (1.28 m) to rotate the aircraft nose-up. Dunlop supplied the wheels and multi-disc brakes controlled by Maxaret anti-skid units. Irving provided the enormous circular braking parachute, ejected from a container in the upper 'pen-nib' fairing between the engine nozzles. The canopy was capable of being reefed to avoid control difficulties in a crosswind.

The positive rotation achieved by extending the nose leg could be selected either before or during the take-off run. It significantly shortened the minimum take-off distance. Although the longitudinal control provided by the horizontal tails was excellent, their moment arm behind the main gears was short, and use of these surfaces alone would have been less effective, besides increasing drag.

As in so many other areas, TSR.2 broke new ground as far as Britain was concerned in the design of the flight-control system, although it followed the technology pioneered with the North American A-5 Vigilante almost a decade earlier. In fact, the Vigilante pioneered the same overall layout, with a sharply tapered high-lift wing mounted on top of a long fuselage which was narrow past the tandem cockpits and much wider downstream of the engine inlets. In TSR.2, above and below this wide rear fuselage, was a total of four door-type airbrakes, which were exceedingly powerful when fully opened.

The one feature of the Vigilante flight controls not adopted was the use of spoilers in both the upper and lower surfaces of the wings. In contrast, the TSR.2 wing could hardly have been simpler, with no fences and no movable surfaces at all except the flaps. This was possible because of the simple yet radical design of the tail. It almost resembled that of a missile, with three fully powered surfaces (one vertical, two horizontal), and no fixed surface at all. The

The night would have been TSR.2's natural environment thanks to its advanced terrain-following radar, sophisticated navigation system and all-weather capability. No aircraft, before or since, has been designed to fly so low, so fast.

Above: When Jimmy Dell stepped out of of XR219 after his first flight, on 15 January 1965, he said, "the aircraft actually handled like a Lightning and one had to be careful not to exceed the specified limits for the prototype."

P.17A had featured a modest fin and rudder and two large ventral fins. TSR.2 had a single 'stab' vertical, adopted (again as in the Vigilante) after evaluating twin vertical surfaces mounted at an oblique angle. The delta tailerons operated together for control in pitch and differentially for control in roll. Of course, at Mach 2.25 the angular limits were very small, but these were progressively opened out until at the landing the possible authority was tremendous. Moreover, when the flaps were lowered the taileron power was further enhanced by unlocking small geared elevators.

The avionics debacle

The surfaces were governed by the pilot via the outstandingly capable flight-control system. Developed by Elliott Flight Automation, this included the autopilot, a digital computer and the pilot's HUD. In 1956 the Ministry of Supply, noticing that three US firms were developing airborne digital computers, funded a British counterpart known as DEXAN (Digital EXperimental Airborne Navigator). By 1957 two types of airborne digital computer were well advanced in development, but the ridiculous belief that no more manned aircraft would be required threw these on the scrap heap. Accordingly, when such a device was needed for TSR.2 the Ministry decided that Britain could not produce anything in time, so Elliott had to take a licence for the Autonetics Verdan, as used in the Vigilante, even though this could not meet the requirements of low-level operation. Elliott modified Verdan into the TSR.2's version, and later into the 920M family which were even sold for use in US aircraft. One wonders what might have been achieved with a sensible British aerospace programme.

H. M. Hobson was the prime contractor for the flight-control power units. Of course, although Britain had pioneered fly-by-wire electrical signalling since the late 1940s, notably with Boulton Paul's Tay-Viscount, the signalling to the power units was partly electronic but mainly mechanical. The overall system was principally of a quadruplex nature, although parts were triplex. Particular care was taken to route the parallel flight-control linkages and hydraulic systems as far apart as possible, to lessen the chance of a single hit by a shell or missile rendering the aircraft uncontrollable.

Above: Flying with the gear down, XR219 displays the type's powerful blown flaps. The TSR.2 was the first aircraft to use full-span blown flaps. A similar system was eventually used on the Buccaneer, but it was far less powerful than that intended for TSR.2.

Right: TSR.2 boasted a 37-ft (12.2-m) wingspan and a planned maximum take-off weight of 95,900 lb (43500 kg) – the former equivalent to a Spitfire but the latter far heavier than a fully loaded Lancaster. Despite this, its handling in the air was always exemplary.

The main power systems were typically state of the art. Each engine drove a hydraulic pump, and a third was driven by the Bristol Siddeley Cumulus APU (auxiliary power unit) mounted immediately in front of the weapons bay. To reduce system weight the cut-out pressure was 4,000 psi (281 kg/cm²), and the fluid was the fireproof ICI Silcodyne H. The main electric power circuits were 400-Hz AC, energised by a 55-kVA Rotax alternator on each engine, mounted on a Plessey constant-speed drive.

Emergency oversight

Most of the accessory power systems and their gearboxes could be reached standing on the ground via doors under the broad rear fuselage. Remarkably, in what the media called an "all-singing, all-dancing" aircraft, no emergency ram-air turbine or monofuel power unit was fitted, emergency power being available only from windmilling engines. For use on take-off, or whenever maximum power was demanded, an 80-Imp gal (364-litre) tank of demineralised water was fitted between the jetpipes.

The engines themselves were impressive, especially in full afterburner. Whereas the P.17A would have had inlets under the wings, as in the F-111 (initially with disastrous results for the US

aircraft), Vickers extended the ducts to the forward fuselage, well ahead of the wing. Undoubtedly, this helped to avoid the F-111's protracted problems with engine inlet airflow. Each inlet was a semicircular D-shape with a sharp lip on which shockwaves were focused by a translating (axially-sliding) centrebody. A short way downstream were two auxiliary inlets, with aft-hinged doors open at low airspeeds in an arrangement similar to that used on contemporary Sukhoi aircraft. Prime contractor for the inlet system was Joseph Lucas. At the other end

of the propulsion system the nozzles were varied in profile and throat/exit area by a 'fueldraulic' system with multiple actuators.

The weapons carriage of TSR.2 was confused by several misleading statements by ministers. Among these were "It will carry air-to-air missiles", and "a weapon being developed for TSR.2 will also be applicable to the V-bombers" (the weapon was Martel, which was never applicable to any V-bomber), and "TSR.2 will carry an air-launched ballistic missile."

Nuclear strike role

Returning to the real world, the original requirement was to carry either a single Red Beard nuclear weapon in the bomb bay or two of the tactical bombs (later designated WE.177) superimposed in the internal bay and two more on the inboard pylons. In the nuclear role the outboard pylons were not fitted, but auxiliary tanks could be carried either in the weapon bay or on the inboard pylons, whichever arrangement was available.

In the conventional role the normal internal load would have been two triple clusters of 1,000-lb (454-kg) HE bombs carried in the weapons bay. If necessary, at the cost of reduced

maximum airspeed, singles or tandem pairs of similar bombs could be carried on the four wing pylons. Alternatively, each pylon could carry an AJ.168 Martel attack missile (the carriage of the TV guidance pack had not been decided) or a multi-tube rocket launcher of which several forms were to be available.

A TSR.2 mission

From the outset, TSR.2 was designed to operate completely independently of ground facilities other than fuel. Thus, it was to be able to fly missions from austere forward bases which, as already noted, did not need a paved runway. Fuel was to be flown in and stored in giant flexible bags. BAC designed a four-wheeled GSV (general servicing vehicle) in support. Running on a very wide range of fuels, this could tow the aircraft on the ground, supply air-conditioning, pneumatic, electric and hydraulic power, function-test each aircraft system, and provide hydraulic power to drive a high-capacity pump to feed fuel from the bag storage.

Two further vehicles were to be provided which, like the GSV, fuel bags and everything else, were to be air-portable in an Argosy C.1.

Slowing TSR.2 down was always a concern for the designers. Its four huge airbrakes, combined with a large braking chute, were intended to stop the aircraft, and were a vital element in TSR.2's intended short-field capability.

One was a self-powered heavylift trolley, able to load any weapon or change an engine, or even a wing. It also served as a servicing platform from which any part of the aircraft could be reached. Height to the fin-cap antenna was 24 ft (7.32 m). The other vehicle was a universal testing trolley, towed by the GSV, with which the onboard systems, especially the avionics, could be checked out before each mission. It was written into the OR.343 requirement that, with its support vehicles, a TSR.2 could be maintained at instant readiness for 30 days.

During mission planning the navigator would collect all navigation information, and build the complete flight plan. This would then be translated by keyboard to a punched tape, which the navigator would then take to the aircraft and feed into the Verdan computer. This could be done using onboard battery power.

Cockpit

Pilot and navigator would climb aboard via either ladders or a large platform wheeled up beside the cockpits. They would strap into their Martin-Baker Mk 8A seats. The Mk 8 was a rocket-assisted seat designed expressly for this aircraft, with zero-height zero-airspeed capability. The ejection circuit was computer-controlled. If initiated by the navigator, his alone departed, with no delay, and the pilot's canopy remained untouched. Initiated by the pilot, both canopies would be jettisoned, followed by the navigator's seat and, a fraction of a second later, the pilot's.

Of course, both cockpits were pressurised and air-conditioned, prime contractor for this system being Sir George Godfrey and Partners, with Normalair pressure controllers. Humidity was controlled, and, unless otherwise commanded, Teddington Aircraft Controls subsystems maintained temperature at 15°C. The air-cycle packs

On flight five, on 14 January 1965, Beamont suffered an undercarriage problem in XR219 whereby the main gear bogies locked in the 'up' position – that is, with the wheels hanging down almost in line with the undercarriage leg. Beamont landed safely with the aid of the TSR.2's precise taileron controls. However, undercarriage vibration problems continued.

British Aircraft Corporation TSR.2

XR222 (prototype KO.4) was due to fly in July 1965. Like all nine TSR.2 prototypes it had a full test programme mapped out for it until 1968, at least. XR222 was to be tasked with longitudinal handling and auto-stabilisation testing. It would then undertake envelope expansion flying followed by auto-ILS trials at Boscombe Down. XR222 was lucky. It escaped the breaker's yard to languish at Cranfield for many years until removed and restored at the Imperial War Museum's Duxford airfield.

Radar

For TSR.2 Ferranti designed the world's first practical terrain-following radar, which was reputed to have a range in excess of 40 miles (64 km). The radar also had 'look into the turn' capability for true TF flying down to 200 ft (61 m). Unlike other radars of its generation the new mono-pulse Ferranti set was all transistor, which contributed to its light weight of only 230 lb (104.3 kg).

Powerplant

The tried and trusted Olympus was radically redesigned by Bristol Siddeley for the TSR.2, resulting in the Olympus 320-22R. The engine was designed to produce in excess of 19,600 lb (87.22 kN) thrust dry and over 30,000 lb (133.5 kN) with reheat. Only the General Electric YJ93-GE-3, developed for the XB-70 Valkyrie, was more powerful. An unrealistic official requirement for the engine to sustain Mach 2.2 for 45 minutes imposed excessive structural demands on the engines which lead to catastrophic failures until the dynamics of the new high-pressure compressors were explored and understood.

TSR.2 weapons

TSR.2 was intended from the outset as a vehicle for dumb bombs, albeit nuclear ones. It was at one time proposed to equip the aircraft with the Blue Water stand-off missile, but Blue Water was cancelled in 1962. TSR.2 was wired for the short-range TV-guided Martel and no doubt other more sophisticated weapons would have been added. However, its prime role was nuclear strike carrying Britain's Red Beard and subsequent WE177 tactical nuclear bombs. At one stage BAC did propose an AAM-equipped version of TSR.2 for the CAF, to serve as a long-range interceptor after Canada's own CF-105 Arrow was cancelled. This version would have carried a mix of Sparrow and Falcon missiles and there is no doubt Sidewinder AAMs could have been easily integrated.

Reconnaissance role

A sophisticated sensor fit (a term not then invented) was planned for the TSR.2, to conduct pre- and post-strike reconnaissance. Its primary system would have been an EMI-developed, Q-band SLAR – which also acted as an aid to the onboard INS/Doppler navigation system. EMI was also involved in producing an infra-red linescan for TSR.2 which could be fitted with an HF datalink – another revolutionary development for the time. A conventional (but climatically-controlled) camera pack could also have been fitted.

Cockpit

The TSR.2 was designed for high-speed, low-level flight. The Triplex Safety Glass Company developed a transparency that could withstand a 3-lb (1.36-kg) birdstrike at near supersonic speed. The transparency also had to remain stable at very high temperatures (up to 150°C/302°F) as the pilot's HUD was projected directly onto it. The canopy also incorporated a gold layer to protect the crew against nuclear flash.

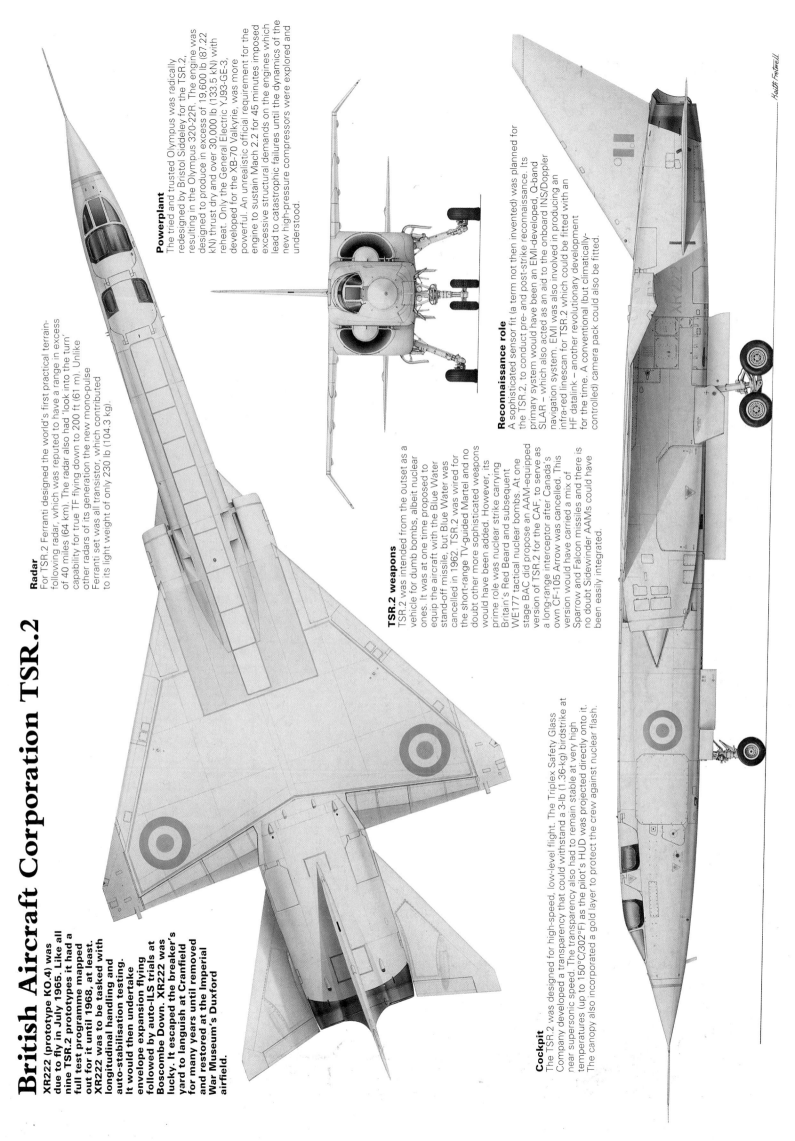

Keith Fretwell

were completely duplicated, excess heat from both the cockpits and the electronics racking being removed by Marston Excelsior fuel-cooled heat exchangers. Separate pipes were provided for the crew's ventilated suits.

Engines were started pneumatically, taking air from a ground cart. At a forward base TSR.2 could have operated completely autonomously. Battery power would have been used to start the APU, which by itself could provide not only compressed air to start the main engines but also hydraulic and electric power and ground air-conditioning. With either main engine started, the APU could be switched off. All necessary systems power would be available, cross-bleed being used to start the second engine.

Quick reaction capability

If not done previously, when loading the flight plan into the computer, the navigator would then run up and align the Ferranti inertial platform and check that it knew the exact starting position and had this linked to the central computer. It was a requirement of OR.343 that, at any time, with no support other than the vehicles forming part of the weapon system, TSR.2 should be airborne within five minutes of a previously planned mission being authorised.

Thus, there would be no lengthy ground testing or running up of the engines. The latter would have burned a lot of fuel, and even with the parking brake engaged it was impossible to hold a TSR.2 with one engine giving more than MIL (maximum dry, i.e. non-afterburning) power. Before moving off the crew would close their individual canopies, hinged down from the rear and latched. To taxi a TSR.2 the pilot used nosewheel steering. It was eventually found possible to steer after a fashion by applying quick jabs of left or right brake, but any attempt to use differential braking in a smooth manner brought the aircraft to a stop.

Lined up on the runway, or a dirt strip on some distant tropical island, the pilot would select 30° flap, with full blowing. He could then go from idle to full reheat in about 2.5 seconds. For minimum run the nose leg would not be extended until speed was passing through the 90-kt (165-km/h) level. Taking maximum take-off weight and maximum afterburning thrust in each case, the TSR.2 had 65 lb (0.29 kN) of thrust for each 100 lb (45 kg) of weight, whereas the figure for the F-111A was only 37 lb (0.16 kN). Thus, 145 kt (269 km/h) would be reached very quickly, and the TSR.2 would be airborne in something between 1,000 and 3,000 ft (305 and 914 m), depending on weight, airfield height and ambient temperature.

With gear retracted the initial rate of climb could exceed 50,000 ft/min (254 m/s), and if necessary the climb could be continued to 50,000 ft (15240 m). During a textbook 1,000-nm

(1844-km) sortie, the initial climb would be checked at 23,000 ft (7000 m) and the aircraft would cruise-climb at Mach 0.92 to about 26,000 ft (7925 m), at a distance of about 630 nm (1167 km). Reheat would then be selected, and the aircraft climb at Mach 1.7 to nearly 50,000 ft upon entering hostile territory, when a steep dive would be made at Mach 1.7 followed by 600 kt (1106 km/h) indicated to the penetration height of 200 ft (91 m).

Low-level leader

Thirty years ago no other aircraft in the world could cross hostile territory at Mach 0.9 at 200 ft; in fact, the TSR.2 was to be cleared to Mach 1.2. This was substantially lower than the permitted limit for the F-111A, which was its nearest rival, and a further factor that would have been much in the minds of the crew was that the specification for the US aircraft did not demand the ability to resist severe birdstrikes at maximum speed at low level. Moreover, it seated the crew side-by-side, so the chance of a windscreen birdstrike was roughly doubled.

En route navigation was accomplished by the most comprehensive suite of avionics ever packaged into a British aircraft, all linked to and through the duplicate computers. It was a highly flexible system giving total autonomy for the demanding task of flying from the 800-nm (1475-km) to the 1,000-nm (1844-km) point just 200 ft above the ground at Mach 0.9 across

TSR.2 airframe

Above: Today, preserved at the Aerospace Museum, Cosford, XR220 stands in silent judgement on those who failed it. There is little doubt that had the programme gone ahead TSR.2s might still be flying in RAF hands (at the very least) today.

Below: To the rear of the navigator's cockpit was the TSR.2's main avionics bay. Entirely new ground was broken by all the UK firms involved in TSR.2 systems R&D.

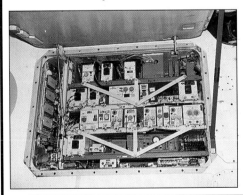

Above: The TSR.2's ventral weapons bay was intended to carry a single tactical nuclear bomb, in the days when such weapons were still bulky and heavy items.

Above right: The complex main gear was developed by Electro-Hydraulics and made from exotic materials for increased strength.

Left: The nose gear could be raised by 30 in (76.2 cm) increasing the angle of attack for short take offs.

Right: The brakechute was housed above and between the huge afterburner nozzles.

Above: In the TSR.2's wing bleed air from the engines was feed into plenum chambers along the wing leading edge, then out over the flaps.

Above: The Olympus 22R was the key to TSR.2's performance, but in the early days it was unreliable and dangerous.

hostile territory no matter what the terrain or weather. Even today, the TSR.2 is probably the most 'penetrable' aircraft ever built, with the possible exception of the USAF's stealthy aircraft of a later generation.

The primary navigation system comprised the Decca Doppler combined with the Ferranti inertial system and Smiths air-data system. The computers, in which all the navigation data was already stored, continuously calculated ground speed and drift using the Doppler, and heading and velocity from the inertial platform. These data were continuously displayed to the navigator as distance to go along and across track to the next stored waypoint. At TSR.2 speed the errors were likely to be measured in feet, but the possible length of the mission dictated that repeated precise fixes were fed in from the largest single avionics item, the EMI SLAR.

This looked out on either side through 90-in (2.74-m) antennas between fuselage stations 207 and 280. Approximately every 100 miles (160 km) it would be used to provide an actual fix to be overlaid on the computed fix on the navigator's display.

TF systems

The above systems took care of the horizontal plane. During the final low-level phase of the mission, control in the vital vertical plane required different systems. The pilot flew looking ahead through his Rank-Cintel HUD, on which was presented all the information he needed. One item would be terrain clearance, provided by the dual STC (Standard Telephones and Cables) radar altimeters. Crucial information on the terrain ahead was provided by the Ferranti monopulse forward-looking

radar which, in addition to giving the pilot a picture, also fed into the terrain-following system the range at which a line projected directly ahead would intercept the ground (if at all), and the angle of the terrain at that point.

This information was fed to the dual Elliott Automation autopilot which flew the aircraft automatically. Called a ski-toe locus, it functioned as if the aircraft were fitted with a long leaf spring sticking out in front which could, like a ski, carry it over obstructions and even over mountains. Such features as radio masts could automatically be flown around rather than over. Thus, the crew could fly the aircraft at 200 ft without visual reference. The navigator would watch his big-screen display giving computed and actual radar position, his digital along/across distance/time readouts and a moving-map display, and the pilot would watch

In total, XR219 spent 13 hours and three minutes in the air, but more than twice that in taxiing trials and ground running. A full flight test programme was mapped out for it, XR220 and the other seven development aircraft (XR221/27, KO.3/9) before the project's sudden end.

Below left: Flight 16, Beamont's last flight in the TSR.2, was intended for limited roll exploration and Beamont engaged in partial and Dutch rolls up to 90°. Then, as a final fillip, he rolled the aircraft once right through 360°, much to the surprise of the chase crew.

the terrain ahead (if he could see it) while looking through the HUD and occasionally looking at his own moving-map display and the various flight instruments.

As far as possible, everything was automated, for example relieving the crew of housekeeping tasks such as fuel management. The crew's comfort was maximised by a combination of the design of the seats, the excellent environmental system, masks fed from liquid-oxygen storage, the quite high wing loading of 137 lb/sq ft (670 kg/m³), the short span, and the flexural design of the airframe which gave a smoother ride at high speed at low level than in any previous aircraft. The terrain-following was fail-safe; for example, any dangerous system failure would automatically put the aircraft into a programmed climb.

Incidentally, the TSR.2 was theoretically a Mach 3 aircraft. Such a Mach number was not required, and for it to be sustained would have required completely different materials for the airframe, and especially for the transparencies.

At all times TSR.2 was to carry one forward-looking and two lateral F.95 cameras in the nose. These would be activated as the target was approached. At a pre-computed point, the aircraft would be automatically established in a climb at a constant pitch-rate to give an exactly known trajectory. Again automatically, the nuclear weapon would be armed by the Elliott weapon-aiming computer, and released at a pre-determined angle. Thus, it would arch over towards the target, while the aircraft made a tight wing-over manoeuvre to return the way it had come. This, and the alternatives of level laydown (using a para-braked bomb), loft bombing, or level attack from medium altitude, could all be done blind. A dive/toss attack required visual reference to the target.

Red Beard, the original UK tactical bomb, required a high-altitude release in a toss manoeuvre, in turn requiring the TSR.2 to leave the safety of low level for a zoom climb to the release point. WE177A was the laydown tactical weapon, initially designed with the TSR.2 in mind, and could be delivered in a low-level pass across the target, using a parachute to retard it, thereby giving the TSR.2 time to escape. It was further envisaged that a limited number of the TSR.2 force would be issued with the high-yield WE177B, to bolster the V-bombers of the strategic force.

Return to friendly skies

Back over friendly territory the TSR.2 might use its Marconi long-range HF radio, while climbing to a little over 30,000 ft (9144 m). From this height it would cruise-climb at Mach 0.92 to about 36,000 ft (10972 m) when 90 nm (167 km) from base. It would then be possible to use the Plessey UHF/VHF radio and ensure freedom from interception with the Cossor IFF (identification friend or foe). Back at its own airfield the approach could be made on the Marconi ILS (instrument landing system). The landing would use 30° flap, the runway being touched at about 165 kt (304 km/h), the braking parachute being streamed immediately to minimise brake temperature.

In a conventional war HE could be delivered on the level, if necessary using parachute retarders or in a toss or dive attack. Depending on the procedure adopted, the delivery could be automatic, measuring target range with the forward-looking radar and feeding this to the Elliott WAC (weapon-aiming computer). Targets of opportunity could be attacked using bombs, rockets or air/surface missiles, using manual visual delivery.

In an alternative mission, reconnaissance, the aircraft could be equipped with a large pallet fitted into the weapon bay. This could be fitted with an EMI Q-band high-definition SLAR, with MTI (moving-target indication, in which only objects moving relative to the ground are detected). This would give coverage out to 10 nm (18.5 km) on either side of track, the results being recorded on special film. A second sensor would be active optical linescan (giving a thermal picture in which hotter areas could be either darker or lighter) by Hawker Siddeley Dynamics/Mullard, providing day or night target pictures which could be transmitted by radio to a friendly mobile ground station. In addition, up to three FX.126 reconnaissance cameras could be installed. It was intended also to develop a TV reconnaissance system able, like the linescan, to transmit target pictures to a mobile ground station.

Surprisingly, bearing in mind that in 1944 RAF Bomber Command led the world in such matters, nothing was said about radar warning and infra-red warning sensors, ECM (electronic countermeasures), chaff/flare dispensers and other devices to enable the enemy's defensive systems to be outwitted. This may have been on grounds of security, though if the Falklands War is any guide it was because the required funding had been blocked by the Treasury.

The political storm

Thus, although TSR.2 would have incorporated a comprehensive suite of navigation/attack systems, weapons and sensors suitable for a multi-role aircraft, it might still have lacked defensive systems. Tragically, more than 30 years ago neither the media nor Britain's technically illiterate politicians comprehended any of this, and it all seemed an outrageous waste of money. This was gold-dust to the Labour party, who shrewdly saw that it could help them win the general election due in October 1964. Accordingly, before long the general attitude of everyone in Britain – except the tiny minority who actually knew a little about the subject – was "we must stop building aircraft that merely thrill the technicians at the taxpayer's expense."

Moreover, the aircraft itself was increasingly seen as – according to Robert Blackburn, of *Flight International* – "never a fact in the national sense. It was an image, shadowy and distorted. Secrecy is the ideal climate for intrigue and mismanagement." The programme was hardly helped by repeated delays caused by unforeseen technical problems, repeated escalation in the apparent costs, and repeated stupid statements by the ministers who were supposed to be justifying it.

The delays had several causes. In October 1963 the Ministry of Aviation released two photographs of the first TSR.2 looking virtually complete in the erection shop at Weybridge,

The TSR.2 had an unrefuelled range of 1,000 nm (1852 km; 1150 miles) with a high-level transit, supersonic descent and high-subsonic dash to target. With external fuel this figure would increase to 1,500 nm (2778 km, 1726 miles) and to 2,120 nm (3926 km; 2439 miles) with a single refuelling (from a buddy pack-equipped TSR.2).

and announced that it was "negotiating for a full production contract for an initial batch of 30 TSR.2s for squadron service." These would have had serial numbers beginning with XS660. The purpose of this very informative release is hard to fathom. At home, the chief result was that the general public thought the aircraft was about to fly, so the Labour party was handed an extra election bonus when it was still on the ground a year later. On a wider canvas, the Soviet design bureau of Pavel Sukhoi studied the photographs and adopted precisely the same configuration (and almost the same size, weight and power) for its T6-1 prototype.

Conquering Olympus

The most serious cause of delay was a dangerous flaw in the engine. After extensive testbed running, the first flight-cleared Olympus 320X engine was mounted in a twin-inlet nacelle scabbed under a Vulcan test aircraft, its propulsive nozzle making those of the aircraft's original four Olympus engines look tiny. On 3 December 1963 this engine exploded during running on the Filton (Bristol) airfield, destroying both the aircraft and an over-enthusiastic fire tender. A month later a second Olympus 320X exploded, followed by another in the first half of 1964.

Discovering the reason proved particularly elusive. It was soon traced to the redesigned tubular shaft joining the LP (low-pressure) turbine to the LP compressor. Quite early it was clear that this shaft was failing due to overstress and fatigue caused by resonance, but ascertaining the cause of the resonance proved difficult. Not

until August 1964 was it proved that the resonance was excited by the high-pressure cooling air to the central inter-shaft bearing. This blasted radially through holes and impinged on the U-shaft, and at 97 per cent of maximum rpm the frequency of the air jets made the U-shaft ring like a bell.

Although the engine was at once redesigned, nothing could be done to modify the engines actually installed in the first aircraft without causing even further delay. Chief test pilot R. P. 'Bee' Beamont and navigator Don Bowen were faced with making the first flight with engines which, if opened up to near take-off thrust, were exceedingly dangerous. Packed into the tight rear fuselage, and surrounded by fuel, the LP shaft of either engine could have caused instant destruction of the aircraft, particularly on take-off. Keeping them below 97 per cent rpm would have provided insufficient power in the event of loss of an engine, because for the first flight this landing gear had not been cleared to retract.

Painted overall in anti-flash white, with the same pale national markings as the nuclear-cleared V-bombers, XR219 was originally intended to fly from its assembly airfield at Weybridge to the Aeroplane & Armament Experimental Establishment at Boscombe Down. The next decision was that it should begin trials at nearby Wisley, but in April 1964 it was taken to Boscombe by road, in sections. Had it been decreed from the outset that the

assembly line should be at Warton, the home of the former English Electric Aviation, the first flight would have occurred about six months earlier.

Maiden flight

Still in the worrying situation that the engines, already derated, were still unsafe, Beamont and Bowen carried out fast taxi tests from 2 September 1964. These were generally encouraging, although they were punctuated by potentially serious failures of the braking parachute, which on one occasion brought brake temperatures up to 1200°C (2,192°F). At last, at 15.28 on 27 September 1964, Beamont and Bowen took off on the first flight, with gear extended. Beamont had accepted use of 100 per cent rpm for the first two minutes on this first flight only, insisting on safe engines for subsequent flying. Although brief, the first flight accomplished a great deal, not least confirmation of the aircraft's superb handling. Take-off was at 76,300 lb (34610 kg), of which 16,151 lb (7326 kg) was usable fuel.

The only untoward happening on the first flight was a sudden, severe but mercifully brief, lateral judder when the main gears touched the runway. This was a feature of several subsequent flights, until the cause was found and eliminated. This short first flight had covered two circuits and was accompanied by a Lightning flown by Jimmy Dell, who would undertake the

BAC TSR.2

1. Pitot head
2. Radome
3. Forward-looking terrain-following and attack radar
4. UHF aerial
5. ECM aerial
6. Rudder pedals
7. Control column
8. Pilot's head-up display
9. Flight-refuelling probe (demountable)
10. Pilot's Martin-Baker Mk 8A ejection seat
11. Tactical instrument console
12. Navigator's Martin-Baker ejection seat
13. Sideways looking radar
14. Oblique camera
15. Radar altimeter aerials
16. Stand-by pitot
17. Systems ground connectors
18. Avionics equipment racks
19. Air system water separator
20. Liquid oxygen converter
21. Fuel system piping
22. Forward fuselage fuel tank
23. Nose undercarriage
24. Hydraulic retraction jack
25. Ventral Doppler aerial
26. Emergency generator
27. Air conditioning system regenerative heat exchanger
28. Inertial platform
29. Intake movable centre-body half cone
30. Centre-body jack
31. Intake suction relief doors
32. Airborne auxiliary power unit (AAPU)
33. Boundary layer spill ducts
34. Anti-collision light
35. HF notch aerial
36. Centre fuselage fuel tank
37. Main undercarriage
38. Tactical nuclear weapon in ventral bomb bay
39. Main undercarriage leg strut
40. Hydraulic retraction jack
41. Airframe-mounted engine accessory equipment gearbox
42. Hydraulic reservoirs
43. Hydraulic accumulator
44. Bristol Siddeley Olympus 320-22R engines
45. Water injection tank
46. External fuel tank
47. Wing integral fuel tank
48. Starboard navigation light
49. ILS aerial
50. ECM aerial
51. Starboard blown flap
52. Flap actuators
53. Flap blowing air duct
54. Inboard flap drive motor
55. Engine bleed air ducting
56. Dorsal air brakes
57. Airbrake drive motor
58. Airbrake screw jacks
59. Rear fuselage fuel tank
60. Starboard all-moving tailplane
61. VHF/UHF aerial
62. All-moving fin
63. Tail navigation light
64. Cooling air duct
65. Fin hinge post
66. Fin hydraulic actuator
67. Brake parachute housing
68. Hinged parachute door
69. Variable area afterburner nozzles
70. Afterburner duct
71. Tailplane flap
72. Tailplane flap actuator
73. Port all-moving tailplane
74. Tailplane mounting spigot
75. All-moving tailplane hydraulic actuator
76. Port blown flap
77. Ventral airbrakes
78. Fuel vent
79. ECM aerial
80. ILS aerial
81. Port navigation light
82. Port wing integral fuel tank
83. 450-Imp gal (1703-litre) external fuel tank

Some of the troubles that would have been in store for line mechanics on the TSR.2 are hinted at in this picture. The aircraft was large and sat high off the ground. Few of its important components were easily accessible.

later TSR.2 test flights, and a Canberra piloted by John Carrodus, both carrying Warton photographers.

At the end of November the modified engines began running at 100 per cent power, leaving undercarriage clearance as the main problem. Rather than fly another wheels-down flight, BAC elected to wait until the gear had completed the required 10 successful retraction/rotation cycles, followed by five installed in the aircraft while on jigs in the Boscombe hangar. This was finally achieved at the end of December, clearing the TSR.2 to fly again on the last day of 1964.

Flights 2 and 3 encountered violent high-frequency fore/aft vibration which appeared to be due to rapid variation – so-called shunting – in the No. 1 engine thrust. Beamont said it was doubly painful because the frequency, about 35 Hz, was approximately the natural frequency of the human eyeball. The vibration was due to an unexpected oscillation within one of the fuel pumps. When this was replaced, the trouble vanished, as demonstrated on Flight 4, undertaken on 8 January 1965.

Almost as serious was an inclination for one main gear to retract or extend and not the other. This was encountered on Flight 5, on 14 January. As Beamont climbed out of Boscombe Down, he selected undercarriage up, but the

port leg stayed down, as could be seen through navigator Bowen's periscope and confirmed by Dell in the chase Lightning T.Mk 4. The bogie was left hanging in the vertical position. After discussion with the ground, Beamont attempted to lower the gear, and while all three units appeared locked and down, both mainwheel bogies were in the vertical position. There was little choice but to attempt a landing, Beamont combining his extraordinary piloting skills with the beautifully controllable landing qualities of the TSR.2 to effect touchdown at a sink rate of less than 6 in (15 cm) per second, resulting in an uneventful tip-toe landing.

Flight 6 on 15 January was made with wheels down, before the undercarriage retraction problem had been cured, and was intended to provide low-speed handling data and the initial conversion flight for Jimmy Dell. The completion of the latest set of gear trials allowed Dell to take XR219 aloft for Flight 7 on 22 January, but this time the starboard gear remained down. A successful lowering of the other two members allowed a less worrying landing than Beamont had experienced. Low-speed stability and control checks occupied Dell and Bowen on Flight 8 (23 January), while Beamont flew 50° flap landings during Flight 9 (27 January).

On 6 February the undercarriage trials were completed again, and with Beamont at the controls the TSR.2 began to increase the envelope, pushing out incrementally to the flutter limit of 500 kt IAS.

The remaining 13 flights were undertaken without any serious problems with the

Even in the short space of time it actually spent in the air, the single TSR.2 prototype accomplished far more than had been initially envisioned. With a total of nine aircraft in the test programme there is little doubt the aircraft's few problems would have been quickly solved.

following highlights: Flight 12 – first flight for pilot Don Knight, heavy landing fractured port undercarriage jack although sink rate was within limits; Flight 13 (16 February) – Dell took the aircraft to 30,000 ft and Mach 0.9; Flight 14 (22 February) – Beamont and Peter Moneypenny transferred XR219 to Warton, including a photo-shoot and the aircraft's first supersonic flight (to Mach 1.12) along the way; Flight 16 (26 February) – Beamont undertook low-level high-speed flights down to 200 ft (61 m) through the Pennines and rolled the aircraft for the first time; Flight 17 (7 March) – Dell took XR219 to 600 kt IAS; Flight 18 (also on 7 March) – sortie aborted due to massive fuel leak in fueldraulic system; Flight 19 (11 March) and Flight 20 (12 March) – more fuel leak problems, low-level data.

During some of these flights the TSR.2 had landed on a foam path to test its ability to land on this fire-retardant surface. Following a brief lay-up to replace various items and attention to the fuel leaks, XR219 returned to the sky for the final phase of testing: Flights 21 and 22 (26 March) – Dell flew numerous landing patterns to establish that the post-landing oscillation problem had been cured, utilising the circuits for simulated single-engine conditions; Flight 23 (27 March) – familiarisation sortie for Don Knight; Flight 24 (31 March) – roll/yaw optimisation sortie by Dell.

Political decisions

A successful first flight was the last thing the Labour party wanted, and it countered with ever more horrifying estimations of TSR.2 cost. It was notably assisted by the inevitable British climate of secrecy and amateurism, Aviation Minister Julian Amery telling the Commons he could not remember the estimated programme cost. During his election campaign, Denis Healey stormed "TSR.2 will only drop ordinary high explosive on tanks and bridges... new anti-aircraft weapons will be able to shoot it down by the time it is in service, so at £16 million an aircraft it is going to make all Mr Amery's other blunders look like chickenfeed." Conservative ministers said £16 million was "an exaggeration by a factor of 10", while declining to reveal any actual costs.

Once in office, the Labour ministers called the aircraft "this inherited monster ... which has already gone on long enough," and later proclaimed that it was "not the duty of the defence forces to act as a wet nurse to the overgrown and mentally retarded children in our

economy." Technology Minister Anthony Wedgwood Benn said the aircraft industry (just the British one) was "like taking pennies from a blind man's tin." On 10 March 1965 test pilot Beamont was booked to give the Bamwell Memorial Lecture before the Royal Aeronautical Society; it would have been undesirable to the government for someone with authority to state how outstanding the TSR.2 was, so he was forbidden to give the lecture. Of course, he had previously gained full security clearance for it, but how could he argue with the TSR.2's customer?

At last, after Prime Minister Harold Wilson had explained to the public what a useless aircraft TSR.2 was, and that it was "far too early to say whether it will succeed or not," Chancellor James Callaghan announced cancellation of the whole programme in his budget speech on 6 April 1965, tucked quietly between an extra sixpence tax on cigarettes and four shillings on whisky.

There followed months of accusation and counter-accusation, and ever wilder assessments of what TSR.2 would have cost, and how many millions would be saved by the switch to equipping the RAF with 50 General Dynamics F-111Ks. These 'savings' ignored the fact that buying a British product would have kept the money in Britain, and also returned a large fraction to the Treasury in taxes, while buying a foreign product meant that all the money would leave the country and benefit only the economy of the supplier.

The question of cost

Unlike the situation in the USA, where the public can usually have confidence in the cost figures reported to Congress by the armed forces and their industrial suppliers, the British love of secrecy has to this day made it impossible to assess the financial side of the TSR.2 programme with any confidence. Everyone had a huge axe to grind, and was concerned with proving a particular argument.

To give a flavour of the credibility of the official figures, ministers and former ministers gave assurances that the total programme cost for TSR.2 (seldom explaining what they meant) would have been 14 different sums varying from £105 million to £1,000 million. In a written Commons answer on 1 February 1967, Defence Minister Healey said, "The total capital cost of the [F-111] programme is of the order of £135 million," but in the Defence Debate three months later the figure was revised to £336 million. In the end, Britain decided to withdraw its forces from locations east of Suez, and in January 1968 cancelled the F-111K purchase.

After such a hate campaign against the British industry, and TSR.2 in particular, the new government had little choice but to call for immediate destruction of the 49 aircraft in the factories, scrapping of the materials and dismantling of the assembly jigs and tooling. Even an offer of a fixed-price £3 million programme to continue test flying with XR221, the third prototype, to develop the navigation, attack and reconnaissance systems, was refused, even though such systems were bound to be needed in the future.

XR219, the only TSR.2 to fly, had completed the first phase of flight testing with outstanding success in 24 flights, in the hands of

Above: When the end came for TSR.2, most reminders of the project were swept away with indecent haste. Many incomplete airframes were scrapped, along with all the jigs. XR222 survived, however. It was rebuilt and transferred to the Cranfield College of Aeronautics in October 1965. In 1978 it was saved by the Imperial War Museum and is now on display at Duxford.

Right: XR219, the most auspicious TSR.2, met a sad fate. It became a target for gunnery and warhead research at Foulness. It was largely destroyed by 1977 and scrapped in 1982.

three pilots and three navigators. In his final assessment of this phase Beamont wrote "..the flying qualities of this aircraft are ideally suited to its design roles, and it is potentially a highly successful design."

XR219 was eventually removed by road to the Proof and Experimental Establishment facility at Shoeburyness, where it was partially reassembled in 1968. The option of flying it to its new home was firmly ruled out by the government. Between 1973 and 1975 it was used as a ballistics target, and its remains were finally scrapped in 1982. The second aircraft, XR220, had been delivered to Boscombe Down in September 1964, but was damaged when it fell of a trailer. Jimmy Dell was ready to take it aloft for its first flight on 6 April, the day of the programme cancellation. The aircraft now resides in the Cosford Aerospace Museum. The mostly complete airframes of XR221 and XR223 also went to Shoeburyness, from where they were disposed of as scrap in 1972-73, while XR222 was presented to the Cranfield College of Aeronautics in October 1965. It spent most of the following years outside until, in 1978, it was presented to the Imperial War Museum at Duxford, which has since restored it to display condition. Other fragments from the production line remain, chiefly at Shoeburyness and the PEE ranges at Pendine. A gutted fuselage section is with the DRA at Farnborough and other parts are at Halton.

One cannot help feeling regret, not only at the abysmal management of this exceedingly important programme by successive British governments and the scientific civil service, but also at the customer's determination to make the specification as challenging as possible, mainly in order to avoid considering the excellent naval aircraft which was much later

Only two complete TSR.2s survive today: XR220 at Cosford and XR222 at Duxford (illustrated). Various components linger at the RAF School of Technical Training, Halton, and on scattered MoD ranges. Yet enough survives of the project to serve as a constant reminder of the tragedy, waste and sheer folly that was its premature and pointless cancellation.

adopted. Again, nobody appeared to consider the effect of such a history on the British aircraft industry. In an increasing number of countries around the world a thriving aerospace industry is regarded as the leading edge of technology development, spurring on the nation's technical capability on a wide front. In Britain, in contrast, of the 60 firms making the largest contributions to TSR.2, 57 have ceased to exist.

A twist in the tail is that, when Britain threw its own aircraft on the scrap-heap and bought the F-111, the Sukhoi design bureau, with the agreement of the customer, completely redesigned the T6 prototypes. The short-span fixed wing with blown flaps and downturned tips (as noted, a clone of TSR.2) was replaced by pivoted swing-wings exactly like the F-111. Later, general designer Mikhail P. Simonov said, "We are proud of our Su-24, but we would have been equally proud had we adhered to the original configuration. In many ways it was superior." **Bill Gunston**

USAFE 1970-1979

During the 1970s the USAFE was a vital piece in the chess game of the Cold War. With the need for funds to fuel the war in Southeast Asia diminishing, the United States Air Forces in Europe became one of the main recipients of new equipment, and by the end of the decade many of the once-ubiquitous Phantoms had been replaced by A-10s, F-15s and F-111s.

On 1 January 1970 the United States Air Forces in Europe (USAFE) had 57,000 personnel and 770 aircraft, which was approximately half the number assigned in 1961. As the decade unfolded the command was in a settled position, having bedded down its forces in neighbouring countries, following the French withdrawal from the North Atlantic Treaty Organisation (NATO) and the enforced departure of USAF assets from bases in France. USAFE had suffered a lack of re-equipment as the ongoing commitment to the conflicts in Vietnam, Laos and Cambodia had the over-riding need for the majority of new equipment programmes. However, senior staff were acutely aware of the need to maintain the forces in Europe at an acceptable level of deterrence, to prevent the Soviet Union and its allies from crossing the Iron Curtain while the US was actively engaged in hostilities on the other side of the world.

At the start of the 1970s, USAFE was composed primarily of F-4 Phantoms in the ground attack role, plus specialist versions of the McDonnell Douglas design dedicated to tactical reconnaissance. The command also had a number of ageing F-100 Super Sabres, whose days in front-line service in Europe were decidedly numbered. Defence of central Europe had for many years been vested in the F-102 Delta Dagger, although the majority had been replaced by the F-4E version of the Phantom, with just one unit retaining the 'Dagger' as the decade opened. USAFE also operated a mix of specialist aircraft to perform airborne command post, tactical air control, and special operations, as well as a widely dispersed VIP and communication fleet.

USAFE had the primary role of maintaining the security of Western Europe as part of NATO. To perform this duty the command was under the control of both the United States Air Force and the US European Command (USEUCOM), while at the same time being part of NATO. During peacetime or unilateral military activity, USAFE was a component of USEUCOM, while the organisation would have come under direct control of NATO's Allied Air Forces Central Europe (AAFCE) in the event of a major confrontation with the Soviet Union or any of the Warsaw Pact nations. To ease responsibility for European activities, the commander of USEUCOM was also the CinC of AAFCE. Headquarters USEUCOM was located at Stuttgart, West Germany, with the command responsible for the integration of all US military assets in Europe into a cohesive, operational package.

Headquarters USAFE was located at Lindsey Air Station, Wiesbaden, West Germany in January 1970, with three numbered Air Forces co-ordinating activities within their geographical regions. The 3rd Air Force at South Ruislip Air Station, UK was solely responsible for assets located within the United Kingdom, while the 17th Air Force at Ramstein Air Base, West Germany controlled units within the northern area of Europe extending from West Germany to Belgium, the Netherlands and Norway. The remaining USAFE components were under the jurisdiction of the 16th Air Force at Torrejon Air Base, Spain. Ironically, the 16th AF had the largest operational area, as its responsibility extended from Spain to Turkey, but had the smallest fleet of aircraft, composed of just one fighter unit directly under its control. The 3rd and 17th AF were both components of the 4th Allied Tactical Air Force (4th ATAF), which was a NATO organisation with fighter units from the RAF, Belgian, Dutch and West German Air Forces operating regularly with those of USAFE. The 16th AF was part of NATO's Allied Forces Southern Europe (AFSOUTH), with the Air Forces of Spain, Italy, Greece and Turkey.

4th ATAF

USAFE forces within the northern and central region of Europe were also part of the Supreme Headquarters Allied Powers Europe (SHAPE) with headquarters at Mons, Belgium. SHAPE itself was responsible for a chain of command incorporating land, sea and air assets from the member countries composed into the Allied Forces Central Europe (AFCENT). Air units were themselves further refined into the Allied Air Forces Central Europe (AAFCE), which was directly responsible for the 4th ATAF. Apart from the 3rd and 17th Air Forces, the 4th ATAF included elements of the 32nd US Army Air Defense Command, as well as the 1st Canadian Air Group, and the German Air Forces 1st and 2nd Air Force Divisions.

As will become readily apparent, the area of responsibility of USAFE was not restricted to the continent of Europe, for the command was allocated the control of certain support types stationed in northern and central Africa, as well as those in Saudi Arabia and Iran. Among the elderly types operated were the C-47 Skytrain in service at eight locations, and the C-54 Skymaster at five. These were only in service for the first half of the decade, as most were withdrawn and flown back to the USA for storage and eventual disposal, or transferred to local air arms.

At the start of the decade, the 81st TFW had two squadrons of F-4Cs (92nd TFS illustrated). These were retained until 1973.

The 81st TFW operated the Phantom in the standard fighter-bomber role. The F-4D served from 1969 to 1979.

Illustrating the 'smart' capability of the F-4D, this 91st TFS aircraft takes off carrying an AVQ-23 Pave Spike laser designator, GBU-10 Paveway I LGB and GBU-8 HOBO electro-optical bomb.

3rd Air Force

The backbone of fighter capability was provided by the F-4 Phantom which began arriving in Europe in October 1965 for service with the 81st Tactical Fighter Wing at the twin bases of RAF Bentwaters and Woodbridge, initiating the transition from the F-101 Voodoo. At the time the 81st TFW was the only USAFE unit to operate the F-4C version exclusively in the conventional fighter role, although the 401st TFW at Torrejon AB, Spain later converted to the version. Other F-4C squadrons were dedicated to Wild Weasel defence-suppression duties. During the first part of 1971, the 81st TFW began preparing aircraft for transfer to the Spanish air force, with 36 F-4Cs being involved. The 81st TFW's initial equipment was composed of 72 F-4Cs from the latter part of the FY 1964 order book, although the displaced Phantoms were replaced by two dozen

The Fairchild A-10 was first delivered to the 81st TFW in 1978, the aircraft initially being painted in the 'Mask-10A' two-tone grey camouflage.

After about 30 aircraft had been delivered in grey, A-10s began arriving with the 81st TFW in April 1979 in the 'Charcoal Lizard' scheme. When the wing's last squadron was formed on 1 January 1980, it had two at Woodbridge and four at Bentwaters.

Below: The 10th TRW at Alconbury shed two of its three RF-4 squadrons in 1976. This aircraft flew with the 30th TRS, which deactivated in April.

Above: In 1972 **USAFE** units adopted wing tailcodes instead of squadron codes. This 30th TRS RF-4C, previously wearing the 'AS' code, was repainted with 'AR' for the 10th Tactical Reconnaissance Wing.

Below: The yellow fin stripe and 'AT' codes signified the 32nd TRS. Due to a reduction in reconnaissance requirements, the 10th TRW deactivated two squadrons. The 32nd TRS was the first to go in 1 January 1976.

FY 1963 airframes along with a handful of older aircraft from FY 1964 production. The F-4C remained in service with the 91st and 92nd TFS at Bentwaters only until the summer of 1973, when the aircraft were transferred to the 401st TFW at Torrejon AB, Spain, upon receipt of the F-4D. The 78th TFS at Woodbridge had received the F-4D during the late spring of 1969.

The 81st TFW was assigned tailcodes 'WR', 'WS' and 'WT' as the form of unit identification at individual squadron level. The Air Force changed the system completely during August/September 1972 in compliance with order AFM66-1, which required tactical units to adopt wing-level tailcodes. In place of the three different tailcodes displayed by 81st TFW aircraft, the wing selected 'WR' as its two-letter identifier. It is worth mentioning that the majority of USAFE units were allocated tailcodes whose first letter denoted the base, such as 'A' for Alconbury, 'B' for Bitburg, 'H' for Hahn and 'W' for Bentwaters/Woodbridge. The second letter of the system consisted of the letters 'R', 'S' and 'T' for most USAFE squadrons, with Bentwaters presenting 'WR', 'WS', and 'WT' on its F-4Cs.

In June 1976 the 81st TFW received three brand-new unmarked F-4Es which were delivered to Bentwaters, but moved to Woodbridge soon afterwards. A further six arrived one month later, although all remained parked in a corner of base in storage, under the care of the 81st TFW. After spending more than two months at the base without having flown, the F-4Es were reassigned to the 50th TFW and delivered to Hahn AB.

Thunderbolt II

The wing was slated to become the major operator of the Fairchild Republic A-10A Thunderbolt II, with the first three aircraft being delivered to Bentwaters on 24 August 1978. The 81st TFW retained the F-4D until 1979, having received many of it initial complement of 72 A-10As to equip four squadrons. At Bentwaters the 91st and 92nd TFS were joined by the 510th TFS, which was activated on 1 October 1978, while at Woodbridge the 78th TFS had the 509th TFS added on 1 October 1979. The latter was only in residence for four months before being transferred to Bentwaters in exchange for the 91st TFS. The sixth and final A-10A squadron to form was the 511th TFS which was activated at Bentwaters on 1 January 1980. The six squadrons were

allocated regular deployments to four forward operating locations in West Germany, stationed at Sembach AB (FOL 1), Ahlhorn AB (FOL 2), Leipheim AB (FOL 3), and Norvenich AB (FOL 4). Crews routinely deployed to these locations to overfly designated sections of West Germany to familiarise and memorise the layout of the terrain and any specific landmarks. The primary objective was for pilots to be so familiar with their designated areas that they would be able to detect any build-up of an enemy's camouflaged heavy armour and tanks if the Warsaw Pact nations made a thrust across the Iron Curtain into West Germany.

The 10th TRW had the distinction of being the first USAFE unit to receive the Phantom when it accepted delivery of its first RF-4Cs in May 1965. The unit operated three squadrons of RF-4Cs, although the gradual reduction in the need for tactical reconnaissance resulted in the 32nd TRS being inactivated on 1 January 1976, followed three months later by the 30th TRS. The 1st TRS remained at Alconbury, operating the RF-4C throughout the decade. The 527th Tactical Fighter Training and Aggressor Squadron was formed at Alconbury on 1 April 1976 with the first eight F-5Es being airfreighted into the base inside a C-5A in May

USAFE – 1 January 1970

Headquarters, USAFE

Lindsey AS, West Germany

7101st Air Base Wing, Wiesbaden AB, West Germany
no sqn	C-118A, VC-118A, C-131D, T-39A
7005th ABS	C-131D, VT-29B, VT-29C, T-39A at Stuttgart/Echterdingen Airport, West Germany
7104th ABS	VC-118A at Chièvres AB, Belgium for CinC HQ SHAPE

3rd Air Force

Headquarters South Ruislip AS, United Kingdom

HQ 3rd Air Force, RAF Northolt
Comms Flt	C-54E, C-54M, VT-29B, VT-29D	

10th Tactical Reconnaissance Wing, RAF Alconbury
1st TRS	RF-4C	'AR'
30th TRS	RF-4C	'AS'
32nd TRS	RF-4C	'AT'
no sqn	T-33A	

20th Tactical Fighter Wing, RAF Upper Heyford
55th TFS	F-100D/F
77th TFS	F-100D/F
79th TFS	F-100D/F

48th Tactical Fighter Wing, RAF Lakenheath
492nd TFS	F-100D/F	'LR'
493rd TFS	F-100D/F	'LS'
494th TFS	F-100D/F	'LT'
Base Flt	T-39A	

66th Tactical Reconnaissance Wing, RAF Upper Heyford
17th TRS	RF-4C	to Zweibrucken AB on 12 January 1970
18th TRS	nil	to Shaw AFB on 15 January 1970

81st Tactical Fighter Wing, RAF Bentwaters
78th TFS	F-4D	'WR'	at RAF Woodbridge
91st TFS	F-4C	'WS'	
92nd TFS	F-4C	'WT'	

513th Tactical Airlift Wing, RAF Mildenhall
10th ACCS	EC-135H
Alpha Sqn	C-130E rotations from USA
Bravo Sqn	C-130E rotations from USA
no sqn	C-47D, VC-47D

16th Air Force

Headquarters Torrejon Air Base, Spain

16th Air Force, Torrejon AB, Spain
Comms Flt	C-54E, C-97K, VC-118A, T-39A

Direct Reporting
7250th ABS, Ankara AS, Turkey – no aircraft assigned
39th Tactical Group, Incirlik AB, Turkey
no sqn	C-131A

40th Tactical Group, Aviano AB, Italy
7207th ABS	rotational tactical fighter deployments
no sqn	VT-29B, VT-29C, U-6A

41st Tactical Group, Cigli AB, Turkey
no sqn	aircraft assignment unknown

401st Tactical Fighter Wing, Torrejon AB, Spain
307th TFS	F-100D/F

353rdTFS	F-100D/F
613th TFS	F-100D/F

406th Tactical Fighter Training Wing, Zaragoza AB, Spain
weapons training school and range support – no aircraft assigned
7206th Support Group, Athens Airport, Greece
7206th ABS	C-47D, VC-47D, C-131D

7473rd Combat Support Group, Moron AB, Spain
no sqn	no aircraft assigned

In addition to the regular units located within the southern part of mainland Europe, there were a number of aircraft assigned to the 16th Air Force for convenience, including some stationed in Africa and the Middle East. These included a C-123B with the Air Attaché at Kinshasa, Zaire, and a VC-47D assigned to the Air Attaché at Tananarive, Madagascar. The Joint US Military Aid Group (JUS-MAG) at Barajas Airport, Madrid, Spain had a VC-47D; the Military Air Advisory Groups (MAAG) at Addis Ababa/Haile Selassie, Ethiopia was operating a VC-54G; and its counterpart at Mehrabad Airport, Teheran, Iran flew a C-47A and a C-54G. The US Liaison Office (USLO) at Sale Airport, Rabat, Morocco also had a VC-47D. At Dhahran AB, Saudi Arabia, the US Military Training Mission was operating a mix of C-54Ds and C-54Es. Finally the 1141st SS at Capodichino Airport, Naples, Italy had a VT-29B and a VT-29D on behalf of the Allied Forces Southern Europe (AFSOUTH).

17th Air Force

Headquarters Ramstein AB, West Germany

17th Air Force, Ramstein AB, West Germany
Comms Flt	T-29B, VT-29C, VT-29D, T-33A, T-39A, UH-1P, HH-19B, UH-19B

Direct reporting
32nd TFS	F-4E	'CR' at Camp New Amsterdam, the Netherlands (Soesterberg AB)
7th SOS	C-47A, C-130E-I, UH-1P at Ramstein, West Germany
7406th OS	C-130A-II at Rhein Main AB, West Germany
7407th OS	WB-57F at Rhein Main AB, West Germany

26th Tactical Reconnaissance Wing, Ramstein AB
38th TRS	RF-4C	'RR'
526th FIS	F-102A	

36th Tactical Fighter Wing, Bitburg AB, West Germany
22nd TFS	F-4D	'BR'
23rd TFS	F-4D	'BS'
39th TEWS	EB-66C/E	'BV' at Spangdahlem AB
53rd TFS	F-4D	'BT'
525th TFS	F-4E	'BU'

50th Tactical Fighter Wing, Hahn AB, West Germany
10th TFS	F-4D	'HR'
81st TFS	F-4C	uncoded
496th TFS	F-4E	'HS'

86th Tactical Fighter Wing, Zweibrucken AB, West Germany
17th TRS	RF-4C	'ZR'

322nd Tactical Airlift Wing, Rhein Main AB, West Germany
TAC Rotation	C-130E from USA
ANG Rotation	KC-97L from USA
no sqn	VC-47D, VT-29D

601st Tactical Control Wing, Sembach AB, West Germany
no sqn	no aircraft assigned

7405th Support Group, Wiesbaden AB, West Germany
7405th SS	C-97G

7350th Air Base Group, Templehof Central Airport, West Berlin, Germany
no sqn	no aircraft assigned

The 17th Air Force was assigned control of the 7240th SS at Gardermoen AB, Oslo, Norway with a VT-29B for the commander of Headquarters Allied Forces Northern Europe (AFNE), as well as a VT-29B for the US Air Attaché at Helsinki Airport, Finland.

The 1st TRS (blue) was the lucky survivor of the Alconbury tactical reconnaissance wing, although it finally succumbed to cuts in 1987.

To provide dissimilar air combat training for USAFE, the 527th Tactical Fighter Training Aggressor Squadron was established under the 10th TRW at Alconbury.

The 527th TFTAS F-5Es wore a variety of Warsaw Pact-style camouflage. In addition to UK-based operations, they regularly flew from Decimomannu in Sardinia.

with the 55th TFS completing the conversion process by the autumn of 1971. The wing eventually operated almost all the production run of F-111Es with the exception of a few examples engaged on various test programmes. The tailcode system selected was within the range 'UR', 'US' and 'UT', although the prefix letter was changed to 'J' in 1971, to avoid using 'US' which could have been misconstrued for 'unserviceable'. The code 'UH' for Upper Heyford was chosen as the wing identifier when AFM66-1 was issued.

Phantoms to Lakenheath

At Lakenheath, the 48th TFW had lost half of its complement of F-100s by the beginning of 1972 in preparation for the arrival of the F-4D Phantom. The remaining Super Sabres left for the USA in batches at regular intervals, with the final F-100Ds leaving on 31 March 1972, followed two weeks later by the last three F-100Fs. The first F-4D arrived on 13 January 1972, with a further 25 being received by the summer of 1972 before deliveries were halted. The situation remained unchanged until January 1974, when deliveries resumed, although it was not until the summer that there was a major influx of aircraft. Many of these were fitted with a long range aerial navigation (LORAN) system, which were distinguishable by the siting of a 'towel rack' along the spine. Many of these aircraft had served in Southeast Asia where the LORAN system was a valuable aid, although it was not required in Europe, so the equipment

1976. A total of 20 Tiger IIs was assigned, painted in five different camouflage patterns, each designed to accurately represent the scheme of a MiG or Sukhoi fighter in service with one of the Soviet Union's allies. The squadron hosted dissimilar air combat training (DACT) courses at Alconbury with up to a dozen visiting USAFE aircraft deployed for short periods. The first course was for the 401st TFW in October, with four F-4Cs and their crews spending a week training with the F-5s. The 36th TFW was the major user of DACT, its F-15s frequently operating from Alconbury. In addition, the 527th TFTAS went 'on the road' to train squadrons at their bases in mainland Europe.

The 3rd Air Force possessed two wings flying the F-100 Super Sabre in January 1970, the 20th TFW at Upper Heyford and the 48th TFW at Lakenheath. All the aircraft had adopted the Vietnam-style dark green and tan camouflage scheme, with the 48th TFW aircraft displaying the two-letter tailcode system of unit identification. The 20th TFW officially moved from RAF Wethersfield to Woodbridge on 1 December 1969, with their aircraft returning to the USA at the same time, enabling the unit to make preparations to receive the F-111E. Considerable upgrading of the infrastructure at Upper Heyford was necessary before the first two F-111s were delivered to the 79th TFS on 12 September 1970. The 77th TFS followed,

Two 3rd AF wings retained the F-100D at the start of the 1970s. The 20th TFW at Upper Heyford left its aircraft unmarked.

Right: 'Aardvarks' first appeared in Europe in September 1970, with the first deliveries to the 20th TFW. The wing operated the F-111E.

The 'Liberty Wing' (48th TFW) at Lakenheath also had F-100Ds. 'LR' tailcodes were worn by the 492nd Tactical Fighter Squadron.

Seen in October 1970, this F-111E wears the 'UR' tailcode initially assigned to the 79th TFS of the 20th TFW at Upper Heyford.

Three squadrons of F-111Es provided USAFE with its nuclear muscle for much of the decade. The red fin-stripe was allocated to the 77th TFS.

Wearing the badge and 'LS' tailcode of the 493rd TFS, this F-100D was typical of the 48th TFW aircraft which served at Lakenheath until 1972.

In 1971 Upper Heyford changed its 'U' tailcode prefix to 'J'. This changed to the wing-wide designator 'UH' in 1972.

The 48th TFW exchanged its F-100s for F-4Ds in 1972. This is the commander's aircraft, with multi-coloured fin-stripe.

was removed and placed in storage. The wing had received its full complement of F-4s by the end of the summer, although the unit was the subject of a major exchange of aircraft soon afterwards. Most of the LORAN aircraft, along with a small number of F-4D-30 versions which were capable of firing the Maverick missile, were transferred to the 52nd TFW at Spangdahlem AB, West Germany. In exchange, the 48th TFW received F-4Ds from Spangdahlem, which included several early production versions from FY 1964 and 1965. Other F-4Ds were received from the 81st TFW at Bentwaters and Woodbridge. The 48th TFW applied tailcode 'LK' to its aircraft initially, although the 314th Tactical Airlift Wing at Little Rock AFB, Arkansas laid claim to this identifier, so the 48th TFW chose 'LN' instead, with the new letters appearing from July 1972.

The withdrawal of United States forces from Vietnam, and later from Thailand, enabled the Air Force to take stock and instigate a modernisation programme for Europe. The Soviet Union had developed light, medium-range missiles, capable of delivering a nuclear warhead to the cities of Europe from behind the Iron Curtain. In particular, the SS-20 was seen as a potential threat to the safety of Western nations in Europe, with the first examples becoming ready for service in the spring of 1977. To counter the threat, the Pentagon decided to base the F-111F in England, with the 48th TFW at Lakenheath being selected as the most suitable unit. The F-111 had been the subject of much political debate, as during testing it was found to have major shortcomings. Despite being allocated a fighter designation, the design was decidedly a bomber which was capable of long-range, all-weather deep penetration of enemy territory using its terrain-following radar to hug the ground. The first production F-111A series featured a pair of Pratt & Whitney TF30-P-3 engines each producing 18,500 lb (82.30 kN) of thrust, which did not offer an extensive range when fully armed. Subsequent versions of the F-111 were much

more capable of performing the long-range fighter-bomber role. The F-111F version was powered by the TF30-P-100 rated at 25,000 lb (111.21 kN) each, offering a maximum range of almost 3,000 miles (4828 km), which could be extended with the assistance of tanking.

Ready Switch

The F-111F was in service with Tactical Air Command, with all production versions operated by the 366th TFW stationed at Mountain Home AFB, Idaho. Under an elaborate project named Exercise Ready Switch, the delivery of the F-111s to Lakenheath was to be part of a three way re-equipment programme whereby approximately 90 F-111Fs would be flown to the 48th TFW. The Lakenheath-based F-4Ds were reassigned to the 474th TFW at Nellis AFB, Nevada, enabling the latter's F-111As to join the 366th TFW at Mountain Home AFB. The project began in March 1977 and took almost a year to complete. The first three F-111Fs were delivered to Lakenheath on 1

141

A Decade of Air Power

Above: The 10th ACCS of the 513th TAW at Mildenhall operated the EC-135H 'Silk Purse' theatre command post fleet.

Left: To rapidly bolster USAFE forces, the 48th TFW upgraded to the F-111F in 1977 under Operation Ready Switch.

March 1977, with these initially being hangared as maintenance trainers for the first weeks of their residency. The number of F-111F aircraft involved was more than could be comfortably accommodated by the three existing squadrons. The 495th TFS was activated on 1 April 1977 with the dual role of being both an operational unit and the 'Aardvark Academy', performing replacement training for aircrew new to the type. The wing had received its full complement of aircraft by 1978 when it was declared to NATO as being fully operational.

Along with the F-111Es of the 20th TFW, the F-111Fs were the major strike force in Europe to form the core of a nuclear deterrent within NATO. It has been unofficially stated that the F-111 was one of the few NATO weapons systems which the Russians considered to be a real threat, as crews were confident they could strike deep into Soviet territory with a high degree of survivability. Coincidental with the arrival of the F-111s, the base at Lakenheath, along with many other NATO fighter stations in Europe, began to see the construction of hardened aircraft shelters.

Reconnaissance relocations

The 66th Tactical Reconnaissance Wing was resident at RAF Upper Heyford on 1 January 1970. The unit had no aircraft, since the RF-101Cs of the 18th TRS had been flown back to the USA during the latter half of 1969, and the 17th TRS and its RF-4Cs were in the process of relocating to Zweibrucken AB, West Germany. The 17th TRS was officially activated at Zweibrucken on 12 January 1970, with the 18th TRS being reformed at Shaw AFB, South Carolina three days later. The parent wing was inactivated on 1 April 1970 following the transfer of its administrative responsibilities for the air base at Upper Heyford to the 20th TFW.

The 513th Tactical Airlift Wing was the major USAFE unit at RAF Mildenhall, and had the 10th Airborne Command and Control Squadron as its only flying unit. The 10th ACCS was activated on 1 January 1970 with five EC-135Hs, although the aircraft had been located at Mildenhall since 1965/66 with assignment to the 7120th ACCS which inactivated on 1 January. The EC-135 operation, which was nicknamed 'Silk Purse', provided an airborne command and control capability with a direct link to its US-based counterpart that was known as 'Looking Glass'. The aircraft were initially flown on a relay system, with an aircraft airborne for eight hours before being relieved by a replacement. 'Silk Purse' provided 24-hour-a-day airborne coverage of western Europe for the Commander in Chief of USAFE to organise operations in the event of ground control centres being destroyed. The aircraft were fitted with a host of receivers and transmitters, with a number of aerials and antennas installed above and below the fuselage, as well as at the wingtips. The aircraft were also fitted with a trailing wire aerial which was installed in a housing beneath the fuselage at the wingroot. Internally there were banks of consoles with a battle staff of specialist personnel to decode and transmit data to ground centres and strike aircraft. Operations were frequently conducted with a general onboard to take control of activities. During their period of service at Mildenhall the aircraft were upgraded with additional features to enhance their capabilities. The EC-135Hs were subsequently re-engined, with the water-injected Pratt & Whitney J57 jet powerplants being replaced by Pratt & Whitney TF33 turbojets, although this did not occur until after 1979. The aerial relay system proved unnecessary, with the aircraft instead being manned at readiness on the ground to respond to an emergency if required.

The 513th TAW was activated as a Troop Carrier Wing at Everux AB, France in April 1966, although its presence in mainland Europe was short-lived as it was relocated to Mildenhall three months later when US units were moved from French soil. The unit took up residence at Mildenhall ostensibly to oversee the operations of the rotational C-130 Hercules on 90-day periods of temporary duty from the USA. Initially this involved participation by C-130A, B and E models from several Tactical Air Command (TAC) units in residence at the same time. The system changed in the spring of 1967 with two entire squadrons in residence, assigned to either the Alpha and Bravo Squadrons, although the titles were unofficial. The duration of rotations changed from 90 to 60 days during the latter half of 1969. A further change took place in December 1969 when the two-squadron system was reduced to just one, Bravo Squadron being the survivor.

Among the units involved were the 64th TAW of Sewart AFB, Tennessee (later at Little Rock AFB, Arkansas and redesignated as the 316th TAW in May 1971), 313th TAW of Forbes AFB, Kansas, 314th TAW of Little Rock AFB, Arkansas, 316th TAW of Langley AFB, Virginia (unit transferred to Little Rock AFB in May 1971), 317th TAW of Pope AFB, North Carolina (until redesignated from the 464th TAW in August 1971), 463rd TAW of Dyess AFB, Texas, 464th TAW of Pope AFB, North Carolina, and the 516th TAW of Dyess AFB, Texas (renumbered 463rd TAW in June 1972). TAC provided the aircraft and personnel until 1 December 1974 when the fleet of Hercules was transferred to Military Airlift Command (MAC). The transfer from one command to another had no real effect on the method of operations. Occasionally the rotation was performed by a composite detachment of more than one unit, although this was not common. There were at least two instances when the front-line forces were augmented by reservist aircraft and crews.

MAC takes over

The operation remained under USAFE control until 15 January 1976 when MAC formed the Military Airlift Center Europe at Ramstein AB, West Germany with direct responsibility for airlift functions within the continent. The rotational C-130s were no longer part of the 513th TAW, but were retained by MAC during their time at Mildenhall. MAC formed the 435th Tactical Airlift Group at Mildenhall on 1 July 1975 as a subordinate unit of the 435th TAW at Rhein Main AB, West Germany, with the former assuming control of the rotation from January 1976. A further reorganisation of MAC operations in Europe with the reformation of the 322nd Air Division at Ramstein occurred on 23 June 1978. The division became the parent organisation of the 435th TAW as well as the 435th TAG, with the latter being redesignated as the 313th TAG on 15 September 1978.

Whereas the C-130E performed the bulk of duty during the first half of the decade, the two rotations performed by the reserves included the C-130A and B models. MAC began receiving the C-130H in 1975 with the 463rd TAW at Dyess AFB operating this version. These began to participate with the Bravo rotation from May 1976.

16th Air Force

As stated, the 16th Air Force had the largest area of operations within USAFE, although it possessed the smallest number of aircraft. Overseeing US Air Force assets stationed within the countries bordering the Mediterranean, the 16th AF had as its sole fighter contingent the 401st TFW at Torrejon AB, Spain with three squadrons of F-100 Super Sabres. The unit took up residence at Torrejon in April 1966 with its aircraft, which were still in theatre on 1 January 1970. The unit was on the threshold of upgrading from the elderly fighters to the F-4E, and the first Phantoms were assigned to the 307th TFS by May 1970. The 353rd and 613th TFS received their F-4Es soon afterwards and the three squadrons adopted tailcodes 'TJ', 'TK', and 'TL', which were outside of the accepted USAFE system. The unit realigned its squadron designations on 15 July 1971, upon the 307th and 353rd TFS being transferred to Homestead AFB, Florida and Myrtle Beach AFB, South Carolina, respectively, in exchange for the 612th and 614th TFSs. The two new squadrons assumed the tailcodes of the units they replaced. However, in line with AFM66-1, the unit adopted tailcode 'TJ' as its two-letter identifier.

All three squadrons began converting to the F-4C from October 1973, with aircraft received from the 81st TFW at Bentwaters. The displaced F-4Es were transferred back to the USA, with many subsequently being reworked to F-4G standard later in their careers. The F-4Cs were themselves only operated for five years, as the wing transitioned to the F-4D beginning in 1978.

Mediterranean responsibilities

The 401st TFW was tasked with defence of not just Spanish air space but extended its area of responsibility to encompass Italy and Turkey, and undertook regular deployments to Aviano AB, Italy and Incirlik AB, Turkey. The fighter capability of the 16th AF was frequently bolstered by the presence of USAFE squadrons from the UK and Germany deployed to Aviano AB, Incirlik AB, and Zaragoza AB, Spain for weapons training deployments on local ranges. In addition, these bases played host to deployments of fighter squadrons from the USA.

At the beginning of the decade the 16th Air Force was responsible for a variety of VIP, communications and liaison types including C-47 Skytrains, C-54 Skymasters, C-118 Liftmasters, C-131 Samaritans, and T-29s. The C-47s and C-54s were approximately 25 years old, and were long overdue for replacement. Gradually these veterans were withdrawn from service, with the last C-47s being retired by the autumn of 1973. Likewise, the C-54s were withdrawn soon after the C-47s. The need for VIP and communications aircraft scattered throughout the 16th Air Force region decreased as the elderly types were withdrawn, although certain key locations were allocated a C-12A.

Within 16th Air Force control were a great many facilities which were important to the efficient running of USAFE, but which did not have combat aircraft directly assigned. Among these were Hellenikon AB, Greece and Iraklion AS in Crete; San Vito de Normanni AS in Italy;

As 16th AF's only major aircraft-operating unit, the 401st TFW at Torrejon operated Phantoms for most of the decade, having transitioned from the F-100 in early 1970. The initial equipment was the F-4E, which served with the 307th (later 612th, illustrated below left), 353rd (later 614th) and 613th TFS (illustrated below right). Due to requirements elsewhere, the wing was then given the old F-4Cs from the 81st TFW in 1973, before its capabilities were partially restored in 1978 with the delivery of F-4Ds (illustrated above).

Ankara AS, Incirlik AB and Izmir AS in Turkey; and Zaragoza AB in Spain.

USAFE has had an interest in Greece for several decades, its base at Hellenikon Air Base (formerly Hassani Airport, adjacent to Athens Airport) overseeing activities since 1948. Prior to that the facility was operated as a staging field for Air Transport Command flights between Italy and the Middle East. US interest in the region was primarily to promote stability, as both Greece and Turkey bordered potentially hostile nations which were supported by either the Soviet Union or China. Hellenikon Air Base housed a small communications fleet of which the 7206th Support Group was the primary unit to control activities. The majority of US traffic to transit the base was airlifters on resupply flights, although SAC operated detachments of RC-135s from the base, with the 922nd Strategic Squadron being formed on 1 July 1978.

Communications base

On the holiday island of Crete the US had facilities at Iraklion Air Station from October 1954. The primary role of the station was to house radio and communications equipment, although USAF aircraft were occasional visitors. The 6930th Radio Group was active from April 1958 until October 1978 as part of the USAF Security Service. Iraklion supplied general support for 6931st Electronic Security Squadron, as well as administering the tenant organisation in the locality. The base also provided servicing for aircraft visiting from elsewhere in USAFE. From October 1978 Iraklion conducted liaison for US activities in Crete as well as providing service for the US Embassy in Athens, with the 7276th Air Base Group as its operating unit.

The primary US facility in Italy was Aviano Air Base, although USAFE has several smaller sites scattered throughout the country. Among these was San Vito de Normanni Air Station near Brindisi in southern Italy. The base was assigned to the USAF Security Service until October 1978 when it became part of USAFE.

The 6917th Radio Group was in residence until October 1978 when the primary unit became the 7275th Air Base Group. Apart from providing a landing facility in southern Italy, the base was strategically positioned to monitor activities in Libya following the take-over by Muammar Khadaffi at the end of the 1960s.

Turkish installations

USAFE has long considered Turkey to be vital to the security of Western Europe, for the nation physically bridges the divide between Europe and the Asia across the Bosphorus. In addition to bordering its traditional enemy Greece to the west, the Turks have enjoyed little more than strained relationships with Bulgaria to the northwest. Much of the northern area borders the Black Sea with the huge Soviet Union (at it was then) naval fleet, while the northeast faced the Soviet Union directly. To the east and south are Arab neighbours Iran, Iraq and Syria. Such a geographical location ensures that Turkey is a major crossroads, an important overland oil supply route, and an ethnic melting pot. Not surprisingly, the US has invested heavily in listening stations close to the borders to enable intelligence gathering to be conducted from the comparative safety of its NATO member. Numerous USAFE facilities were located in Turkey, with three which were considered major facilities, albeit without any combat elements directly assigned.

Ankara AS, located close to the capital city of the same name in central Turkey, became a USAFE facility in May 1955. Ankara was established as an administrative headquarters without any flying operations, having as its primary mission the provision of support for US military and diplomatic agencies in Turkey. Within the city of Ankara were a great many US military facilities, including the Headquarters of The United States Logistics Group (TUSLOG) which was located within the central area, but which moved to the air station in May 1973.

Without doubt the single most important military base in Turkey was Incirlik AB, located near the southern city of Adana. The base was assigned to USAFE in February 1955 with no combat aircraft permanently assigned, although the facility hosted numerous squadrons for exercises and for weapons training on the near-by ranges. The base was administered by the 7216th ABG which became a combat support group in July 1962 before being redesignated as the 39th Tactical Group in April 1966. The base had housed visiting squadrons from both SAC and TAC, with the latter basing F-100s and F-105s during periods of crisis in the region. By 1970 Incirlik was most frequently occupied by squadrons of fighters from the 3rd and 17th Air Force which deployed for weapons training away from the cluttered skies of northern Europe. The 401st TFW at Torrejon AB frequently detached F-4s to Incirlik as part of the unit's mission to perform defence of various regions of the 16th Air Force. The UK-based F-111s were the most prolific visitors, sending regular detachments to Incirlik.

The US began to assign personnel to the vicinity of Izmir upon the formation of the Allied Land Forces Southeast Europe in September 1952, followed 13 months later by the arrival of the Sixth Allied Tactical Air Force. Initially these were supported by the US Navy, with Det 2 7206th ABS administering USAF interests in the region. USAFE assumed control of all US and NATO entities in the Izmir area from January 1956 through the 7266th Support Squadron. The air base at Cigli became part of USAFE in July 1962, with US and other NATO aircraft deployed for exercises. The 41st Tactical Group was organised in April 1966 to control visiting US aircraft, until inactivated on 30 June 1970 when the Turkish air force assumed control of Cigli AB. The 7241st SS was activated in July 1970, and was subsequently upgraded to air base group status.

Construction in Spain

Zaragoza AB was a small Spanish air force facility when the US began construction work to enlarge and improve the base in September 1954. Unlike the majority of other facilities in the 16th Air Force, Zaragoza had combat assets located, with the 531st FIS flying F-102As from September 1960 until its withdrawal in April 1964. The base had also hosted SAC bombers on rotation, until July 1964 when the base was placed on standby status. The facility was maintained on a caretaker basis in January 1966, and reassigned to USAFE in April 1966. The loss of access to facilities in Libya in 1969 resulted in the USAF making use of the Bardenas Reales air-to-ground bombing and gunnery range from February 1970. The range was extended to include a dart tow air-to-air gunnery capability for USAFE and Spanish air force units from April 1971.

16th Air Force operated a number of C-47s, C-54s, C-131s and T-29s at various locations in Europe, Africa and the Middle East for the Military Air Advisory Groups (MAAG) and Embassy Flights, although these were costly to maintain, particularly in isolated locations far from larger USAF facilities. These aircraft were gradually replaced beginning in 1975 by the C-12A, which was painted in a VIP scheme and therefore blended in far more effectively while operating from civilian airports.

17th Air Force

USAFE combat assets were almost evenly split between UK-based units operating long-range fighter-bombers under the control of the 3rd Air Force, and a similar number of units under 17th Air Force whose aircraft included air-defence fighters. Those aircraft based in the 17th Air Force region were closest to the perceived enemy of the day, for fighter bases behind the Iron Curtain, particularly in East Germany and Czechoslovakia, were only a few minutes' flying time away from NATO military complexes. The composition of USAFE was established such that those under 17th Air Force control would be the first line of defence, and the 3rd Air Force would have the heavy retaliatory strike capability. The third line of defence was located within the United States, which would provide reinforcements to the European theatre. The Warsaw Pact forces were similarly disposed to those of USAFE, with Soviet MiG-21 'Fishbeds', MiG-23 'Floggers' and, later, MiG-29 'Fulcrums' standing alert at numerous forward locations, while long-range Su-24 'Fencers' were on standby to penetrate deep into NATO airspace.

The air defence community had almost completed its re-equipment programme, four squadrons of F-102 Delta Daggers having been replaced by the F-4E Phantom. The Dagger has served faithfully in Spain, although these squadrons had been withdrawn several years earlier, leaving three in West Germany and one in the Netherlands. The 32nd FIS was stationed at Soesterberg near the Dutch city of Utrecht, and the 496th, 525th and 526th FIS were located at Hahn AB in the Hunsruck, Bitburg AB in the Eifel mountains, and Ramstein AB. To enable a change from pure interceptor to the general fighter role, the four were redesignated as tactical fighter squadrons between 1 July 1969 and 1 April 1970. The 32nd, 496th and 525th had completed the withdrawal of their F-102s before the end of 1969, while the 526th FIS performed its last operational mission with the Dagger on 1 April 1970. The sortie involved four aircraft, which upon completion effectively ended the service career of the F-102 in USAFE. The squadron began ferrying its aircraft back to the USA on 15 April for service with the Air National Guard, with the last batch leaving the following day.

Ubiquitous Phantom

The retirement of the F-102 enabled the F-4 Phantom to reign supreme within Europe, as the type constituted all the tactical fighter and tactical reconnaissance squadrons of the 17th Air Force by the middle of 1970. The 26th Tactical Reconnaissance Wing at Ramstein AB was composed of the single squadron of F-102s, which soon received the F-4E, along with the 38th TRS flying the RF-4C. The 17th AF reorganised its fighter and reconnaissance assets in 1973, with the 26th TRW being transferred the short distance to Zweibrucken AB, while the 86th TFW moved from Zweibrucken to Ramstein AB. The 26th TRW took with it the RF-4Cs of the 38th TRS to join company with those of the 17th TRS to consolidate the two reconnaissance squadrons under the same wing.

The only USAF unit in the Netherlands, the 32nd TFS at Soesterberg (Camp New Amsterdam) had converted from the F-102 to the F-4E in 1969.

Despite its general fighter designation, the 32nd TFS remained an air defence squadron. It reported direct to 17th AF.

After nine years in the F-4E, the 32nd TFS transitioned to the F-15A in late 1978, following the 36th TFW to complete USAFE's F-15 allocation.

Zweibrucken had previously been a Canadian facility until closed to flight operations. The base became part of USAFE on 29 August 1969, with the 86th TFW reactivated on 1 November of that year. The 86th had been designated as an air division (defence) to control the four F-102A units located in the Netherlands and West Germany, until 14 November 1968 when the parent organisation was downgraded to become the 86th Fighter Interceptor Wing and was inactivated the same day. The three Germany-based squadrons were reassigned to their respective host units on 1 November, while the 32nd FIS was allocated as a direct reporting unit of Headquarters 17th Air Force.

The 86th reformed on 1 November 1969 as a tactical fighter wing, gaining the 17th TRS from RAF Upper Heyford in January 1970. The 81st TFS arrived from Hahn AB in June 1971 with its mix of conventional F-4Cs, together with slightly over a dozen dedicated to the suppression of enemy air defences role with the appellation Wild Weasel. The 17th TRS had tailcode 'ZR' and the 81st TFS quite naturally adopted 'ZS'. However, under AFM66-1 the code changed to 'ZS', with the RF-4Cs briefly applying this before the unit changed to 'ZR'. The 81st TFS was only resident for 18 months until it relocated to Spangdahlem on 15 January 1973.

The 36th TFW at Bitburg AB was responsible for three squadrons (the 22nd, 23rd and 53rd TFS) flying the F-4D, along with the 525th TFS which had converted from the F-102A to the F-4E during the autumn of 1969. These were allocated tailcodes 'BR', 'BS',

At the start of the 1970s the 26th TRW was operating from Ramstein AB, hence the 'RR' codes on this 38th TRS RF-4C.

The 36th TFW was a five-squadron wing at the start of the decade. The 'BR' codes were worn by the F-4Ds of the 22nd TFS.

Although assigned to the 36th TFW, the 23rd TFS was based at Spangdahlem. It was reassigned to the 52nd TFW on 1 January 1972.

Above and below: The 1973 reshuffle of assets in Germany resulted in the two RF-4 squadrons (38th TRS, above, and 17th TRS, below) being co-located at Zweibrucken under the 26th TRW.

Three of the 36th TFW F-4D units were based at Bitburg, including the 53rd TFS (above). Four of the wing's aircraft are seen below, including two 53rd and a single 23rd TFS aircraft.

Across the US armed forces the 1976 bicentennial celebrations resulted in many special schemes. The 36th TFW, by then operating F-4Es, painted their aircraft with special tail markings.

'BT' and 'BU', respectively. The 7149th TFW was activated to administer Spangdahlem AB when the 49th TFW relocated to the USA in July 1968. This situation remained until September 1969 when the temporary wing inactivated and the base at Spangdahlem became a satellite of the 36th TFW. By that time the 39th Tactical Electronic Warfare Squadron had formed with the EB-66C/E at Spangdahlem, having activated on 1 April 1969. The squadron was allocated tailcode 'BV', which was the next available in sequence. The dual operation of both Bitburg and Spangdahlem Air Bases by the 36th TFW enabled the unit to transfer the 23rd TFS to the latter on the last day of December 1971. The transfer coincided with the activation on 31 December 1971 at Spangdahlem of the 52nd Tactical Fighter Wing, which had the 23rd TFS and 39th TEWS directly assigned.

Phantom transfers

The 22nd and 53rd TFS upgraded to the F-4E during 1973 with aircraft transferred from the 401st TFW at Torrejon AB. In turn, the F-4Ds of the 22nd TFS were passed on to the 81st TFW at Bentwaters, while many of the 53rd TFS aircraft joined the 10th TFS at Hahn, enabling the latter to transfer its early production F-4Ds to Bentwaters. The swap was an exercise in 'tidying up' the command, enabling Phantom aircraft from similar production batches to be grouped together, thereby easing spares holding and maintenance work.

Despite being assigned to their new parent wing, the two squadrons retained their Bitburg codes until the summer of 1972 when 'SP' was

applied to the unit under AFM66-1. The elderly EB-66s of the 39th TEWS were disposed of between September and December 1972; some made the long journey to join the 388th TFW at Korat RTAFB in Thailand, while others were flown back to the USA for storage and eventual disposal with the Aerospace Maintenance and Regeneration Center at Davis-Monthan AFB, Arizona. Others continued their service career at Shaw AFB, South Carolina with the 363rd TRW, which was the training unit for tactical reconnaissance and electronic warfare crews. The departure of the B-66s enabled the 39th TEWS to inactivate on 1 January 1973, providing sufficient time for the 81st TFS to be relocated to Spangdahlem from the 26th TRW at Zweibrucken.

The 23rd TFS retained the F-4D for the remainder of the decade, and the 480th TFS was activated on 15 November 1976, also with the F-4D. The squadron began conversion to

the F-4E at the end of 1979. The 81st TFS, which had performed the defence-suppression role for many years, converted to the F-4G and F-4E as a hunter/killer team. Whereas the F-4C was slightly modified for the role, the F-4G Wild Weasel was completely reworked to enable it to be highly effective in the detection of enemy emitters as well as being equally capable of launching the AGM-45 Shrike anti-radiation missile at these targets. The 52nd TFW received its first F-4Gs in March 1979 for service with the 81st TFS.

The Eagle arrives

Bitburg received a visit by an F-15A of the 58th TFTW from Luke AFB, Arizona in January 1976 in readiness for the wing to begin preparations for the Eagle's assignment to the unit. The 36th TFW continued to operate the F-4E until April 1977, when the wing began to receive the F-15A and B. The first Eagle for the

36th TFW was a TF-15A (as the two-seater was designated at the time) which arrived on 5 January 1977 to become a maintenance trainer. The designation TF-15A became F-15B on 1 January 1978. The first squadron to convert was the 525th TFS which received its complement during the spring of 1977, and was followed by the 53rd TFS and the 22nd TFS.

The 50th TFW at Hahn AB had operated three tactical fighter squadrons in the traditional manner for many years, being equipped with the F-100D/F until 1966 when the first F-4Ds arrived. The unit was reduced to two squadrons when the 417th TFS was repatriated to the USA in July 1968, along with the 49th TFW and its three squadrons from Spangdahlem AB. The concept was to have the four units stationed in the USA, but committed to NATO with an annual exercise involving them returning to Europe under Crested Cap. The first such exercise took place in 1969, and others followed annually. Gradually the composition varied as other units assumed the place of the four dedicated squadrons. The gap left by the departure of the 417th TFS was filled in November 1968 by the direct assignment of the 496th FIS along with its F-102As. The latter unit sent its Daggers back to the USA towards the end of 1969 when it began converting to the F-4E, becoming a tactical fighter squadron on 1 January 1970.

Wild Weasels

The 81st TFS exchanged its F-4Ds for a mix of conventional F-4Cs and a number of defence suppression examples, with the transition commencing in December 1969. The wing was composed of the 10th, 81st and 496th TFS, although only two applied squadron-level tailcodes. The 10th TFS selected 'HR' and the 496th TFS applied 'HS', while the 81st TFS aircraft remained uncoded due to the impending transfer to Zweibrucken AB. In 1972 the 50th TFW adopted tailcode 'HR'. In 1973 the 10th TFS was involved in a reshuffle of aircraft between units, with its aircraft being transferred to the 81st TFW, in exchange for F-4Ds from Bitburg AB. The 10th TFS began converting to the F-4E in July 1976, and the 313th TFS was activated on 15 November 1976 as the third squadron, also with the F-4E.

As stated, the 86th TFW reformed at Zweibrucken on 1 November 1969 and moved to Ramstein AB on 31 January 1973, assuming control of the 526th TFS which had converted from the F-102A to the F-4E early in 1970. The 526th had been a fighter interceptor squadron until 1 April 1970 when it changed designation to become a TFS. The 86th TFW was composed of a single flying squadron, although it was also responsible for a mixed fleet of VIP and communications aircraft and helicopters which was in residence for the Headquarters 17th Air Force as well as for Headquarters USAFE. These included various versions of the VT-29, a single T-39A and almost 20 T-33As, together with a handful of elderly UH-19Bs and HH-19B Chickasaws. These VIP and communications types were operated by the 26th TRW during the unit's assignment to Ramstein. The H-19s were retired from service during the summer of 1971, with the T-33As being withdrawn

between 1972 and 1973. Some were transferred to the Turkish air force under the Military Aid Program (MAP), with others returning to the USA for storage. USAFE T-29s and C-131s were frequently exchanged between units in Europe, those at Ramstein being no exception. Ramstein also received seven C-118As along with a VC-118A between August and October 1973, the majority arriving from Wiesbaden. The VIP and communications aircraft at Ramstein were assigned to various squadrons; the T-39s are believed to have been with the 7055th Operations Squadron which was active between 31 March 1973 and 15 September 1976, while the C-118As were with the 7086th Operations Squadron which was formed on 1 June 1973. Despite the C-118s being withdrawn, the squadron remained active until 1 April 1978, its duties having been assumed by the 58th MAS (see under MAC). In May 1977 the squadron received five VC-140B Jetstars which previously had been operated by the 89th MAW at Andrews AFB, Maryland. Initially the Jetstars were assigned to the 89th MAW Overseas Location Alpha (OL-A), although this was eventually disbanded when the aircraft joined the 58th MAS. The unit also took delivery of a C-12A at the same time.

HQ move to Ramstein

Headquarters USAFE was located at Lindsay Air Station near Wiesbaden until late 1972 when the organisation began relocating to Ramstein, consolidating activities with the headquarters of NATO's 4th Allied Tactical Air Force at the same location. HQ USAFE was accommodated in the buildings which previously housed the Headquarters 17th Air Force, which in turn moved to Sembach Air Base. The relocation of HQ USAFE was finally completed on 14 March 1973. The 7101st Air Base Wing operated more than a dozen communications and VIP aircraft on behalf of HQ USAFE, some of which moved to Ramstein during 1972 and 1973.

The 7101st Air Base Wing at Wiesbaden was not under direct control of the 17th Air Force despite being located within the centre of its area of responsibility. Instead, the unit reported directly to Headquarters USAFE, as its primary tasks included the transportation of senior personnel throughout the European region, as well as providing a courier network to the major sites within its area. The wing operated a fleet of T-39As, together with seven C-118As and VC-118As, and at least two C-131Ds. The USAFE Command Centralized Courier system was established in December 1970 with regular weekly connections linking Wiesbaden to Greece, Italy, Spain, Turkey and the UK. Each of these courier flights was connected with a series of localised services to ferry mail, light cargo and passengers, thereby reducing considerably the necessity of using civilian airlines. The success of the service led to the formation of an Operation Creek Guardlift in April 1971 involving the rotation of Air National Guard C-97G and C-121C/G squadrons at Torrejon AB, Spain. The two aircraft detachments were formed to link Torrejon with several US facilities in Italy and Sardinia.

The 7101st ABW remained the major unit at Wiesbaden until 31 May 1973 when the 601st

Conversion to the F-4E for the 36th TFW occurred in 1973. The wing then comprised the 22nd, 53rd (illustrated) and 525th TFS.

The 36th's fifth squadron was the 39th TEWS, operating a mix of electronic warfare Destroyers from Spangdahlem. This is an EB-66C.

The three squadrons of the 36th TFW converted to the F-15A from April 1977, this being a 'yellow-tail' from the 53rd TFS.

Tactical Control Wing was transferred from Sembach AB, assuming control of the various communications and VIP aircraft. These types were only assigned to the 601st TCW for two months as most were moved elsewhere when the wing was relocated to Wiesbaden to prepare for the arrival of dedicated counter-insurgency forces. The 20th Tactical Air Support Squadron was activated on 1 October 1973 as its first flying unit, although its complement of OV-10A Bronco aircraft did not commence delivery until almost one year later. The unit received the CH-53C from January 1975 and was assigned to the 601st TASS. The CH-53s were used for Special Forces missions and to transport mobile Tactical Air Control Centers within Europe. The period of residency for the 601st TCW at Wiesbaden was relatively short, as the wing returned to Sembach AB on 1 January 1976 along with its two flying squadrons.

Radar sites

The 601st TCW began life as a group when it was formed at Sembach on 15 February 1965, before being upgraded to wing level on 1 July 1968. The reorganisation enabled the unit to take responsibility for five 412L Aircraft Control and Warning System sites located at Doebraberg, Erbeskopf, Giebelstadt, Kindsbach and Wasserkruppe on 1 November 1968. These had previously been a component of the 86th Air Division (Defense) at Ramstein AB. Early in 1970 the 601st TCW was tasked with the

The 81st TFS and its defence suppression F-4Cs had moved from Hahn to Zweibrucken before settling at Spangdahlem as part of the 52nd TFW.

This 52nd TFW F-4D carries a red star on the splitter plate to signify a MiG kill, and bicentennial fin-stripe.

The 480th TFS was activated at Spangdahlem in 1976 with the F-4D to raise the number of F-4 squadrons to three.

The 39th TEWS was reassigned to the 52nd TFW in 1972, although the squadron was deactivated during the year. This is an EB-66E.

The 52nd TFW employed a mix of conventional Phantoms and Shrike-armed Wild Weasel F-4Cs (illustrated) in the defence suppression mission. Originally flown by the 81st TFS, the F-4Cs were later redistributed, this being a 480th TFS aircraft (red fin-stripe).

F-4Es arrived to replace F-4Ds with the 480th TFS right at the end of the decade. The aircraft were used to partner the F-4G in hunter/killer teams.

The dedicated F-4G introduced a dramatic rise in defence suppression capability compared to the F-4C. The 781st TFS received its first in 1979.

In 1970 the 50th TFW at Hahn had three Phantom squadrons flying three variants (F-4C, D and E). The F-4D unit was the 10th TFS, an example of which is shown here carrying a Pave Spike laser designator.

additional role of developing a forward air controller capability, with three Cessna O-2As being airlifted into Ramstein in February. Despite assignment to the 601st TCW, the three Skymasters remained at Ramstein, where they were operated until transferred to Wiesbaden when the wing moved in May 1973. One O-2 was lost in an accident in September 1974, and the other two joined the US Army Europe's Berlin Brigade in February 1975. The 601st TCW returned to Sembach at the end of 1975. Additional OV-10s were delivered during the second half of 1975 with approximately three dozen eventually assigned, and the 20th TASS was joined by the 704th TASS which was activated on 4 July 1976.

The joint civil/military airport at Frankfurt/Rhein Main has been synonymous with transport operations for several decades,

and came to prominence in 1948 when it became the principal Western base of the famous Berlin airlift. Subsequently, Rhein Main became the major port of entry for cargo and passenger flights into Germany. The base was administered by the 7310th Tactical Airlift Wing until 1 January 1970 when the 322nd Tactical Airlift Wing was reformed as the major unit at Rhein Main. The wing inherited responsibility for the C-130 Hercules rotation, which operated in much the same way as that at Mildenhall, with squadrons deploying for 60 days at a time. The 435th Military Air Support Wing had functioned at Rhein Main since being formed on 1 July 1969 to control airlift operations, although the rotational aircraft were administered by the 322nd TAW. This changed on 30th June 1975 when the 322nd TAW inactivated and was replaced by the 435th MASW,

which was redesignated at a tactical airlift wing the following day. The 322nd TAW did not remain dormant for long as it was reactivated as the 322nd Air Division at Ramstein on 23 June 1978. The reformation of the 322nd Air Division as part of Military Airlift Command instead of USAFE enabled MAC to control its Europe-based assets more effectively. The C-130 rotations to Rhein Main continued until September 1977 when the last unit returned home. On 1 October 1977 the 37th TAS reformed at Rhein Main with 18 permanently assigned C-130Es. In addition, the 435th TAW became responsible for the 55th AAS (see below) as well as the 7405th SS, until this unit became part of the 7575th Operations Group.

Rhein Main had communications and VIP types in residence at various times, including the VC-47D and VT-29D. The C-47 was

Right: The 496th TFS at Hahn had always been an air defence squadron, and had converted from F-102s to F-4Es in 1969. It flew the variant throughout the decade.

Below: In 1976 the 50th TFW standardised on the F-4E, with the 10th TFS (illustrated) converting from the F-4D. The 313th TFS was activated the same year to restore the wing to three squadrons following the departure of the 81st.

retired in September 1972 and the T-29 was exchanged for a C-131A in June 1972. The 7111th Operations Squadron was formed on 1 February 1972 to operate these and later a VIP-configured C-9A, although its tenure was brief since the unit was inactivated on 1 February 1975.

Rotational 'Strats'

The 322nd TAW also gained control of Operation Creek Party. This involved the fort-nightly rotation of KC-97L Stratofreighters from Air National Guard squadrons which were in residence to provide an inflight-refuelling capability for USAFE fighters, thereby freeing SAC's hard-pressed KC-135 fleet for duty in Southeast Asia. The operation began on 1 May 1967 as an interim measure, but became so suc-cessful that it continued for 11 years until finally being terminated on 28 April 1977. The 181st ARS, Texas ANG had the distinction of per-forming the final Creek Party rotation. The operation was composed of four aircraft for the first few years, but was increased to between five and seven 'Strats' later. All seven KC-97L squadrons were involved, each undertaking two weeks in residence before being relieved on sta-tion and returning home. On a few occasions there were aircraft in residence from more than one squadron, although this was not common. Refuelling operations were normally restricted to the 'race tracks' over and around Germany, and the vintage KC-97s usually provided fuel for F-4 Phantoms on training sorties.

The Iron Curtain divided the two Germanies and the Federal Republic faced not only the German Democratic Republic but also Czechoslovakia. The need to maintain updated and accurate details of the military strength and disposition of the forces in the Warsaw Pact was an ongoing requirement for NATO, to which end the US Air Force dedicated a sizeable effort. Some assets, such as the strategic recon-naissance RC-135 aircraft of the 55th SRW, were operated openly either in international air-space or over friendly territory to gather elec-tronic and signals intelligence. Others were flown in a more clandestine manner with air-craft thinly disguised to enable them to operate without attracting undue attention. Among these was a mixed fleet of C-97s and C-130s, which were operated together with some RB-57s. The 7406th and 7407th Support Squadrons were formed at Rhein Main in May 1955 oper-ating the RB-50 and RB-57, respectively. The 7406th SS traded in the RB-50s for the C-130A-II in 1958. There has been much specula-

tion that these C-130s flew regular sorties between Rhein Main and Templehof Airport, Berlin via the three transit routes which were designated as international airspace across East Germany. The C-130A-II also periodically vis-ited Hellenikon AB, Athens, so presumably the squadron monitored activities in countries neighbouring Greece. The aircraft were fitted with camera equipment located behind sliding doors in the underside of the fuselage, which enabled them to obtain imagery during their sorties while looking ostensibly like any other regular cargo aircraft. The C-130As were replaced in 1971 with C-130B-II 'Sun Valley II' Sigint-gathering versions of the Hercules. Seven were delivered between October 1971 and January 1972, with three others assigned by June 1972, although one was dispatched to the USA in mid-year. The C-130Bs were only sta-tioned in Germany for a short time since the squadron was inactivated on 30 June 1974.

High-altitude Canberras

The B-57s flown by the 7407th SS included the RB-57D model which was in residence from mid-1959 until 1964, and the much-mod-ified RB-57F high-altitude version which joined the squadron early in 1965. These air-craft were fitted with high-resolution camera equipment to photograph areas of interest while flying along the border with East Germany. The RB-57Fs had their reconnaissance prefix changed to weather reconnaissance, becoming WB-57Fs later in their career. The WB-57s had been withdrawn by 1972 and flown back to the USA to briefly join the 58th WRS at Kirtland AFB, New Mexico before being placed in stor-age. The 7407th SS inactivated on the same day as its sister unit the 7406th SS.

The third unit was the 7405th SS, which formed at Wiesbaden on 10 May 1955. This unit operated a handful of specialist C-97G air-craft devoted to Sigint operations. Among the external modifications applied to these C-97s was the addition of various small aerials above the forward fuselage, and a large circular fairing positioned beneath the wingroot. Details of the modifications carried out have not been made available; the designation EC-97G has been mentioned, although this has not been listed on official records. Approximately six were operat-ed by the squadron, one of which was with-drawn during December 1969 followed by another in February 1970. The remaining four continued in service until the mid-1970s, when two were retired in early 1975, and the final pair departed Rhein Main for storage in

February 1976. The 7405th was redesignated as an operations squadron and moved to Rhein Main on 31 December 1975. The unit gained three anonymous C-130Es at the end of 1975 which were modified for photographic recon-naissance operations under project Pacer Coin. The unit appears to have remained direct-reporting until 1 July 1977 when the 7575th Operations Group was activated. The three C-130Es were painted in the same camouflage scheme as regular Military Airlift Command Hercules, thereby ensuring they did not attract attention when flying regular sorties along the Berlin corridors. One report suggests the C-130s were fitted with a huge camera lens measuring 100 in (254 cm), and therefore capa-ble of obtaining high-quality photographs of distant locations while in transit over East Germany. The destruction of the Berlin Wall in 1989 and the subsequent reunification of East and West Germany saw the aircraft cease their regular flights to Templehof Airport, and all three return to the USA. The 7405th OS was inactivated in November 1990.

Air Commandos

The 7th Special Operations Squadron was formed at Sembach AB on 1 July 1964 as an air commando squadron operating a few all-grey C-47s and some C-123Bs. The squadron received the first examples of the C-130E-I 'Skyhook I' on 27 February 1968 which were dedicated to the Special Forces role. The air-craft were painted in a black and dark green camouflage scheme which was specially designed by 3M to absorb and reduce radar sig-natures. Their noses were fitted with the dis-tinctive Fulton recovery system yoke, altering the clean contours of the aircraft and giving rise to speculation that they were a version of the HC-130. Internally, the modifications included a terrain-following radar to enable low-level night sorties to be performed safely. The unit was redesignated as a special operations squadron on 15 July 1968, before moving to Ramstein AB exactly one month later. The Skyhook C-130s replaced the C-123Bs, although at least two of the C-47As were retained by the squadron until May 1973, when they were finally retired from service and returned home for disposal. A pair of U-10B Super Couriers was operated during 1970, with suggestions that they may have been stationed at either Ramstein or Sembach with the 7th SOS. Their time spent in Europe appears to have been relatively short, as the two Couriers had been placed in storage at AMARC by mid-

Above and left: The 86th TFW moved from Zweibrucken to Ramstein in early 1973, complete with a single squadron of F-4Es (526th TFS, red fin-stripe). This was later joined by a second squadron (512th TFS, yellow fin-stripe). The 86th was also responsible for staff/VIP transport for HQ USAFE and HQ 17th AF.

Iran was to occupy the US greatly in the latter part of the decade. Here Hahn F-4Es are seen at Shiraz AB in 1977, during one of the last exercise deployments to the nation.

Below: The 'HS' tailcode was worn only briefly by the 496th TFS, until order AFM66-1 dictated that the wing adopt a universal 'HR' tailcode.

The 601st Tactical Control Wing operated the OV-10A Bronco in the forward air control role from 1973. Initial deliveries were in light grey.

Broncos were flown by the 20th TASS, the aircraft changing to 'lizard' camouflage in the late 1970s. The 601st also had CH-53Cs for transporting ground control teams.

1972 sporting the unit markings of the 317th SOS, 1st SOW based at Hurlburt Field, Florida.

The squadron had a small rotary-wing element of UH-1Ps, which was replaced by two twin-engined UH-1Ns in July 1971. The 7th SOS remained at Ramstein until 15 March 1973 when the squadron moved to Rhein Main to join the 322nd TAW. The C-130E-Is were re-engined with the Allison T56-A-15 in 1975, thereby becoming similar to the C-130H, although the designation applied was C-130E (CT) for Combat Talon. This changed again in 1977 when the aircraft became the MC-130E (Combat Talon).

VIP duties

The UH-1Ns remained at Ramstein with assignment to Detachment 2, 67th ARRS, although the helicopters were frequently flown in the VIP role rather than being used exclusively for rescue duties. The UH-1Ns remained part of MAC, painted in a normal green and tan camouflage until late in 1974, when they received a smart VIP scheme consisting of dark blue overall with a white cabin roof and engine cover. Despite remaining part of MAC, the helicopters carried the USAFE emblem on the fuselage. The 58th MAS formed at Ramstein on 1 September 1977 with control of the VIP assets including the C-12A, VC-140B and the CT-39A, along with a VC-135B which was flown to transport the commander of USAFE and other senior military figures within Europe.

In July 1948 USAFE formed the 7350th Air Base Group at Templehof Central Airport in West Berlin to administer the massive influx of supplies which flowed into the city by air from West Germany following the closure by the Soviet Union of all surface links with the outside world. Templehof became the major hub, handling thousands of flights under Operation Vittles. Subsequently, Templehof remained the main USAFE terminal for West Berlin although it was confined to military airlift traffic from September 1975.

SHAPE support

The 17th Air Force administered the US aviation assets operated by Headquarters of the Supreme Headquarters Allied Powers Europe (SHAPE) located at Mons in Belgium. The commander of SHAPE was allocated a C-118A for many years until August 1977, when the Liftmaster was finally withdrawn having been replaced by a C-9A which was fitted out for the VIP role. These were assigned to the 7104th ABS at Chièvres AB, Belgium along with a small number of US Army UH-1s for local VIP duties. The US European Command (USEU-COM) at Stuttgart, West Germany was assigned a small fleet of VIP and communications aircraft drawn from the US Army and Air Force, including the C-131D, VT-29B, VT-29C and T-39A flown by the 7005th ABS. The C-118 at SHAPE, as well as the aircraft of USEU-COM, were allocated to the 7101st ABW until May 1973 when control was transferred to the 601st TCW for just three months before joining the 86th TFW. Despite the change of wing control, the aircraft were unaffected and remained at Chièvres and Stuttgart, respectively.

The only flying component stationed in the Netherlands was the 32nd TFS at Soesterberg AB which, as stated earlier, exchanged its F-102s for the F-4E at the end of 1969, and which operated the Phantom until 1978. The squadron was jointly tasked with the air defence of the Netherlands airspace as well as being integrated into USAFE. The 32nd TFS began receiving the F-15A/B in September 1978.

Military Airlift Command

Although the majority of aircraft were assigned directly to USAFE, there were other commands with assets stationed in Europe but whose ultimate control remained with their headquarters in the USA. Among these was Military Airlift Command, which had air rescue assets located across Europe as follows:

40th Aerospace Rescue & Recovery Wing, Ramstein AB, West Germany

Det 1	HH-43F	RAF Alconbury, UK
Det 2	HH-43F	RAF Upper Heyford, UK
Det 3	HH-43F	RAF Lakenheath, UK
Det 4	HH-43F	Ramstein AB, West Germany
Det 5	HH-43F	Hahn AB, West Germany
Det 6	HH-43F	Incirlik AB, Turkey
Det 7	HH-43F	Torrejon AB, Spain
Det 8	HH-43F	Bitburg AB, West Germany
Det 9	HH-43F	RAF Wethersfield, UK
Det 10	HH-43F	Aviano AB, Italy
Det 12	HH-43F	RAF Woodbridge, UK
Det 13	HH-43F	Spangdahlem AB, West Germany
Det 15	HH-43F	Zaragoza AB, Spain

Here an HC-130N of the 67th ARRS refuels an HH-53C of the same unit. The unit also supported an HH-3 detachment on Iceland.

Performing local rescue and fire-fighting duties for tactical bases were the HH-43F Huskies of the 40th ARRW. Two were located at each base.

The first rescue Hercules variant in Europe, the HC-130H, lacked tanking capability but had the Fulton recovery system fitted.

Rescue aircraft from the US were occasional visitors to Europe, used to bolster the rescue forces. This is an HC-130N.

Prior to the delivery of the C-9A, the Convair MC-131A Samaritan was the principle air ambulance. This is a 439th MAG aircraft.

The 55th Aeromedical Airlift Squadron received the C-9A Nightingale in 1972, allowing the retirement of the MC-118 and MC-131.

Each of the detachments was assigned a pair of HH-43F Huskies for local fire-fighting duties. The Huskies were withdrawn by May 1973, with some being scrapped locally, while a few were returned to the USA for storage. The parent 40th ARRW was inactivated on 30 June 1973, responsibility for European rescue operations being assigned to the 39th ARRW with headquarters at Eglin AFB, Florida. The Aerospace Rescue and Recovery Service (ARRS) had three aerospace rescue and recovery squadrons stationed within the USAFE area of operations, consisting of the 57th ARRS at Lajes AB in the Azores with the HC-130H; 58th ARRS at Wheelus AB, Libya flying the HH-3E; and the 67th ARRS at Moron AB, Spain with the HC-130H and HC-130P. Responsibility for providing a single-aircraft HC-130 detachment to Keflavik, Iceland was shared between the 57th and 67th ARRS. The 67th ARRS was in residence at Moron AB, Spain only until 15 January 1970, when the unit transferred to RAF Woodbridge, UK. The HH-3Es were also relocated to RAF Woodbridge, following the withdrawal of all US military and civilian assets from Libyan soil during the winter of 1969/70. The 67th ARRS had received the HH-53C by February 1973, enabling the HH-3Es to be relocated to Keflavik for assignment to Detachment 14 of the squadron. The HH-3Es were stationed at Keflavik by July 1973. The 67th ARRS began making preparations to exchange its HH-53Cs for the advanced HH-53H at the end of 1979, with first deliveries due to take place during the following year. The departure of the 67th ARRS from Moron resulted in the USAF having no dedicated rescue capability in Spain, and Detachment 9 of the 67th ARRS was formed at Zaragoza AB with the HH-1H. USAFE fighter squadrons regularly deployed to the base for weapons practice, so there was a need for a rescue capability to respond to the loss of an aircraft on the range.

Aeromedical evacuation (Medevac) throughout Europe was performed by the 55th

Aeromedical Airlift Squadron which was part of the 439th MAG based at Rhein Main. Its C-118A and C-131A were operated in full MAC markings with the addition of a red cross painted on the tail. The aircraft were mostly flown on a scheduled basis to all the major facilities in Europe to collect patients for transportation to Rhein Main. One of the main US military hospitals in Europe was located nearby, at Wiesbaden, where sick and injured service personnel were taken prior to being repatriated to the USA aboard C-141s especially outfitted for the Medevac role.

The first C-9A arrived for service with the 55th AAS in June 1972, with three others following. The delivery of new equipment enabled the C-118As to be transferred to other units in Europe, while all but one of the C-131s were reassigned to the Air National Guard, SAC and Air Training Command. The Medevac equipment was removed and the interior was changed to a passenger configuration with airline-type seating fitted throughout.

Strategic Air Command

Strategic Air Command had withdrawn its permanently assigned assets from Europe during the 1960s when the Reflex B-47 bomber rotations ceased. However, SAC was the sole operator of the huge fleet of KC-135A aerial tankers, and was therefore tasked with providing worldwide inflight refuelling with aircraft on temporary duty in Europe and the Pacific region. The major SAC tanker facility in Europe was Torrejon AB, Spain, where the 98th Strategic Wing was formed on 25 June 1966 to co-ordinate activities throughout USAFE. The location of Torrejon in the western area of USAFE necessitated the unit maintaining a detachment in the UK with four KC-135As forward deployed. Detachment 1 was

located at Upper Heyford during the second half of the 1960s, but the need for additional space to construct hardened aircraft shelters and other infrastructure for the planned F-111 assignment forced the tankers to relocate to Mildenhall. The detachment moved to its new base in August 1970, although Mildenhall had been the primary diversion airfield for Upper Heyford's tankers. The detachment was also responsible for the rotational RC-135C and D models which routinely operated in Europe. Mildenhall assumed a greater importance for KC-135 operations in Europe beginning in 1975, with the base eventually becoming the major location for tankers.

The 98th SW finally inactivated on 31 December 1976, responsibility for SAC tankers in Europe having passed to the 306th SW which had formed at Ramstein AB on 15 August 1976. The location of the parent wing at Ramstein, and having operations performed from Mildenhall, created problems for routine communications. The problems were further exacerbated as there was a need for a second forward base to house additional tankers in the UK. Late in 1977 the European Tanker Task Force was formed at Mildenhall to co-ordinate the air refuelling requirements within Europe, which were provided by aircraft and crews drawn from squadrons all over the United States. The 306th SW officially moved to Mildenhall on 30 June 1978, with the 7th Air Division (SAC) assuming an overview of operations and providing the necessary link between the strategic wing and SAC headquarters at Offutt AFB, Nebraska.

SAC personnel had evaluated 18 airfields in the UK and finally selected RAF Fairford as its second tanker base in June 1978. Operations began on 15 November 1978 when the 11th Strategic Group was formed, with the first two KC-135s arriving on 13 September 1979. SAC tanker operations at Torrejon finally ceased when the 98th SW inactivated although there was an ongoing requirement for tankers to be available to provide aerial refuelling for USAF

SAC's two high-fliers were both visitors to Europe in the 1970s. Shown left is one of the 1975 U-2C deployment to test the ALSS equipment, while above is a 9th SRW SR-71A, wearing the legend 'Bodonian Express' on the tail following an unscheduled diversion into the Norwegian airfield at Bodø.

RC-135s of several variants provided the main electronic intelligence gathering capability. This aircraft is an RC-135C, the most numerous variant to be seen at English bases during the first years of the decade.

Strategic Air Command's main contribution to USAFE was the provision of inflight-refuelling assets in the shape of the KC-135A.

Proudly wearing its 'Milky Way' sash, a KC-135A gets airborne from Mildenhall in a pall of smoke. This English base became the centre for SAC's European operations, housing U-2s, SR-71s and RC-135s in addition to much of the tanker fleet.

aircraft in transit across the Mediterranean Sea. Zaragoza AB had KC-135s in residence on occasions, usually weather diversions from Torrejon, or aircraft in temporary residence for exercises. SAC formed the 34th Strategic Squadron on 1 August 1978 with KC-135s assigned for short duration, from Mildenhall initially, although Fairford assumed the duty of providing aircraft once the 11th SG became operational.

Electronic snoopers

USAFE had tactical reconnaissance aircraft in-theatre to conduct pre- and post-attack target assessment photography, along with specialised intelligence platforms to gather Elint and Sigint while operating close to the borders with the Iron Curtain countries. However, for several decades SAC had performed the majority of intelligence-gathering missions with its highly modified fleet of aircraft. These included the RB-47 which was withdrawn from service as SAC took delivery of the RC-135. The 55th SRW at Offutt AFB, Nebraska was allocated the task of providing the aircraft and personnel for deployments to both Europe and the Far East. The wing received three RC-135Ds from 1964 which were modified former MATS C-135As. Other surplus airframes were converted for specialist reconnaissance duties, although it was not until 1963 and 1964 that the Air Force placed an order for 10 dedicated RC-135Bs. The airframes were constructed by Boeing before being flown to the E-Systems Inc. facility at Greenville, Texas for the modification and installation of the extensive reconnaissance suite. The designation was not used, as the aircraft became RC-135Cs prior to delivery. The aircraft began to emerge from Greenville in 1967 and two distinct versions appeared at Upper Heyford soon afterwards. The RC-135s were not painted but instead were in natural metal finish.

RC-135s were also operated from bases in Alaska with the 6th Strategic Wing, although the unit did not enjoy a good safety record, as

several were lost. Operations in Europe faired much better, with no losses. The RC-135s were frequently updated with the installation of the latest sensors to facilitate the acquisition of electronic and signals intelligence while operating openly from either international airspace or over friendly territory. Sorties were frequently flown over the Baltic Sea, as well as off the Soviet coast above the Arctic Circle. The RC-135Cs were extensively modified between 1973 and 1975, resulting in the two versions becoming the RC-135U 'Combat Sent' and RC-135V 'Rivet Joint'. The new designations were applied to differentiate between the two distinct roles which the two types performed. The RC-135M version was flown by the 55th SRW primarily on operations over Southeast Asia, and later from Kadena AB, Okinawa for duties off the coast of the Soviet Union. These aircraft did make rare visits to Europe.

High-fliers

SAC also operated the two most sophisticated reconnaissance aircraft in the US Air Force inventory, the SR-71A and the U-2R. Both flew at incredibly high altitude to gather their intelligence data, although there the similarity ended. The U-2R was a single-seat, subsonic, glider-type aircraft whose huge straight wing enabled a phenomenal rate of climb and the ability to cruise for many hours using the minimum of fuel. The SR-71A was a two-seater which flew in excess of Mach 3 and therefore was almost impossible to intercept. Both types were operated in Europe during the 1970s, and the SR-71A made its first visit to the UK in August 1970 when a single aircraft made a brief stop at Upper Heyford while monitoring the Arab-Israeli ceasefire. A pair of U-2Rs refuelled at Upper Heyford shortly afterwards during a flight to the region. They returned to Upper Heyford in December 1970 while on their way back to the USA. The 9th SRW at Beale AFB, California operated the SR-71As, while the 100th SRW at Davis-Monthan AFB, Arizona was the unit assigned the operational U-2Rs.

Additional U-2R visits occurred in October 1972 when one was in residence for a week at RAF Wattisham, which was an air defence fighter base in eastern England and did not normally host US Air Force operations. During that month the Soviets announced they were airlifting large numbers of troops to the Suez Canal Zone, which started alarm bells ringing in the major capitals of the Western world. The presence of the U-2R at Wattisham was almost certainly in connection with this threat, and may well have been a joint US/British operation. The Soviet stance so concerned the United States government that forces were raised to a Level Three Nuclear Alert on 24 October 1972. The Soviets responded by removing their forces from the region, enabling the USAF to gradually return to its normal peacetime stance.

Middle East interest

Other U-2s made refuelling stops at Upper Heyford in 1973 and at Mildenhall in January 1975. Most flights were in connection with events in the volatile eastern Mediterranean region, including Egypt, Israel, Lebanon and Syria, as ongoing hostilities and terrorist activity was a major problem. In particular, the Soviet backing of Egypt and Syria threatened the fragile stability of the whole Middle East region. SAC had operated a pair of SR-71As on a non-stop sortie from Griffiss AFB, New York to overfly Egypt and Israel in October 1973 during the Yom Kippur War. The mission, which was carried out in great secrecy, was exhausting for the crews and could have posed a major problem if either aircraft had developed technical faults, for most of the flight time was over water.

The USAF had requested the use of an air base in the UK to launch its SR-71s, but this had not been approved by the Heath government. Undeterred, the Pentagon continued to lobby for a site in the UK for SR-71 detachments. As a thinly veiled evaluation, the Air Force announced it was to 'attempt' to establish a new

Above: Throughout the 1970s the C-141A StarLifter was the workhorse of the aerial resupply effort into Europe, the majority of flights terminating at either Mildenhall or Rhein Main.

Left: A rare but pleasing sight in the 1970s was an Air National Guard KC-97L tanker, this example being from the Utah ANG. It had made a diversion into Mildenhall during a Creek Party deployment.

world speed record for the Atlantic crossing in September 1974 with the aircraft landing at the Farnborough air display where it would be placed on public view for the first time in Europe. At the completion of the event the SR-71 flew to Mildenhall where it remained for a few days until it returned to Beale AFB, establishing another speed record, this time from London to Los Angeles in slightly less than four hours. Apart from showing the aircraft to a wide audience in Europe, the flights paved the way for operations to begin from Mildenhall later in the decade. SR-71 operations began at Mildenhall in April 1976 with a 10-day deployment, which was followed by other brief visits. A U-2R was flown to Mildenhall in June 1977 and remained for many months, initiating the type's residence. Detachment 4, 9th SRW had been formed at Mildenhall in 1978 to man the U-2 operation to monitor activities in northern Europe, and therefore it was sensible for the unit to expand its coverage to include the SR-71s. Towards the end of decade the SR-71 became almost a permanent feature at Mildenhall, with a 'barn' erected in 1980 to house the aircraft.

U-2 deployment began in 1976 with periodic visits to Mildenhall to enable operations to be flown within the relative safety of international airspace. The U-2s performed long sorties of anything up to 10 hours, their valuable 'take' later removed from the sensor bay for processing and dissemination. The development of advanced technology for the acquisition of intelligence resulted in the U-2 receiving various different sensor packages. The first U-2R fitted with the new Remote Tactical Airborne Sigint System (RTASS) arrived for operations at Mildenhall in 1978 for duty with Detachment 4. The system was installed in superpods mounted beneath the wings. Other aircraft were fitted with superpods containing all manner of aerials and antennas. On 29 December 1979 Det. 4 increased its complement to two U-2Rs, when a second aircraft was delivered. Gradually the U-2 operation became permanent, with the situation remaining little changed until the first TR-1As were delivered to RAF Alconbury in 1983. The TR-1A could perform the majority of duties previously conducted by the U-2R, and the latter aircraft returned to the USA. The removal of the U-2 from Mildenhall

did not see the inactivation of Det 4, as the unit continued with the ongoing SR-71 operation.

Prior to the formation of Det 4 at Mildenhall, SAC began operating U-2Rs at RAF Akrotiri, Cyprus which was ideally located to maintain a close watch on the nations in the eastern Mediterranean. Understandably, the British government was reluctant to admit to the operation and the U-2s rarely received any publicity, although it would seem obvious that data obtained by the USAF was shared with both parties. U-2 operations were conducted from Akrotiri from at least January 1975, when a U-2R made a refuelling stop at RAF Mildenhall, ostensibly on a flight to Cyprus. The U-2s were operated by the 100th SRW until 30 September 1976, when the aircraft were relocated to Beale AFB to join the 9th SRW thereby consolidating the operations of both types under a single organisation. The 9th SRW established Detachment 3 at Akrotiri soon afterwards, with a single aircraft permanently assigned.

Radar location

Apart from the U-2R, SAC operated the older U-2Cs, which were the original aircraft obtained in the mid-1950s. These were painted the same matt black as the U-2R and SR-71 fleets. The Air Force had developed the Advanced Location and Strike System (ALSS) which was designed to detect and pinpoint the exact position of a threat emitter. Tests in the USA were of limited success, although the Air Force was convinced ALSS could be made to work and that it would offer an improvement in performing precision air-to-ground strikes. The Air Force decided to evaluate ALSS in Europe where there was a dense threat emitter environment, to establish the feasibility of integration into an existing command and control network. Exercise Constant Treat began in May 1975 with five U-2Cs being deployed to RAF Wetherfield, having been repainted in an attractive two-tone grey scheme. A ground station and five remote sites were set up in Germany, with each test mission involving three aircraft flying racetrack patterns. The tests proved inconclusive, for a series of malfunctions and breakdowns caused sorties to be aborted. The aircraft returned home during the summer,

except for one which crashed in Germany on 29 May. Nevertheless, ongoing development lead to the Precision Location and Strike System (PLSS) which eventually became operational.

Intercontinental Resupply

The distance between the United States and Europe dictated a regular 'air bridge' to resupply USAFE bases with all manner of equipment. Non-urgent commodities could be ferried across the Atlantic by sea, although this was limited, as military equipment, spare parts, mail and passengers were considered to be vital to the efficient running of the military and could only be transported by air. The Air Force was the primary operator of these transatlantic flights, with the Military Air Transport Service (MATS) performing the majority of sorties. A variety of aircraft types was obtained, including some which were basically civilian airliners with cargo doors fitted.

It became clear that the military should become more flexible, with the ability to deploy to areas of potential conflict with the necessary equipment to intervene and prevent an escalation of tension. However, there were only a limited number of elderly types in service, such as the C-124 Globemaster II and C-133 Cargomaster, which were capable of ferrying tanks and armoured vehicles over intercontinental range. During the mid-1960s the C-141A StarLifter began to enter service, and MATS was reorganised as Military Airlift Command (MAC) in January 1966. The C-124 and C-133 were commonplace throughout the 1960s, although the completion of C-141 deliveries enabled the Globemaster to join the reserves or be retired. The StarLifter offered the capability of delivering a heavy payload nonstop far more quickly over intercontinental range, but the aircraft could not accommodate outsized loads such as the latest battle tanks. To rectify this shortfall in airlift capacity the Air Force obtained the C-5A Galaxy, which made its European debut in July 1970 when a exam-

At the beginning of the decade the elderly Douglas C-124 Globemaster was still used on transatlantic freight flights.

Another veteran was the C-133 Cargomaster, which was retired from service in 1971. This 436th MAW example is seen transiting through Malta.

Right: The 7101st Air Base Wing operated this C-97G Stratofreighter on general transport missions from Stuttgart and Chièvres.

Above: One of many overseas ANG deployments saw the F-100Ds of the Indiana Guard at Lakenheath in 1976.

Right: CONUS-based RF-4C units regularly sent aircraft to Alconbury. The 'JO' codes signified the 363rd TRW at Shaw AFB.

Left: C-130s from US units were sent to Europe to man the Bravo Detachment at Mildenhall. This aircraft is from the Dyess-based 463rd TAW.

Above: Standard C-121Cs were rare to see in Europe during the 1970s. This aircraft flew with the 193rd TEWS of the Pennsylvania ANG.

ple from the 436th MAW at Dover AFB, Delaware visited Lakenheath. Delivery of the C-5A was sufficiently advanced by 1971 to enable the C-133 to be completely retired from service, and the entire fleet was withdrawn between March and August 1971. The C-124 continued to soldier on in service for a few more years, the last example visiting Europe in April 1974.

Fighter reinforcement

During the 1950s and 1960s the Air Force dispatched squadrons of fighter aircraft during periods of tension between NATO and the Warsaw Pact, as well as for exercises. In some instances the fighters were dismantled and flown across the Atlantic for reassembly. Such a labour-intensive operation was not ideal, and was almost as slow as transporting them by sea. Others were flown via the northerly route involving refuelling stops in Canada, Greenland, Iceland or the United Kingdom. The quickest alternative was inflight refuelling, whereby squadrons of fighters could be ferried to Europe in a matter of hours. The practice involved crews preparing themselves both physically and mentally, as the prospect of many hours spent in a cramped cockpit over an endless stretch of water was daunting, to say the least. Very few fighter aircrew had performed aerial refuelling regularly, although it was commonplace for SAC bomber personnel. SAC possessed the majority of tankers for its bomber fleet, although TAC, PACAF and USAFE had operated a few elderly KB-29s and KB-50s until their withdrawal in the early 1960s. The Air Force realised that fighter crews would need to deploy rapidly to reinforce Europe in time of

tension, and would therefore need to be familiar with the technique of inflight refuelling. In addition, flight operations over the empty skies of North America were vastly different from those experienced in Europe, particularly as the weather conditions in the UK and Germany were unpredictable and changeable.

Coronet deployments

In August 1964 the Air National Guard undertook Exercise Ready Go, involving the deployment of 20 F-100C/F Super Sabres from the District of Columbia ANG, along with a mixed complement of 12 RF-84Fs of the Alabama, Arkansas and Mississippi ANG. The F-100s deployed to Hahn and Ramstein AB, while the RF-84Fs were in temporary residence at Toul-Rosières AB, France. The deployment was a test to evaluate the speed with which a reinforcement of reserve assets could be flown non-stop to Europe. In 1968 the 67th TRW at Mountain Home AFB, Idaho flew a squadron of RF-4Cs to West Germany for a deployment. The following year saw the four F-4D squadrons, which were stationed in the USA but dedicated to USAFE, return as part of their dual basing agreement. The annual Crested Cap Exercise involved inflight refuelling, which by this time had become commonplace since it was part of the training programme for all pilots. Subsequently, the Air Force instigated a regular series of Coronet deployments under the Chequered Flag series of exercises, involving US-based active-duty and reserve aircraft being flown to Europe to familiarise crews with operations likely to be encountered. Although some squadrons were deployed to US installations in Europe, many were to facilities of other NATO

members such as the Italians, West Germans, British, Belgians and the Dutch. The practice of deploying to nominated Co-located Operating Bases enabled crews to operate from unfamiliar facilities while gaining valuable experience of integrated flight procedures. The bases, which numbered approximately 50, were equipped with the infrastructure to accommodate the Coronet deployments at short notice.

The E-3 Sentry has not been directly assigned to USAFE, although there have been numerous occasions when US Air Force 'AWACS' have operated in support of campaigns and exercises. Initially the type was allocated the designation EC-137D, with the prototype being presented to senior NATO personnel during a March 1975 European tour that included visits to Mildenhall and Ramstein. The designation E-3A was applied soon afterwards. Deliveries to the 552nd AW&CW at Tinker AFB, Oklahoma got underway in March 1977. The Sentry was stationed at Keflavik, where it replaced rotational EC-121T Constellations which had operated patrols from the base for many years.

Other locations

Although technically outside the jurisdiction of USAFE, US facilities north of the Arctic Circle and in the Atlantic were closely tied to European operations.

The Danish-controlled bases at Sondrestrom and Thule Air Bases in Greenland alternated between SAC, MATS and Air Defense Command (ADC) at various times during their

A Decade of Air Power

The 57th FIS at Keflavik flew the F-4C for five years in the defence of Iceland. The island and its base were a vital transatlantic staging post for the reinforcement of Europe.

The 57th FIS was the last active-duty user of the F-102 Delta Dagger, transferring to the Phantom in 1973. This example is seen firing an AIM-4 Falcon missile, and demonstrates the high-conspicuity red tail worn for flights over ice.

In 1978 the 57th FIS upgraded to the F-4E, reverting to the 'ADC Gray' scheme worn by earlier air defence aircraft. Iceland-based interceptors worked with EC-121s and E-3s.

operation. Both were located on the giant ice-cap and therefore required special methods of operations for the majority of the year when weather conditions were unfavourable to flight operations. Although they were outside the USAFE area of responsibility, Sondrestrom hosted in temporary residence ADC interceptors and SAC bombers which were committed to the defence of Europe. Interceptors were assigned periodically to maintain a ground alert facility when needed, although these were not common due to the harsh environment. The majority of aircraft using the bases were in transit between North America and Europe. Likewise, Thule AB was primarily concerned with SAC and ADC operations, although the facility housed two fighter interceptor squadrons between July 1958 and July 1965. The base provided control of air rescue operations in the northern Greenland area. The Ballistic Missile Early Warning Systems (BMEWS) became the principle element supported by Thule AB from 1966, with the 12th Missile Warning Squadron activated in January 1967.

Atlantic outpost

The naval station at Keflavik, Iceland was an important outpost which had a direct bearing on the security of USAFE, even though the base and its operational units were not part of the organisation. Keflavik became a naval station in July 1961, and ADC was the primary USAF operator. The 57th Fighter Interceptor Squadron was formed in April 1954, with the F-102A and T-33A assigned during 1970. The Delta Dagger was withdrawn in 1973 when the squadron received the F-4C. The unit began upgrading to the F-4E in March 1978. The primary duty of the unit was the air defence interception of Soviet bombers penetrating the Icelandic military air defence identification zone. The squadron participated in monitoring all unidentified traffic transiting the Faroes/Iceland Gap, in conjunction with the Norwegian air force and the RAF, among others. Keflavik also housed deployments of airborne early warning EC-121s from Stateside active-duty and reservist units, until the E-3 Sentry became operational. The 960th Airborne Warning & Control Support Squadron was

formed in September 1979 with E-3s rotated on a regular basis from the 552nd AW&CW at Tinker AFB, Oklahoma to provide coverage.

Located approximately one-third of the distance between Portugal and New York, the joint Portuguese/US facility at Lajes Field in the Azores provided necessary refuelling support for aircraft in transit across the Atlantic. The base was jointly used by British and US forces until it was returned to the Portuguese, whereupon both governments retained rights of transit for military aircraft. The US has continued to use the base with the rights renewed periodically. The base was administered by MATS and later MAC, with the C-54G-equipped 1605th Support Squadron activated in January 1967. No other US aircraft were in residence, although the base had a large volume of traffic as well as Navy patrol squadrons on temporary duty.

Southeast Asia commitment

The start of the 1970s saw the United States heavily involved in the protracted war in Southeast Asia, with hundreds of thousands of personnel committed to a seemingly endless conflict which was controlled by politicians and senior military figures thousands of miles from the war zone. The war involved hundreds of fighter and bomber aircraft stationed in South Vietnam, Thailand and the Philippines, along with hundreds more in support including airlifters, tankers, rescue elements and observation types. The drain on assets and resources to sustain combat operations limited the scope for expansion elsewhere. Furthermore, the need for additional squadrons and equipment to replace losses ensured that certain elderly aircraft remained operational longer than anticipated. Despite this, the level and lethality of USAFE was maintained sufficiently to remain an effective deterrent.

The USAF had been established as a war-fighting machine, whose forces were dedicated to striking back in the event of hostilities. Gradually, the military had evolved to add other roles, including that of humanitarian relief. Apart from providing intervention forces to bolster those of allied nations, the US military increasingly found itself transporting urgently needed supplies into areas devastated by war or

natural disaster, as well as ferrying civilians and refugees from these areas. They were also prepared with contingency plans and arrangements for the evacuation of its personnel from areas which could possibly pose a threat to their safety. In many cases these plans required modification to suit the location in which the threat was posed. USAFE was in such a situation as the decade arrived. In September 1969 Muammar Khadaffi successfully lead a military coup against the government of pro-American King Idris in Libya. The Khadaffi regime declared the country an Arab republic with a revolutionary council filled with the usual anti-Western rhetoric, particularly against the United States. The Libyans wasted no time in making their unfriendly assertions, with an announcement on 16 January 1970 that all foreign military personnel, particularly the US and British, should vacate their desert bases. In addition, Khadaffi ordered out all American oil companies. USAFE had a huge installation at Wheelus Air Base near Tripoli, which housed various units including the 7272nd Flying Training Wing with the F-100C and F models for aerial target towing. The command had deployed its fighter aircraft to practise weapons delivery and gunnery firing over the ranges located in the sparsely populated desert. Even before the Khadaffi ultimatum, the wing had relocated its Super Sabres to Lakenheath as a precaution, although it took the US until June 1970 to complete the evacuation of its forces. To replace the loss of Wheelus and its ranges, the US commenced use of the Bardenas Reales range near Zaragoza in Spain.

Jordanian alert

During the latter part of 1970 the situation in Jordan developed into a civil war with dissidents attempting to overthrow the Hashemite government and its ruler King Hussein. Fighting between government forces and rival factions inevitably created civilian casualties, with an urgent need for medical supplies and additional personnel to treat the injured. The C-130 Bravo rotation at Mildenhall was placed on alert to respond to Operation Fig Hill. The C-130Es of the 347th TAS, 516th TAW from Dyess AFB, Texas, which was in residence at the time, were joined in September 1970 by a

Above and right: C-130s were used by both the 435th TAW and the Bravo Detachment for ferrying equipment around Europe, and for tactical support of the US forces based in-theatre.

USAFE was naturally concerned with events in the Middle East during the 1970s. A number of C-130s were maintained in this desert scheme for rapid deployment if required.

The 7th SOS at Rhein Main flew a number of special Hercules variants on Special Forces support missions. This is the unit's standard equipment: the MC-130E Combat Talon.

For weather reconnaissance USAFE used occasional detachments of WC-130H aircraft.

Another weather recon type that was an occasional visitor to Mildenhall was the WC-135B.

composite detachment from the 313th TAW at Forbes AFB, Kansas and the 464th TAW at Pope AFB, North Carolina. The C-130s deployed to Jordan towards the end of September and remained until the end of October, most of the aircraft receiving a large red cross of the tail.

Middle East watch

As stated previously the USAFE area of responsibility was not confined to Europe, for it was logical to assign small US Air Force activities to the command for convenience. This included parts of Africa, and the Middle East. The ongoing tension between Israel and her Arab neighbours was of particular interest to USAFE as well as the US Department of Defense. The United States and certain European allies had carried out a resupply of weapons and equipment prior to the Six Day War in June 1967. On that occasion the Israelis decimated the air arms of the neighbouring forces. Tension remained high, and the Israelis received considerable improved hardware including the A-4 Skyhawk and the F-4E Phantom. The Arab nations also received an influx of replacement weaponry, including the latest combat fighters from the Soviet Union. The Israelis captured some strategically important land during the 1967 War including the Golan Heights in Syria, the Egyptian Sinai Desert and the West Bank from Jordan. The continued occupation caused much consternation in the Arab world, as the holy city of Jerusalem was the prize of the West Bank. With dialogue out of the question there seemed little alternative but for the Arabs to regain the territory by force. With the two superpowers supporting the opposing sides, there was a distinct

probability that world peace could be jeopardised by an escalation of conflict in the Middle East.

On 6 October 1973, when the Israeli nation was celebrating the holiest day of the Jewish calendar, the forces of Egypt crossed the Suez Canal, while to the northeast the Syrians invaded the Golan Heights. The surprise combined offensive quickly gained ground and the Arabs, with superior ground equipment and a vastly superior personnel numbers, threatened to annihilate Israel. In addition to much offensive weaponry, both the Egyptians and Syrians had received a modern air defence network which caused many Israeli aircraft to be lost during the early days of the battle. The United States responded quickly by supplying aircraft withdrawn from operational units, including a dozen C-130E Hercules, several dozen F-4E Phantoms, and A-4 Skyhawks. Collectively the fighters numbered almost 150 airframes, which were ferried across the Atlantic by way of an air bridge supported by air refuelling assets strategically placed at bases on the East Coast of the USA, at Lajes Field in the Azores, and along the Mediterranean.

MAC air bridge

In addition, MAC ferried ammunition and spare parts, together with tanks, armour and helicopters which were quickly impressed into service. The massive resupply effort, combined with a lack of additional equipment being supplied by the Soviet Union to the other side, resulted in the Israelis routing the advance and recapturing much of the lost territory. USAFE supported the war indirectly by supplying air refuelling capability with some of its KC-135s.

The CIA claimed that the Israelis were

preparing to fit nuclear warheads to their Jericho ground-launched, medium-range rockets which could be used against Cairo and Damascus as a last resort. To determine if the reports were true, two SR-71As flew non-stop from the USA to overfly Egypt and Israel on 13 October 1973. The imagery confirmed the report. The US administration agreed with their Soviet counterparts to take whatever measures were necessary to end the conflict. A UN resolution calling for a ceasefire was met with minor infringements and an advance by Israeli troops. The Egyptians requested the US, Soviet Union and others enforce compliance, although the Russians refused to join, and instead suggested they would intervene with their Red Army. Such a prospect was met with alarm by the US, who placed its military on alert worldwide. This included USAFE units which were armed with live weapons and made ready to respond to any provocation by the Kremlin. Faced with the prospect of a direct challenge from the US, the Soviets cancelled their plans and another potential confrontation was avoided.

Force modernisation

Throughout the 1970s the US was not involved in any combat operations following the withdrawal of its forces from Southeast Asia. The decade was one of consolidation which enabled aircraft from the 1950s, such as the C-47, C-54, C-124, C-133, F-100, and F-102, to be completely retired from flying duty. Their place was taken by newer, more capable types such as the A-10, C-12, C-5, F-15 and the F-16 entering service with USAFE. The decade opened with USAFE still operating three wings of F-100s, although their retirement was fairly rapid, with all three fighter versions of F-4

USAFE – 31 December 1979

Headquarters USAFE

Ramstein AB, West Germany

7005th ABS	C-12A, T-39A at Stuttgart/Echterdingen Airport, West Germany
no sqn	C-9A at Chievres AB, Belgium for CinC HQ SHAPE

3rd Air Force

Headquarters RAF Mildenhall, United Kingdom

10th Tactical Reconnaissance Wing, RAF Alconbury		
1st TRS	RF-4C	'AR'
527th TFTAS	F-5E	
20th Tactical Fighter Wing, RAF Upper Heyford		
55th TFS	F-111E	'UH'
77th TFS	F-111E	'UH'
79th TFS	F-111E	'UH'
48th Tactical Fighter Wing, RAF Lakenheath		
492nd TFS	F-111F	'LN'
493rd TFS	F-111F	'LN'
494th TFS	F-111F	'LN'
495th TFS	F-111F	'LN'
81st Tactical Fighter Wing, RAF Bentwaters		
78th TFS	A-10A	'WR' at RAF Woodbridge
91st TFS	A-10A	'WR' at RAF Woodbridge
92nd TFS	A-10A	'WR'
509th TFS	A-10A	'WR'
510th TFS	A-10A	'WR'
511th TFS	A-10A	'WR' formed on 1 January 1980
FOL 1	A-10A rotations at Sembach AB, West Germany	
FOL 2	A-10A rotations at Ahlhorn AB, West Germany	
FOL 3	A-10A rotations at Leipheim AB, West Germany	
FOL 4	A-10A rotations at Norvenich AB, West Germany	
513th Tactical Airlift Wing, RAF Mildenhall		
10th ACCS	EC-135H	
Bravo Sqn	C-130E rotations from USA	

16th Air Force

Headquarters Torrejon Air Base, Spain

no sqn	C-12A

HQ TUSLOG Ankara AS, Turkey	
no sqn	no aircraft assigned
39th Tactical Group, Incirlik AB, Turkey	
no sqn	no aircraft assigned
40th Tactical Group, Aviano AB, Italy	
no sqn	rotational tactical fighter deployments
401st Tactical Fighter Wing, Torrejon AB, Spain		
610th TFS	F-4D	'TJ'
611th TFS	F-4D	'TJ'
612th TFS	F-4D	'TJ'
406th Tactical Fighter Training Wing, Zaragoza AB, Spain		
weapons training school and range support – no aircraft assigned		
7206th Support Group, Athens Airport, Greece		
no sqn	no aircraft assigned	

Many of the outlying USAF operations which were operating liaison

and communications types in 1970 had been withdrawn or no longer had aircraft assigned. The C-12A had fairly widespread use within the 16th Air Force, including some located in Africa and the Middle East. These included the Military Training Mission in Jeddah and Dhahran, Saudi Arabia; the Military Air Advisory Groups (MAAG) at Mehrabad Airport, Teheran, Iran; Monrovia in Liberia; Addis Ababa/Haille Selassie Airport, Ethiopia; and Lagos, Nigeria.

17th Air Force

Headquarters Ramstein AB, West Germany

Direct reporting		
32nd TFS	F-15A/B 'CR' at Camp New Amsterdam, the Netherlands (Soesterberg AB)	
26th Tactical Reconnaissance Wing, Zweibrucken AB		
38th TRS	RF-4C	'ZR'
36th Tactical Fighter Wing, Bitburg AB, West Germany		
22nd TFS	F-15A/B	'BT'
53rd TFS	F-15A/B	'BT'
525th TFS	F-15A/B	'BT'
50th Tactical Fighter Wing, Hahn AB, West Germany		
10th TFS	F-4E	'HR'
313th TFS	F-4E	'HR'
496th TFS	F-4E	'HR'
52nd Tactical Fighter Wing, Spangdahlem AB		
23rd TFS	F-4D	'SP'
81st TFS	F-4E/G	'SP'
480th TFS	F-4D/E	'SP'
86th Tactical Fighter Wing, Ramstein AB, West Germany		
512th TFS	F-4E	'RS'
526th TFS	F-4E	'RS'
601st Tactical Control Wing, Sembach AB, West Germany		
20th TASS	OV-10A	
601st TASS	CH-53C	
704th TASS	OV-10A	
7350th Air Base Group, Templehof Central Airport, West Berlin, Germany		
no sqn	no aircraft assigned	
7575th Operations Group, Rhein Main AB, West Germany		
7th SOS	MC-130E	

MAC units in Europe

322nd Air Division, Ramstein AB, West Germany

435th TAW Rhein Main AB, West Germany	
37th TAS	C-130E
55th AAS	C-9A
58th MAS	C-12A, CT-39A, VC-135B, VC-140B at Ramstein AB
7405th OS	C-130E

Aerospace Rescue & Recovery Service units in Europe

39th Aerospace Rescue & Recovery Service Headquarters Eglin AFB, Florida

67th ARRS	HC-130H/N/P, HH-53C at RAF Woodbridge, UK
Det 2	UH-1N at Ramstein AB, West Germany
Det 9	HH-1H at Zaragoza AB, Spain
Det 14	HH-3E at Keflavik AB, Iceland

At the start of the 1970s the Douglas VC-47 was standard equipment for many staff transport flights. The type also equipped some of the Embassy and MAAG flights, including those of Spain (above) and Libya (below).

Performing a wide range of light transport duties, including the rapid ferrying of reconnaissance film and staff transport, was the North American T-39 Sabreliner which served with a number of USAFE units.

Phantom becoming the most prolific type in service.

USAFE supported several evacuation airlifts during the 1970s, following internal strife between factions opposed to their governments. Among these was the tension between the Greek Cypriots in the south of Cyprus and their traditional enemies the Turkish Cypriots in the north. MAC C-130s on duty in Europe during 1975 were called upon to provide emergency airlift operations. Two years later the MAC airlifters were involved in an evacuation during the civil war in Ethiopia. One of the traditional allies of the United States in the Middle East was Iran, where the Shah had adopted a Western style of leadership that directed the people from traditional Islamic ways. Iran had permitted the US to operate listening stations on its territory to monitor activities within the

Soviet Union. There were no US aircraft stationed in Iran apart from a handful of C-12As of the Military Air Advisory Group (MAAG). The US supported the massive expansion of the Iranian air force with military advisers and technicians operating in Iran to train IIAF personnel.

A movement away from the Shah and his Western ways was fomented by traditionalists, particularly the holy men who had been sent into exile. Gradually there was an uprising against the Shah, with much anti-American rhetoric fuelled by the Ayatollahs. During 1979 the US decided it would be prudent to evacuate all non-essential personnel from Iran, and MAC was called upon to provide the necessary transportation. The MAAG Iranian C-12s were also withdrawn, most being temporarily assigned to the 58th MAS at Ramstein.

The US State Department had maintained relationships with certain Arab nations in the Middle East, particularly those with oil wealth and influence such as Iran and Saudi Arabia. Both had provided stability and were necessary for the US to act as go-betweens in negotiations with some of the less level-headed leaderships in the Arab world. The State Department operated a series of courier flights between the USA and the Middle East during 1972 and 1973 with a handful of C-130Es. The aircraft were part of Headquarters Command with assignment to the 1115th MAS stationed either at Eglin AFB or Hurlburt Field, Florida. The unit was formed on 23 July 1968 and operated until inactivated on 31 December 1973. The squadron was parented by the 1115th MAG which was located at Bolling AFB, District of Columbia.

Initially the unit flew two C-130Es which were periodically attached to the Bravo rotations at Mildenhall. The aircraft were painted in the same camouflage scheme as the remainder of the C-130s present, thereby attracting little interest from the casual observer. However, they were eventually repainted with a white upper surface and tail, grey underside and an attractive blue cheatline. The US flag was prominently applied to the tail. After service with HQ Command, the two C-130s were

Providing occasional AWACS support for USAFE were the EC-121Ts of the 552nd AW&CW. These were based at Keflavik on rotation from the US.

USAFE operated a large number of support aircraft at its bases throughout Europe, although the numbers dwindled during the 1970s. Two key types in the early years were the Douglas C-54 (above) and Convair T-29 (below). The turboprop-powered Beech C-12 King Air largely supplanted the latter, while the old Douglas was retired completely.

A handful of C-118s remained in USAFE service in 1970, including for VIP (below) and staff transport duties. The aircraft shown above was serving with the 1605th Air Base Wing when it was seen at Mildenhall in 1974.

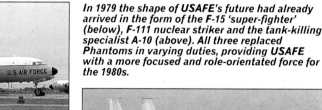

In 1979 the shape of USAFE's future had already arrived in the form of the F-15 'super-fighter' (below), F-111 nuclear striker and the tank-killing specialist A-10 (above). All three replaced Phantoms in varying duties, providing USAFE with a more focused and role-orientated force for the 1980s.

reassigned to TAC, having been joined by a pair of former 7th SOS C-130Es. The latter two aircraft flew several State Department courier flights during the final two years before the 1115th MAS inactivated. The flights originated at Andrews AFB, Maryland and staged through various European bases including RAF Mildenhall on their journey to Saudi Arabia.

Bomber visits

One aircraft type which was not based in Europe during the period was the B-52, although the Stratofortress made visits to European bases for exercises. The annual bombing and navigation competition between SAC and the RAF brought B-52s to the UK each year, while other aircraft visited to participate in some of the large-scale NATO exercises. These consisted of the B-52D and G models almost exclusively, as the B-52H was virtually non-existent within Europe. The former pair undertook conventional bombing techniques which could be practised in conjunction with other European air arms. The majority of other USAF combat and direct-support types were located in Europe at sometime between 1970 and 1979, with the F-106 Delta Dart making its one and only appearance (except for participa-

tion at the 1961 Paris air show) during the period. Six F-106As from the 5th Fighter Interceptor Squadron at Minot AFB, North Dakota were at Hahn AB in 1975 for the annual Anumn Forge series of exercises.

Throughout the second half of the decade, the Soviets' stock of mobile SS-20 nuclear surface-to-surface missiles was increased, with hundreds located in East Germany pointing at NATO facilities and the industrial heartland of Europe. The US advantage in missile numbers was gradually eroded, and by 1975 the Russians were reported to have gained the lead. The elderly TM-76 Mace and TM-61 Matador missiles of the 1960s had long since been withdrawn, with the US largely relying upon its US-based Intercontinental Ballistic Missiles (ICBMs) buried deep in the silos of the central states. On 12 December 1979 NATO declared that it was going to deploy 572 new nuclear missiles to Europe. One hundred and eight Martin Marietta Pershing II missiles were to be located in West Germany, while 464 cruise missiles would be distributed in purpose-built hardened accommodation in five countries. The Pershing missiles were to be located exclusively in West Germany at Mutlangem, Neckarsulm and Neu-Ulm. The General Dynamics BGM-

109G Tomahawk cruise missiles were to be positioned at Greenham Common and Molesworth in the UK, Florennes in Belgium, Comiso in Sicily, Wueschheim in West Germany, and Woensdrecht the Netherlands. The basing of the missiles in Europe was a tremendous bargaining chip, although it eventually cost millions of dollars and alienated large sections of the population in Europe.

The strength of USAFE had changed slightly from 57,000 personnel and 700 aircraft on 1 January 1970 to approximately 60,000 with 600 aircraft 10 years later. The number of installations had shrunk slightly, with the Air Force no longer occupying RAF Wethersfield as a flying station, although the facility was maintained on a standby basis. The Air Force had departed from Wiesbaden in West Germany, having been replaced by the US Army. The Turkish base at Cigli had also been vacated by USAFE. The modernisation programmes of the 1970s had largely been completed, although USAFE was making plans for the introduction of the next of the teen series of fighters to enter service. The F-16 had yet to become a resident, although the type had been presented to senior USAFE officials.

Bob Archer

INDEX

Picture acknowledgments

Front cover: Harry S. Gann. **4:** Imperial War Museum, The late Sqn Ldr N. Hearn-Phillips via Roy C. Nesbit (RCN), RAF Museum. **5:** The late Sqn Ldr J.E. Archibald via RCN (two), Imperial War Museum, Roger Hayward via RCN. **6:** J. Muncie via RCN, The late Sqn Ldr J.E. Archibald via RCN, Imperial War Museum (two). **7:** Imperial War Museum (two), The late Sqn Ldr J.E. Gibson via RCN. **8:** M.C. Bateman via RCN, Aerospace, RCN, BAe via RCN. **9-10:** Imperial War Museum. **12:** Wg Cdr A. Gadd via RCN. **13:** The late Wg Cdr F.E. Burton via RCN (two). **14:** Imperial War Museum, Aerospace. **15:** Imperial War Museum (three). **16:** Aerospace (two), Charles E. Brown Collection/RAF Museum. **17-19:** Imperial War Museum. **20:** USAF (two). **21:** USAF, Larry Davis Collection, Randy Jolly. **22:** via Robert F. Dorr (four). **24:** via Robert F. Dorr (three), Aerospace. **25:** Larry Davis Collection (two), via Robert F. Dorr, Warren M. Bodie. **26:** USAF (two), Warren M. Bodie (two). **27:** USAF, Norm Taylor Collection, Larry Davis Collection, Warren M. Bodie. **28:** Warren M. Bodie (two), Vic Rajani via Warren M. Bodie, Ken Sumney via Warren M. Bodie. **29:** Ken Sumney via Warren M. Bodie (two), Warren M. Bodie. **30:** Ken Sumney via Warren M. Bodie (three), via Robert F. Dorr. **31:** via Robert F. Dorr, Warren M. Bodie, USAF, Ken Sumney via Warren M. Bodie. **32:** David W. Menard, Norm Taylor Collection, USAF via Larry Davis. **33:** Budd Butcher via Larry Davis (two), H.G. Martin via David W. Menard. **34:** Budd Butcher via Larry Davis (two), Lt Col A. Bruder via Larry Davis. **36:** USAF via David W. Menard, William J. Balogh via David W. Menard, Ron Picciani via Larry Davis. **37:** Joe Michaels via Larry Davis, Kevin L. Patrick, Randy Jolly. **38-39:** MBB via Michael Stroud, Dr A. Price. **40:** Aerospace (three), MBB via Michael Stroud (two), Bundesarchiv via Dr A. Price, Bruce Robertson. **44:** Aerospace (two). **45:** Aerospace (three), Patrick Laureau. **46:** Aerospace (all). **47:** Aerospace (six), Bundesarchiv via Dr A. Price. **48:** Dr A. Price (two), Aerospace (two), Bundesarchiv via Dr A. Price. **49:** Aerospace (two), Dr A. Price (two), MBB via Michael Stroud. **50:** Dr A. Price (four), Aerospace (two), Imperial War Museum. **52:** Aerospace, Dr A. Price (two), MAP. **53:** Aerospace (three), Dr A. Price. **54:** Aerospace (two), Dr A. Price, Bundesarchiv via John Weal. **56:** Bundesarchiv (four), Aerospace. **57:** Dr A. Price. **58:** Aerospace (three), Bundesarchiv via John Weal. **59:** Aerospace, A&AEE, USAF. **60:** Dr A. Price, Bundesarchiv, Aerospace (two). **61:** Bundesarchiv (two), Aerospace. **64-66:** Aerospace. **67:** Werner W. Gysin (three), P.H.T. Green. **69:** P.H.T. Green (three). **75:** Jim Winchester (two). **76:** Aerospace (four), Jim Winchester. **77:** Bundesarchiv, Jim Winchester (five), Aerospace (two). **78:** Will Plenti via Warren Thompson (WT), John Mikus via WT. **79:** Ed Cooke via WT, Joe Dishonch via WT, Aerospace. **80:** Randy Presley via WT, Malcolm Pearson via WT, Wesley Jacobson via WT. **81:** Ralph Ritterman via WT, Chester Lamb via WT, Otto Kopf via

WT. **82:** USAF, Jim Upchurch via WT, David Symes via WT. **83:** Bill Turley via WT, Harold Turley via WT, Ed Edelen via WT. **84:** E.J. Lloyd via WT, Eugene 'Mule' Holmberg via WT, Ed Edelen via WT, V.W. Martin via WT. **86:** John Ferebee via WT, George Terry via WT, Bob Fahey via WT, Art Beasley via WT. **87:** Otto Kopf via WT (two). **88:** Kent Savage via WT, John Tabor via WT. **89:** Jim Upchurch via WT, John Hughes via WT, John Ferebee via WT. **90:** Robert D. Carter via WT, USAF, USAF via WT. **91:** James Carter via WT, Larry Davis, Robert Hook via WT. **92:** Lloyd Irish via WT, Richard Frailey via WT, Larry Guarino via WT. **93:** USAF, Al Gamblin via WT, Bruno Giordano via WT. **94:** Kent Savage via WT, Robert Nicklaus via WT. **95:** Dick Seger via WT, Ralph Reed via WT, Ken Koon via WT, USAF. **96:** Don Mansfield via WT, John Thomson via WT. **97:** Bob McDermott via WT, USAF. **98:** Harry S. Gann, McDonnell Douglas. **99:** Harry S. Gann, US Navy. **100:** via Terry Panopalis, Harry S. Gann. **101:** Robert E. Kling, Harry S. Gann. **102:** McDonnell Douglas (two), Harry S. Gann. **103:** McDonnell Douglas (two), Harry S. Gann (two). **104:** Aerospace (three), Robert E. Kling. **105:** McDonnell Douglas, Robert E. Kling, Aerospace, Douglas R. Tachauer. **106:** Chris Ryan, Robert E. Kling, McDonnell Douglas, Harry S. Gann, USMC. **107:** McDonnell Douglas, Harry S. Gann (two), Joe Zerbe. **109:** Ted Carlson/Fotodynamics (two), USN (two), Harry S. Gann (two). **110:** Harry S. Gann, Frank B. Mormillo, McDonnell Douglas. **111:** McDonnell Douglas, Harry S. Gann, Aeropsace. **112:** Harry S. Gann (three). **113:** Bruce R. Trombecky, Harry S. Gann, Peter R. Foster, Ted Carlson/Fotodynamics Norris Graser. **114:** Robert E. Kling (two), Werner Münzenmaier, USN (two). **115:** Frank B. Mormillo, Harry S. Gann, de Napoli and Mancini Collection. **116:** Harry S. Gann, Frank B. Mormillo, Ted Carlson/Fotodynamics, Peter R. Foster. **117:** Harry S. Gann (two). **118-121:** Commonwealth Aircraft Corporation. **122-123:** BAC. **124:** via Peter R. March, Bristol Siddeley (two), BAC. **125-127:** BAC. **128:** Simon Watson (three), BAC. **129:** BAC. **130:** BAC, BAe. **132:** BAe, BAC. **133:** Simon Watson (eight). **134:** BAC, BAe. **135:** BAe. **136:** BAC. **137:** Austin J. Brown/APL, Aerospace, Tim Senior. **138:** Dylan Eklund, Arthur Davies via T. Panopalis, Peter R. March. **139:** Stephen Kill, Di Napoli/Mancini Collection Larry Davis (three). **140:** Peter R. Foster, Di Napoli/Mancini Collection (two). **141:** Peter R. March (three), Stephen Kill, Dylan Eklund (two), Larry Davis. **142:** Jim Rotramel via Larry Davis, Peter R. March. **143:** Larry Davis, R. Jenner Hobbs, Dylan Eklund. **144:** via T. Panopalis, Di Napoli/Mancini Collection, Larry Davis. **145:** Larry Davis (five), Peter R. Foster, Di Napoli/Mancini Collection (two). **146:** Larry Davis, Keith Wilson, USAF via Larry davis. **147:** Di Napoli/Mancini Collection (two), Larry Davis (four), Stephen Kill, Dylan Eklund. **148:** Stephen Kill, Larry Davis. **149:** Larry Davis (four), Di Napoli/Mancini Collection (two). **150:** Peter R. March (two), Keith Wilson, Di Napoli/Mancini Collection, Dylan Eklund, B. Redfern. **151:** B. Redfern (three). **152:** Peter R. Foster, Di Napoli/Mancini Collection. **153:** Peter R. Foster (three), Peter R. March (two), Godfrey Mangion, Di Napoli/Mancini Collection. **154:** via T. Panopalis, 57th FIS, Peter R. March **155:** B. Redfern (two), Di Napoli/Mancini Collection, Peter R. March (three). **156:** Godfrey Mangion (three). **157:** Aerospace, Godfrey Mangion (two), R. Jenner Hobbs, USAF via Larry Davis, Peter R. Foster (two).